D0812153

HARVARD MIDDLE EASTERN STUDIES 5

HARVARD POLITICAL STUDIES

published under the direction of the Department of Government in Harvard University

EGYPT in search of Political Community

AN ANALYSIS OF THE INTELLECTUAL AND POLITICAL EVOLUTION OF EGYPT, 1804–1952

NADAV SAFRAN

HARVARD UNIVERSITY PRESS
Cambridge, Massachusetts
1961

LIBRARY
OF
MOUNT ST. MARY'S
COLLEGE
EMMITSBURG, MARYLAND

© *Copyright 1961 by the President and Fellows of Harvard College*
All rights reserved

Distributed in Great Britain by Oxford University Press · London

Library of Congress Catalog Card Number 61–13742

Printed in the United States of America

To Frank E. Manuel

Preface

This is a study of some of the grave problems encountered by Egypt in the course of her endeavor to carve for herself a place in the modern world. But while the analysis developed in this book centers specifically on Egypt, it is cast in a frame that, in this author's view, is applicable to many other contemporary societies. For only few of the problems discussed in this inquiry are relevant solely to Egypt. Many of them are shared in varying degrees by Egypt's sister Arab countries. Others are, *mutatis mutandis*, problems confronted by all developing countries. It is therefore hoped that this study may prove of interest to and invite comments from not only the specialist in Middle Eastern affairs but also from the student of comparative government and politics.

Like so many authors before me, I can only testify that a book of this sort owes so much to so many that it is impossible to acknowledge all the debts. I cannot, however, fail to thank Professor H. A. R. Gibb and Professor Rupert Emerson for their encouragement and help when this book was in its preliminary stage, and my friend L. Carl Brown for his unstinting and tireless assistance at its birth. A Sheldon Traveling Fellowship enabled me to gather much of the material used in this study; a partial leave from current teaching work granted by the Department of Government, Harvard, and a research subsidy from the Center for Middle Eastern Studies, Harvard, gave me the leisure to put this book into shape. To the benevolent authorities presiding over these institutions I am grateful. Mrs. Margaret Fitzgerald and Miss Brenda Sens have typed the manuscript and Mrs. Judith Walzer and Miss Ellen Gordet have helped in editing it. Miss Kathleen Ahern, of the Harvard University Press, has labored in preparing the manuscript for the press far beyond the call of duty. To all these graceful ladies I hereby express my gratitude. Finally, this book owes so much to my wife that it would have been impossible without her.

NADAV SAFRAN

Cambridge, Massachusetts, 1961

CONTENTS

PAGE

EGYPT
IN SEARCH
OF POLITICAL
COMMUNITY

INTRODUCTION

This is an interpretive study of the political evolution of Egypt from the beginning of the nineteenth century, when that country entered the modern era of her history, until the revolution of 1952. Its central topic, however, is the evolution of ideas in Egypt during that period. Underlying the choice to focus attention on the intellectual evolution are three historical-sociological propositions, which form the analytical frame of this study.

The first and basic proposition is that a political community cannot be viable and stable unless it is founded upon a more or less generally shared set of ideas, modes of thinking, norms, and values (which will also be referred to in this study as belief-system, ideology, world-view or *weltanschauung*). Such a belief-system interprets for the various groups in the community the world they live in, justifies the institutions under which they live, and helps regulate relations between them. From ancient Israel to the most recent country to have undergone civil war, the historical record demonstrates that every actual political breakdown was foreshadowed by the disruption of the common belief-system. From Plato to Hegel, from Aristotle to Max Weber, normative and analytical political thought has dwelt on the crucial function of shared myths, beliefs, norms, and values in cementing a political community. A Machiavelli, analyzing dispassionately the tactics of political survival and expansion in a society in political flux, may tell his Prince that he need not share the beliefs of his subjects. But he would be careful to emphasize that it is nevertheless important that he should appear to share them, and he would insist, at any rate, that, ultimately, the only sound and enduring political community is one that is founded on the *virtú* of its citizens. A Hobbes may employ a formidable ingenuity in attempting to work out a theory of the state based solely on the idea of force acting on man's fears, but he would be compelled to introduce surreptitiously the supposition of a consensus on a minimum of ethical and rational principles.[1] A Marx, delighting in "unmasking" the rationalizations of political philosophers, may point out that the state has its roots and its *raison d'être* in economic exploitation of class by class, but he would have to admit tacitly that in each historical stage, an ideological "superstructure" manages to legitimize this exploitation so that the overthrow of the state at any given stage could not take place before the related "superstructure" had been deliberately undermined through intellectual criticism. In short, force may be a necessary element for the state — it may even be its essential characteristic, as Max Weber indicated in his famous and widely accepted definition.[2] Its effectiveness in the long run, however, depends on its being legitimized within a generally acceptable belief-system which, as Rousseau phrased it, could "transform power into right and obedience to it into duty."

The second proposition is that there is an intimate connection between material realities — economic, social, and political conditions — and modes of thought, ideas, norms, and values. A certain complex of material conditions suggests a certain kind of world view and excludes others. Conversely, some types of belief-systems are suitable to some kinds of economic, social, and political situations and not to others. This is quite different from the vulgarized versions of Marx's views on the relations between "substructure" and "superstructure." For one thing, the "material conditions" envisaged in our second proposition are more comprehensive than purely economic conditions. Moreover, the connection between material conditions and belief-systems that we envisage applies to broad types of both, as will be seen presently, rather than to specific conditions and specific ideologies. Finally, there is no presumption that a complex of material conditions would of necessity lead to the actual formulation of the type of belief-system that it suggests — not, at least, in the short historical run of three or four generations, which is the span of the present study. Briefly, then, there is a connection between material realities and belief-systems to the extent that a drastic change in the former may make a particular belief-system obsolete, require its modification or replacement, and suggest the direction it should take. Such ideological reorientation may take a long time to materialize, if it does at all; meanwhile, the community, deprived of a valid belief-system, may become the victim of disorder and confusion and have to be kept together by sheer force or by some temporary expedient.

The third proposition at the basis of this study suggests that there is one experience which most, if not all, societies must undergo, and which nearly always exerts such pressure on the existing belief-system as to disrupt it and lead to the breakdown of the political community. This experience is one in which a society, starting from a position of adherence to a theologically oriented belief-system, first comes under the impact of modern science, technology, economics, and methods of organization, and so faces the need to reformulate its belief-system to give it a human orientation. In applying the terms, "theological" and "human" to belief-systems, we do not differentiate between systems that do or do not have a place for the deity and religion, but between those in which the ideas, values, and norms they encompass are viewed as having their foundation in objective, "given," transcendentally "revealed" truth, and those in which these values are viewed as having their foundation in truth that is ascertained by the human faculties, including, as the case may be, ideas about the deity and religion. Why such a transition is made necessary by modern science, technology, economics, and methods of organization is apparent: These disciplines testify to man's ability to understand and manipulate his natural and human environment by means of principles which *he* has discovered or learned. The reason why the transition is so difficult is that belief-systems, in general, by virtue of the function they fulfill in a community, become part of the community's consciousness of itself, a means of identifying and distinguishing itself from others, and they therefore acquire a certain sanctity which makes them more resistant to change than material conditions. Some Western societies today, for example, can visualize fantastic changes in the material conditions of life in the future, yet they tend to assume that their present belief-systems will remain the same. To the community itself, its established belief-system is never the relatively temporary and changing phenomenon that it in fact is, but is regarded instead as the culmination and final result of the historical process. And if this is the case with belief-systems in general, how much more is it with systems that are avowedly considered as revealed and sacred?

The relevance and application of these three propositions to Egypt will be indicated in the following brief statement of the problem to be examined in this study:

Egypt was heir to a belief-system based on Islamic doctrine which had evolved over a period of many centuries parallel to the evolution of her material conditions, and which served as the foundation of her political community. Both belief-system and material conditions had been crystallized by the beginning of the Ottoman occupation, and changed very little in the next three centuries. By the beginning of the nineteenth century, the basic character of Egyptian government and the structure of the economy and society began to undergo very rapid change under the impact of renewed contact with Europe, while the belief-system remained frozen. An increasingly widening gap developed between reality and ideology which undermined the existing political community and threatened to condemn Egyptian society to a permanent state of instability and tension, unless the gap were bridged by means of a readjustment of the traditional belief-system or the formulation of a new one capable of serving as a foundation for a new political community.

With some important modifications concerning the source and tempo of the change, and the political circumstances under which it took place, the problem as stated above is not unlike that which faced Western societies when the medieval Christian *weltanschauung* was undermined by modern economic development, science, and philosophy. If it is kept in mind that Islam, from the beginning, had been much more involved than Christianity in social and political life and that Western societies spent several centuries and went through a dozen civil and international wars and revolutions before they finally managed to reestablish fairly viable belief-systems and political communities, it could not be expected that Muslim Egyptian society would have found a solution to the problem two or three generations after it first became aware of it. This study, therefore, is not intended to measure results, but to analyze the precise nature of the conflict between traditional ideology and modern reality, the efforts made to meet the problem, and the difficulties encountered in the process, with the purpose of discovering the sources of Egypt's past difficulties and the requisites of an eventual solution.[3]

Part One

MODERN HISTORICAL EVOLUTION VERSUS THE TRADITIONAL BELIEF-SYSTEM

CHAPTER 1

The Islamic Ideological Background

For many centuries before the nineteenth, Egypt had belonged culturally, without any ambiguity or reservation, to a larger Islamic society whose chief characteristic was a religious attitude to life. William James has described such an attitude as the belief that there is an unseen order, and that man's supreme good lies in harmoniously adjusting himself thereto. Applied to Islam, this general description must be accompanied by the qualifications that Allah, and only Allah, is responsible for the unseen order, and that His revelation to Muḥammad is man's guide in the endeavor of adjusting himself to that order. With such provisions, this definition would represent a minimum upon which all Muslim sects agree, although the *Sunnī* * (orthodox) view, which prevailed in Egypt, would insist on adding that revelation is the *only* guide.

James points out that in the religious attitude to life, values, norms, ideals, and ideas are viewed as founded on a given order which is both objective and transcendental. The modification attributed to Sunnī Islam stipulates further that, in the orthodox view, not only the formative principles but even the specific formulations of values, norms, ideals, and ideas relating to all aspects of man's life are objectively given by divine revelation. This is a fundamental tenet of Islamic doctrine that will be encountered repeatedly in the detailed analysis that follows.

Of central importance to the preceding formulation in its modified form, are five specific concepts each of which will be examined closely in order to point out its political ideological implications. These concepts are: Allah, nature, man, Muḥammad, and the divine revelation.[1] In examining them, attention will be focused on their historical evolution as well as on their final Sunnī formulation, because the Sunnī view of these concepts developed dialectically, in opposition to the antecedent *Mu'tazilah* view, and can, therefore, be best understood in contrast to them. Also, the Mu'tazilah views,

* The transcription system followed by the author will be found under "Chief Foreign Alphabets" in *Webster's New Collegiate Dictionary*, 2nd ed. (G. C. Merriam Co.). Names of cities, such as Cairo and Beirut, for example, and certain current words (bey, pasha, and so on) have been left in anglicized form.

though not orthodox, are worth recording since they had a special appeal to some modern Egyptian and Muslim thinkers.

The question of the characteristics of Allah, and of His relation to man and to nature, was the subject of heated and vigorous discussion in the course of the second and third centuries of the *Hijrah*. Even earlier, in the first century, the question of divine determinism or free choice of man had been raised in connection with the attitude to be adopted toward the rule of the Umayyads. This problem was generalized and carried to the level of abstract discussion only after the translation of the Greek classics, and as members of the conquered peoples in Syria and Mesopotamia who had been trained in Greek dialetics challenged the Muslims to defend the seemingly naive concepts of their faith. In its new version, the question was put in the form made familiar by Jewish and Christian theological disputations: Is man the creator of his actions? If he is, how can this be reconciled with God's omnipotence and omniscience? If he is not, how can a righteous God hold him responsible for them? The Qur'ān itself is undecided on this point; it contains verses affirming man's free will, and still more numerous verses signifying that he is a helpless tool in the hands of God.

The group of Muslims that rose to answer the challenge of the detractors of Islam was called the Mu'tazilah. Strictly speaking, its members were not philosophers. They did not erect a total conceptual system, but started from the premises of belief in God, in the creation, in Allah's revelation to Muḥammad, and in the authenticity of the truth of the Qur'ān; and they attempted to expound them. They believed, however, that God, His word, and His order were rational, which amounted in fact to having reason sit in judgment over the Qur'ān and the Tradition. They thus reinterpreted allegorically those verses of the Qur'ān that seemed to contradict reason, and discarded as unauthentic those traditions that did not suit their logic.

The Mu'tazilah tried to answer the problem of freedom of choice and justice by explaining that man is, in fact, the creator of his own actions by means of a contingent power that God originally placed in him. God merely knows these deeds by a contingent knowledge as each action is performed. Similarly, God has implanted in nature its generative and reproductive powers, but has prescribed for them regular and unchanging rules of operation.

Once the Mu'tazilah committed themselves to this position, the logic of their argument compelled them to take a rational stand on many other related questions. Thus, for example, if the Qur'ān is to be understood by reason, the ethical principles it proclaims must have a rational foundation. The Mu'tazilah followed this logic and asserted that good and evil are that intrinsically, and not because the Qur'ān had arbitrarily defined them as such. What the Qur'ān did was to proclaim them for the benefit of the generality of mankind. Even before the Qur'ān, men were under the obligation to follow these rules by using their reason, and they would be rewarded and punished accordingly in the next world. Similarly, if God's work is rational, it followed, then, for the Mu'tazilah, that everything God does must be for the benefit of his creatures; otherwise, there would be a superfluity in His work that is opposed to wisdom. The Mu'tazilah did not deny that certain acts of God seemed to be nonbeneficial, and even harmful, but they ascribed this apparent contradiction to the inability of man's mind as yet to perceive God's larger design in His deeds.

Other points in the teachings of the Mu'tazilah are of strictly theological interest and need not concern us here. Suffice it to say, for purposes of later reference, that they fought vigorously against any anthropomorphic notion of God and for His absolute unity. They reinterpreted all the Qur'ānic verses that refer to God's hands, speech, sight, throne, and so on, and labored hard to merge into the divine essence the qualities attributed to God in order to avoid any coeternal attributes. They did not hesitate to go against popular sentiment and declare that the Qur'ān had been created in time, because otherwise it would mean that the Qur'ān was associated with Allah in eternity. For the rest, the Mu'tazilah did not differ from the other Sunnī thinkers except that they were more inclined toward the *Ḥanafī* school of law, noted for its advocacy of a somewhat freer use of reason in working out the system of the Law.

On the whole, the Mu'tazilah had reached a position rather close to modern conceptions of natural law, although, it should be emphasized, it was not identical with them. Its adherents were not averse to limiting divine omnipotence in favor of reason. Goodness is universal, is discoverable by reason, and is binding even upon God Himself. Man was made free, nature was made autonomous, and superfluity in God's work was excluded, so that the law of causation prevails in both the material and the moral universes. The Mu'tazilah differed from the exponents of the modern theories of natural law by their belief in the Qur'ān as the word of God. For, quite apart from the ethical principles it proclaimed, the Qur'ān contained certain specific positive laws that could not be said to have an intrinsic foundation but had to be accepted by virtue of their being divinely sanctioned. Thus, ultimately, it is not reason which encompasses the Qur'ān, but the Qur'ān which encompasses reason; it follows that no legislation can be initiated that has its sanction in reason only, but must always refer back to specific Qur'ānic texts for its justification.

The views of the Mu'tazilah school, which were accepted and fostered by ruling circles for nearly two generations in the ninth century, were subsequently abandoned and their proponents persecuted, until the alternative and much less rational views of their opponents finally prevailed. These latter views, modified in turn by the influence of *Ṣūfī* thought and practice, gained acceptance as the orthodox doctrine from the twelfth century onward.

The main characteristic of the reaction against the Mu'tazilah was an overwhelming emphasis on the omnipotence of God and the utter inscrutability of His will. The spokesmen of the reaction — al-Ash'arī and his school — dissected the entire material world as it moves in space and time into atoms and their accidents. Some Ash'arites maintained that, although accidents are transitory, substances endure; but others made no such distinctions, contending that substances, like accidents, are nothing but points in space and exist only for a time. Allah creates the world anew every moment so that its condition at a given moment has no necessary connection with that which preceded it or that which follows. This means that there is a series of worlds, each following the other, which merely present the appearance of one world; any semblance of causality proceeds from the fact that Allah, in His inscrutable will, does not choose to interrupt the usual course of events by a miracle, which He is able to do at any moment. Thus, the theoretical line between the miraculous and the usual was almost entirely obliterated, since both represent specific acts of creation and since the inscrutability of the divine will does not permit any assurance of constancy in the repetition of the usual.

While this concept denied any efficacy to nature, man was granted a certain distinction in his ability to assent to the works accomplished through him by God and to claim them as his own. This distinction is purely empirical and has no ontological implications. It is based on the observable distinction between — for example — the act of writing, which involves the assent of the subject, and the act of shivering which does not. Otherwise, the act of writing is reduced to its component parts, each of which is made separately dependent on God. He puts in man the desire to write, moves his hand, creates in the pen the power to imprint the writing on the pad, and so forth. The only relation between one step and the next is the accidental fact of succession.

Contrary to the Mu'tazilah, the Ash'arites did not recognize the possibility of any ethical principles existing independently of the

Qur'ān. Good and evil are what they are only because God said so, and it is quite conceivable that He might have said the contrary and made murder, for instance, a good deed. All that is known of God's will is from its statement in the Qur'ān. As to His nature, while He sees, hears, speaks, and does all the things the Qur'ān says He does, we must not understand these activities in human terms, though we know not how else to understand them. All the predicates of perfection apply to God, except that they apply to Him in a different and higher sense than to His creatures. Respecting the Qur'ān, the Ash'arites distinguished between the eternal word in God and in the Book as man possesses it, which was revealed in time.

The broad implications of these views are evident. We shall examine some of their more specific consequences later, but we must complete now the Sunnī picture of God, man, and nature by introducing the Ṣūfī contribution.

The Ṣūfī reaction against the doctrine of the Ash'arites was different from the opposition of the school of al-Ash'arī to the views held by the Mu'tazilah. The Ṣūfīs did not reject the principles of the Ash'arite doctrine, but, feeling unable to endure the spiritual chasm which that doctrine created between man and God, attempted to bridge it by shifting the emphasis in religious life from the mind to the heart. They accepted the doctrine that Allah works all in all, but preferred to dwell on His loving and illuminating nature rather than on His arbitrary will. Accordingly, they developed a theory of knowledge founded on feeling, in which love serves as the *trait d'union* between God and man. Man's soul is conscious of knowledge that comes to it from without, but its true essence consists of certain internal states of feeling, inclination, and disinclination, the most essential of which is love, which lifts man up to God. Knowledge of God, then, is possible, but it is acquired by intuition (*ilhām*) rather than by study. The way to seek it is through spiritual striving, removing blameworthy qualities, severing all earthly ties, and yearning fervently for God. God will turn to him who turns thus to God, and will take charge of his heart and illumine it with knowledge. The secret of the heavenly kingdom (*malakūt*) will be revealed to him; the veil of error will be lifted from the "surface of the heart" so that the essences of divine things will shine in it as if reflected in a mirror.

On the basis of these views, the Ṣūfīs developed a theory of a universal order. The individual Ṣūfī strives in his path (*ṭarīqah*) within two hierarchies, one visible and the other invisible. In the visible one, the Ṣūfī has his place among a multitude of brethren of varying degrees of spiritual illumination and power, all seeking a path to God according to the teachings and traditions of their particular order. Besides these separate and visible organizations, there is one single, ultimate, and invisible hierarchy that governs the world. At its head is a great saint, presumably the greatest of the time, chosen by God and given miraculous powers above all others. He is the axis — *quṭb* — of the world. He wanders in the world, often invisible and always unknown, performing the duties of his office. From him the hierarchy descends in gradually widening numbers, and the whole system forms a saintly board of administration by means of which the invisible government of the world is carried on.

The views and practices of Ṣūfism met at first with staunch opposition by Sunnī jurists and doctors, but the continued success of Ṣūfī teachings among the people proved that they answered a deep emotional-religious need, and, in due course, they were incorporated into the main orthodox body of Islam. The incorporation was not achieved by means of a synthesis between the two doctrines; rather, the two were allowed to persist side by side. An epistemology was developed which allocated to each of them an independent realm. Al-Ghazzālī, who is credited with having effected the reconciliation between Ṣūfism and the doctrine of the Ash'arite school, divided all knowledge into two categories: religious knowledge (*'ulūm dīniyyah*) and rational knowledge (*'ulūm 'aqliyyah*). Religious knowledge is granted to prophets by revelation (*waḥy*) and to saints by intuition (*ilhām*). Rational knowledge is of two sorts, axiomatic (*ḍarūrī*) and deduced (*muktasab bil-ta'allum wal-istidlāl*). Deduced knowledge may deal with affairs of this world (*dunyawiyyah*) or with the next world (*al-ākhirah*). The difference between deduced and intuitive knowledge is that the latter involves a "removing of the veil" — a matter outside of man's control. Between intuited and revealed knowledge, the difference is that revealed knowledge is conveyed by the angel messenger who can be seen by the prophet, whereas intuited knowledge is cast into the subject (*qadhf*) without his knowing how. Religious knowledge, whether obtained by revelation or intuition, is received by others on authority and by tradition (*bil-taqlīd wal-sunnah*).[2]

The effect of the Ṣūfī doctrine was to restore to man a worth and dignity which the Ash'arite emphasis on the divine omnipotence and God's arbitrary will had completely denied him. Man has latent in him a substance worthy of losing itself in the Divinity provided he exerts himself to that end in the right way. On the other hand, the Ṣūfīs did away with the world even more thoroughly than did the Ash'arites, who had brought everything in the objective world to the central point of the inscrutable will of God in creation. The Ṣūfīs dissolved everything both in being and in thinking into the yearning after the One Beloved Being.

We have so far discussed the most important elements of the unseen order as viewed by the Sunnī Muslims without considering the way in which the individual was to adjust to it. As previously indicated, two concepts are of relevance here: the concept of the Prophet and that of his message.

In his own eyes, Muḥammad was a mere man. He claimed no special miraculous relation with the Divinity beyond that of being the chosen receptacle of God's message. Whenever not guided by revelation, he believed himself fallible in thought and deed. In the course of time, however, his life came to be considered the ideal, and his personality the quintessence of perfection, human and superhuman. The legends of the ages made of him "the great ascetic, the intercessor with God for the believers, the mystic saint, the miracle worker with knowledge of the hidden, the descendant of Adam and heir of his spark of divine substance, the cause of creation, and the hub of the universe." [3] Muḥammad's personality has had a deep hold on all Muslims to the present day, as may be seen in the continuing literary process of its enrichment. Modern writers endow him with the qualities of the accomplished diplomat, the great revolutionary, the model statesman, the born democrat, the strategist of genius.[4]

Muḥammad has been viewed by all Muslims as the seal of the prophets, which means that God's message to mankind as revealed to Muḥammad is complete and final. Muḥammad's apostleship is consequently viewed as the most crucial event since the Creation. For the Muslim, this mission marks not only the beginning of his own history but also the start of man's metaphysical career. The Prophet's mission does not, like that of the founder of Christianity, represent an episode in a drama which had its beginnings in original sin; he represents, rather, the last and most perfect of sporadic manifestations of divine mercy expressed through the sending of messengers to men. Prior to him, men were not laboring under the metaphysical consequences of the Fall; they were immersed in ignorance — *jāhiliyyah* — or had swayed from the truth proclaimed by earlier prophets. By setting forth the complete and perfect revelation of God, Muḥammad's message offered mankind the chance of a new start in the pursuit of its destiny.

What is the nature of the message revealed through Muḥammad? The Qur'ān and the Tradition of the Prophet's sayings and deeds contain a prescribed belief, a ritual, homiletics, legal maxims and injunctions, socio-political norms, and ethical principles. We have already considered the elaboration of the prescribed belief into dogma. The ritual need not detain us here; all we need mention, perhaps, is that its emphasis lies in overwhelming formality. Prayer, for instance, is not a personal invocation or communion with God, but consists of a sequence of formulas that are recited in coordination with a sequence of exactly prescribed movements of the body. All the other elements of the Qur'ān and the Tradition are best examined in their systematic elaboration in the form of the law — the *Sharīʿah*.[5]

The Sharīʿah is a vast system of norms and regulations encompassing all areas of the Muslim's life — his religious duties, regulations concerning ritual cleanliness, food, and dress; laws of family, inheritance and endowment, contracts and obligations; criminal, fiscal, constitutional, and international law. Theoretically, the Sharīʿah derives entirely from the Qur'ān and the Tradition of the Prophet's deeds and sayings. Its purpose is not to determine the relations between men, but to define the standards of right and wrong in all matters considered by God as ethically relevant. Whether or not something is ethically relevant is known not only from its being specifically mentioned as such in the Qur'ān and the Tradition, but also from its being implied in the texts and principles of these two sources. Implications are discovered by the use of analogy and, in case of uncertainty, the consensus of the community or of its learned leaders is decisive. In the process of working out the implications, the theory continues, certain minor differences arose among various schools due to their use of different traditions and different analogies; all of the schools are, however, orthodox, and four have survived to the present day.

The historical reality of the development of Muslim law is quite different from this formal doctrine of the Sharīʿah. This fact would have little importance from our point of view if all Muslims, or, more specifically, if Egyptian Muslims, continued to profess the formal theory. We are not interested in a critique of the doctrine of Islam as such, but in Islamic concepts as elements of an ideology. But since criticism of the discrepancy between the formal doctrine of the Sharīʿah and its historical development has found its way into Egyptian consciousness, it is important to examine this discrepancy in order to be able to assess the Egyptian view of it.

Historically, far from originating as a set of theoretical deductions, the Sharīʿah was built up by taking over and "islamicizing" elements of the law prevailing in countries conquered by the Muslims. Thus, portions of Arabian, Byzantine, Persian, Nestorian, and Jewish laws and usages were taken over and incorporated into the Sharī'ah by reading them into the Qur'ān and the Tradition, or by inventing traditions for the purpose. The administrative decisions of Umayyad officials, based on personal opinion and current custom with scant reference to the Qur'ān, played an important role in mediating the acceptance of local usages, and they were also taken as sources in themselves. This process took place on a large scale during the first two-and-a-half centuries of Islam, continued at a slower pace during the following century-and-a-half, and from then until recent times nearly came to a stop, though it never ceased absolutely.

Although, ideally, the Sharī'ah encompasses all aspects of the Muslim's life, in actual fact it was never integrally applied. For reasons we need not discuss here, the governments very early took the administration of criminal justice away from the Shar'ī courts. Events gave the Shar'ī constitutional doctrine the character of a fiction or of a retrospective sanctioning of the status quo almost in the very course of its formulation. The fiscal laws were hardly ever applied, and in the law of contracts and obligations the Sharī'ah had to relinquish an ever-increasing share to practice and custom. Only the laws of personal status, inheritance, and endowment have been applied with any consistency throughout Muslim history.

More important than these factual failures, however, is the persistence of the ideal represented by the Law — that man ought to be guided in all his activities by the moral purpose expressed in the divine Book. Constant efforts were made to reconcile the deviations with the ideal. For example, the vast number of secular legislative initiatives that Muslim rulers assumed from early times were justified as acts of administration permitted by the Sharī'ah to assure its application. Multitudes of legal fictions — *ḥiyal* — were invented to make acts alien or inimical to the Sharī'ah conform to its letter and acceptable in practice. These efforts may strike the observer as insincere, but a more noteworthy observation is the remarkable persistence of the ideal of the law.

The ideal of the good life according to the Sharī'ah has always been viewed as capable of realization only collectively. Ideally, the collectivity should include the whole community of Muslims organized in a single unit. This principle was asserted from the outset when, after the death of the Prophet, many Arabian tribes who had attempted to shake off their political allegiance to the central authority without renouncing the faith itself were compelled by the sword to return to the political fold. Later, jurists made desperate attempts to maintain the fiction of a single community in the face of the inexorable breakdown of the political unity of the Muslim empire. When even this became impossible, after the destruction of the Baghdad caliphate, the requisite of political unity was reluctantly surrendered, but not the principle of spiritual unity through uniform laws, and certainly not the collective idea. The collectivity was simply reduced and made a concomitant of the political unit, whatever that happened to be.

This brief survey of the main concepts of the Muslim attitude to life should enable us to clarify some of the more specifically political concepts of the Islamic heritage. A good transition between the two is provided by the Islamic view of history, a concept which is not articulated as such in the ideas of Islam but which can be easily derived from them.[6]

The Islamic theory of history is characterized by three distinctive traits deriving from the concepts just examined. First, the conception of Muḥammad's mission has led to a pessimistic view of history. Until the appearance of the Prophet, it was possible to view the historical process as a progress toward a perfect revelation of God's will. A succession of divinely inspired messengers from Adam to Muḥammad had arisen to relay God's word to the various nations in terms suitable to the circumstances of the times of their appearance. Each messenger confirmed the mission of his predecessor, cleared it of distortions it had suffered, and expanded it. Something like this view is expressed in the Qur'ān itself. But with the appearance of Muḥammad, this process came to an end. Since Muḥammad was viewed as the "seal of the prophets," no further perfection could be expected in the statement and interpretation of the divine will. Henceforth, history could move only on or below the level to which Muḥammad had raised it and, as a matter of fact, the chances that it would remain on that level were poor. For the generation of the Companions of the Prophet had his unfailing guidance in interpreting the word of God, and the next generation had the benefit of the guidance of the Companions who had preserved the Tradition of the Prophet's deeds and sayings with which they had been directly acquainted. From then on, however, the further removed a generation was from the source of inspiration, the dimmer and more uncertain the guidance became, and the lesser were its chances of being able to live according to the perfect message of God.

It is clear that, in the Islamic view, perfection is to be sought in the past, to which all present activity must refer for justification. This view became the most important principle of the legal science and the guiding idea in the science of the Tradition — Ḥadīth. It was brought to its logical conclusion in the "closing of the gates of *ijtihād*" — independent inquiry — in the fifth Islamic century: once the divine law had been elaborated and completed, once the perfect message had been seized in its entirety and set down, it was idle, indeed it was evil, to expect any improvement on it. Henceforth, the best that could be hoped for was *taqlīd* — imitation of the past masters.

The other two traits of the Islamic view of history derive from the conception of God. Since nature and man were denied any efficacy and since God's will is inscrutable, it is vain to look for causes and effects, for "laws" in history. The philosophy of history, which in the West had its origins in theodicy and was developed by natural law and sociology, was denied any foundation in Sunnī Islam by the a priori renunciation of man's ability to understand the operation of the divine will. Between the poles of Creation and the Last Judgment, there is nothing but the inscrutable will of God. Works of history are thereby reduced to the chronicle of events and the narration of wonders without any unity or connection beyond their tacit, common reference to God's will.

The last trait of the Islamic view of history suggests itself from what has been noted in the preceding paragraph. Since the events of history are manifestations of the divine will, only one easy step is needed to legitimize facts of history and to take them as norms. To be sure, God has already revealed once and for all His will-as-norm through His Prophet, and what history provides is only His will-as-fact. But, through His Prophet, God has also provided Muslims with the instrument to effect the passage from fact to norm: by the consensus of the community (*ijmā'*), current facts may become inviolable norms; and, since this consensus need be tacit only, it is easy to see how history, which is of so little import in other respects, becomes, paradoxically, a source of legislation. This process can be seen in operation most clearly in the theory of the state.[7]

In theory, the doctrine of the state is an integral part of the divine law, and for this reason the state it envisages must be immutable and perfect. Hence, there is no need for Islamic political thought to concern itself with the dynamics of the state in the abstract, or with comparative constitutions. Its function becomes simply the systematic description of government and the statement of its normative doctrine. It can envision the fortunes of the state in terms of one relation only: its prosperity, decay, or fall depend entirely on the extent to which it conforms to the extrinsic divine norms. This picture has been modified by reality in some important respects, but Islamic political thought never escaped the notion that the good state could not be established on any basis other than the virtue and good will of government and community and their compliance with the norms of the Law. Artificial mechanisms, checks and balances, guarantees and controls, equilibrium of interests, and so on, always remained alien to it.

The Islamic concept of the state is well described by al-Ghazzālī, when he says: "Surely one of the purposes of Allah was the good organization of the religious life; and this organization is not attainable without an *imām* [leader, that is, caliph] whose authority will be obeyed." [8] This definition stresses the two most important principles in Islamic political doctrine and points out their different sources. The first subordinates state and government to the overriding purpose of promoting life according to the precepts of God; the second principle identifies Islamic government with the form of government known as *imāmah*, or caliphate. But, while the first principle derives from the essence of Islam, the second is based on the *historical* precedent established by the leaders of the community immediately after the death of Muḥammad. The modes of appointment of the first four caliphs and the tradition of their behavior also supplied Muslim jurists with the elements for the elaboration of the complete doctrine of the caliphate, after rationalizing them and finding support for them in Qur'ānic verses and in the traditions.

The function of the caliph has been summarized by Muslim jurists in the formula of "protecting the faith and governing the world." [9] Among other things, this function includes the responsibility for maintaining public order, defending and expanding the frontiers of Islam, assuring the application of the Law, and defending the purity of the faith against heretics.[10] The caliph is the successor of the Prophet in the leadership of the community. He is also the representative of the Law and is indispensable for its fulfillment. There can be only one caliph at a time. In his role as "ruler of the world" his power is absolute. All authority is vested in him; all acts of his subordinates are carried out in the name of the authority which he delegates to them.[11] Apart from the caliphate there are no public bodies in Islam which carry their own authority. The one that came nearest to it was perhaps the function of the judicial system of the Sharī'ah (*qaḍā'*), but even this could not develop a truly independent position because of limitations on its procedure which forced it to depend on the central government.

But the caliph is not a sovereign in the modern sense of the term. He has no legislative power in the proper sense and is himself subject to the Sharī'ah like any other Muslim. Theoretically, the legislative function ceased with the death of Muḥammad; and, in so far as the Prophet's legislation needs interpretation for purposes of specific application, the prerogatives of the caliph in this matter are neither more nor less than those of every other Muslim. The caliph does, however, have the right and the duty to issue from time to time administrative decrees necessary for the purpose of applying the Sharīʿah, and this right includes the all-important prerogative of prescribing for the individual *qāḍīs* the spheres of their jurisdiction, which amounts practically to the right of prescribing the extent to which the Sharīʿah is to be actually applied.[12] Later in this study we shall see how this opening provided Muslim rulers with an excuse for legislating and for carving up whole areas of the Sharīʿah and placing them under noncanonical legislation.[13]

Because of their immediate relation to power politics, the terms of the appointment of the caliph and the conditions of his tenure have been the cause of violent sectarian strife and, even within Sunnī Islam, were subject to many modifications and disputes. This aspect of the theory of the caliphate was most instrumental in weakening the notion that the specific details of state organization are divinely ordained.

In its initial formulation, the doctrine asserted that the candidate for the caliphate is installed by virtue of a contract — *bayʿah* — made between him and the representatives of the community, the men with the power to "loosen and bind." This is in no way a form of social contract because sovereignty does not reside in the people or its representatives, but only in God. The people do not create the function of the caliphate; neither does the caliph derive his authority from their representatives. This contract is simply a procedure prescribed by God, Who bestows the authority on the caliph. It merely signifies that the would-be caliph agrees to take upon himself the functions of his office, and that the representatives of the community bind themselves to obey him as long as he is capable and willing to fulfill these functions. Should he be incapacitated or should he prove to be wicked and evil-doing, the contract lapses and the people "*may* turn away from him and give allegiance to somebody else."[14] Further requirements were of a formal nature: the candidate must be of legal age, strong in mind and body, versed in the religious knowledge and apt in leadership and war; he also had to be a descendant of the clan of Quraysh.

It will have been noticed that the doctrine made no provision, short of revolution, for the correction or replacement of the caliph should he violate the contract or otherwise cause it to lapse. This is the clearest instance of the neglect of the "engineering" side of government by Islamic political doctrine, and the most significant in terms of its results. Because of this omission, almost all the requirements of the doctrine had to be greatly modified. The first amendment made the *bay'ah* valid even if it were concluded with the candidate by only one "qualified" person.[15] This development practically made the caliphate a hereditary office in one family. Next came the renunciation of the requirement of the unity of the caliphate, provided the different caliphates were separated by sea.[16] This modification was obviously made to accommodate the reality of the existence of a separate caliphate in Spain. In time, as the real power of the caliphs weakened, and as the realm of Islam was repeatedly torn by civil wars, the doctrine was further modified to insist on absolute obedience even to a barbarous and evil caliph in all but a command to violate the major prescriptions of the faith. In justification, a tradition was produced which said that one day of civil strife is worse than sixty years of tyranny.[17] Next came the legitimation of the tenure of caliphs even in the event that they should be deprived of all power and should become creatures of strong men, provided that the holder of the real power recognize symbolically the authority of his puppet by having his name mentioned in the Friday sermon — the *khuṭbah* — and stamped on the coins.[18] Finally, after the Mongolian invasion of Baghdad and the destruction of the 'Abbāsid caliphate, the concept of the caliphate ceased to signify a specifically regulated form of government and came to mean any government in which the ruler commits himself generally to govern in accordance with the Sharī'ah and to foster its application.[19]

All these changes of doctrine involved the transformation of several important principles in Islamic political thought, which we shall have to examine more closely. But the one principle of cardinal importance which remained constant was that, under all circumstances and despite all changes, the Sharī'ah remained the essence of the Islamic state. In the final account, all original forms and requirements were thrown overboard, but the state remained Islamic and could be called a caliphate only if the ruler committed himself to govern in accordance with divine law and to promote its application.

One of the principles that suffered an important transformation is the concept of the relation between authority and power. In theory, the caliph does not have any legislative power since all legislation is divine and is contained in the Sharī'ah. However, the caliph's relation to the Sharī'ah is not one of simple submission to the law and supervision of its application; his authority is necessary in order to give it validity. The Sharīʿah is intrinsically valid as the word of God; but it acquires practical validity only by passing through the channel of the caliph's authority. For instance, a Muslim cannot perform a valid act or contract, even if this be done according to the Sharīʿah, unless it is sanctioned by the caliph or his delegate. Thus, while the caliph's authority itself derives from the Sharīʿah, it is at the same time indispensable for the validation of its application. Hence, the caliph is not only the temporal ruler and the protector of the faith, but the keystone of the whole legal structure of the commonwealth. This, incidentally, partly explains the persistent adherence of Muslim theorists to the institution of the caliphate long after it seemed emptied of its content.

Although the authority of the caliph has a divine origin, it in turn requires power for its validation. It is not that Islamic theory initially conceived of authority and power as distinct; but it naturally assumed that power accompanies authority and is one of its necessary manifestations. This attitude has its roots in the psychology of a conquering people and in the historical fact that the caliphs of the first two centuries were the holders of both authority and power. It also explains the perplexity which overtook Muslim jurists when power starkly presented itself as independent of authority in the subsequent centuries. When this happened, their first reaction was to rejoin power and authority by means of the fiction of allegiance, *khuṭbah*, and coinage; and when this arrangement was nullified by the destruction of the Baghdad caliphate, they conferred the sanction of authority upon power, on one condition. The beginning of this crucial transformation is well expressed in the writings of al-Ghazzālī.

Long before al-Ghazzālī's time, effective power had passed entirely from the hands of the caliphs to military leaders and *condottieri* who made and unmade caliphs at will, and even killed them.[20] This situation raised questions about the validity of these leaders' power and of the caliph's authority, and, consequently, about the practical validity of the Sharīʿah. On the validity of power and authority, al-Ghazzālī came to the conclusion that:

> The *wilāyah* (government) in these days is a consequence solely of military power. Whosoever he may be to whom the holder of military power professes allegiance, that person is the caliph. And whosoever exercises independent power while he shows allegiance to the caliph by mentioning his name in the *khuṭbah* and on the coinage, he is sultan, whose orders and judgments are executed in the several parts of the earth by a valid appointment.[21]

In other words, al-Ghazzālī tried to legitimize power by submitting it symbolically to authority, at the same time that he sought to confirm authority by linking it to power. He defended his position by referring to the relation between authority and the practical validity of the Sharī'ah:

The concessions that we make are involuntary, but necessity makes permissible that which is prohibited. . . . Who is there . . . who would argue for the voidance of the *imāmah* in our days because of the lack of the requisite qualifications? . . . . Which is better, that we should declare that the *qāḍīs* are divested of their functions, that all appointments are invalid, that no marriages can be legally contracted, that all executive actions in all parts of the earth are null and void, and that the whole creation is living in sin — or to recognize that the *imāmah* is held by a valid contract, and that all acts and jurisdictions are valid given the circumstances of the times. . . . ? [22]

From this position, it was only one step to the justification of power in itself. This step was taken when the destruction of the Baghdad caliphate simplified the triangular situation of authority, power, and the Sharī'ah. The theory that emerged and won acceptance as Sunnī proclaimed that all power comes from God and derives authority from this fact. But while all power is legitimate, there may be good and bad government. Good government is that which promotes the divine law, and may be called the *imāmah*, or caliphate; any other government is tyranny because it gives play only to irascible human nature.[23] The crowning legitimation of power came with its being made the heir to the caliphate in conferring practical validity on the Sharī'ah.[24]

In its preoccupation with the question of the caliphate, Islamic doctrine paid very little attention to the political destiny of the ordinary Muslim citizen. At first, it tended to leave him at least some discretion by allowing him to withhold his allegiance from the illegitimate and tyrannical caliphs; but even this right was soon withdrawn from him and he was enjoined to obey any caliph or sultan, no matter how he acquired power or how he exercised it. Modern Muslim writers tend to make a great deal of the *bay'ah* — the contract with the caliph; the *ijmā'* — consensus of the community or of its self-appointed learned spokesmen; the Qur'ānic injunction to command what is good and prohibit what is evil; and the Prophet's recommendation of *shūra* — consultation, deliberation. They present these principles as evidence that Islam recommends some sort of popular democracy and popular representation limiting the absolutism of the ruler.[25] It is not my intention to prescribe for Muslims the limits of their right to interpret Islam as they wish, or to deny the social value of such current interpretation. Nonetheless, it must be seen that, historically, the *bay'ah* did not and could not have the meaning of a social contract in the context of the total Islamic doctrine; *ijmā'* was not a programmatic concept, but rather an *ex-post-facto* legitimation of situations of fact by virtue of a divine assurance that the community shall never agree on the wrong; the injunction to command what is good and prohibit what is evil has been reduced for the individual to inner moral commendation or reprobation and has been institutionalized, in its application to the community, in the office of the market inspector with some auxiliary police functions; [26] that, in its context, the *shūra* is an expedient recommendation — two minds are better than one — rather than a moral or political obligation; and that, at any rate, it was never institutionalized and was erratically practiced. In short, it should be emphasized that, historically, the Sharī'ah did not provide for the political self-fulfillment of the Muslim as it did for the realization of his moral potentialities.[27] Politics remained alien to him, and the notion grew that it was thoroughly contaminated with sin. The great jurist Abū Ḥanīfah had to be whipped into assuming the office of judge of Baghdad. The only specific civic obligation that the Sharī'ah imposed on the Muslim was that of answering the call for Holy War — *Jihād* — when issued by the caliph, and this was nothing more than a particular instance of the Muslim's general obligation to obey the ruler.

Although the Muslim had no political rights, he was endowed with many personal rights. This does not mean that any rights were attached to his person as a human being; rather, like the Benthamite conception, the rights of the Muslim are created by the Law — the obligations of one are the rights of others, and vice versa — with the difference that in Islam these rights and obligations have a divine sanction and no new rights can be created since the Law has been given once and for all. The property right of a Muslim, for instance, creates for others the obligation to respect it. To them it becomes *ḥarām*— prohibited. The mode of acquisition of such right is prescribed by the Law; in this instance, booty, a concession by the caliph, and work confer the right of property. But these factors do not confer that right by virtue of a causative relation, such as Locke conceived between labor and property, but are the revealed indications that the Owner of all property wishes to confer that particular property upon the beneficiary. Naturally, the divine sanction implies that violation of any rights is not only a crime punishable by earthly authorities, but is also a sin punishable by God.

The same pattern applies to the status and condition of the Muslim in the community. Although all Muslims are equal before the Law, this equality does not derive from any intrinsic right of the individual as such; it is a juridical right which the Law confers upon the Muslim qua Muslim. Non-Muslims are subject to legal discrimination: if they are scriptuaries — *dhimmīs* — they have to pay a special tax symbolizing recognition of their submission to the Muslims; all other non-Muslims are to be offered Islam or the sword.

The primary state of the Muslim is freedom — *ḥurriyyah*: a foundling is considered free until the contrary is proved; a Muslim may do everything unless it be prohibited by the Law; the prohibitions of the Law are significantly called *ḥudūd* — limitations upon this primary state of freedom. But, here again, this conception of freedom is not founded on the inherent status of man as man, nor is it related to an ontological free will, which Sunnī theory denied to the Muslim. Rather, it is a legal status, and it refers to the position of a man who is independent vis-à-vis his fellow men in the eyes of the law; one who is not subject to any trusteeship with regard to the exercise of his legal rights and the fulfillment of his duties. That is the reason why such freedom is not incompatible with the recognition of slavery. Slavery, in this case, does not imply any natural destiny of certain people, as Aristotle understood it, but a state of more or less complete legal dependence on the master. It can be seen, too, how such a conception of freedom may coexist with the ontological determinism of Sunnī Islam: God has simply prescribed that a Muslim be treated as a responsible, independent creature vis-à-vis his fellow Muslims.

This, then, is an analysis of the most important and politically relevant elements of the Islamic ideology, which constituted the basis of the Egyptian political community at the beginning of the nineteenth century. The detailed analysis of the concepts of Allah, nature, man, the Prophet, the Book, and the theory of the Sharī'ah illustrates the generalization made at the beginning of this chapter about the objective, "given," transcendental character of the Muslim view of the world. On the other hand, the analysis also reveals that, within the Islamic ideological heritage as received by Egypt, there were certain possibilities for individual or collective human initiative in setting up subjective norms. Some of these were due to gaps in the system itself, others to historical precedent established in disregard of some of its norms. The most important of these possibilities lay in the spheres of politics and administration, and it is through them that elements of innovation were to infiltrate the citadel of the Islamic ideological system. It is therefore worth our while to review them.

It will be recalled that the Law considered certain human activities as being ethically neutral because they had not been mentioned in the Qur'ān and the Tradition. I pointed out the whole sphere of what we call civil rights as an example of this kind of activity. It follows that there is nothing in theory to prevent the ruler or the community from establishing a whole set of norms in that sphere. It is conceivable, indeed, that such norms may even gain some sanction by virtue of the Sharī'ah's empowering the ruler to set up "administrative" laws necessary for the effective carrying out of the Law. Another opening, which also serves to strengthen the first, was the concept of the consensus of the community allowing the establishment of new, and the lapse of the old, norms. Moreover, since the Shar'ī fiscal law was hardly ever applied, the ruler could initiate his own laws without violating precedent. The same can be said of the tradition of rulers themselves administering summary justice in the sphere of criminal law, especially in the very vague field of "political crimes."

LIBRARY
OF
MOUNT ST. MARY'S
COLLEGE
EMMITSBURG, MARYLAND

CHAPTER 2

The Political, Economic, and Social Transformations, 1804-1882

At a time when the West was ushering in the age of the great discoveries, the Renaissance, and the Reformation, Egypt was settling down to one of the longest periods of isolation and economic and cultural stagnation since its conquest by Islam. Muslim civilization in general, primarily urban and centered in rich valleys or in peripheral regions cut off from one another by large expanses of desert, needed its naval control and coastal accesses for its material prosperity. With the development of Portuguese, then Dutch and British, naval power, mastery of the seas passed into new hands and the Muslim empire became increasingly fragmented. The resultant economic stagnation reinforced the static cultural orientation which had already begun to manifest itself in Islam, and which considered all knowledge as "given" and the process of learning an accumulation of the known rather than a process of discovery. Within the Muslim community, Egypt suffered most acutely from the isolation because the discovery of the Cape route diverted transit trade from its territory and reduced it to a backwater province of the Ottoman empire, deprived even of those few contacts with the West that took place at its periphery. Thus, for three centuries after the Ottoman conquest, Egypt went into its own medieval slumber from which only the campaign of Napoleon and its aftermath awoke it.

At the beginning of the nineteenth century, Egypt entered a period of rapid transformation which revolutionized its entire economic, social, and governmental structures within a relatively short time. However, unlike the transformation of the medieval Western civilization, the change in Egypt did not proceed gradually, organically, and indigenously, but was the result of the initiative of individual autocrats in imposing certain reforms on a reluctant population in an effort to emulate particular aspects of Western civilization. The material changes were therefore not preceded or accompanied by an intellectual reawakening, as they had been in the West, but proceeded independently while the ideology prevailing at the beginning of the process remained unchanged. It was not until the last quarter of the nineteenth century that the discrepancy between the traditional ideology and the implications of the new reality began to provoke intellectual discomfort and to elicit some attempts to reconcile it. But since this happened at a time when Western powers encroached upon Egypt and eventually dominated it politically, the problem of ideological adjustment was fused with the problem of resisting foreign political encroachment to form a "synthetic" perspective that distorted both problems. Ever since then Egyptians have been prone to discuss ideological questions more in terms of their implications for the struggle against alien powers than in terms of their own merits, and to look for ideological implications behind the politically motivated drive and domination of foreign states. This whole subject will be discussed in greater detail later. For the moment, we must turn to a brief review of the material transformations that took place in Egypt from the beginning of the nineteenth century to the beginning of the British occupation in 1882. Of course, there can be no question of giving here a detailed internal history of Egypt during that period. The purpose of this chapter is rather to draw the main lines of economic, social, and political developments in this formative phase in the life of modern Egypt in order to establish the general objective challenge of modern conditions to the traditional view of life, and particularly its concept of the socio-political order. We shall endeavor mainly to draw the outline of the emerging new structure which provides the frame for subsequent historical and ideological development; and in the process we shall point to such changes as affected particularly and directly the traditional Muslim institutions, and the tendencies which influenced significantly the subsequent ideological evolution.

1. *Development under Muḥammad 'Alī*

When Muḥammad 'Alī came to power in the wake of the confusion following the withdrawal of Napoleon's expedition, Egypt had completed nearly three hundred years of a life of medieval stability under Ottoman dominion. The regime under which it had lived, while not prescribed in its details by the Islamic doctrine, was, on the whole, quite in harmony with it and with the Islamic view of life.[1] The main division of society was that between rulers and ruled; the former enjoyed the spoils of power while the rest of society operated under its own traditional institutions almost independently of the rulers. In the eighteenth century, the ruling class was composed of a nominal Ottoman governor and a ruling military aristocracy of Mamluk beys. The country was divided into feudal domains which provided these beys with the revenue to support themselves and their retinues of horsemen. The beys did not perform any social or judiciary functions in their domains, as did their medieval European peers; they were rather like absentee owners, interested only in the collection of the revenues from their domains and leaving the care of their interests to their bailiffs, or *multazims*. Otherwise, they spent their time politicking and warring among themselves, raiding the neighboring provinces, or simply enjoying their lot. The Ottoman governor, as representative of the sultan, appointed the *qāḍīs* according to the requirements of the Sharīʿah, and these officials ran their courts autonomously and collected for themselves the fees for cases brought before them.

The ruled were organized in their turn into a multitude of small, closely knit, religious-social-economic units. In the countryside, the unit was the village; in the towns, it was the guild. These units were headed by their respective *shaykhs*, who were responsible for the taxation and behavior of their people and formed the only point of contact between rulers and ruled. Villages and guilds were affiliated with their own Ṣūfī order and ran their lives according to long-established custom, the guidance of the *shaykhs* of their orders, and the legal regulations administered by the *qāḍīs*.

Such public institutions as schools, mosques, charity houses, public fountains, and so on, were established and supported by private endowments. Although rulers often contributed to such institutions, they did not do this as part of their function as rulers, but as acts of piety and generosity traditionally expected from men of means.

Relations between rulers and ruled were thus restricted to the minimum, since power played almost no social function at all. The true leaders of the community were the *shaykhs* of the orders and the *ʿulamā'* — religious leaders and teachers — who had a rich, independent, and powerful stronghold in the mosque-university of al-Azhar. The whole scheme was thus admirably suited to the compromise that Islamic doctrine had made with power by recognizing its legitimacy and prescribing obedience to it, as long as it allowed the Sharīʿah to care for the affairs of Muslims and promote their eternal well-being.

The harmony between ideology and reality depended, then, on the fact that the holders of power were content to let society run itself on the basis of its autonomous institutions and the regulations of the Sharīʿah, and could be maintained only as long as that fact endured. As long as wars consisted of massive duels between two armies of mercenaries and as long as the material substance of power consisted of a few thousand lightly armed professional soldiers, there was, on the whole, little or no reason for the rulers to intervene in the affairs of their societies beyond collecting the customary taxes to maintain themselves and their retinues. But as armed conflicts began to acquire the character of "national" wars, and as the material substance of power expanded concomitantly, it became necessary for the ruler who wished to hold his own to broaden his control and extend his regulations to ever more spheres of his subjects' lives.

This process had begun in Europe with the "enlightened despots" of the seventeenth and eighteenth centuries, who, in a do-or-die competition, had set new levels of power based on massive armies and navies sustained by an unprecedented expansion of the purview of governmental functions. The centralization and streamlining of the administration, uniform laws, mercantile policies of developing the economy by deliberate planning and investment, the construction of roads and development of the means of communication, the spread of education and the promotion of science and technology — these and other factors came to be viewed as bearing great relevance to material power and, therefore, as necessary and legitimate fields of concern for the state. When Napoleon came to Egypt with his citizens' army and his large team of scientists and savants in order to bring Britain to her knees by threatening her empire in India, the process had reached a height which was not to be exceeded until World War I.

The European rulers of the eighteenth century had felt compelled to outdo each other in the process of expanding the basis of power since failure to do so might mean the loss of their kingdoms, as the partition of Poland dramatically illustrates. Muḥammad ʿAlī found himself faced with a similar imperative once he had maneuvered his way to power and entertained the ambition to hold on to it. The French expedition had ended the centuries of isolation of Egypt and drawn it inexorably into the arena of world power politics. If Egypt were not to fall again to another expedition issuing from Europe, power of European quality and on a European scale was needed as a deterrent. And if the prospect of another European assault was somewhat remote due to the mutual jealousies of the great powers, it was at any rate certain that the Ottoman sultan would not allow Muḥammad ʿAlī, a parvenu former Albanian officer and tobacco dealer, to retain Egypt unless ʿAlī put himself in a position to be able ultimately to cross swords with him. To build up the power necessary to meet these contingencies out of a backward society of slightly over two million people and a medieval economy, nothing short of a complete revolution could suffice.[2] With ruthless determination, amazing resourcefulness, and demonic cunning and energy, Muḥammad ʿAlī proceeded to bring about just such a revolution.

In general, it can be said that Muḥammad ʻAlī was more successful in tearing down the traditional political, social and economic structures than in building new ones in their place. This is said not only because many of the tangible results of his work — his factories and arsenals, his army and navy, his commercial enterprises, his school system, and so on — collapsed once he was assured the hereditary rulership of Egypt and at the same time was decisively checked in his expansionist designs, but because most of what survived and endured in his work bore the mark and the defects of having been hastily erected with the single purpose of power expansion in mind. Be that as it may, there is no doubt that in the final account, Muḥammad ʻAlī made Egypt into something radically different from what it had been at the beginning of his reign and that this difference upset irremediably the previous harmony between reality and ideology.

Muḥammad ʻAlī needed money to realize his projects and, in setting out to get it, he revolutionized the whole economic and social structure of Egypt with a few bold strokes.[3]

In agriculture, he destroyed forever the big land-owning Mamluk beys and expropriated nearly all the country's land. He then redistributed it in hereditary tenures to individual fellahin, making them individually responsible for rents and taxes, and gave large tracts to members of his family, high officials, and other people who were willing to put newly reclaimed land to work. Thus he brought down, in fact, the whole feudal system of land tenure and started the new pattern of land distribution that was to characterize Egypt. He introduced large-scale cotton cultivation for export and so bound Egypt's economy to the international market and defined its character as a single-crop economy.

In industry, he was the sole owner of the new large-scale enterprises which he had founded for profit as well as to equip his armed forces. But he also established his own monopoly over the production, sale, and purchase of certain goods, notably textiles and textile yarns, the violation of which was punishable by flogging, hard labor, or death. Even women and children working in their own homes became, like everybody else, salaried employees of the "state." By thus separating work from capital, reducing the masters and craftsmen into wage workers, and eliminating the traditional limitations on occupation, movement, and membership in craft associations, Muḥammad ʻAlī undermined the whole traditional corporate system.[4]

Muḥammad ʻAlī extended his monopoly over the field of large-scale commerce as well. Apart from textiles, several other commodities were sold exclusively by his agents. Altogether, almost the only large-scale merchants allowed were foreigners who enjoyed special privileges and rendered him service in the field of export-import. In 1840, for example, there were only six big Egyptian commercial firms in Alexandria compared with forty-four foreign. In Cairo, at the same time, there were only sixty-three *small* merchants who were Turks or Egyptians.[5] This *étatisation* of both commerce and industry, which spared only the foreigners, was largely responsible for the long delay in the development of an indigenous industrial and mercantile bourgeoisie — a factor which was to have some important consequences for the political and economic evolution of Egypt up to present times.

The management of the new monopolies, which replaced the traditional, feudal pattern of economic organization as well as of other new functions of state, involved a fundamental change in the character of state administration. The new administration was a precursor of the modern state bureaucracy, in the precise technical sense of the term as used by Max Weber,[6] in so far as it embodied the basic principle of separating the administrators below the ruler from the ownership of the means of administration. In other respects, Muḥammad ʿAlī's administration remained his own personal adjunct. It consisted essentially of a multitude of officials acting as his continually instructed and controlled agents rather than as a machinery with an established hierarchy of authority, fixed offices with clearly defined functions, set procedures and rules, a staff acting impersonally, and all the other characteristics of a large-scale bureaucratic organization. However, since the highly personal administration he preferred was so heavily dependent on the attention of the ruler, even Muḥammad ʿAlī, with all his energy and jealous power, found himself compelled to delegate some of his authority and to take other steps which had the effect of moving gradually closer to the modern state bureaucracy.

In order to manage his enterprises, run his administration, and staff his armed forces with officers, Muḥammad ʿAlī needed large numbers of educated personnel, including some with an education in wholly new modern subjects. To meet this need, Muḥammad ʿAlī began by leaning heavily on foreigners while taking measures to provide for himself an indigenous educated class. He tapped the meager resources of al-Azhar, improvised a state-managed school system, imported teachers for his technical schools, sent student groups to Europe, and allowed mission schools to operate. In all this, he not only laid the foundations of the modern Egyptian system of education, but also largely set its pattern and defined its character.[7]

It was he who started the two separate systems of religious and secular schools that were to contribute heavily to dividing Egyptian opinion later, and it was he who started the tradition of gearing education to the production of officials and state employees.

These developments in the sphere of economy, administration, and education had important effects on the stratification of Egyptian society. Muḥammad ʿAlī often rewarded his assistants in the enterprises that he undertook with large land grants. These assistants, together with members of his own family, came to form a new landed aristocracy instead of the military aristocracy of the Mamluk beys. Muḥammad ʿAlī's vigilance at this stage prevented the new aristocracy from developing independent centers of power based on its estates, but, under his successors, it managed to acquire a formidable position in Egyptian political life. At the highest echelons, most of the new aristocrats were Turks; but on the other levels, Muḥammad ʿAlī's great need for officials opened to Egyptians avenues of social mobility on a scale unknown hitherto. Formerly, Egyptians could move up the social ladder to a very limited extent through the religious institutions. Now, the creation and expansion of secular civil and military services engendered the beginnings of an entirely new class with a unique outlook and experience.

In addition to the indirect effects that his innovations had on the traditional belief system, Muḥammad ʿAlī renewed the process of large-scale direct encroachment by the state on the religious institutions. He taxed *waqf* (religious endowment) property for the first time in Muslim history, confiscated much of it, and prohibited the creation of new family—as distinguished from charity—*waqfs*. By establishing the tradition of the ruler's appointing the head of al-Azhar to replace election by his colleagues, he permanently weakened the power of the *ʿulamāʾ* in order to deprive them of the opportunity of taking independent action against him.[8] He not only started an educational system that was independent of the religious institutions, but harnessed the religious schools themselves to the service of his power schemes. From institutions providing the ABC's of salvation, he turned the *kuttābs* into essentially elementary schools providing the ABC's for further schooling and eventual service in government.[9] It is true that he left untouched the system of religious courts, even though he had a very low opinion of them, in order not to raise complications with the Ottoman sultan to whose hands the jurisdiction over these courts ultimately reverted; but he established two courts independent of Muslim Law in Cairo and in Alexandria to settle commercial disputes and had criminal justice administered almost exclusively by the executive authorities in a summary fashion.

All these developments under Muḥammad 'Alī had little or no consequence in the field of cultural activity. The religious educational establishment had failed to produce any work of value for centuries before, with the possible exception of al-Jabartī's history, completed in the early half of Muḥammad 'Alī's reign. The newly established secular education was too recent and too technically oriented to contribute anything to cultural life. Muḥammad 'Alī had founded a printing press in Bulāq in 1822 — it is still in existence today — which produced 243 books in the first twenty years of its existence. By far the largest group of these books, however, consisted of military and naval manuals; only two works of literature were printed.[10]

In the sphere of politics, Muḥammad 'Alī's power was absolute. He had systematically destroyed all centers of potential independent action and prevented the development of any new ones. The memory of his massacre of the Mamluks cast around him a shadow of terror which was sufficient in itself to paralyze any budding opposition.[11] It is true that, to the delight of his Saint Simonian advisers, he institutionalized the practice of consultation and discussion before undertaking any public business, but in the final account the decision was his and his alone.[12]

Muḥammad 'Abduh, about whom we shall say a great deal later, summarized Muḥammad 'Alī's activities in the political and social sphere on the occasion of the centenary of his accession to power in these terms:

> He was a man of cunning and intuition. He would use the army and some factions which he had attracted to himself in order to cut every head among his opponents; and then he would again use the army and some other faction against those who had been with him and had helped him against the previous opponent and would wipe them off and so on until all the strong factions were crushed. Whereupon he turned against the heads of the noble houses until he left no head sheltering a conscience [*sic*] . . . Finally he turned against any remaining manifestation of life among individuals in the country at large leaving no head that knows itself without severing it from its body or without exiling its bearer and all his village to the Sudan where he perished.
>
> He then elevated to high positions the mean in the towns and villages, as if he recognized in them kin with his own "noble" origin, so that all the nobles were humbled and nothing remained in the country save instruments of his will which he used to collect soldiers and wealth by any and all means. Thereby he wiped out any element of good life such as opinion, will and personal independence in order to make the entire Egyptian realm one big feudal domain for himself and his children, where it had been many domains under many princes. . . .[13]

2. *The Age of Ismā'īl*

The relative lethargy that characterized the last years of Muḥammad 'Alī's reign was followed by a short period under 'Abbās I which was marked by outright reaction against almost everything European. But under Sa'īd and Ismā'īl, and particularly the latter, the efforts toward modernization were resumed with renewed vigor. Muḥammad 'Alī had been illiterate until the age of forty, and his appreciation of Europe outside the spheres of technology and organization was bound to be limited. Ismā'īl, by contrast, had received a princely education which included three years of study in France. When he came to power in 1863, his aspiration was no less than the transformation of Egypt into a part of Europe.[14] He shared Muḥammad 'Alī's desire for power and attempted in his turn to build an Egyptian empire by expanding southward into the Sudan, equatorial Africa, and Abyssinia; but while his great predecessor had built only arsenals and factories, Ismā'īl built operas, palaces, and promenades as well, adopted French as the language of his administration, and introduced modern legal codes. He wanted to be accepted as an equal among European princes and liked to think of himself as having a *mission civilisatrice*. In pursuit of this mission he opened the Sudan, abolished slavery, and gave full assistance to de Lesseps in the construction of the Suez canal.

Under Ismā'īl, private ownership of land came to replace completely the system established by Muḥammad 'Alī, who considered all the land of Egypt as vested in himself. In 1871, under the pressure of financial difficulties, Ismā'īl offered to recognize absolute ownership of all lands distributed in tenure by Muḥammad 'Alī to all those who paid six years' taxes in advance. This, and the recognition of the right of foreigners to own land, which Sa'īd had granted previously, marked the final break with the feudal system and the establishment of the capitalist system of landed property. From the reign of Muḥammad 'Alī through that of Ismā'īl, the area under cultivation was expanded from 3,050,000 feddans in 1813 to 4,743,000 in 1877, thanks to 8,400 miles of new irrigation canals; an increasing share of the land was devoted to cotton cultivation.[15] Cotton exports reached 3,000,000 *kantars* in 1880 as against 350,000 *kantars* thirty years earlier. Another industrial crop, sugar cane, was developed on a large scale but at the cost of further restricting cultivation of staple products and of increasing Egypt's dependence on the world market.

The first railroad had been built under 'Abbās in 1851, between Cairo and Alexandria. By 1880 there were 1,300 kilometers of rail and 5,200 kilometers of telegraph cables. In 1866 the port of Alexandria was enlarged and developed and the Suez Canal was opened for international traffic. A score or more steamship lines touched Egyptian ports. Currency was stabilized. Modern commercial and mortgage banks were established and experienced a spectacular growth in the mid-sixties.

The economic opportunities opened up by all these transformations and by Ismā'īl's lavish spending, attracted large numbers of foreigners who had an important role in the infusion of Western ideas and customs. From 3,000 in 1836, the number of foreigners grew to 68,000 by 1878. They settled mainly in the larger cities whose appearance they helped to transform. A few years later, Lord Cromer was to describe Cairo as a combination of Mecca and a stillborn Rue de Rivoli.

Education was once more vastly expanded, and energetic if unsuccessful efforts were made to improve its quality. School attendance reached its peak in 1875 after the reorganization of the system of education undertaken by the devoted and capable 'Alī pasha Mubārak. During that year, 4,685 religious elementary schools were registered with an attendance of 111,896 pupils; three higher religious schools with 15,335 students, and thirty-six civilian schools, supported by *waqfs* and by the government, with 4,778 students.[16] Provisions were made for allowing distinguished students from the religious elementary schools to continue their education in the secular schools. In 1872, after having despaired of reforming al-Azhar, Ismā'īl opened the college of Dār al-'Ulūm with the aim of training teachers in modern subjects as well as in the traditional subjects taught at al-Azhar, and with the hope that the college would eventually replace the erstwhile conservative university as the main center of Islamic influence. A year later the first school for girls was founded under the patronage of Ismā'īl's wife and was soon followed by another in 1875. But, with all this progress, public education could not free itself from the old methods which emphasized facts and memorizing, nor liberate itself from its extreme utilitarian bent. The whole system remained centrally directed in every respect, and the graduates were immediately channeled into government service. Between 1865 and 1875, 63 per cent of the graduates of civilian schools were absorbed in the army, and another 19 per cent in the civil service.[17]

An advance of greater consequence in education took place through the expansion of the activities of missions in Egypt. The number of mission schools not only multiplied under Ismā'īl, but their example stimulated the creation of communal and private schools. By 1878, there were over two hundred missionary and private schools, and 52 per cent of their student body was of Egyptian nationality.[18]

Ismā'īl exerted great effort in his attempt to reform the judicial system of Egypt. His Armenian minister, Nubār pasha, successfully negotiated with the European powers the establishment of mixed courts to adjudicate civil and commercial matters when one or both of the parties were foreigners, to replace the previous practice of allowing the consul of the nation to which the foreigner belonged to handle such cases.[19] The law applied in these courts was a modified version of the French civil and commercial codes, and these were adopted soon afterwards for the country at large to insure uniform justice. This development caused whole generations of students, lawyers, and judges to look to France and Europe as sources of inspiration for legal principles and practice, and so was instrumental in instructing Egyptians in the constitutional foundations of modern Western law, and in the ideas of national rights, sovereignty of the people, and civil liberties which became the basis of the nationalist movement. It also prepared the ground for substituting modern secular codes for Shar'ī law in one sphere after another, even though Ismā'īl contented himself for the moment with the technical reorganization of the Shar'ī courts along modern lines, the codification of the laws of personal status and inheritance, and the uniform application throughout the country of the Ḥanafī legal "code."

Ismā'īl's prodigality, the opportunities opened by his attempt to establish a modern administration, and the relative liberty that prevailed in Egypt in comparison with the Hamidian tyranny that prevailed in their homeland, attracted to Egypt large numbers of Syrian Christians who had studied in Christian missionary colleges in their own country and who now became pioneers in many fields of cultural endeavor. They founded the first Arabic daily newspaper and other periodicals and began the process of creating a simplified, flexible, and direct language to suit the purposes of journalism. They provided the spark needed to set off a literary renaissance which in turn contributed to the rise of the nationlist movement in Egypt.

In the political sphere, important developments occurred during this period which awakened for the first time a consciousness of the ideological challenge imposed by the new conditions and at the same time stimulated the first attempts to meet it. Sa'īd and Ismā'īl had obtained from Constantinople the recognition of a larger autonomy for Egypt. Ismā'īl used this increased independence to contract large loans at exorbitant rates to finance his vast projects, and, when he had exhausted his credit, the usual results followed: bankruptcy, foreign control, disturbances, and foreign occupation. But, also as usual, Ismā'īl had been forced in the wake of his financial embarrassment to make concessions that put definite limitations on his absolute power and on the power of his successors. We have already mentioned his offer to recognize absolute ownership of the land to all those who paid six years' taxes in advance. Another concession was forced on him by his foreign creditors, compelling him to rule through a responsible ministry which drastically curtailed his power, particularly when foreign controllers were joined to the cabinet. The public treasury, which had always been indistinguishable from the ruler's private wealth, was now separated from it and both were submitted to the control of the cabinet and the British and French officials representing the creditors. Ismā'īl had set up consultative representative assembly as a showpiece in imitation of civilized governments; but his repeated recourse to it to support him in imposing new taxes aroused the assembly to claim a real voice in the affairs of the government.[20] This experiment, together with the spread of education, the establishment of a press, the emergence of a new middle class of officials, professionals, and a landed bourgeoisie, the constant exaction of taxes, and the foreign intervention, produced the first stirrings of public opinion and of civic political activity, and the first attempts to grapple with the results of the changes that we have described.

CHAPTER 3

Challenge and Response: The First Formulations

The cumulative effect of the developments that we have described amounted to nothing less than a complete transformation of the basic character of the life and organization of Egyptian society. Such a transformation undermined the traditional Islamic ideological system which had served as the foundation of the political community, and, in the absence of an alternative belief system, the stability, indeed the very existence, of the political community became increasingly precarious. Whereas sheer force and an inevitable delay in the crystallization of popular awareness had enabled Muḥammad ʿAlī to preserve a semblance of a community, these props could not suffice for long, and by the end of Ismāʿīl's reign and the beginning of his successor's they had drastically weakened, leaving the community vulnerable to the forces of disintegration.

It is not our intention here to analyze in detail the complicated process of corrosion which consumed the authority of the governments of Ismāʿīl and his successor, Tawfīq. This has been done adequately by a number of historians and is, at any rate, of secondary importance in our interpretive scheme, which views this process merely as the occasion for making clear the consequences of the basic conflict between the belief-system and the implications of the new reality. Rather, an elaboration of the nature of the conflict itself in specific terms, first objectively, and then as it appeared to those political and intellectual leaders who first expressed an awareness of it, constitutes the primary task in this chapter. Nevertheless, in order to understand why the conflict developed when it did and why the first reactions to it took the form they did, the following events are worth recalling.

In the first place, Ismāʿīl's declaration of bankruptcy in 1876 had severely damaged the prestige of the government, which had become an increasingly vital factor in maintaining control of the people as the more fundamental grounds for eliciting obedience were undermined by the changing conditions. The humiliation of bankruptcy was aggravated by the fact that the financial crisis brought Ismāʿīl and his government under the formal control of foreign powers; and in his attempt to escape this control by warning the powers that their imposed regulations contravened the Muslim tradition, Ismāʿīl succeeded only in increasing the popular alarm and invoking a spectre that would haunt him and future rulers as well. Moreover, Ismāʿīl's financial difficulties had led him to resort to such depredatory taxation that many peasants preferred to abandon their beloved land and flee rather than submit to his endless exactions. In the cities there was a state of semi-famine in the years 1877–1878. Misery and hunger naturally disposed people to believe that something was amiss in the world they inhabited and to attribute the blame to those responsible for the most recent disturbance of the status quo. Finally, the general development of the preceding half-century, the spread of education and contact with Western ideas of government, had given rise to a new group of officials, professional men and educated people of public spirit who could, for the first time in Egypt's history, articulate their views on political and social conditions.

The transformations in the conditions of life of Egyptian society constituted a challenge to traditional Islamic doctrine on several levels. The basic challenge consisted of a contradiction between the Islamic world view and the world view implicit in the new conditions of life. These conditions implied an outlook on life which, like the modern European *weltanschauungen*, conceives the world of human affairs as essentially self-contained; whereas the traditional Islamic — like the Medieval Christian — outlook views it as determined and guided by an extrinsic transcendental authority. It is true that those Egyptians who had been most affected by the new conditions of living did not necessarily formulate at once a consciously explicit and comprehensive theory that embodied an outlook of the world as self-contained, but their failure to do so only blurred the underlying contradiction without eliminating it, causing all the more unease and confusion. For, as Dilthey [1] pointed out, world views are not the product of thinking per se, but proceed from the conduct of life and from life experience in general. Their articulation in conscious cognitive and normative systems is a very important step in the intellectual development of mankind and is a necessary condition for their becoming the basis of a political community; but world views can make a strong impact on society even as simple sets of psychological inclinations without conscious formulation.

Another challenge to traditional ideology found expression in the sphere of law and ethics. In a certain sense, the challenge here may be viewed mainly as a concrete manifestation of the conflicting world views that we have just discussed. But it should also be seen as the actualization of a conflict that has resided *in potentia* in the traditional doctrine of the Sharīʻah ever since its formulation. For that concept, with its notion of the Sharīʻah as nothing less than the final and complete spelling out of the objective divine revelation of the Qur'ān and the Ḥadīth, sought to impose on human affairs forever a specific system which had in fact developed out of the historical conditions of the early centuries of Islam. That historical reality subsequent to the formulation of the doctrine did not expose this fiction was due to the fact that reality itself, the basic social structure, and the organization and character of the economy of Muslim communities, remained for so long fundamentally unchanged. When this ceased to be the case, after the transformations wrought by Muḥammad ʻAlī and his immediate successors, the long-delayed conflict fell due, manifesting itself in a sense of perplexity due to the lack of Sharʻī directives in very many new situations and in an uneasiness about the adequacy of existing directives. This led the rulers to assume the initiative in summarily constricting the sphere of the Sharīʻah and introducing new legal codes and court reforms that suited their personal notion of progress or their immediate political purposes. And this action, in turn, fostered an attitude of indifference and hostility to the law, so prejudicial to the consolidation of a political community, that was to be the bane of modern Egyptian society.[2]

On another level still, the conflict between traditional doctrine and the implications of modern reality manifested itself in the sphere of power. It will be recalled that the later Sunnī view on the subject was characterized by the willingness to legitimize all power on the grounds of the basic philosophical view that all things happen by the will of Allah and on the basis of a specific Qur'ānic text to the effect that Allah bestows dominion on whomever He wishes. This disposition, however, was implicitly related to the tendency to absolve power of any public function beyond the maintenance of order and the appointment of *qāḍīs*, and to leave to the Sharīʻah the task of regulating the other aspects of life. As long as power had actually confined itself to its own sphere, its legitimation regardless of how it was achieved was plausible, since it still permitted society to live according to the Sharīʻah. But as power began to reshape society according to its own chosen ends without regard to Islamic doctrine, as it enlarged its purview to encompass the education, livelihood, and life of the people, and as it began to substitute its own laws for the dictates of the Sharīʻah in one area after another, it became clear that to legitimize such power would be to turn the Sharīʻah into an instrument of the state, and thus reverse the distribution of functions that had been from the beginning at the basis of Islamic doctrine. Such a reversal, though not impossible to conceive, could not, at any rate, take place as a matter of course, especially under circumstances in which most of the population was still mainly tradition-bound. A new interpretation of the principles of legitimation of power was urgently needed. A regime that flouted the old principle without providing a new one could compel the subjects to obedience but could hardly elicit the allegiance which is needed for the stability of the political community.

In addition to these considerations, the subject of power presented another problem, this one mainly externally inspired but one which frequently assumed predominant importance. The traditional doctrine had proclaimed the legitimacy of all power on the ground that all power came from Allah. In so doing, however, it appeared to ignore altogether the possibility that superior power might fall to the lot of the infidels. Perhaps this was due to a propensity of Muslims to associate superior worldly power with Islam ever since the brilliant military triumphs that came after the death of the Messenger; or perhaps it was simply the result of a provincial Muslim perspective, not surprising for the time in which the doctrine was formulated. At any rate, as the irresistible encroachment of European nations on Muslim territories in the nineteenth century drove home ever more forcefully the realization of the overwhelming supremacy of Western Christian power, the notion that all power came from Allah, otherwise so consistent with the absolute divine determinism of traditional doctrine, became extremely difficult to maintain. To do so would be tantamount to legitimizing the oppression of Muslims by infidels, a conception for which Muslims were totally unprepared either psychologically or doctrinally.

Other religious world views were able to deal with similar difficulties in their own terms. The ancient Children of Israel, although they considered themselves God's chosen people, could still conceive of themselves being dominated by idol worshippers because they viewed history as a drama in which an intelligible design of God unfolded in interaction with the actions of men. Saint Thomas Aquinas could contemplate with equanimity the prospect of Christians living under a pagan ruler because he believed with Aristotle that it was possible to have a commonwealth based on natural justice. But traditional Muslim doctrine, having annihilated historical causality and natural justice in the inscrutable omnipotence of Allah, could offer neither hope of redemption from, nor a satisfactory explanation for, the possibility of subjugation by alien, less virtuous powers. And the prospect was all the more frightful since Muslims, accustomed by the concept of *jihād* and conditioned by their view of their own past to look at military and political domination as a prelude to religious domination, were inclined to ascribe the same motive to the military and political expansion of the Christian Western powers. Present-day Western readers may tend to regard such fears as altogether absurd. It is therefore necessary to recall that the agitation stirred in Europe every time a Christian nationality revolted against Ottoman sovereignty, the concern and solicitude of a presumably secularist France for Christian minorities, missions, and holy places, and the actions and proclamations of statesmen like Gladstone or heads of state like Alexander II invoking the obligation of Christian solidarity, were not calculated to assuage Muslim suspicions and apprehensions.

These, then, were the elements of conflict between the new reality and the traditional Islamic world view that afflicted Egyptian society in the last quarter of the nineteenth century, when the conflict was first articulated. One of the characteristics of that articulation, and one that has drawn particular attention and comment from Western analysts, was that the leaders of opinion in Egypt who finally bestirred themselves to take stock of the conflict and to suggest a remedy concentrated mainly on its power aspects even though the conflict existed in fact on several other and perhaps more significant levels, as we have just seen. Theories have been advanced attempting to explain this phenomenon on the grounds that power does in fact occupy a central place in Muslim outlook. W. C. Smith,[3] for instance, makes an essential distinction between the nature of the challenge faced by Christendom in the sixteenth century and that faced by the Muslim world in the nineteenth, and argues that, whereas in the case of Christianity the challenge consisted of the problem posed by science and philosophy to the essential Christian dogma, in the case of Islam the challenge consisted *essentially* of the problem posed by the realization of the supremacy of non-Muslim power. Because Islam asserts itself more as a way of life than as a dogma, Smith contends, it is more impervious to rational attacks than Christianity, but is on the other hand much more sensitive to psychological challenges, such as the sudden realization of its inferiority in terms of worldly power.

Actually, there are more immediate explanations of the preoccupation with power at this and at subsequent stages of the ideological evolution of Egypt which leave unaffected our proposition that the challenge of modern conditions to traditional Islamic ideology was on the comprehensive ground of world views, ethics, and law, as well as power.

In the case of the first articulation of the nature of the conflict, with which we are concerned at present, the problem of power was emphasized simply because that problem was more obvious *at that particular moment* than the more abstract problem of theological-rational conflict. Since the modernization of Egypt had been imposed from above, and had none of the social and intellectual bases that underlay the modern evolution of Europe, the spirit of modern science and philosophy had made very little headway by the time depredation, semi-famine, bankruptcy, and other abuses of government on the one hand, and foreign encroachments, on the other, compelled attention to the problem of power. Subsequently, as the new concepts of science and philosophy became more widespread, the conflict was indeed moved to the level of rational against theological principles and the problem became, *mutatis mutandis*, not unlike that of Christianity at the dawn of the modern age. When preoccupation with the problem of power reappears later, it will be clearly seen as constituting one of the consequences of the failure to resolve the rational-theological conflict.

But even as things stood at the end of Ismā'īl's reign, the conflict could not be formulated purely as a question of power without involving concern with broader implications, because the traditional view of power was an integral part of a whole religious, philosophical, historical, legal, and political system. The fact of reexamining the question implies from the outset a break with the conception of the Islamic doctrine as complete, final, and immutable. Nor could any attempt to absolve Allah from responsibility for the subjection of Muslims to unbelievers be made without involving a whole new theodicy which would modify the notion of absolute, arbitrary divine omnipotence, and so open the door for a critical view of history as self-impelled. And if causation were restored to history, could ethical values remain without intrinsic meaning? These questions do not exhaust the possible implications of a revision of the traditional concept of power, but they indicate sufficiently that such a revision must unavoidably lead to a far-reaching reappraisal of the whole Muslim view of life. The first articulation of conflict and suggestions for its remedy to which we now turn, show that their authors, al-Afghānī and his disciples, were certainly aware of the ramifications of the problems of power even though they failed at this stage to cope with them adequately.

Jamāl al-Dīn al-Afghānī (1839–1897) [4] was born in Afghanistan, according to his own account, where he received an unusually broad Islamic education, an education which he constantly supplemented throughout his life. In his early manhood he served as minister to a contender for the throne of Kabul who was eventually defeated by his British-supported rival. Soon after, al-Afghānī set out on a leisurely pilgrimage to Mecca and stopped for a while in India; but his sojourn there was cut short by an expulsion order. Henceforth, he was seized by the idea that European imperialism presented a mortal threat to the Muslims and made it his life mission to awaken the still-independent Muslim countries to the danger, and to incite them to unite and reform their views and their life to face it. As he saw it, the danger was not merely loss of independence — it was the destruction of Islam itself; and whatever excuses the imperialist powers used to justify their expansion were only so many disguises to cloak the offensive of Christianity against Islam which had begun with the Crusades.

Al-Afghānī became convinced that the power of the Europeans was a function of science and technology, methods of organization, and diplomacy. To counter their onslaught, Muslims must begin forthwith to adopt and develop the same means to the utmost extent. This proposition was not in itself new to the Muslim world; in Egypt it had already received thorough application in the work and career of Muḥammad ʻAlī. What was new, however, was that a religious leader had given it his sanction and now sought to enlist science and technology in the cause of defending Islam itself. This constituted a revolution in Muslim thought. For it brought back to the world of human affairs a recognition of causality which had been banished by traditional doctrine, and thus foreshadowed the re-evaluation of the status of the doctrine itself.

Al-Afghānī did not shy away from the implications of his views. He advocated outrightly the reopening of the gates of *ijtihād*, vehemently rejected unquestioning submission to the authority of the medieval school, urged a return to the spirit of the true primitive Islam, denounced fatalism and passiveness, and condemned the superstitions and abusive mystic practices which distorted the true faith. He was never able, however, to bring himself down from this level of generalities to specific reformulations of Islamic principles. One reason for his inability to do so was that he believed that the Christian powers would not allow the Muslims to reform unless Muslims took the necessary political measures to hold them at bay. Chief among these measures, according to al-Afghānī, was a union of all the Muslim countries, or at least a mutual defense alliance among their rulers — in short, pan-Islamism.

Another reason for remaining on the level of generalities was that, judging from his only published book,[5] al-Afghānī did not seem to have the philosophic mind, the intellectual equipment, or the temperament necessary for a thorough theoretical reformulation of Islamic doctrine.

But whatever al-Afghānī's shortcomings as a theoretician, they did not prevent him from being a great teacher and from having a remarkable charismatic appeal which inspired all those who came in contact with him. These qualities enabled him to exert an enormous influence on the ideological development of Egypt, where he had come at the invitation of the chief minister in 1871, following his expulsion from Constantinople on the accusation of teaching heretical views. He settled down near the mosque-university of al-Azhar and soon attracted a substantial number of eager students with whom he studied certain Muslim philosophical works which had long been abandoned in al-Azhar and were still viewed with suspicion. He introduced his students to some translated Western works and was particularly fond of Guizot's *History of Civilization in France*, from which he endlessly drew practical lessons about civic virtues, duties, and rights, and about what makes the greatness of nations. He encouraged his students to come down from the ivory tower of scholastic studies, to take a stand on worldly subjects, and to express their opinions on them in writing. In this way he managed to impart by word of mouth many of the ideas which he had failed to set forth in writing; and, like Socrates, he was fortunate in having his Plato in the person of Muḥammad 'Abduh — of whom we shall hear a great deal later.

But al-Afghānī was too much a born political agitator to remain content for long with mere teaching; and the opportunities for more exciting endeavor did not fail to present themselves. As the consequences of Ismā'īl's profligacy began to manifest themselves in more oppressive taxation, bankruptcy, and foreign intervention, all sorts of reformers, agitators, and generally discontented people were drawn to al-Afghānī. It is said that he founded a Masonic chapter to serve as a cover for his political activities which numbered three hundred members, among whom was the young crown prince Tawfīq; [6] and it is certain that he encouraged and supported several journalistic endeavors dedicated to opposition to the khedive — an unheard-of step in Egyptian history.

Al-Afghānī had fathered the idea of pan-Islamism as the only means to stave off Christian attacks while the Muslim countries reformed themselves. He soon realized, however, that Muslim rulers themselves often abetted the designs of the enemies of Islam by their gullibility, irresponsibility, and corruption. Consequently, he drew the inevitable conclusion that restraints must be imposed upon the rulers' powers, even though he did not show any particular preference as to the forms these restraints should take. In Egypt he supported the Constitutionalists who sought to bring the khedive under the control of an elected assembly; in Persia he had sought to restrict the shah's power through the religious leaders. In both cases he was willing to resort to any other means. One report maintains that he, the champion of opposition to Western intrusion in Muslim affairs, consulted the French representative in Egypt with the idea of inducing the European powers to press the Ottoman sultan to depose Ismā'īl and appoint Tawfīq in his place.[7] He also plotted with some of his students, including young Muḥammad 'Abduh, to assassinate Ismā'īl. And in the last days of Ismā'īl's rule, as depression and agitation reached their height, he did not hesitate to address an audience in Alexandria in the following terms:

> You, o poor peasants. You split open the heart of the earth in order to bring therefrom sustenance to yourself and your folk. Why don't you also split the heart of your oppressor? Why don't you split open the hearts of those who eat away the fruit of your labor? [8]

After the deposition of Ismā'īl and the accession of Tawfīq finally materialized in 1879, it looked for a time as if al-Afghānī and his supporters were about to have their way. Al-Afghānī was consulted on all sorts of subjects by the young, well-meaning khedive, who assured him that he, al-Afghānī, was the repository of his own hopes for Egypt. But al-Afghānī was impatient for action and urged Tawfīq to get rid of the palace advisers inherited from Ismā'īl who counselled caution and fostered the young khedive's timidity. Tawfīq failed to move as far and as rapidly as al-Afghānī had wanted him to do, and when the British, French, and Italian representatives joined members of the palace guard in warning Tawfīq against the possible dangers to his own person in following and not following his fiery adviser, the khedive, characteristically, reversed his stand and expelled al-Afghānī from Egypt.[9] But this action only postponed for a brief while the consequences that it was meant to avoid. For al-Afghānī's disciples continued his political activity and two years later many of them joined the 'Urābī uprising which threatened to bring down the khedive and the whole political order that he headed. Only the intervention of the British saved him from that fate.

In addition to al-Afghānī and his disciples, another group, to whom we have already alluded as "the Constitutionalists," [10] attempted to meet the challenge of the new conditions as it manifested itself in the sphere of power, only from a different point of view.

Al-Afghānī had been concerned with the problem of power primarily in terms of the threat posed by the superior might of the expanding Christian countries, and in terms of the general ideological implications that this threat might hold. His involvement in the internal problem of power was more a consequence of his concern with checking foreign intrusion than of an awareness of the intrinsic problem of its legitimation. The Constitutionalists, on the other hand, though they were at times involved in the question of foreign intrusion, were in fact chiefly preoccupied with establishing a new basis for the legitimation of power within the political community.

It is true that the Constitutionalists did not explicitly and consciously perceive the problem in any broad theoretical frame that showed an awareness of the conflict between the traditional view of power and the new conditions, and of the implications for the political community of the absence of a suitable principle of legitimation. Such awareness is rarely found even among the several generations of more sophisticated politicians and thinkers who succeeded them. Rather, the Constitutionalists, including high-ranking officials and notables, were a group who, having been exposed to a certain degree to Western influence, had come to think of constitutionalism, representative assembly, and ministerial responsibility as inherent features of civilized and efficient government. Nevertheless, though the implications of their position might not have been worked out in great detail, the Constitutionalists were making a practical beginning toward the establishment of a new procedure of legitimation of power. More important, their initiative was encountering a receptivity and support among the newly emerging press and leaders of public opinion that promised eventually to make explicit and popularize some of the principles implicit in the practical constitutional arrangements. Such support was forthcoming not only from the many Western-educated Christian Syrian writers, but also from good Muslims, including men from al-Afghānī's school. Thus, Muḥammad 'Abduh, in 1880, wrote a long article in *al-Waqā'i' al-Miṣriyyah*, the official government gazette which he edited at the time, arguing in Islamic juridical terms the merits of constitutionalism, and concluded by saying: "From here we learn that the inclination of some people to demand a *shūra* (meaning here a parliamentary assembly) and to reject absolutism does not come simply from a desire to imitate the foreigner, but is in accordance with what the Sharī'ah requires."[11]

In these words 'Abduh may have been trying to soothe the anxiety of the conservatives who feared any foreign importation, or he may have been himself convinced that the Sharī'ah enjoins *shūra*.

The fact remains that the Constitutionalists had drawn their ideas from Europe, directly or through the intermediary of Turkish Liberal statesmen who had forced a constitution upon the sultan in 1876. Sharīf pasha, the leader of the Constitutionalists in Egypt, had, for instance, spent nearly six years studying in France as a member of a student mission sent by Muḥammad 'Alī, during which he witnessed and was impressed by the revolution of 1848. Later, as a high-ranking official and a Turk, he was in touch with developments in the Ottoman empire and the Western-inspired and largely Western-pressed reforms undertaken by fellow-Ottomans like 'Ālī, Fu'ād, and Midḥat. The entire Constitutionalist movement in Egypt developed, it will be recalled, from the modest representative assembly that Ismā'īl had established in an obvious effort to imitate European constitutional rulers.

The Constitutionalist movement was not destined to have the chance of a trial at this stage in Egyptian history. Before it had managed to make any substantial headway, it was caught up, willy-nilly, in the rising tide of the 'Urābī revolution and accordingly shared its fate. We have mentioned before that the movement began when members of the initially comically timid representative assembly set up by Ismā'īl began to clamor for increased authority when he turned to them for help in imposing new taxation. Eventually, Ismā'īl responded generously to these clamors when he thought that he would thereby be in a better position to ward off the pressure of his creditors and the interference of the French and the British in directing the government. On the one hand he sought to use the assembly to sabotage the work of the Ministry which he no longer controlled, and on the other hand he wanted to impress on everybody that the legitimate representatives of the country were behind him. In spite of his schemes, Ismā'īl was finally deposed; but the assembly remained with enlarged powers and an appetite for more. It demanded that the government be formally responsible to it. Particularly, it demanded the right to approve the budget, and thus came in conflict with the newly established Anglo-French Commission of the Debt. In this way the Constitutionalists became associated with resistance to the foreigners, and their leader, Sharīf pasha, found himself cooperating intermittently with 'Urābī and his fellow-rebels. In 1882, Sharīf accepted the presidency of a Ministry which had been imposed by the rebels on the khedive, and took the revolutionary step of summoning the assembly into session without a convocation from the khedive. But his suspicion of the methods of the 'Urābists prevented him from collaborating wholeheartedly with them and thus saved him personally from the consequences of revolt when the debacle came. The Constitutionalist movement itself, however, was silenced — at least for the next quarter of a century.

We have seen that the movement of al-Afghānī as well as that of the Constitutionalists became entangled with the 'Urābī uprising and failed, in the immediate sense, with its collapse. For this reason and because the 'Urābī uprising led to such important international consequences, historians have tended to look at those two movements as relatively minor episodes within the main drama of the 'Urābī revolution. In the perspective of the present study, however, the order of importance to be attributed to the movements and the revolution needs to be drastically revised. Partial, rudimentary, shallow, and general as their endeavor was, the Afghānists and the Constitutionalists at least addressed themselves in fact, if not always consciously, to the basic problem of ideology and the political community. On the other hand, if viewed in terms of its internal significance, the revolution remains only the expression of a haphazard mixture of concrete complaints and fears, inchoate general discontent, and vague and contradictory aspirations that could only lead to what was described by Milner as "the complete dissolution of Egyptian society in the summer of 1882," [12] and could be met only by the imposition of a superior force of some kind.

The 'Urābī movement had started when a few Egyptian army officers led by Colonel 'Urābī sent a petition to the Minister of War protesting against the privileged position of their Turkish and Circassian colleagues and demanding redress. Mishandled by the authorities, the petition led to a mutiny involving a few battalions. From this moment on, fear of reprisals pushed the compromised officers into more and more drastic action in order to protect themselves, and led them gradually to widen their demands and their platform in order to enlist the support of various groups. Thus they first imposed on the khedive a Minister of War of their choosing and then an entire cabinet. They supported the demands of the Constitutionalists for a parliamentary assembly, became mouthpieces for the Afghānī partisans in seeking to bind the country more closely to the Ottoman sultan the better to resist foreigners, and, without regard to consistency, adopted the slogan "Egypt for the Egyptians" that had been launched by an Egyptian-Jewish nationalist publicist. They pleaded the case of the plain soldier and championed the cause of the small farmer, who was reeling under the burden of taxation. Within a brief time they succeeded in stirring up the whole country behind them so that, in the words of a contemporary Egyptian witness of ambivalent sentiments toward the 'Urābists, "Everybody fancied himself 'Urābī and 'Urābī fancied himself everybody; classes were dissolved and the high and the low got mixed and there was no making heads or tails of it."[13] But although the 'Urābists managed to achieve in practice full control of the government, they were not able to control the forces they had unleashed. There followed wave after wave of violence, disorders, *jacqueries*, and arson, which reached their height in the massacre and looting of Alexandria in June of 1882 and provided, among other things, an excuse for the British forces to intervene, crush the rebellion, and occupy the country.

It would be a mistake to conclude from the genesis and step-by-step unfolding of the events, as some observers have done, that the 'Urābī revolution was mainly the handiwork of a few frightened agitators. 'Urābī and his associates were able to arouse all sectors of the population only because these had been for some time past restless under a political order that not only oppressed them but was alien to them. Here was, in fact, a perfect illustration of one of the basic propositions of this book, that a political order that lacked a foundation in shared views could only have a precarious existence. Since the Egyptian regime had radically diverged from the traditional belief-system, it had lost any claim to the allegiance of the people and was able to exact obedience from them only as long as force and prestige were in its command. When these were challenged by the 'Urābī movement, there was nothing left to prevent the "breakdown of Egyptian society." Yet it remains true that 'Urābī's movement was basically a negative one with no understanding of what the real ailments of Egyptian society were or how to cure them. This is, perhaps, the reason why it left little trace after it was suppressed, despite the efforts of the men of the 1952 revolution to rescue it from oblivion. In contrast, certain aspects of al-Afghānī's teachings and the aspirations of the Constitutionalists were revived and pushed forward soon after their initial setbacks.

Part Two

MAIN TRENDS OF IDEOLOGICAL EVOLUTION

CHAPTER 4

The Making of Modern Egypt: Economic, Social, and Cultural Evolution under the Occupation (1882-1922)

The British occupation of Egypt in 1882 opened a new, crucial, and intricate phase in the country's political evolution. The British had landed in Egypt for the declared purpose of restoring the authority of the khedive, which had been shaken by the rebels, and of establishing a modicum of order in the administration and finances of the country in order to forestall any attempt by other powers to intervene and gain ascendancy in an area of vital importance for British imperial communications. Despite the shadows that subsequent history seems to cast on them, it appears clear to anyone who is acquainted with British politics of the period that the British government's declarations of its intention to evacuate the country promptly, made even as the British troops were marching on Cairo and repeated often thereafter, were sincere. However, these declarations had come from the government leaders in London, who had mistakenly, but excusably, thought that the recent disturbances in Egypt constituted a limited uprising, made possible by the ineptitude and ruthlessness of some oriental despots, fomented by a relatively few frustrated men, and joined by larger sections of a population driven beyond the limits of endurance. The British agents on the spot, however, thought differently of the situation once they had a close look at it.

It was, perhaps, a measure of the insight of the great British proconsul in Egypt, Lord Cromer, that he perceived that what had just taken place was no simple uprising due to specific abuses but rather a collapse of the entire political order that had emerged since the days of Muḥammad 'Alī — a collapse brought about by failure of the government to earn for itself any claim to the people's allegiance. It was, perhaps, a measure of Cromer's limitation that he believed Britain, an alien occupying power, could preside over the rehabilitation of a genuine political community on the basis of "civilized" values and "Christian" ethics. But it was surely a measure of the absurd self-deception to which pious intentions and a colonial administrator's mentality can lead that he thought the British could achieve this purpose solely by the administrative, financial, and technical reforms to which London had largely confined its representatives in Cairo in its concern not to extend the goals of the occupation too far beyond what would be necessary to ensure its own political and economic interests.

These, however, are only reflections on the limited role the British occupation authorities could play over the long run in the basic conflict between the traditional belief-system and modern reality. Actually, there was a good deal that could be done within the frame of the occupation before that limit would be reached. The entire development since the days of Muḥammad ʻAlī needed to be consolidated and a more accurate notion of the practical meaning of modern government had to be conveyed to rulers and ruled alike. Since the momentarily inexorable fact of the occupation had drastically reduced the possibilities of political activity and discouraged any impulsive militant action, it became relevant for Egyptian intellectual leaders to concentrate on achieving a deeper appreciation of the basic ideological problem. It seemed possible that a start might be made toward the solution of the problem without its proponents getting hopelessly entangled in immediate political conflict and diverted from their purpose. All this was in fact largely realized. The years from 1882 to the first World War constituted, indeed, a truly formative period in the ideological and historical evolution of modern Egypt. The ideological developments will occupy our attention after a brief consideration of the record of the occupation in the economic and social spheres and a general description of the cultural activity during that period.

One of the most important developments that took place during the nineteenth century and continued under the British was the very rapid growth of the population. The newly gained security of life and property, the development of communications, the application of minimal measures of sanitation, and, above all, the introduction of cotton cultivation with its immense demand for labor that could be easily performed by children, provoked a demographic explosion that enlarged the population of Egypt from about 3,000,000 in 1800 to 6,800,000 in 1882 and 11,300,000 in 1917.[1] Thanks to the vast irrigation projects undertaken by the British, it was possible for a while to expand the crop area to follow rather closely the growth of population. From 4,743,000 *feddans* in 1877, the crop area was increased to over 7,700,000 *feddans* in 1911, even though the cultivable area did not exceed 5,203,000 *feddans* in 1913.[2] But after the second decade of the twentieth century, as the population continued to grow and little new land could be brought under the plow or converted to perennial irrigation, Egypt began to feel the pressure of overpopulation.[3]

Under the firm hand of the British, the economy of the country was expanded and stabilized. Cotton cultivation was increased and reached 22 per cent of the crop area in 1913, accounting for 93 per cent of the total value of Egypt's exports in 1910–1914. Public finances were put in order after Ismā'īl's bankruptcy, and private financing was expanded. Railroad construction continued and there were 4,800 kilometers of rail in 1909 compared with 1,300 kilometers in 1880. All these developments, together with the security provided by the presence of the British, fostered a great boom in foreign investment. By 1914, the total capital of joint stock companies was estimated at L.E. 100 million ($500 million), 92 per cent of which was invested by foreigners.[4]

Egyptian nationalists are fond of contrasting the remarkable achievements of the British occupation in the spheres of agriculture, finance, and communications with the dismal record it made in public education in order to substantiate the charge that the British were mainly interested in those improvements that enabled them to exploit the country economically. If we accept public education as the only test of disinterested endeavor, then the nationalists' charge must stand. For it must be said that public education expanded extremely slowly under the British and continued to be purposely geared, for most of the period under review, toward producing government officials. Its development was deliberately limited to the administration's capacity to absorb its graduates. Apart from the traditional *kuttābs*, there were only sixty-eight government-supported primary and secondary schools in 1914 when the population counted much more than nine million. And it was not the case that the Egyptians were not eager for education; their demand for it was well reflected in the mushrooming of private and missionary schools. In 1914 there were 739 private Egyptian schools with an attendance of 99,000, and 328 communal and missionary schools with 48,000 pupils.[5]

Student missions continued to be sent abroad on a scale equal to that of Ismā'īl's days, but there was now a great policy shift with respect to the country to which they were sent and in the subject matters studied. In the whole previous history of student missions, 80 per cent had studied in France and 96 per cent had learned technical subjects; under the British, however, 75 per cent were sent to Britain and 65 per cent took up subjects related to the humanities and the social sciences. Besides these governmental missions, hundreds of students studied on their own in Europe, particularly in France.[6]

The British refrained from undertaking any large-scale social reform largely because of their peculiar legal position in Egypt until World War I. (Theoretically the country was still under the suzerainty of the Ottoman empire, and the only justification for the presence of the British was to restore order and to secure the debtors' interests.) For the same reason, and out of care for the religious sensitivities of the people, they were even more careful to refrain from interfering with any subject that was even remotely connected with the religious institutions and traditions. It is true that they reformed the *kuttāb* system, enforced the abolition of slavery, and introduced the national courts, but all these things had already been initiated during the previous regime. Altogether, it is important to keep in mind that the basic patterns and trends of Egyptian economy and society had already been established by the end of Ismā'īl's days and that the role of the British has been more one of consolidation and extension than of initiation. By the time they came to Egypt, the basis of the economic structure had been changed from a feudal to a private one; the economy had become attached to the world market through specialization in cotton cultivation and export; and the foundations for further economic development had been laid in the form of social capital, financing institutions, and a judicial and administrative framework. The country had been unified under a central government and a Western-style administration had been established. Western education had been introduced in addition to the modified traditional system, and had been geared to supply the state with civil servants. Foreigners had been encouraged to settle in the country, and Western technology, manners, and fashions had gained a strong foothold, particularly in the cities. The pattern of social stratification had already emerged: at the top was the ruling class, composed of a Turco-Egyptian landed aristocracy, and at the bottom a *tiers état* in which a new middle class of professionals and officials was prominent. A high and low "clergy" divided between the two classes. A native mercantile and industrial bourgeoisie had been conspicuously absent ever since the time of Muḥammad 'Alī, whose monopolization of commerce and industry had left room only for foreign traders and entrepreneurs. In all these respects the British administration was responsible for many quantitative changes and a systematic development. Where progress had been sporadic and uncertain, it was given stability and planning, and was secured against the kind of relapse that occurred at the end of Muḥammad ʻAlī's days, during the reign of Abbās I, and in the last years of Ismāʻīl's rule. Where certain institutions had already been adopted, the British strove to make them work, and where gaps had been left, they tried to close them. Above all, by the example of their administration, their efficiency and devotion, their vigilance, and such actions as the abolition of the *kurbāj* (whipping) and forced labor, the British communicated to Egyptians (it is hard to gauge how deeply and how extensively) the notion that power is a social function and not simply domination; that office is a public service and not a fief to be exploited in return for personal service to a prince; that the people are really equal before the law and that their rights, even if unstated in constitutions, can exercise a restraint on the power of the government.

In the cultural sphere, modern Egyptian literature, which had had its hesitant and fumbling beginnings at the time of Ismāʻīl, finally reached the highroad of decisive development during this period. This was not, of course, a sphere for which the British were primarily responsible, but they had created an environment and an atmosphere that encouraged constructive work and thought, and for most of the period they allowed ample freedom of expression. The continued immigration of Syrian intellectuals, the maturation of some of the students trained by al-Afghānī, and the return of mission students from Europe who had received a thorough education in the humanities provided several crops of writers with varied viewpoints and interests; and economic development and the multiplication of schools gave birth to a substantially large public endowed with the leisure, education, and interest to form an audience, a "market" for the writers' products. The result, measured against the situation preceding it, was a true literary and intellectual renaissance.[7]

There had begun, in Ismāʻīl's day, a movement to revive and republish Arabic literary masterpieces from the period before the decline. This movement was accelerated during the occupation and inspired a school of influential and accomplished poets which included men like al-Bārūdī (1840–1904), Ṣabrī (1885–1923), Shawqī (1868–1932), Ḥāfiẓ (1871–1932), and Muṭrān (1871–1949). It was a sign of the vitality of the budding cultural life that, brilliant and established as this school was, it was challenged just before the first World War by another school of young poets who criticized its excessive imitation of classical models, forms, and themes, and the weak intellectual and social commitment of its members. That school included men like Shukrī (1886–), al-Māznī (1889–1949), and al-ʻAqqād (1889–) — the latter two even better known for their prose work — all of whom began their work in the third decade of the occupation but produced most of it in the period since then.

The whole literary activity of the period fed and has continued since to feed on the translation of Western works, which had begun before the occupation and flourished under it. Most popular were the works of Lafontaine, Molière, Racine, Rousseau, Bernardin de Saint-Pierre, and the French romantic writers from the second half of the nineteenth century, especially Anatole France and Hugo. Translations were followed by adaptations and imitations and finally by original creations, and, in the process, the novel and the play made their first entrance into Arabic literature. The pioneers of this literary movement were men like 'Uthmān Jalāl (1829–1898), who adapted de Saint Pierre's *Paul et Virginie* in blank verse and translated Racine's *Esther*, *Iphigénie*, and *Alexandre le Grand* into colloquial verse; Adīb Isḥāq (1856–1885), who adapted *Andromaque*, *Charlemagne*, and *La Belle Parisienne*; Aḥmad Fāris al-Shidyāq (1804–1887), who wrote *al-Faryāq*, a work heavily inspired by Rabelais; Jamīl Mudawwar (1862–1907), who wrote a historical novel after the fashion of Fenelon's *Aventures de Telemaque*; and Jurjī Zaydān (1861–1914), who poured out no less than twenty-two Muslim historical romances after the fashion of Dumas and Scott, in addition to his other voluminous efforts.

On the broadly philosophical side, the Syrian *émigrés* did most to acquaint Egyptians with eighteenth and nineteenth century Liberal and scientific French and British currents of thought. Faraḥ Anṭūn (1874–1922) issued the review *al Jāmi'ah*, which was devoted to spreading French thought, particularly the ideas of eighteenth century rationalism, anticlericalism, and revolution. Ya'qūb Ṣarrūf (1852–1927) edited the widely read review, *al-Muqtaṭaf*, devoted to the popularization of modern sciences, natural and social, which served as an instrument for spreading the theories of Darwinian and Spencerian evolution. Jurjī Zaydān published the monthly *al-Hilāl*, where he wrote an endless number of articles on Western history and the history of science. Shiblī Shumayyil (1860–1916) started a school of thought devoted to the philosophical interpretation of evolution, inspired by Buchner and Spencer, which has had an unbroken chain of adherents until recent times. Among the Egyptian Muslim writers, Fathī Zaghlūl worked most on introducing Western political thought and sociology with translations that included Le Bon's *L'Esprit de la société*, Bentham's *Principles of Legislation*, and Edmond Demolins' *A quoi tient la superiorité des Anglo-Saxons*. He was followed by Luṭfī al-Sayyid, editor of the daily *al-Jarīdah*, the apostle of the philosophy of Liberalism and utilitarianism in Egypt, whose ideas we shall examine more closely later.

Parallel to the spread of Western literature and ideas, there was a revival of interest in the Egyptian, Arab, and Muslim past which was linked to the emergence of modern nationalism and to the increasing awareness of the need to reinterpret Islam in the light of modern conditions. On the secularist side, Jurjī Zaydān once again led the way with his five-volume history of Arab civilization and his four-volume history of Arabic literature; Shawqī wrote romances which sought to express the splendor and glory of ancient Egypt, such as his *'Adhrā' al-Hind* and his *Maṣra' Kliubaṭrah*; and Ḥāfiẓ wrote poems on various pharaonic subjects. On the religious side, Muḥammad 'Abduh and Rashīd Riḍa went back to the formative period of Islam in their attempts to establish the foundations for a reform of the faith.

This general cultural awakening was reflected in the very extensive development of the press under a liberal British censorship policy. In 1898, one hundred sixty-nine papers and journals were reported to be in existence, and two hundred and eighty-two in 1913.[8] Many of these were unstable enterprises, but quite a few were publications of importance. Among the latter were the journals mentioned before, several women's magazines, and a few relatively big dailies — *al-Ahrām*, *al-Muqaṭṭam*, *al-Liwā'*, *al-Mu'ayyid*, *al-Waṭan*, *al-Jarīdah* — which represented various shades of political opinion and devoted one or more columns to literary work and fundamental ideological discussion.

The entire cultural activity of the period was dominated by two problems, each of which may be seen as having undergone two phases: One consisted of the question of evolving an appropriate style and technique for modern literature. Here, two schools faced each other in the first phase: one was composed of the partisans of the medieval Arab *littérateurs* who scorned simplicity and favored a recondite style, studded with obscurities and graced with literary allusions and erudite wit typical of a courtly culture; the other was composed primarily of Western-educated Syrians who advocated a simple, direct language, hospitable to colloquial and arabicized foreign words. Their language has been described by their opponents as French written in Arabic. Neither of these schools was able to prevail, and victory went to a third, represented by a group of young writers which emerged during the second decade of the twentieth century and practiced a style that succeeded in preserving spontaneity and communicability without sacrificing entirely the continuity of the language or beauty of expression.

The other problem overshadowing the cultural activity of the period was the struggle between new ideals, ideas, norms, and values and the traditional Islamic conceptions — that is to say, the problem which constitutes the main subject of our study. Here, of course, there could be no question of relatively quick solutions, as in the case of the problem of style. The best that could be expected was a clear and comprehensive formulation of the problem and some concrete beginnings toward its resolution; and indeed these took place during this period. Before this happened, however, there was a preliminary phase which appears in retrospect to have been mainly an interval spent in acquiring and learning new ideas, during which the battle of conflicting ideas was diffused and lacked coherent centers of gravitation. We mention this phase only because it helps in explaining the one that followed; there is no reason for us to enter into it.

We have seen that the challenge presented by the new conditions of life to the traditional belief-system affected in principle all the chief elements of that system, but that the first responses to the challenge concentrated on the question of power. But we have also argued that the traditional view of power could not be considered without involvement in other aspects of the belief-system of which it was an integral part, and we found an illustration in al-Afghānī's simultaneous concern with the problem of power and revolt against basic aspects of the traditional doctrine. Now, one of the reasons why al-Afghānī's revolt was not followed by concrete, positive reformulations was the still low level of culture, especially among those followers of the Master who were concerned about the condition of religion. Twenty years after the occupation, enough books had been translated and enough had been written, particularly by Western-educated Syrians, to bring a wealth of new ideas and perspectives within reach of all.

Another factor that made possible comprehensive formulations of the ideological problem and of at least tentative solutions was, strangely enough, the materialization of the long-feared threat of foreign domination in the form of what seemed for most of this period the inexorable fact of the British occupation. At first, the occupation was met by the population with something like despair and a feeling that the world had come to an end. But gradually the devil proved to be less terrible than the thought of him. Far from attacking the Muslim religion, as the Egyptians had feared, the British encroached on the remnants of Muslim institutions and the existing religious traditions much less than the Muslim rulers who had preceded them; and as their various projects unfolded, most sections of the population found good practical reasons for tolerating their presence. The *fellahin* were the object of a special solicitude as they were effectively freed from forced labor, the *bastinado*, and excessive taxation arbitrarily collected; but the landlords too, benefited from the extensive irrigation projects undertaken by the British, and everybody, in general, enjoyed the rare experience of a fair and orderly government. A magistrate, a social reformer, and intellectual leader like Qāṣim Amīn did not hesitate to write bluntly that Egypt had never enjoyed as much freedom and justice as under the British.[9]

All this did not mean that the initial religiously inspired fear and suspicion of the British, as of non-Muslim powers in general, wore off completely for any but a tiny section of the Muslim population. Such deep-rooted feelings die hard, and we shall have occasion to see them manifested in many guises. But within the context of an occupation that seemed unshakable, the behavior of the British was such that it dulled the edge of the initial suspicion sufficiently to permit the bulk of the population to go about their daily concerns in peace, and to enable a few of its leaders to turn their attention from the problem of power in its immediate and narrow aspects to the broader ideological implications contained therein.

The result was that two major trends, destined to be of crucial importance in the evolution of Egypt during the first half of the twentieth century, were formulated during this period. At first they seemed to have much in common, and the men responsible for them at times collaborated with each other; but as they developed and crystallized, they became increasingly alternative and competing platforms. One approach, formulated by Muḥammad ʿAbduh and modified by Rashīd Riḍa, spoke for a reformist Islam; the other, formulated by Muṣṭafā Kāmil and Luṭfī al-Sayyid, promoted a nationalist ideal to which was attached a rationalist liberal philosophy.

CHAPTER 5

Reformist Islam

Muḥammad 'Abduh (1849–1905)

The life of Muḥammad 'Abduh has been studied extensively by many writers.[1] Born to a farmer in lower Egypt, he received his elementary religious education from various *shaykhs* and tutors and entered al-Azhar in 1866. In 1872, he met al-Afghānī, whom he followed for the next seven years. In 1879, 'Abduh was appointed teacher in the college of Dār al-'Ulūm, but was dismissed for his political views that same year, when al-Afghānī was expelled from Egypt. 'Abduh was ordered to return to his village and abstain from political activity. Two years later, following a political change, he was called back to Cairo to edit *al-Waqā'i' al-Miṣriyyah*, which, though the official gazette, he was able to use as an organ for presenting the reform subjects dear to his heart. With the outbreak of the 'Urābī uprising, 'Abduh found himself on the side of the rebels, assisting the movement with his word and pen and advising its leaders. After the debacle, he was sentenced to three years and three months of exile. He joined al-Afghānī in Paris where, in 1884, they both published the reformist, pan-Islamic, revolutionary review *al-'Urwah al-Wuthqā* (The Most Firm Bond). The review was shut down after eighteen issues, and 'Abduh went to Beirut where he gave up his political activity and led a quiet, scholarly life. At the end of his term of exile, he returned to Egypt reconciled to the British, and was appointed judge in the National Courts, and then counselor in the Court of Appeal. In 1894 he was appointed member of a newly formed Committee of Administration of al-Azhar which aimed at reforming that institution. 'Abduh became its moving spirit, but the opposition of the conservative *'ulamā'*, supported by the khedive, frustrated his projects. Despite heroic efforts, remarkably courageous stands,[2] and the support of Cromer, he was compelled to resign from the Committee, having managed to introduce only a few administrative reforms. In 1899, 'Abduh was appointed Grand Mufti of Egypt, a position he held to the end of his life despite the intensive and often unscrupulous machinations of his enemies.[3] In the same year he became a member of the Legislative Assembly, which he hoped to see develop into a full parliamentary body.

His most important writings consist of a theological treatise—*Risālat al-Tawḥīd*—published in 1897; a commentary on the Qur'ān, on which he worked to the end of his life without finishing it; and his polemics about Islam and Christianity and their respective attitude toward science and civilization published in *al-Manār* in the course of 1901, and later issued in book form. He was familiar with some translated Western works and missed no chance to broaden his education. He learned French when he was past forty in order to read original works, and when visiting in Switzerland he diligently attended lectures at the University of Geneva. His interest lay primarily in the fields of social ethics, history, philosophy, and education. A great admirer of Herbert Spencer, he visited him in England, and translated his work on education from a French version. He was also an admirer of Tolstoy and wrote him a letter expressing his sympathy when the great writer was excommunicated.

Early in his career, when still a student of al-Afghānī, Muḥammad 'Abduh had been as obsessed as his master with the immediate problem of power rather than with the broader implications of the ideological crisis. Measures that he advocated concentrated mainly on defensive necessities, and the opinions that he expressed about other subjects were based more on broad generalization than on concrete thought and evidence. For instance, in an article published in *al-Ahrām* in 1876, he said:

> The *'ulamā'*, who are the spirit of the nation, have failed so far to see the benefit of the modern sciences. They continue to busy themselves with what might have been suitable for a time that is long gone by, not realizing the fact that we are living in a new world. . . . We must study the affairs of other religions and states in order to learn the secret of their advancement. . . . We see no reason for their position of *wealth and power* except their progress in education and the sciences. Our first duty, then, is to endeavor with all our might and main to spread these sciences in our country.[4]

After his experience with the 'Urābī movement and his activity early in his exile, he became convinced of the futility of impulsive and violent methods and began to see the problems facing Egypt and the Muslim countries not so much in terms of a threat of the material power of the West as in terms of a challenge of the intellectual, social, and ethical dynamism underlying that power to an Islamic superstructure no longer suitable to the present age.

Once he was allowed to return to Egypt, 'Abduh set out to revise systematically some of the orthodox conceptions which he felt prevented Islam from serving as a valid and effective foundation for a modern community. He consistently kept this practical purpose in mind and tried, whenever possible, to avoid provoking abstract theological discussions which were likely to lead to sectarianism and strife and to defeat his intentions. For the same reason he attempted throughout his work to couch his formulations, which often had revolutionary implications, in conservative terms, and to follow the logic of his argument only to the point necessary to achieve the practical aim behind it. But this excessively pragmatic and cautious approach, wise and perhaps inescapable as it might have been in the short run, relied too much on a restraint which was essentially subjective. It did not draw boundaries based on principle, and therefore made it possible for others, invoking his authority, to expand or restrict his principles beyond anything he himself had anticipated.

'Abduh's most revolutionary enterprise was, of course, his reinterpretive initiative. He rejected vehemently the orthodox view that the doctrine and law of Islam had been formulated once and for all by the medieval doctors, and insisted on the right of every generation to go back to the sources and understand them according to its own lights:

> Islam turned the hearts of men away from exclusive attachment to the customs and practices of the fathers . . . it qualified those who accept blindly the words of their predecessors with folly and levity, and it called attention to the fact that precedence in time is not a sign of knowledge nor a mark of superior intellect and wisdom. . . . Indeed, later generations have a knowledge of past circumstances and the possibility of reflecting upon them and profiting from their lessons which their ancestors did not have.[5]

With this conception, 'Abduh reversed the easy and tempting conception of Islam as the immutable doctrine and law of God in favor of a more difficult and more dangerous one. To be sure, he believed in the absolute truth of the Qur'ān, but, as we shall see, the meaning of this truth relied heavily on the use of reason.

'Abduh not only defended the right of later generations to go back to the sources of Islam and understand them according to their own lights, but he also diverged radically from the orthodox view of what these sources were. The Qur'ān he naturally accepted as the primary source; but regarding the Sunnah — Tradition of the Prophet — he considered only a minute number of *hadīths* (particular traditions), mostly concerning the life of the Prophet, as genuine,[6] discarding implicitly as later inventions most of what orthodoxy had accepted. The value of the whole Sunnah itself was anyway greatly discounted by 'Abduh's conception of prophecy, which tended to restrict the infallibility of the Prophet to his activity as transmitter of the divine message.[7] Outside of this function, which is his proper one, the Prophet is subject to human failures and errors. Although 'Abduh was inclined to view Muḥammad in his "extra-prophetic" activity as a great social reformer, this did not give his activity any authoritative character. As for the traditional third source of doctrine, the consensus of the community, there could, of course, be no question of Muḥammad 'Abduh's accepting it, since it would *ipso facto* rule out all his activity. The unanimity he would accept was that of universal reason, which, after the Qur'ān, was to him the main source of doctrine.

The most consequential of Muḥammad 'Abduh's teachings, aside from his assertion of the right to reopen Islamic doctrine to new inquiry, was his definition of the relation between reason and religion. Basically, 'Abduh viewed this relation as a symbiosis which is best calculated to serve man's nature as a thinking and feeling being. Reason approves the credentials and weighs particular beliefs and rulings of religion, even as reason allows religion to respond to man's innate craving for contact with the metaphysical universe. Religion, on the other hand, endows the conclusions of reason with the affective power that gives them vitality and puts a brake on attempts of reason to speculate on the nature of divine "things in themselves." 'Abduh's conception of the relation between reason and religion implied also a general shift of emphasis from the traditional legalism and preoccupation with the divine, to the human and ethico-social aspects of religion. He was in agreement with ibn-Khaldūn in regarding religion as indispensable for the achievement of individual and social happiness, and with al-Ghazzālī in viewing it as an affair of the heart, in relation to which the outward forms are only secondary. But he went beyond both men in advocating restraint of the religious passion by means of reason, having learned from the history of the Ṣūfīs the abuses to which this passion may otherwise lead:

> Religion is a general sense, the province of which is to discover means of happiness that are not clearly discernible to reason. But it is reason which has the final authority in the recognition of this sense, in directing its exercise in its appropriate sphere, and in accepting beliefs and rules of conduct which that sense discovers for it. How can the right of reason to do this be denied when it is reason which examines the proofs of these beliefs and rules in order to arrive at a secure knowledge of them and to be assured that they emanate of certainty from God? [8]

Elsewhere, 'Abduh applied this rule more specifically to the Tradition of the Prophet:

> There is general agreement among Muslims that in case of conflict between reason and what has been given as Tradition, the conclusions of reason are to be given preference. Two possibilities remain with regard to the Tradition: either to acknowledge its genuineness while confessing inability to understand it and resigning the matter to God's knowledge, or to interpret it so that it would, in a sense, agree with what reason has established, without, however, doing violence to the rules of the language.[9]

In his major theological work, 'Abduh applied the same rule, though in a somewhat modified form, even to direct revelation. He argued that it is the duty of reason, once it has accepted a prophet as true, to believe all that he reveals, even though not all of the true meaning of the revelations can be understood. This does not mean that something impossible must be accepted — such a thing cannot be contained in the message of prophets. If the apparent sense of a passage contains what seems, nevertheless, to be a contradiction, then,

> reason must believe that the apparent sense was not intended. It is then free to choose between interpretation of the passage consistently with the rest of the words of the Prophet . . . and between resigning the matter to Allah and His knowledge.[10]

'Abduh's faith that reason cannot ultimately be in contradiction to revelation, despite appearances to the contrary, was a crucial aspect of his teachings. Though he cautiously limited reason so as to exclude excessive metaphysical speculation about "things in themselves," his position permitted and encouraged Muslims to indulge in rational study and inquiry without fearing that they might thereby deny their faith or be considered as renegades by their fellow-Muslims. And both the pursuit of rational inquiry and the assurance of remaining within the fold were necessary if a humanistic, dynamic belief-system appropriate to the conditions of a modern society were to be worked out and at the same time have a chance of gradual acceptance by the existing, still-traditional society.

The impulse 'Abduh gave to the development of Egyptian thought was particularly effective because he did not confine himself to these general concepts, crucial as they were, but took the initiative in suggesting some concrete revised theories. In the sphere of ethics, for example, it was necessary to have criteria for judgment that could be applied to the constantly varying situations arising from the new conditions of life. 'Abduh attempted to meet this need by taking the radical step of disassociating ethics from any *necessary* connection with revelation and founding them entirely on a rational principle. In order to avoid the thorny question of the relation between the absolute and the divinity, he did not resort to an absolute, natural-law principle, as the Mu'tazilah had done. Instead, he took advantage of the Arabic terms for beautiful and ugly — *ḥasan* and *qabīḥ* — which are applicable in that language to the expression of value as well as aesthetical judgments, in order to evolve a utilitarian theory of ethics based on common aesthetics. Although tastes may differ in many circumstances, 'Abduh argued, there is no doubt that everybody recognizes certain things as beautiful — flowers, for instance — and other things as ugly — the sight of a mutilated corpse, for example. The qualities of beauty and ugliness are attributed to these things because of the sensation of satisfaction or revulsion they awaken in us. In the same way, he wrote:

> Voluntary actions may also be distinguished as beautiful or ugly according to the idea of their utility and harmfulness. Distinctions of this sort are possible only to man. For some actions are pleasurable in themselves yet are judged ugly because of their harmful consequences. . . . All these distinctions the human reason is capable of making. . . . They are recognized as the causes of happiness and misery in this life, as the grounds for the progress or decline of civilization, and the strength or weakness of nations. They can be discovered by human reason and the senses without the aid of revelation.[11]

Having thereby established an intrinsic social principle for ethics, 'Abduh retraced his steps to explain the connection between ethics and revelation. The purpose of revelation is not to endow arbitrarily certain acts with the character of good and bad, as traditional doctrine maintained, but to help fallible reason by defining some of the good and bad acts on the basis of the utility principle. Thus, continuing his discussion after the passage just quoted, 'Abduh went on to say:

> The actual history of man has shown that very few peoples have done so, and even among these peoples there is no agreement regarding individual actions. The needs, rivalries, and temptations of the mass of mankind are so powerful, that reason has proved to be a not infallible guide. History has shown the need for prophets who would draw a code of morals and doctrines agreeable to God to serve as means for securing happiness in this life and in the hereafter.[12]

Elsewhere in the same treatise he wrote:

> Religion is the most potent factor in the formation of moral traits, not only for the mass of the people, but also for the chosen few. For its hold

upon souls is stronger than the hold of reason which is the distinguishing trait of the latter [the chosen few].[13]

It may be said, then, that 'Abduh's view of ethics evolved as a reciprocal theory whereby whatever is socially useful is ethical, and even enjoys the benefit of implicit divine sanction, as long as it does not conflict with injunctions specifically revealed. On the other hand, the revealed injunctions are themselves to be understood in terms of the principle of utility, according to which they have been intended to secure the happiness of men here and in the hereafter.

If, in the case of speculation about the divinity, 'Abduh insisted on setting limits, however weak, on the purview of reason, and if in the sphere of ethics he endeavored to check to some extent the conclusions of reason against the given injunctions of revelation, in the realm of science he dared to do away with any restrictions whatsoever:

The summons of Islam to reflection in regard to the creation was wholly unlimited and unconditional because of the certainty that every sound speculation leads to belief in God as He is described in the Qur'ān without over-emphasizing His transcendence or defining His nature.[14]

The length to which 'Abduh committed himself becomes more noteworthy when we realize that by "science" he meant not just the natural sciences but what are now called the social sciences as well. Thus Spencer's theory of social evolution, for instance, with its concomitant social and moral implications, was viewed by 'Abduh as part of science, as will be seen presently.

To establish the reconciliation between science and Islam, it was necessary to modify the traditional emphasis on the arbitrary will of God in favor of a concept that would underline regularity in the functioning of nature. This 'Abduh did by reinterpreting the traditional notion of the *sunnah* (custom) of God which, in the traditional doctrine, held primarily the function of distinguishing normal occurrences from miracles,[15] to give it a meaning that permitted scientific causality. Thus, God is the constant creator of the universe, but in this activity, He follows a regular, unchanging custom which may be studied and formulated into scientific "laws":

The *Qur'ān* makes such references to the origin of the universe . . . of creation, and so on, in order to arouse the intellect to follow its natural course in discovering the original state of things and the laws which govern them. . . . The Qur'ān does not restrict the mind in these things in any respect but it summons in many verses . . . which amount to as much as half the Qur'ān . . . to the contemplation of God's signs in nature.[16]

The last two quotations illustrate something of the weakness of the foundations underlying 'Abduh's well-meaning support of free scientific investigation. He was confident that the results of such investigation would always harmonize with revelation; but this confidence was based on an act of faith — a deduction from *à priori* premises — rather than on conclusions founded on an understanding of the true spirit of science. Starting from the premises that revelation is truth as spoken by God and that science is truth as revealed in nature, he, understandably, reached the conclusion that the two could not contradict each other. To substantiate this conclusion, he and his followers did what many Christian thinkers did under similar circumstances, particularly in the latter part of the nineteenth century: they endeavored to find in the revealed texts intimations of the latest scientific phenomena or laws. But this undertaking only shows another misunderstanding of science as a static, given set of conclusions, rather than as a process, a method of pursuing truth, in which the results are only relatively valid and always open to revision. For 'Abduh and his followers, the misunderstanding was compounded by the fact that they were apparently unaware of the difference in the degree of certainty characterizing the conclusions of the natural and the social sciences. Thus they attempted with equal zeal to find in the Qur'ān hints about the "laws" of social evolution and about bacteria. All these weaknesses had important practical consequences, but it need only be noted for the present that by giving his sanction to free investigation on the basis of wrong premises, 'Abduh was opening the door to ideas and forces that he had not quite intended to let in.

From our analysis of 'Abduh's ideas so far, it is natural to expect him to attempt to restore causality in the realm of human affairs by endowing man with a measure of freedom which the orthodox doctrine, with its marked emphasis on the arbitrary will of God, had totally denied him. Here, of course, the problem was more complicated than in the realm of nature because of the factor of human volition; and 'Abduh approached it with a characteristic caution that produced ambivalent results. Man, said 'Abduh, "is conscious of his voluntary actions. He weighs their consequences by means of his reason, assigns values to them, and then performs them by a certain power within himself. All this, the man with sound reason and senses knows without need of proof and without a teacher to instruct him. . ." [17] At the same time, 'Abduh continued, man learns from his experience that there is in the universe a power greater than his own whose conduct is beyond his comprehension. This should not, however, cause man to underestimate his ability to control his own actions and direct the exercise of his natural power. For "the divine law is based upon this truth, and only by means of it can responsibilities be imposed. Whoever denies this denies at the same time the locus of faith in his own soul which is his reason. . . ." [18] More than that, man need not, and should not try to know, because that would be prying into the secrets of the universe which have been forbidden to him.[19]

'Abduh refrained from basing man's freedom on any ontological principle and founded it on a semiagnostic, pragmatic consciousness in order to avoid the complications in which the Mu'tazilah became involved. In so doing he liberated man from the shackles of traditional religion, reaffirmed more emphatically man's moral responsibility, and dealt a blow to the spirit of passiveness. But he missed the opportunity of making freedom a guiding principle in the reinterpretation of Islam and, in the political sphere, the foundation for a universal doctrine of right. 'Abduh's pragmatic positivism thus released the Muslim from the narrow confines of traditional Islam but provided him with little guidance as to the roads he should follow.

The last statement may perhaps serve as the best summary of 'Abduh's work. He had an abundant confidence in the effectiveness and self-evidence of reason that is reminiscent of the faith of the eighteenth century. If only reason were "correctly" applied to the material of religion, as well as to all other aspects of life, there could be no doubt that its results would be universally recognized. That is why he was a fervent believer in the magic power of education, especially as he cleared the way for it by his revolt against the authority of the medieval school, his restoration of causality in nature and in society, his assertion of man's liberty of choice, his emphasis on the social-utilitarian nature of ethics, and, finally, by his reassertion and definition of the rights of reason in all spheres of life.

Although politics and the problem of power had been his main preoccupation at the start of his career, 'Abduh made little attempt to deal with political doctrine as such after his return to Egypt and his reconciliation with the British. Later in his life he was to explain this abdication in these words:

There is another thing that I called for while all the people were blind to it, whereas it is the foundation of their life in society and the cause of all their weakness and humiliation; and that is the distinction between the government's right to the people's obedience and the people's right that the government be just. Yes, I was among those who appealed to the Egyptian nation to be conscious of its rights with regard to the ruler when this had not occurred to it for more than twenty centuries. . . . We have proclaimed that openly when despotism was at its height, when tyranny gripped its whip and when the oppressor's fist was of iron and all men were indeed slaves to him. . . . [Today] I still call to my view about religion and demand the completion of the reform of the language. . . . As for the question of ruler and ruled, I have left it to the disposal of fate and to the hand of God to manage, for I have learned that this is a fruit that needs planting and many years of growth before it can be collected. It is this planting that needs care and attention at the present, and God is our help.[20]

Nevertheless, 'Abduh made some marginal remarks and comments that are as remarkable for the attitude and the limitation they reveal as for their contribution to political thought. Here, as in much of his work, there is an eagerness to assimilate current Western ideas and institutions into their nearest Islamic equivalents. The limitation, which is more pronounced here than elsewhere in his work, is a failure to pursue to the end the implications underlying some of the conceptions he sought to assimilate, with the result that assimilation is accomplished only on a formal and superficial level, making his work vulnerable to unintended uses. He asserted, for example, that love of the fatherland is a religious duty,[21] which accorded very well with the aims of the nationalists. But he still maintained that the community of the believers — the *ummah* — is the basic political unit, a thesis which the nationalists vigorously denied. More revealing still is his conception of sovereignty and representative government, which constitutes his most important specifically political contribution.

'Abduh maintained the traditional Islamic concept that sovereignty belongs unquestionably to God, Who revealed His sovereign will in the Book. But his reassertion of the freedom to inquire into the meaning of God's word opened the possibility for a "secondary sovereignty," to be exercised by the interpreters. That secondary sovereignty he attempted to equate with the modern theory of representative government, for which he endeavored to find support in the Qur'ān. Thus, when in his exegesis of the Qur'ān he reached *sūrah* IV, verse 62: "O ye who believe, obey God and obey the apostle and those among you invested with authority. . . ." he interpreted "those . . . invested with authority" to mean "the men of position and influence such as the *'ulamā'* and the leaders, who are known in the language of the day as representatives of the nation. . . ." To them are to be referred all judicial, administrative, and political affairs, including the revision of the Sharī'ah, which they will determine "according to the principles of divine law concerning the promotion of the beneficial and the avoidance of evil, and in harmony with the conditions of time and locality.[22] Prior to that, he wrote in the official governmental gazette: "Representative government and legislation by representatives chosen by the people are entirely in harmony with the spirit and practice of Islam from the very beginning." [23]

Here 'Abduh's usual reservations and ambiguity are puzzling. On the one hand, he reasserts the traditional principle that sovereignty belongs to God and he therefore insists on the restriction that any "legislation" should be based on the principles of the Sovereign's divine law and that it should be undertaken with the participation of the *'ulamā'*. On the other hand, he seems to imply that the limitation imposed by the divine law consists only, or mainly, in the principle of promoting what is beneficial and avoiding what is evil, interpreted in the light of circumstances of time and place — in other words, social utility — and that on this basis the Sharī'ah itself is to be modified by the representative assembly which may include only a few *'ulamā'* among its members. On which of these sides is the stress to be laid? From 'Abduh's blanket endorsement of representative government elsewhere it seems obvious that he meant to lay stress on the more permissive side. But in any case it cannot be denied that partisans of out-and-out parliamentary government based on the sovereignty of the people needed to make only a formal and minor modification in their theory to be justified in invoking the authority of 'Abduh: they needed only to recognize that the divine law is sovereign before proceeding to alter it.

Another piece of marginal theorizing by 'Abduh, that is both interesting and revealing, if of less practical consequence, is the attempt he made in his commentary on the Qur'ān to evolve a theory of history integrating his conception of the prophecy with certain current notions of progressive evolution. Societies, according to this theory, are organic growths which go through stages of evolution analogous to those experienced by the individual. In their infancy, societies are ruled entirely by their physical needs and by the instinct of self-preservation. There is little time or leisure for higher concerns and for the development of the arts of civilization. Gradually, however, men in society learn from their experience some of the principles governing their corporate life and rise from childhood to the years of discernment and to the capacity to receive prophecy. "This shows that the *sunnah* of God with respect to nations is identical with that in respect to individuals and is one of gradual progress from weakness to strength and from imperfection to perfection. . . ." As the desires and passions of men grow, society is faced with a danger from some or all of its members comparable to the danger that youth faces from the development of its passions. And just as God gives reason to youth, when its passion threatens to lead it astray, so He gives to societies the guidance of prophecy at a stage when expanding knowledge and consciousness of its power become a source of danger to it. Revelation is accommodated to the moral and intellectual capacity of each nation to which the prophets are sent. The age of prophecy brings light and happiness to all those who accept it; but

> . . . the farther the nation gets from the time of the prophet, the more the hearts become hardened and the minds darkened, lust prevails and learning declines, religion is corrupted by its teachers and differences appear on account of political influences and political leadership. This stage continues until the people reform themselves and return to obeying revelation.[24]

The philosophical and methodological incompatibilities involved in this scheme are obvious. They follow inevitably from the attempt to merge a conception of active providential intervention in history and a religious view of ethics as the main determinant of the well-being or misery of society with some naturalistic and strictly sociological views of history. Thus, ʿAbduh declares that progress is the *sunnah* of God in history; yet, at the same time, he maintains the traditional view of the Prophet's message and age as the unsurpassable acme of perfection. The former view embodies the eighteenth and nineteenth centuries' concept of progress as the law of history, meaning essentially the unlimited perfectibility of man and society; whereas the latter cannot conceive of an attainment higher than that of Muḥammad's age and message. The first looks forward to the intensification of prevailing trends because they bring men nearer to the golden age; the second aspires to reverse prevailing trends in order to return to a golden age. In his eagerness to find a place in Islam for what seemed to him to be a "scientific law," Muḥammad ʿAbduh adopted the "law" of progress, but because of his commitment to the traditional view of the Prophet's mission, he was compelled to restrict the applicability of that law to the ages preceding Muḥammad's appearance. This restriction, however, denied the validity of the conception of progress as a *law* of history and nullified ʿAbduh's purpose.[25]

A similar difficulty is reflected in his use of the theory of evolution. In its many Western versions this theory conceives of progressive development as inherent in the life of societies; it is a process of automatic growth in accordance with some specific social "laws of development." Here, as with the idea of progress, 'Abduh adopted the Western notion as far as the age of "adolescence," but then shifted his ground to allow for an Islamic concept. From the time of the appearance of Muḥammad, history no longer follows a definite progressive path according to its own social laws, but is given to ups and downs and is contingent upon men's following the moral laws. 'Abduh explained this shift from organic social determinism to moral determinism by calling it "reaching the stage of adulthood," but in so doing he was using arbitrary analogy for causality.

'Abduh's ideology and program as a whole gained support only among a tiny group of reformers, but many disparate and general ideas of his had an influence on Egyptian thought and development that can hardly be exaggerated. His reconciliation of reason and science with religion, weak and pregnant with difficulties as it was, made possible a development of Egyptian thought and literature which could not otherwise have been achieved without an immediate, painful, and total break with Islam. Much of that thought and literature carried some of 'Abduh's ideas far beyond what he had intended, and this in turn provoked a reaction among some of his followers, who attempted to limit his views to even narrower confines than he did. Both schools could lay claim to his authority because his thought did indeed lend itself easily to radical and conservative interpretations. For he had reopened most effectively the gates of inquiry into some of the basic traditional principles but had been much less helpful in suggesting concrete alternative formulations. On the crucial question of the role of reason, for instance, he upheld fully its competence to serve as the guide in individual and social life provided its conclusions were referred to revelation for verification. But such verification, we know, is not absolute since in case of irreconcilable conflict the matter is to be "left to Allah and His knowledge." And, in any case, does not his assurance that the conclusions of reason and science could never conflict with revelation tend to make superfluous the attempt at verification?

The same ambiguity is evident in 'Abduh's thought on the crucial question of the role of Islam in the social and political order and has equally led to radically opposite views invoking his authority. On the one hand, his theory of the subsidiary, proclamatory role of revelation in the sphere of ethics, his tendency to view history as developing under its own laws, his rejection of the authority of popular *ijmā'* for the *ijmā'* of reason, and his ambivalence about the infallibility of the Prophet outside of his function as divine messenger — all these tend to lead, and did in fact lead, to a concept of Islam as not concerned immediately and directly with the social and political order. This view may find confirmation in a statement 'Abduh had made to W. S. Blunt, British Egyptophile writer, in which he said that the best sort of government for Egypt under the occupation would be a parliamentary system after the British model, and did not mention anything about religion except to say that the prime minister should be Muslim.[26] On the other hand, this reference can be dismissed as a temporary expedient under the circumstances of the occupation; and it could be pointed out, instead, that 'Abduh always spoke of and to the *ummah* in the traditional sense of the community of all Muslims; that while admitting that specific regulations for the social and political orders may vary in time, he insisted that they should at any rate be inspired and approved by revelation; and, finally, that he insisted that the Qur'ān should be supreme sovereign even if its word was open to interpretation. These and similar arguments could, and did, lead to the view that a reformed Islam — but an Islam that dominated directly the political and social orders — was, on 'Abduh's authority, the only guarantee of a good and viable community.

Muḥammad Rashīd Riḍā (?–1935) [27]

Muḥammad Rashīd Riḍā was Muḥammad 'Abduh's leading disciple until his death and afterwards. He was also his biographer, the editor of his works, and the man who more than anyone else carried on his tradition and interpreted his doctrines. Born in Syria, Riḍā was educated in Tripoli where he received his diploma of *'ālim* (religious scholar) in 1897. He had been inspired by what he had read in the revolutionary review, *al-'Urwah al-Wuthqā*, and, upon finishing his studies, he arrived in Egypt where he attached himself to Muḥammad 'Abduh until the latter's death. Soon after his arrival in Cairo, he founded the review *al-Manār* (The Lighthouse), first published as a weekly and then as a monthly, in which he sought to perpetuate the tradition of *al-'Urwah al-Wuthqā*, but without its policy of agitation, which, under British rule, was no longer possible. The review sought to foster reform of various aspects of life, and its concern was Islam and the Muslim countries in general, with special emphasis upon Egypt. Beginning with its third year, a section was dedicated to 'Abduh's commentaries on the Qur'ān and to decisions on matters concerning law and religion. Riḍā did the largest part of the writing in *al-Manār*, but contributions were received from supporters and sympathizers. Judging from the somewhat technical character of its argumentation and the quality of its documenta-

LIBRARY
OF
MOUNT ST. MARY'S
COLLEGE
EMMITSBURG, MARYLAND

tion, *al-Manār* was patently addressed to a small, cultivated Muslim minority. The review had considerable influence on a group of periodicals and on some societies inspired by similar ideas. Among the first were *al-Majallah al-Salafiyyah*, *al-Zahrah*, *al-Fatḥ*, *al-Jam'iyyah al-Islāmiyyah*, *al-I'tiṣām*, *al-Murshid al-'Arabī*, and *al-Sha'ā'ir*.[28] Most of these journals were short-lived, but some were able to draw contributions from the best writers of the time. *Al-Manār* also had an undoubted influence on such societies as *al-Rābiṭah al-Islāmiyyah*, *Jam'iyyat al-Shubbān al-Muslimīn*, *Jam'iyyat al-Hidāyah al-Islāmiyyah*, and *Jam'iyyat Makārim al-Akhlāq al-Islāmiyyah*.[29] In addition, Riḍā and his supporters formed their own society for propaganda and guidance — *Jam'iyyat al-Da'wah wa-al-Irshād*. The peak of the influence of Riḍā and *al-Manār* was reached in the early twenties, after which both declined rapidly until the Muslim Brotherhood revived some of their slogans and general ideas, while giving them a different meaning.

Riḍā's career covered a span of about forty years and extended chronologically beyond 1922 into another phase of Egyptian intellectual development. We shall have to deal here, however, with all his work until his death in 1935 to avoid breaking the sequence of his thought, and then return to the genesis of Liberal-Nationalist thought at the turn of the century.

Muḥammad 'Abduh's program had included, besides the attempt to reformulate Islamic doctrine which we have already examined, three other aims we have not yet stressed. These were (1) to purify "original" Islam from later accretions; (2) to reform Muslim higher education; and (3) to defend Islam against theoretical attacks. For Rashīd Riḍā, all these elements, and particularly the last, were crucial factors in the development of his thought.

With 'Abduh, the defense of Islam had been directed primarily against Christian thinkers who thought it responsible for the low state of the Muslim countries. Early in Riḍā's career that accusation was taken up by Egyptian thinkers and leaders[30] who advocated wholesale adoption of Western ideas and institutions. The defense of Islam against these Westernizers became the most important consideration in Riḍā's attempt to develop 'Abduh's thought and to give it positive content.

Riḍā was aware that 'Abduh's thought lent itself in many ways to interpretations that might support the ideas of the Westernizers, and he made a desperate effort to banish this possibility without at the same time handicapping the aim of reforming Islam. Further, Riḍā endeavored to restore confidence in Islam by pointing out its glories and advantages, and tried in a practical way to secure his suggested reforms by presenting a political blueprint which had at its center the revivification of the caliphate.

The chief pitfall in ʿAbduh's thought was that, having rejected *ijmāʿ* and restricted the authoritative sources to the Qur'ān and a very few traditions, he had left wide scope for the unhampered operation of reason, which could be, and often was, exploited by the Westernizers to justify their espousal of foreign ideas. This latitude was particularly dangerous in the sphere of ethics where ʿAbduh had severed any necessary relation between revelation and morality. To meet this danger, Riḍā tried, in general, to restrict the scope of reason by greatly increasing the authoritative sources of reference to include a vast number of traditions besides the Qur'ān and by restoring the principle of *ijmāʿ*, which he restricted, however, to the period of the first four caliphs, the "rightly guided ones." These sources taken together, Riḍā claimed, contained the whole body of dogma, all the principles of the faith, a code of ethics, and the practices of the cult.[31]

In his attempt to give specific application to this general concept, Riḍā retreated in the sphere of dogma from the position of moderate rationalism taken by ʿAbduh to one of cautious literalism that exceeded in its restrictiveness even the faint rationalism of the orthodox. To those who worried about the effect on initiative of the concept of arbitrary divine omnipotence that was likely to follow from a literal interpretation of the Qur'ānic dogma, Riḍā pointed out that the Muslims, under the rightly guided caliphs, had been able to achieve mighty deeds without being hampered by this belief, which they accepted without casuistry. Fatalism, he contended, developed only after the later hair-splitting argumentation of the schools.[32] Thus in trying to shut the door on modern philosophy and rationalism, Riḍā was willing to shut out the whole Muslim philosophy as well.

In the sphere of ethics, ʿAbduh had tried to overcome the rigidity of the traditional conception by asserting the autonomous rational-utilitarian foundation of all ethics; at the same time, he had sought to retain a divine sanction for them by equating utilitarian ethics with the ethics of revelation. But by severing any necessary connection between ethics and revelation he had made it possible for the Westernizers to neglect revelation altogether in evolving a system of morals. Riḍā tried to fight that danger by restoring the divinely authorized sources as the only necessary foundation of ethics and by denouncing all systems based on utilitarianism or humanistic rationalism. The Qur'ān and the Tradition, as understood by the Companions of the Prophet, he asserted, contain a complete code of ethics which is best for men because it is the product of divine wisdom.[33] Still, in order to allow for inevitable accommodation to changing conditions, here as in the sphere of the Law, he suggested including among the principles of ethics the concept of *maṣlaḥah* — public interest — itself founded, according to Riḍā, on the authority of the rightly guided ancestors.[34]

'Abduh's rejection of *ijmā'* as an absolute principle had undermined the one foundation that could guarantee a uniform interpretation of the Qur'ān and the Tradition. His confidence in the oneness of right reason was the only assurance that a universally acceptable interpretation of the sources could be reached, and this assurance was easily disproved by the reality of men attaining different conclusions, all in the name of reason. To close that breach, or at least to narrow it, Riḍā reintroduced the principle of the consensus of the Companions as an authoritative source for correct interpretation.[35] But in order to leave open the possibility of readapting the Law, he endeavored to prove that the rightly guided Companions had themselves understood the sources available to them in a progressive way and did not hesitate to overrule the text in the public interest.[36]

But even after broadening the authoritative sources and restricting the scope of reason, Riḍā was aware that as long as the discussion remained on the level of principle he would only have helped his Westernizing opponents. He would have contributed to undermining whatever remained of the traditional legal system by his criticism of its exponents and his rejection of the kind of *ijmā'* upon which it had been based, without providing a specific substitute for it and thereby leaving a vacuum which the Westernizers were bound to exploit. That is why Riḍā put great emphasis from the outset on certain practical steps to work out the principles of his doctrine. In its first year of publication, *al-Manār* advocated the formation of an Islamic Society under the patronage of the Ottoman sultan-caliph, which would have its headquarters in Mecca and branches in every Muslim country, and would have as its objects (1) the uniting of all Muslims in submission to a common system of law, doctrine and ethics, and a common language, (2) the suppressing of harmful teachings, and (3) the spreading of Islam.[37]

Unlike Muḥammad 'Abduh, who had remained almost entirely silent on the subject, Riḍā considered the caliphate an indispensable part of his reform program. This followed logically from his inclusion of the consensus of the Companions as an authoritative legal source. As long as the Ottoman caliphate maintained its precarious existence, however, Riḍā did not dwell much on this question either, but was content to concentrate his main effort on projects of reformulating and unifying the Law, in the belief that this was the first step toward the reformation of the caliphate to restore it according to the tradition of the rightly guided caliphs. But under pressure of the events that resulted in the breakup of the Ottoman empire, the whittling down of the caliphate, and the strengthening of separatist nationalist movements, Riḍā began to concentrate his attention and effort on the problem of the caliphate in an attempt to give the Muslims a practical alternative to the nationalist program of the Westernizers. This effort was summarized in a book, *al-Khilāfah, aw al-Imāmah al-'Uẓma* (briefly, The Caliphate), published in 1923, on the basis of a series of articles written during the preceding years. The book reflects clearly the tense circumstances under which it was written; it is much more a passionate and desperate apologia for Islam than a carefully thought-out theoretical study. Still, it gives an excellent picture of the direction of Riḍā's thought, and provides the substance and spirit of an argument which was to have great significance later.[38]

Riḍā's basic point was an a priori assertion that the Islamic principles of government, being of divine inspiration, are superior to anything the human mind can invent. Therefore, if rightly applied, they can assure the happiness and well-being of mankind in this and in the next life. Thus it was clear to him from the outset that the obvious and undeniable decline of the Muslim world could not possibly be attributed to Islam as such. The fault lay with the Muslims who "deviated from the principles of public law as they had been decreed at the time of the rightly guided caliphs." [39] Had they observed them, all the discords and evils which the community has suffered would have been avoided and Islam would have extended over the whole earth.[40]

How and why did the decline set in? Riḍā's answer is revealing: the first infraction of the principles of Islamic public law was perpetrated by the Umayyads. When Mu'āwiyah forced the recognition of the succession of Yazīd by means of power and money, he replaced the tradition of the Prophet and his Companions with that of Chosroes and Caesar.[41] The caliphate ceased to be elective and became "the plaything of clans and the spirit of domination," upsetting the whole political system of Islam. This distortion was at the root of all the woes that have afflicted the Muslims materially and spiritually ever since.[42]

After the Umayyads, the 'Abbāsids, the non-Muslims, the non-Arabs, and particularly the Turks, each contributed their share to the ruin of Islam, Riḍā continued. The non-Muslims wanted to avenge the conquest of their empires by sowing discord between Muslims and Arabs. The non-Arabs were at the root of the quarrels that broke the unity of the *ummah* and altered the true nature of the *imāmah* and the caliphate.[43] The Turks surpassed them all with their misdeeds: "They tyrannized the country, multiplied the acts of aggression against the people and went as far as killing caliphs on their thrones." [44] Worst of all, they usurped the caliphate from the 'Abbāsids and so took it out of the hands of the Quraysh clan which had been chosen by God to spread the Qur'ān over the world, after it had given Islam its Prophet, its language, and its first adherents.[45]

Finally, Riḍā placed upon the *'ulamā'* a good deal of the responsibility for this sad record of thirteen centuries of illegality and errors: They legitimized the abuses of power, the tyranny and absolutism of despotic governments and unworthy leaders, instead of combating them. Their servility was matched only by their ignorance. They sheepishly allowed the Sharī'ah to be trampled while they sought refuge in the quiet of their mosques and the safety of their homes.[46]

It is not relevant to our purpose to engage in exhaustive technical criticism of Riḍā's historical views, but it is important to underline the extremely moral-idealistic approach to politics that made it impossible for him to draw any practical lesson from past experiences of the Muslims. The fact that a political system had admittedly worked correctly for only forty out of thirteen hundred years did not for a moment lead him to look for weaknesses in its procedural arrangements, but to search instead for villains and wicked plotters. After narrating that sad record of failures and woes, he went on to insist that the caliphate is "the archetype of government, without which no amelioration of society is possible," and that the original Muslim state is "the best state not only for Muslims but for the entire humanity." For, he said, "it combines justice and equality, enforces respect for everybody's interest, prevents evil, orders the good, cares for the minors, the sick, and the invalid, and assists the poor and needy." [47] Decidedly, Riḍā's view of politics was religious — the excellence of a political system is entirely determined by the quality of its ideals, never by how it performs.

This disregard of procedural questions was not confined to his historical analysis but reflected itself clearly in his outline of a fundamental law for a modern Islamic state.

Riḍā's fundamental proposition was that any integral application of the Islamic Law must involve the restoration of the caliphate.[48] After the caliphate, the most important principle of Islamic government is the *shūra*, the Qur'ānic advice of mutual consultation which Rida sought to institutionalize. Any *ijtihād* (independent investigation of the sources), he insisted, must lead to "an organization in the spirit of the modern constitutions so as to subordinate the exercise of the power of the caliph to the respect of the Law and the principle of consultation." [49] He conceded that Islam never had any such formal institution, but argued that Muḥammad had left it to the community to establish its own organization.[50] Sovereignty belongs to God and resides in the principles of the Qur'ān and the Tradition; but the divine Legislator has delegated to the *ulu al-amr* — the men in authority — the right to legislate the particular applications of these principles in accordance with the public interest. Executive power belongs to the caliph, who is elected by the *ulu al-amr*.

Riḍā never made it clear who the *ulu al-amr* are, how they came by their positions, whence they derive their authority, whether they are the same as the members of the consultative assembly, what power the latter have to compel the caliph to remain within the principles of the Law, and what happens in the event the *ulu al-amr* disagree with the caliph on the interpretation of the principles of the Qur'ān. Under these circumstances, Riḍā's assertion that the harmony between the powers in the Islamic state "is so perfect that no discord or animosity could arise which would not be solved immediately by the arbitration of the Qur'ān and the Sunnah" [51] is unwarranted and begs the question.

Riḍā's moralistic approach was so thorough that it overshadowed even such institutionalized "powers" as he mentioned: the *shūra* and the *ulu al-amr*. Even though he equated *shūra* with modern constitutional devices, it seems that what he actually had in mind when he thought of consultation was primarily a kind of moral experience through which the caliph must go before issuing any laws or regulation, and not any device of popular representation and check on the ruler's power. Riḍā explains very little about the *ulu al-amr*, but we know that they must have moral and intellectual qualifications. This was made clear when Riḍā conceded at some point that he was willing to consider the modern parliamentary representatives as the *ulu al-amr* of the Tradition provided they were endowed with those moral qualities on which Islam insists.[52]

In addition to the caliphate, another cardinal principle in Riḍā's thought was the related concept of the *ummah*. Even before the Ottoman empire broke up into half-a-dozen Muslim states, one of his major endeavors had been the restoration of the complete unity of the *ummah*. We have already referred to his suggestion of an Islamic society which would formulate a common dogma, ethics, and law for all Muslims. This suggestion was in harmony with the idea of the Manārists that the primitive Tradition existed in its entirety before the rise of the various schools and sects; that the latter arose and endured for subsequent historical reasons which had ceased to be valid and should therefore be abolished in order to eliminate factors tending to perpetuate disunity among the Muslims.[53]

Naturally, Riḍā and the Manārists looked with marked disfavor on the modern nationalist movements among the Muslims, and they did so on more than one score. Riḍā was one of the few Muslim thinkers in Egypt who saw early and clearly the threat posed by the concept of nationalism to the Islamic doctrine. To be sure, the undeniable appeal of the negative side of nationalism — liberation from foreign occupation — prevented him from condemning it absolutely, except once in 1900.[54] But even though he accommodated himself to this aspect of it on the ground that the liberation and reunification of the *ummah* must, under the circumstances, proceed by degrees,[55] he never ceased to condemn the positive, ideological aspects of the nationalism that prevailed in Egypt and other Arab countries after the turn of the century. Nothing is more dangerous, Riḍā argued, than the desire of the nationalist Westernizers to replace the sentiment of Islamic solidarity with national and racist sentiment.[56] This was, to him, not only a new source of dissension among Muslims, but something close to apostasy. "They count a Muslim and an Arab as a foreigner if he does not belong to the same country as themselves. . . ," Riḍā wrote sarcastically, so that "the *sharīf* (descendant of the Prophet) of the Hijaz or of Syria is no better to them than a heathen from China." [57] Even in their own terms, Riḍā argued, was it not absurd to want to destroy all that constitutes the originality of the nation, that is to say, "its beliefs, its instincts, its morals, its literature, and its emblems," in the slavish pursuit of alien ideas? [58]

One last point before summarizing the position of Riḍā and the Manārists and evaluating its effect on Egyptian thought: 'Abduh had already legitimized the pursuit of science and the adoption of modern technology. Riḍā and his party fully concurred with this position in the public interest. They even reinterpreted one of the major principles of Islam — *jihād* (Holy War) — and internalized it to mean "follow the progress of the foreigner so as to be able to push him back in case of need." [59] Given their extreme opposition to Western ideas and thought, it is obvious from their support of science that they tended to view it as a collection of findings and conclusions and were unaware of the fact that the philosophical and even ethical spirit underlying the scientific method was "subversive" of their views.

Riḍā and his party had placed themselves from the very beginning in the extremely difficult and paradoxical position of conservative revolutionaries. Without rejecting the principle of consensus itself, they had revolted against the medieval consensus which gave the traditional doctrine its final form. As a result, once they had failed to enlist religious opinion in working out a new consensus, they placed themselves, by their own doctrine, outside the mainstream of Islam. They endeavored with all their might to reconcile the various sects and groups and ended up by creating a new splinter. They advocated a critical re-examination of the sources of Islam and of its development, but set their own arbitrary a priori limits on what the sources were and even what was to be deduced from them. They rejected all Western ideas and institutions only to sanction many of them unwittingly or underhandedly: thus they repudiated utilitarian ethics in principle but restored them in practice in the name of *maṣlaḥah* — the public welfare; they criticized the imitators of Western parliamentary institutions, but advocated the adoption of something similar under the guise of *shūra*; they rejected Western thought but urged the adoption of Western science without realizing that it embodied the spirit they had tried to shut out.

But apart from these contradictions, Riḍā and the Manārists had tied their theoretical work to practical political schemes which had very little chance of succeeding under the circumstances of the times. "The Muslims consider, in fact, that their religion does not really exist unless an independent and strong Islamic State is established which could apply the laws of Islam and defend it against any foreign opposition and domination." [60] They were committed to a true caliphate at a time when diplomatic considerations obstructed the possibility of realizing it. When those obstructions were weakened after World War I, the nationalists were already on the way to power, the ideal of Muslim solidarity had been dealt a severe blow by the Arab revolt, the Ottoman empire had been partitioned into a number of autonomous states, and the caliphate was abolished altogether. The failure of the practical schemes on which Riḍā and the Manārists had counted left them with the feeling that they had only succeeded in helping the Westernizers by their attacks on the traditional system. In the case of Riḍā, this feeling drove him gradually away from his initial mild liberalism toward an uncompromising legal and traditional puritanism akin to the spirit of the Wahhabis of Arabia which alienated him from all other groups. His revisionism was too daring for the conservatives, his puritanism too dry for the simple masses, and his restrictions too rigid for the Western-educated. His position grew so weak that his death in 1935 went almost unnoticed.

Liberal Nationalism [1]

Although a radical interpretation of 'Abduh's thought might have served as a starting-point for a mild, enlightened nationalism, it was not from that source that the founders of Egyptian nationalism drew their inspiration. They undoubtedly derived comfort and support from 'Abduh's ideas, but their main source of inspiration was Western Liberal Nationalism which was basically at variance with 'Abduh's fundamental inclination. For that inclination, as Riḍā quite rightly assessed it, was a desire to see a reformed Islam taking a central place in Egyptian public and social life; whereas the Liberal Nationalists sought to reduce religion to the role of mentor of the individual conscience and a medium of personal relationship with the divinity, while trying to found social and political life on the principle of the nation and some of the ideals and values of Western Liberalism. It is precisely because Liberal Nationalism had strong elements of affinity with 'Abduh's thought, while differing from it in fundamental aims, that Riḍā and the Manārists attempted to restate their master's thought and to bolster it with a political doctrine so as to prevent its exploitation by the nationalists. Henceforth, the gap between Reformist Islam, as interpreted by the Manārists, and Liberal Nationalism steadily increased until the two became mutually exclusive.

1. *Muṣṭafā Kāmil (1874–1908)*

Muṣṭafā Kāmil is generally considered to be the founder of modern Egyptian nationalism. This view is correct if we have in mind the nationalist movement; but if we think of the nationalist ideology, the credit must go to Luṭfī al-Sayyid. Indeed, Muṣṭafā Kāmil was a tenacious political agitator, a gifted diplomat, a brilliant orator, and a talented journalist; but he was not at all a political thinker. One looks in vain in his writings and speeches for anything more than general, often rhetorical, references to political conceptions, which he enunciated as self-evident truths. The following excerpt from a speech he made midway in his career provides a good illustration:

> No civilization will rise in Egypt and be of lasting worth unless it is

> built on the nation and by the nation, . . . unless every one of its members realizes that man has certain sacred rights which cannot be touched, that he was born not to be an instrument but to live like a human being, that the love of the fatherland is the highest virtue that can embellish a human being, and that a nation that loses its independence has no honor and her sons have no worth. . . .[2]

Nowhere in the entire speech, or elsewhere, did Muṣṭafā Kāmil elucidate those "sacred rights" in detail nor did he explain and defend the sources from which they derived. One can only assume that he meant them in the Western Liberal sense since he received a thoroughly Western education and moved in Liberal European circles.

Muṣṭafā Kāmil was the son of an engineer who had been educated in the schools established by Muḥammad 'Alī and had spent all his life in government service. The only traditional education ever received by Muṣṭafā was one year of learning the Qur'ān, between the ages of five and six. Following that, Muṣṭafā attended secular primary and secondary schools and then joined the Khedivial Law School. In 1892 he enrolled in a French law school, studied two years in France, and obtained his *License* in 1894. From that time until his death in 1908, he spent at least a few months every year in Europe, where he associated with diplomats, politicians, nationalist leaders, writers, and journalists of Liberal inclinations.

Barely touched by traditional Muslim education, a specimen of the newly arisen middle class with no attachment to previous forms of social organization, Muṣṭafā was instinctively oriented toward the modern concept of the nation-state as the basic political-social entity. Through education, travel, and personal friendships, he lived with part of his mind in Europe; and he gives the impression of having always played to European audiences even when he was addressing his own people. It was not altogether for tactical reasons that, after founding in 1900 the *al-Liwā'* (The Standard) — the daily organ of his party — he thought it necessary to go to the trouble of issuing complete French and English versions.

Nationalism involves a certain element of immediate, intuitive, emotional identification on the part of the individual with the collectivity called the nation. But it also involves an intellectual framework that defines the basis of the nation, the nature of the bond that holds its members together, and their rights and obligations. At its point of origin, in the West, the modern idea of nation had been given various theoretical foundations, ranging from the contractual and historical theories of society of Rousseau and Savigny, through the romantic *volk* conception of Herder and the ethico-political associations of Mazzini, to the blood-and-earth and race myths of the turn of the century. Muṣṭafā Kāmil, however, never attempted to clarify his views about the foundation of the nation, though his speeches and writings sometimes hinted vaguely at various conceptions. His whole effort seems instead to have been directed at fostering and glorifying the sentiment of nationalism. It may very well be that, given his general background he took for granted the Liberal concept of nationalism popular in the latter half of the nineteenth century and therefore thought that his audience was not so much in need of an explanation of principles as of exhortation to commit itself to them.[3] Consider the following excerpts from his speeches:

> Nationalism is a sentiment before which all nations and all communities bow because it is the feeling of the worth and dignity of man, of the bounty of God and His care, of the meaning of existence itself. . . .[4]
>
> Nationalism is the food which the body and soul of Egypt need before any other food. . . . It is the mainspring of all miracles and the principle of all progress . . . it is the blood in the vein of nations and the life of all living things. . . .[5]
>
> Nationalism is the noblest tie for men and the solid foundation upon which great and mighty kingdoms are built. . . . Life is merely transitory and it has no honor without nationalism and without work for the welfare of the fatherland and its children. . . .[6]
>
> Fatherland, O fatherland: To you my love and my heart. To you my life and my existence. To you my blood and my soul. To you my mind and my speech. . . . You, you O Egypt are life itself, and there is no life but in you. . . .[7]

It can be seen from these excerpts that Muṣṭafā Kāmil described patriotism in terms and with a pathos which had hitherto been expressed almost exclusively by religious mystics. Indeed, Muṣṭafā Kāmil, partly because he tended to think of nationalism in the sense of patriotism, partly because he conceived of Islam mainly in individualistic terms, believed sincerely, if somewhat simply, that instead of contradicting each other, nationalism and Islam are in fact complementary:

> There are some who may think that religion opposes nationalism, or that the call of religion has nothing to do with nationalism. But I believe that religion and nationalism are inseparable twins and that he whose heart is possessed by religion would love his fatherland and sacrifice his goods and life for it.

The next lines of this passage give a clearer illustration of Muṣṭafā's conception of Islam:

I do not rely in what I am saying on the teachings of the ancestors, whom the men of the modern age may accuse of ignorance and fanaticism, but I call upon Bismarck, the greatest leader of our time . . . to testify to the truth of this principle. This great man proclaimed indeed with a mighty voice: "if you tore faith from my heart, you will have torn with it my love of the fatherland." [8]

Muṣṭafā Kāmil, clearly, was thinking only of the ethical-emotional aspects of nationalism and Islam, where agreement was conceivable; the doctrinal and institutional implications of the two forces, where harmony was by no means self-evident, never occurred to him. Apparently he took it for granted that Islam was an individualistic religion concerned, like modern Christianity, only with faith and morals. Thus, in the next passage of the speech from which we have just quoted, Muṣṭafā Kāmil went on to speak of the bonds of brotherhood and equality that nationalism formed between Muslims and Copts, unaware that Muslim Law would insist instead on certain prescribed discrimination against non-Muslims.

Muṣṭafā Kāmil's disregard of the foundations of nationalism and his limited view of Islam's role in public life were reflected in his support of pan-Islamism. He did not seem to notice the contradiction between the concept of the *ummah* based on a common religion, which underlies pan-Islamism, and the modern concept of nation — based on secular political, geographical, and other factors — which is at the root of nationalism. That is why he found it difficult throughout his career to understand those who criticized him on this score. In 1897 he explained to a German correspondent that "although the Egyptians know only one homeland, and that is Egypt, it is certainly natural that they should support the caliphal state as a sign of gratitude for its refusal to play into the hands of the British." [9] Ten years later he was still explaining in an article in *Le Figaro*: "Our sympathy with the Islamic peoples is a natural thing and has nothing to do with religious fanaticism. There is not a single enlightened Muslim who thinks for a moment that it is possible to join the Muslim peoples in a league against Europe." [10]

Later in his life, Muṣṭafā Kāmil coupled his agitation for independence with a demand for a constitution and a parliamentary government. But if constitutionalism and popular representation were connected in his mind as essential elements of nationalism, this fact was never made explicit in his writings and speeches. As a matter of fact, during the early part of his career he argued for national independence at the same time that he defended the prerogatives of the khedive. In a speech he made in Alexandria in 1896, for instance, he said, addressing himself to the British nation:

O you great nation. Some men with hidden motives have deceived you [in telling you] that peace and order have not been restored in Egypt and that the khedive cannot rule the country with his men, in order to force you to concede the necessity of the occupation. But know you that it is nothing but pure invention. For peace and order reign undisturbed and the whole nation is loyal to its prince, loves him, and venerates him. . . .[11]

He argued for a constitution for the first time in 1900, after he had discontinued his collaboration with the khedive in disappointment over the latter's timidity in the diplomatic wrangles connected with the Fashoda incident. Even then, Muṣṭafā Kāmil argued for a constitution from expediency rather than from right. Thus, in *al-Liwā'*, October 5, 1900, he demanded a constitution in order "to give liberty and justice solid foundations so that no human hand can harm them." In a speech he made on May 21, 1902, he said that "the constitution means *the granting* (*manḥ*) to the nation of the right to supervise all things and to control all the actions of government. . . ." [12] Writing in *al-Liwa'* on November 6, 1902, after having described the "bankruptcy of the occupation regime" in the various spheres of internal administration, he said:

. . . I believe that all these evils point to the great need of this country for a representative assembly which would have supreme legislative authority. . . . Else, the concentration of absolute power in the hands of one person, whether Egyptian or Englishman, will cause great harm to the country and bring calamities upon it.

It was not until just before his death that Muṣṭafā Kāmil came close to a position of a *right* of popular sovereignty, which, however, he still left unsubstantiated by any argument. In *al-Liwā'* of May 26, 1907, he wrote in an "open letter to the khedive":

. . . No truly patriotic Egyptian will ever consent that Egypt be ruled by His Highness the khedive alone, or by the British Commissioner, or by both of them. He demands that his beloved homeland be governed by the talented and sincere among its children and that the system of government be constitutional and representative.

In an "open letter" to the British prime minister in *Le Figaro* of September 14, 1907, he wrote: "We shall never accept government by whim or tyranny. The only will to which we want to submit is the will of the Egyptian people. . . ."

Muṣṭafā Kāmil was careful to contain his agitation within the limits of the law. He was wary of violence and uprisings after the bitter experience of the 'Urābī movement. He looked to education and the pressure of opinion as the means of achieving independence, particularly after all his diplomatic schemes had ended in fiasco. With respect to the form this education should take, he was frankly and purely occidental. Thus he wrote in *Le Figaro* of July 11, 1906:

> We want to raise our people and acquaint it with its rights and duties and guide it to its right place among the nations by the means of education and enlightenment. We have realized for over a century now that nations cannot lead an honorable life unless they follow the path of Western civilization. We were the first oriental people to shake hands with Europe, and we shall certainly continue along the path we have taken.

The significance of Muṣṭafā Kāmil, then, did not lie in his vague references to an ideology of nationalism, but in his success in stirring large sections of the educated population and mobilizing them behind slogans of independence, patriotism, constitutionalism, and Western education. It was left to Luṭfī al-Sayyid to give nationalism a more solid ideological foundation on the basis of a comprehensive Liberal philosophy, including a doctrine of popular sovereignty, and to rescue it from the pan-Islamic entanglements in which Muṣṭafā Kāmil had left it.

2. *Aḥmad Luṭfī al-Sayyid (1872–)* [13]

Aḥmad Luṭfī al-Sayyid was born in a village of lower Egypt to a family of rich landowners. He went through the *kuttāb* and the primary school and then moved to Cairo for his secondary education, which he finished in 1889. By the time he entered the Law School, he was already deeply impressed by the theories of evolution, having read Darwin's *Origin of Species*, which Shiblī Shumayyil translated in the same year. While still in school he began to write frequently for the newspaper *al Mu'ayyid*, and during a visit to Constantinople in one of his summer vacations he was introduced by Sa'd Zaghlūl and others to Jamāl al-Dīn al-Afghānī. He was graduated in 1894 and entered government service.

Luṭfī started his career as a nationalist leader under the aegis of Muṣṭafā Kāmil. In 1897, when Muṣṭafā, with the help of the khedive, was planning to form his party officially and to found a newspaper, he suggested to Luṭfī that he become editor but only after spending a year in Switzerland in order to acquire Swiss citizenship, and with it the special protection and immunities that foreigners enjoyed under the Capitulations. Luṭfī agreed and went to Geneva. But while there, he met and befriended Muḥammad 'Abduh, which put him on the black list of Muṣṭafā's patron, the khedive. This friendship with 'Abduh and Muṣṭafā Kāmil's advocacy of pan-Islamism proved enough to divide the two men permanently.

In 1907, when Muṣṭafā Kāmil had succeeded in rallying around his party large sections of the population aroused by British harshness in the notorious Denshiway incident, Luṭfī joined a group of moderate nationalists in founding the *Ummah* (nation) Party to counter Muṣṭafā's movement. The party included among its leaders several very rich landowners like Maḥmūd Sulaymān, Ḥasan 'Abd al-Rāziq, Ḥamd al-Bāsil, Sulaymān Abāẓah, 'Alī Sha'rāwī, and others, who had a stake in keeping on good terms with the British. But the party also contained a great many eminent intellectuals, social reformers, and statesmen who had already made a significant impact on their society or were destined to preside over the destinies of Egypt in the following two or three decades. In this group were such men as Fatḥī Zaghlūl, Qāsim Amīn, 'Abd al-'Azīz Fahmī, 'Abd al-Khāliq Tharwat, and Sa'd Zaghlūl, who was an active if not an official member. Luṭfī al-Sayyid became secretary of the party and chief editor of its daily organ, *al-Jarīdah*, and so was in a position to make his voice heard by men of influence as well as by the general public. He devoted several columns of his publication to the discussion of fundamental cultural, social, and political problems and made it the rallying point and training school for a whole generation of young writers. Only a few of the men whose names will appear in this study have not, at one time or other, written for *al-Jarīdah* and benefited from Luṭfī's encouragement. By 1914, when he resigned his editorship (still having forty years of active life ahead of him) he had already merited the title of *ustādh al-jīl* — Teacher of the Generation.

In 1908, the "thinkers' group" of the Ummah Party brought to a successful realization, by means of public subscriptions, the long-discussed project of an Egyptian university. In 1924, when the University, now taken over by the state, launched a vast expansion program, Luṭfī was chosen as its first director. Once again he found himself in a central position to mold opinion and he used it with no less credit than he had his previous post as editor. He left the University twice — first in 1928–1929, to go to another strategic position, the Ministry of Education, and again in 1931–1935, in protest against the dismissal of Ṭāha Ḥusayn by the Ṣidqī government. He finally resigned in 1941 to become an appointed member of the Senate. After 1952 he retired from public life except for occasional attendance at the sessions of the Academy of Arabic Language of which he is still the venerated president.

Apart from his writings in *al-Jarīdah*, selections of which were assembled in books and published several times, Luṭfī put great and persistent effort into translating the works of Aristotle, mainly from the French, in the conviction that Egypt's renaissance, like the West's, must be founded on the spread and assimilation of the classics. He managed to publish the *Ethics* around 1922, *On the Universe* and *On Generation and Destruction* in 1932, *On Nature,* in 1935, and *Politics,* in 1940.

Luṭfī al-Sayyid's creative period as a writer, before he turned to administrative occupations and scholastic work, falls entirely within the period in which he was editor of *al-Jarīdah.* During those crucial formative years he devoted much of his attention to political thought with the purpose of establishing new foundations for a viable political community. He attempted to do so by constructing a nationalist doctrine within the framework of a comprehensive Liberal socio-political philosophy inspired by Aristotle, Rousseau, Locke, Bentham, and Spencer. With Rousseau, he asserted that man ". . . was born free; with free will, free to choose between doing and abstaining from doing anything, free even to live or to die. . . ."[14] But, unlike Rousseau, he did not conceive of the primary state of man as isolation, and society as an artificial creation. To him, man was by nature a social animal and society was an organic, natural creation. He resolved the conflict between man's freedom and the reality of his "chained" position in society by conceiving freedom in an Aristotelian sense as a potentiality: Man is born *for* freedom, but he can realize it only in a society rightly organized for the purpose. These simple premises give some insight into the quality and temper of Luṭfī's mind, the problems he endeavored to meet, and the principles of his practical philosophy. He avoided the highly abstract fiction of the social contract in favor of an organic conception (more suitable to the mystique of nationalism), by endowing the nation (society) with an original life of its own. He met the very important problem any philosophy of inherent rights must face, that of explaining the corrupt past, by suggesting that the individual and group rights were dormant because consciousness of them was lacking and because there was no adequate organization to realize them. Finally, he pointed out that redemption lies in overcoming just those weaknesses of the past, and he justified gradualism and moderation by his view of freedom as an evolutionary process of fulfilling a potentiality rather than as something to be achieved by a single revolutionary act.

Luṭfī conceived of individual rights in terms of interdependent concentric circles reminiscent of Fichte's concept. At the core, there is man's natural freedom of which nobody can deprive him as long as he lives. But since this natural freedom is useless if its expression is hampered, it must be defined and secured by civil rights. To ascertain and protect those rights man must also have political rights in the form of "a respected will in the management of society." [15] But the rights of society, or the nation, are not simply the aggregate of the rights of its members. The nation itself, being a natural creation, has its own "natural rights" quite independently of the rights of its members:

> As for the right of the nation, or its constitution, or its public liberty—this right of the nation is like the right of personal freedom of the individual. Those who say that man was created free—and all men agree about this—must say that the nation too was formed free; because the formation of the nation was a natural act based on man's social nature. . . .[16]

As a matter of fact, Luṭfī was even more emphatic about the rights of the nation than about the rights of the individual. Whereas the rights of the individual are merely potential, society has always exercised its supreme right, although it did so in a misguided way:

> The sovereignty of the people exists in fact even though the laws do not recognize it. Only it is not directed in the right channel because past rules [the rules of Islamic Law] have oriented it towards accepting despotism as the foundation of government. . . .[17]

The correct exercise of the people's sovereignty should include the establishment of a constitutional regime and the separation of powers as advocated by Locke and Montesquieu.[18] The people should also be wary of granting the government any rights or controls beyond what is required for the maintenance of order.[19]

Because he conceived the individual's natural rights as potential, Luṭfī was able to combine them with a utilitarian ethical and political philosophy which he probably expected to be more readily understood than a purely abstract theory of right. He tried to prove that it is in the interest of all concerned to recognize and give practical application to the individual's and the nation's rights:

> The generality of men (*al-kāffah*) have natural, or virtually natural, rights which the legislator should not touch. These rights existed prior to society—assuming that society is derivative—or are the cornerstones of human society if society is, as we believe it is, a product of nature from the time man came into being and until God inherits the earth and its contents. . . . .[20]

Here, then, is an assertion of rights as natural, inherent. In the same pages Luṭfī proceeded to argue that these rights should be recognized in the name of utility:

. . . We believe that love of the fatherland, like love of the family, indeed like any sentiment, is based on utility (*manfa'ah*). Utility is the foundation of all sentiments and actions. Human society stands on mutual usefulness. The individual who sees nothing in society except sacrifices without receiving anything in exchange . . . has no interest in remaining in society. Experience has proved that individuals and groups who found that their losses in society outweighed their gains have resented the social order and sought to subvert it in revenge. . . . The legislator must then leave a number of rights to the generality of men far from the sphere of legislative experimentation. . . . These are the capital of the individual in a civil society without which his devotion to it turns into hatred. . . . These rights consist of (1) the right of personal freedom in its general sense; freedom of thought, of belief, of expression, freedom to teach and to learn — all limited by the freedom of others. . . . (2) the right of equality before the law . . . (3) the right of property. . . , the sanctity of this right being one of the most important pillars of society . . . (4) the right of the people to govern itself according to its own choice. . . . .[21]

Again, thanks to his concept of potentiality, Luṭfī was able to combine a theory of evolution with his principles of inherent rights. Social evolution becomes the process of the gradual realization and substantiation of the latent inherent natural rights. This theory enabled him, in its turn, to explain the despotic realities of the past at the same time that it provided him with the necessary ammunition to overcome it in the name of the ideals of progress, the struggle for survival, liberty, and utility. The reason for the backwardness, despotism, and humiliations of the past is found in the submission to the rigid, static, and distorted teachings of the *salaf ṣāliḥ* (virtuous predecessors) contrary to the law of evolution, with which, Luṭfī insisted elsewhere, the original spirit of Islam was in harmony.[22]

Yes, we have tried the ideas of our *salaf ṣāliḥ* in the near past and the results have been our present condition. There is nothing left for us, then, but to surrender the ideas and qualities which have caused our backwardness and to adopt change and evolution so that we may compete in the struggle of this civilized life. . . .[23]

Consequently, to Luṭfī the main front on which the battle for true freedom and independence should be fought was not that in which the foreign occupier was met with force and numbers, but the spiritual one in which reason faced imposed authority of all sorts, in which the will to a decent life and progress broke the shackles of inherited dogma that bind it:

Our progress towards realizing our natural share in freedom is impossible to achieve even if we possessed the greatest instruments of brutal force and even if our number were many times what it is until we liberate ourselves first from the curse of worshipping uncritically thoughts and ideas on authority, and until we shatter with our own hands the chains which have held our mind in bondage and the fantasies which have prevented us from benefiting from the new ideals. If we could only raise the beacon of freedom in that sphere, in which we are free to act without hindrance or intrusion, we will have made a good start in the task of collecting the strength necessary for the realization and preservation of complete freedom.[24]

On the basis of the "new ideals," Luṭfī frankly rejected all notions of nationalism founded on religion: "We are not partisans of this Muslim League (meaning pan-Islamism) because it is religious, whereas we believe that nationality and the bonds of utility are the bases of political action. . ." [25] He also derided the attempts to link the Egyptians to the Arab or Turkish lineage and considered such acts just as dishonorable as the attempt to break away from the lineage of one's own family.[26] He had his own ethnological conception of the Egyptian nationality based on the principle of the inheritance of acquired characteristics.[27] The three millennia of ancient Egyptian history, he contended, have created a "pharaonic core" which, together with the elements of later Egyptian history, conspired to produce a distinct Egyptian personality. That is the reason why Luṭfī was not afraid that Egypt might lose her personality through wholesale borrowing from the West. Time and the Egyptian core would synthesize the borrowings into something distinctly Egyptian.[28]

Luṭfī's rejection of pan-Islamism in the face of well-known instinctive popular sympathies toward it was not only a radical theoretical departure but also an act of great moral courage. His opposition to it even as a political tool at a time when it appeared to many that Egypt had no other recourse in dealing with the British revealed rare integrity. It also marked the highest point reached by any Egyptian in the emancipation from the obsession with the problem of power as a *religious* issue. The judicious moderation and positive approach that accompanied his firmness and integrity contrasted sharply with the attitude of some of his own supporters who were not averse to resorting to methods that were nearer to vulgar propaganda than to calm reasoning. Compare, for example, the following excerpt from an article by 'Abd al-Ḥamīd al-Zahāwī in *al-Jarīdah* of September 10, 1907:

Pan-Islamism means agreement on the proposition that the Qur'ān is

God's book, revealed to Muḥammad the Messenger of God. But any inquiry into the history of those who share in this agreement will show that it did not prevent them from disagreeing on other things beyond the possibility of reconciliation to the present day. . . . The Muslims have not agreed politically since 'Umar, or religiously since the days after 'Alī. What is this union of people who have differed politically and religiously for thirteen centuries, of people who kill each other and who summon against each other the aid of peoples with fundamentally different faiths? What is the union of people whose factions have not ceased fighting one another from the time of the assassination of their second caliph? What is the union of people whose kings have rejoiced in the disappearance of the realms of other kings among them? What is the union of people whose history tells us that an oriental foreigner like Hulagu could ravage their country at the time of their glory without their joining hands to fight him? . . . What is the union of a people whose history tells us that a Western foreigner like the Crusader could attack their lands without their uniting to expel him until one section of them, having marshalled its energies, was able to repulse him all by itself?"

The political thought of Luṭfī al-Sayyid no doubt contained many contradictions and incompatibilities. The reader may have noticed, for instance, the very tenuous grounds on which he argued for the rights of the nation independently of the rights of individuals. Essentially, he seems to have based these national rights on nothing more than an analogy with the individual, which only begs the question. Also, he often confused civil with political rights, natural right with utility, and natural society with a society which is held together by bonds of utility. It seems incongruous to urge the legislator not to intervene with the "right of the people to govern itself according to its own choice": either he is a legislator by choice of the people — and then the recommendation seems meaningless — or he is a self-appointed legislator and, as such, he already violates the right of the people to govern itself. Further, one may wonder about his using a doctrine of *natural* right of the individual when the same results can be obtained through a doctrine of utility; and one is puzzled about Luṭfī's understanding of the term "natural" as ascribed to the formation of society when he also states that "human society stands on mutual usefulness," and implies that men can leave it when it ceases to serve that purpose. Some of the contradictions may be attributed to the fact that he expounded his thought piecemeal in newspaper articles over a period of four to five years, which made it difficult to spot inconsistencies and correct them. Others may be due to tactical political reasons. For while Luṭfī argued the need for a long-range intellectual and psychological transformation of Egyptian society, he also sought immediate practical reforms and wanted to influence the current action of the ruling authorities. He may have used the utilitarian argument in the belief that it was more congenial to the mentality of the authorities while retaining the argument based upon natural right as more appropriate to the long-range re-education of the public. At any rate, all the theoretical difficulties do not detract from the significance of Luṭfī's contribution. Contradictions could be ironed out later by successors; the important thing is that Luṭfī perceived clearly the problem facing Egyptian society in the matter of erecting a true political community, suggested a direction for its solution, and courageously blazed the trail himself. He realized that what Egypt needed most was a thorough re-education in a new belief-system and did not hesitate to break away entirely from traditional Islamic political concepts. He regarded nationalism as the most suitable answer but consciously fought against those who saw it as nothing more than liberation from a foreign imperialist power, after which all wrongs would be miraculously righted. On the contrary: he suggested a good many ideas which might serve as elements of the comprehensive, positive, and enduring belief-system that he considered to be the main substance of nationalism.

Part Three

THE TRIUMPH OF THE LIBERAL NATIONALIST MOVEMENT

CHAPTER 7

The Anatomy of the Liberal Nationalist Triumph

Despite the enormous influence which some of Muḥammad ʿAbduh's ideas were to exert on the Liberal intellectual and political leaders of Egypt, the totality of his doctrine and his inclination to restore a reformed Islam at the center of the community's life found no response among them. Neither did his doctrine and program make any immediate headway among the orthodox religious leaders to whom they had been addressed in the first place. Riḍā's attempt to rework ʿAbduh's doctrine, rescue it from the Westernizing leaders, and present it as a concrete liberal-Islamic political program had been less than successful in theory and met complete failure in practice.

In contrast, the alternative formulas suggested by Muṣṭafā Kāmil and Luṭfī al-Sayyid seemed to have encountered almost immediate and brilliant success. Only two decades after Muṣṭafā had begun his preaching and less than a decade after Luṭfī had completed his initial formulation, the revolution of 1919 broke out. The whole nation, fellah and pasha, illiterate and educated, Muslims and Copts, men and women, stood behind Saʿd Zaghlūl,[1] fighting with great courage and heavy sacrifice in apparent support of the Liberal Nationalist ideals he represented. The universal character of the uprising surprised not only the British, who had tended to discount the nationalist movement as a somewhat troublesome but inconsequential agitation of school-boys and other marginal elements, but even the most fervent followers of Muṣṭafā Kāmil, who had firmly believed in the depth and miracle-working power of the spirit of nationalism.[2] So impressed were the British by the solidarity and tenacity of the movement that they were compelled, after three years of vain maneuvering, to scrap all their plans for the political future of Egypt and to proclaim its independence in February 1922. This triumph of Liberal Nationalism was crowned the following year by the promulgation of a constitution embodying its ideals as the supreme law of the land, and therefore as part of the ideology of the whole community.

But was there really a Liberal Nationalist impulse behind all the forces that took part in the revolution? Did the uprising mean that Liberal Nationalism in any meaningful sense had been accepted by the country at large?

These questions may be irrelevant from the point of view of strict political and diplomatic history. It may be legitimate to view the revolution as the culmination of the nationalist movement even though it is known that many extraneous motives entered into the situation. All great popular upheavals, it may be said, involve an alliance of disparate forces and motives which converge temporarily on a particular issue; and there is no doubt that in the case of Egypt the issue was Sa'd Zaghlūl and what he stood for.

For a study of belief-systems and ideological evolution, however, these questions are of great importance. They lead into an analysis of all the various forces and motives in the situation, helping us to discover which elements are essential and which are contingent; which views were generally shared among all the forces and which were particular to only some of them. It is impossible to understand or explain the developments that followed without drawing these distinctions, and we shall endeavor to do so by examining the rise and triumph of the nationalist movement in terms of the role and function of the various social classes and forces that contributed to it.

Nationalism in dependent countries has generally two aspects, one negative and the other positive. In its negative manifestation, nationalism is a movement of liberation in the sense of seeking to drive out the dominant foreign power. This feature is shared universally by the various countries as well as among most of the social classes within each country. In its positive aspect, nationalism involves specific concrete ideologies which, though they may have characteristics in common, tend to differ greatly from country to country, from one sector of the population to another within the same country, and from one historical period to another. The type of ideology that may dominate a movement at any particular time depends on the circumstances of each country, on its pattern of social stratification, and on its development. Nevertheless, allowing for local variations, a certain broad regular pattern is discernible in the growth of nationalism in most dependent countries that is basically similar to the one to be observed in Egypt.

Nationalism in Egypt found its first practical expression in the al-Afghānī-'Urābī movement. It had failed to develop into an enduring movement, however, because of its almost completely negative character and its lack of anchorage in a specific social group. But with Muṣṭafā Kāmil and Luṭfī al-Sayyid, nationalism finally developed a positive ideology of secular liberal inspiration and could count on the lasting support of a substantial middle class of professionals, officials, and intellectuals which had emerged in the interim. There are several reasons why the middle class was most responsive to the Liberal Nationalist appeal. This was an entirely new class which had no traditional roots in society and was therefore more receptive to new ideas in general. To qualify for their occupations, its members had to be exposed intensively to Western education. In the case of many — lawyers and government officials, for example — their jobs required them to think in terms of rights, duties, nationality and national jurisdiction, authority and sovereignty, and so on, all of which had become current legal phraseology in an administration using Western codes before they received any general political and ideological significance. Then, never having formed part of the traditional corporate system, and often belonging to independent professions, men of that class were more eager and able to associate themselves with the larger and rather abstract unit called "the nation" than other groups, such as the peasants, who worked and lived in the frame of their "organic" villages, or the old urban tradesmen, workers, and small merchants, for whom the autonomous city quarter, the *sūq* (market), the Ṣūfī order, still provided some social frame, even while the corporations were declining.

To say that the middle class was most responsive to the ideas of nationalism does not mean, however, that the other classes just mentioned were not important for the nationalist movement. Although they were prevented by their lack of education, their immediate social environment, and their traditional cast of mind from understanding and assimilating the modern conception of the nation, not to speak of liberal principles of rights and ethics, they could, nevertheless, contribute tremendous support to the nationalist movement *in its negative aspect* on grounds of their own. For, their resentment of foreign domination and an intense desire to get rid of it had strong and deep roots in their religious view of the world. This view, it will be recalled, showed a world divided into two hostile religious camps: Islam and the unbelievers. In this perspective, the British occupation was not simply a political domination by a foreign nation, but an encroachment on the domain of Islam by a Christian power, based on religious hostility. And if Muslims had been enjoined to fight in order to expand the frontiers of Islam against infidelity, how much more were they duty-bound to fight in order to prevent the reverse from taking place?

Of course, these propositions were not elaborated and discussed all the time by the peasants, workers, and other members of the lower classes. They were rather normative attitudes, implied in their commitment to Muslim tradition in general, and, like all norms, could be and were in fact relegated somewhere to a corner of consciousness and conveniently kept from intruding on the normal business of life, especially when there appeared to be no feasible alternative. But this did not detract from their importance any more than particular violations or temporary neglect detract from any norms in any society. It only meant that the practical attitude of active religious-xenophobic nationalism which these latent thoughts foreshadowed was in the background and needed a catalyst to bring it into action. And this catalyst was provided by the events of World War I and its aftermath.

If this analysis is correct, we will have found the key to the impressive unanimity of the Egyptian revolution. But is there any evidence for it? Considering that the groups with which we are presently concerned were inarticulate at the time of the uprising, and since no one attempted to seek and report their motivation reliably, we have only circumstantial evidence to go by.

In the case of the urban lower classes, that evidence is fairly strong because we have an articulation of their sentiment at a later date in the form of the ideology of the Muslim Brotherhood which they joined *en masse*. And it is significant that the phenomenal growth of the Brotherhood, which cannot be explained unless one assumes that the feelings to which it gave expression had existed long before, took place mainly during World War II and its immediate aftermath, when the provocations were almost identical with those of World War I. In both cases there were running inflation and a very severe shortage of food and goods, from which the urban lower classes suffered most; and in both cases there was a drastic loosening of public morals — all the more shocking to those who derived no benefit from it — which had been induced by the rush for quick profits and the presence of large numbers of foreign troops behaving as soldiers in wartime away from home are likely to behave. But, while in World War II the Brotherhood was already in existence as an organization into which the lower classes could channel their protest autonomously, in World War I they could give vent to their feelings only through the nationalist movement.

As for the fellahin, from whom most might have been learned of the motives and the process that made the revolution unanimous precisely because they were illiterate, lived in relative isolation, and are traditionally passive, the evidence is unfortunately circumstantial to an even greater degree. One fact that appears certain is their adherence to the Muslim principles which we have described. This was confirmed in a recent investigation conducted by a British-trained Egyptian sociologist who found that, in general, religion governs the political behavior of the fellahin, and, more specifically, that even now, "for the villagers, the world is classified into believers and non-believers on the basis of the Moslem faith," and that otherwise "they are hardly aware of concepts like race or class." [3] Apart from these facts, any further evidence must rely on a process of elimination and a general sense of the subject. The theory that the fellahin might have been incited and organized from the city is disproved by the surprise of the nationalist leaders themselves at the general participation of this group in the uprising. Moreover, the very numerous investigations conducted by the British authorities in connection with the trials of culprits who were caught failed to reveal any advance nationalist preparation and agitation among the villagers. It was only after the revolt had broken out that some nationalist leaders in the provinces attempted to guide it as best they could.

Another theory advanced by many observers to explain the motive behind the fellahins' uprising emphasizes the hardships brought upon them by the war.[4] The requisition of produce and animals without adequate compensation, massive mobilization in the Camel Corps and Labor Corps by press-gang methods, in which the fellahin were exposed to injury, death, and plagues, and other exactions and irritations — all these were real and important, but they do not in themselves provide a sufficient explanation. The fellahin had been exposed only recently to worse oppression under Muslim rulers, such as Muḥammad ʿAlī and Ismaʿīl, and were to suffer no less in the depression of the early thirties and in World War II and after, but they did not revolt. Only if the factor of the latent religious resentment against the oppressor is taken into account does the uprising become understandable. The view of the world underlying the religious resentment, diverted and checked by Cromer's "full belly" policy, was brought sharply into focus again by the economic hardships, and perhaps by Britain's war against the Ottoman sultan-caliph, and found an opportunity to express itself in action following the agitation in the cities and the arrest of Saʿd Zaghlūl. Certainly it is significant that in the course of many centuries the fellahin had broken out in widespread revolt only twice before 1919, and in both cases there was also foreign occupation or the impending threat of one. The first revolt broke out in 1800 and was directed clearly against the Christian French occupier; [5] and many local uprisings occurred during the ʿUrābī agitation when there was the impending threat of foreign intervention.

One more social group of major importance remains to be considered and that is the small and — for the most part — Western-educated aristocracy of big landowners. This class had derived enormous material benefits from the occupation. The security of titles and regularization of taxation, the stabilization of finances, the growth of the population, the extensive development of irrigation, and the expansion of cotton plantation that took place during the occupation had increased tremendously the value and yield of the landowners' acreage. There were occasions, for instance, when land value multiplied more than twelve-fold within five years.[6] During the war, the profits that accrued to the big landowners were enormous. Nevertheless, although their wealth increased under the British, or perhaps precisely because they became richer, they resented increasingly their exclusion from decisive political power and eagerly looked for opportunities to gain it. They welcomed the proclamation made during the war of the principle of self-determination, believing that it meant, at last, the transfer of power to their hands. When the nationalist agitation began after the war, they tended to hold back at first in order not to compromise their position with the British; but as the movement gained momentum, most of them joined forces with it, at least outwardly, to assure for themselves a voice in the settlement.

When the revolution broke out, those among the big landowners who were close to the circles of power were as surprised as everyone else at its magnitude, but thought of it as a useful means of extorting concessions from the British, largely to benefit themselves. But when the uprising was followed by strikes, terrorism, constant agitation, boycott of the British commission of investigation, and there seemed to be no prospect of settlement, they grew alarmed at the possibility that the situation might get out of hand and turn into a social revolution. In March 1919, the fellahin had already taken advantage of the anarchy that accompanied the general uprising to sack government as well as landowners' property.[7] In the cities, the workers had begun to organize and had shown disconcerting effectiveness in the general strike of 1919; and the excitement of the general masses had led to ugly riots, looting, and massacres in Alexandria in 1921. Above all, the longer the agitation continued, the more the control of effective positions of power passed into the hands of second- and third-rung nationalist agitators so that even Zaghlūl himself seemed to have lost effective control. It is not surprising, therefore, that members of the landowners' class began to break their uneasy alliance with Zaghlūl and sought to liquidate the whole struggle at the price of a compromise with the British. In this they finally succeeded when they induced the British to issue the February Declaration proclaiming, with certain reservations, the independence of Egypt.

Altogether, then, it appears from the foregoing analysis that the revolution of 1919 and the events that immediately followed could hardly be viewed as an expression of a popular consensus in favor of the Liberal Nationalist ideology in any reasonable sense. What had happened was, rather, that a relatively small class of Western-educated and Western-oriented Liberal Nationalists had managed to ride to a decisive political victory on the wave of two elemental and hitherto inchoate forces that moved the large masses of the people: hatred of a religiously alien power, based on a Muslim view of the world, and excessive economic suffering. But this conclusion, which, it should be admitted, has had the benefit of hindsight, was not apparent to the Egyptian leaders themselves nor to most foreign observers. Concern with the strictly political aspect and consequences of the revolt obscured the variety of motives that lay beneath it. Consequently, the nationalist leaders took the convergence of forces, which had been so largely the result of agreement on the *negative* aspects of nationalism, to signify the expression of a general approval of nationalism in its positive Liberal aspects as well. The first outcome of this misconception was the establishment of a Liberal Nationalist constitution; its other consequences we shall meet later.[8]

CHAPTER 8

The Role of the Nationalist Governments in the Evolution of Ideology

Although the political triumph of the Liberal Nationalists was devoid of the significance that they tended to ascribe to it, it is not without significance for the study of the development of opinion in Egypt. If the triumph of the nationalists did not mean the victory of the Liberal Nationalist ideology, it at least meant the coming to power of a group of people who were motivated by that ideology and who could therefore use the important instruments of the state, such as legislation, public education, and other means, to foster its promotion and general acceptance by the public. This is quite different from the situation which had hitherto existed when the government was in the hands of some outright or disguised despot pursuing essentially personal policies and using the means of state power to further them.

Another change of equal significance derived from the fact that the coming to power of the Liberal Nationalists introduced a much greater element of interaction between government and people than ever before. Hitherto, the policies and actions of government bore no necessary relation to the general disposition of the population and it was therefore impossible to gauge any effect of one over the other in terms of the development of opinion. Ismāʿīl's policy of making Egypt a part of Europe, for instance, indicated little or nothing about the feeling of any section of the community toward it; policy and popular opinion operated on almost entirely separate levels. The rise of national governments and the institution of democratic constitutional procedures, on the other hand, though they did not necessarily cause government action and policy to become expressions of any general will, made them at least more responsive to some sectors of public opinion and gave those sectors the means of exerting some influence. There is therefore much to learn from what a government dared or did not dare do at a given moment and from the justifications it offered in either case.

This does not mean, however, that the study of the actions and policies of the government makes unnecessary any consideration of the evolution of ideas and thought among the articulate leaders of opinion at large, upon whose shoulders the main educative task rested. For in its general actions and policies, the government was likely to be more concerned with getting things done than with educating the public; and in its specific effort in the field of formal public education it was on the whole bound to draw upon the stock of ideas that had been accumulated by writers and leaders of opinion. Even if the men in power had taken upon themselves the task of propounding ideas which they had themselves evolved or imported by means of a massive propaganda or "guidance" effort, they would still have had to depend on the assistance of a large cadre of writers and educators, so that an analysis of the writers' works would still be indispensable. Clearly, then, actions and policies of the new kind of government can be, more or less, an important source for the pursuit of our subject, but not the exclusive source. In this chapter we shall examine some of the major acts of the successive national governments from the point of view of their relation to Islam, traditional and reformist. Other actions of government, formal and informal, that are relevant to the ideological evolution will be considered later, after the analysis of the work of the intellectual leaders that will follow this chapter.

The first and most important act of the nationalists after the proclamation of independence was the elaboration of a constitution. This document was drafted by a committee of legal experts and high officials on the basis of the Belgian Constitution, adjusted to take into account *formal* differences in Egypt's circumstances. It was issued by Royal Rescript, and came into force in 1923. The Constitution enshrined in every respect the principles of Liberal Nationalism, which represented in many instances radical departures from the fundamental principles of traditional Islamic doctrine. However, the significance of this fact was largely discounted by the deliberate adoption of ambiguous terms in the clauses dealing specifically with questions of religion, and by a conscious endeavor on the part of the framers of the Constitution to leave undisturbed the current *practice* in things related to religion even when the principle was altered. The reasons behind this attitude will be discussed later. Its effect was to encourage the notion among the people who were not initiated in Western constitutional theory that the changes introduced had been merely formal.

Article 1 of the Constitution [1] declared Egypt to be "a sovereign state, free and independent," thereby substituting the modern concept of nation-state for the traditional concept of the *ummah*. Further, it precluded the submission of Egypt to any Islamic superstate by declaring that its sovereignty is "indivisible and inalienable." Article 3 granted to all Egyptians equal rights and duties and equality before the law, without distinction of race, language, or religion, thus abandoning formally the principles of Islamic law which discriminate between Muslims, *dhimmīs*, and unbelievers. Article 12 declared that "freedom of conscience is absolute," contrary to Islamic law which prescribes the death penalty for apostasy. Article 23 recognized that "all powers emanate from the nation. . . ," and Articles 24–28 gave Parliament full power of legislation unlimited by any reference to current Islamic law. Article 60 prescribed an oath for the king which committed him ". . . by God Almighty to observe the Constitution and *the laws of the Egyptian people*," and for the representatives an oath of allegiance to the Constitution and the king, thus founding government on a new contract which took no account of the Sharī'ah and its place in the state. Nowhere in the entire Constitution was there any specific reference to the religious law.

Other articles, not necessarily contradictory to traditional Islamic principles, embodied fully the Liberal Nationalist doctrine. The Constitution granted universal manhood suffrage (Article 82), established a two-chambers Parliament (Article 73), ministerial government, and responsibility to the representative assembly (Articles 57–72); provided for decentralization and local representative councils (Articles 132–133), and reaffirmed in many ways the supremacy of the will of the nation over that of the ruler in case of conflict (Articles 35, 37, 39, 41, 88–89, 96, 114, 155). The Constitution proclaimed education to be compulsory and free in its elementary stage (Article 19); it proclaimed the freedom of person, of speech, and of assembly, and guaranteed the inviolability of the domicile and the sanctity of property (Articles 3–16). It placed the liberty and equality established in the Constitution beyond the power of amendment (Article 156).

In clauses that dealt explicitly with matters related to religion, the Constitution was vague and ambiguous. In Article 149 it declared that "Islam is the religion of the State. . . ." without clarifying the meaning of this principle here or anywhere else.[2] Article 12 had declared the absolute freedom of conscience, but Article 13 added to it a puzzling qualification: "The state protects the free exercise of all religions and creeds *in conformity with the usages established in Egypt*. . . ."[3] Finally, Article 153, which dealt with the crucial matter of all the religious institutions and practices, surpassed them all in its vagueness:

The Law regulates the *manner* in which the king *exercises his powers*, *in accordance with the principles of the present Constitution*, in what pertains to the religious establishments, to appointing the religious chiefs, to the *waqfs entrusted to the management of the Ministry of Waqfs*, and, in general, to *matters concerning the cults accepted in the country*. In the absence of a legislative provision, these powers shall continue to be exercised in accordance with the rules and customs now in force. . . .

This article — the only one dealing explicitly with the religious institutions — subordinated the question of the relation between religion and the state to considerations of the distribution of power in these matters within the branches of government; and was vague in both cases. From the words of the first clause, it might be understood that only "the manner" in which power is exercised in regard to the religious institutions and cults of the country is subject to regulation by the law, not the institutions and cults themselves. This vagueness is not clarified by the use of the term "accepted," which may mean tolerated by the will of the legislator and therefore subject to change, or may simply signify a statement of fact implying a limitation on that will. On the other hand, the second clause may be taken to mean a reassertion of the principle of absolute sovereignty of the nation and of the unlimited competence of Parliament in all the affairs of the state, including religion. The article is ambiguous even on the question of the distribution of power in these matters between the king and Parliament. We shall see that in fact it did give rise to constant conflict between the two.

Altogether, it seems that the drafters of the Constitution intended to assert the absolute sovereignty of Parliament and to reduce Islam and its institutions to the level of custom and usage, carrying much weight, but ultimately subject to the sovereign will. This distinction was not made very clear in the text and was too subtle to be noticed, especially since the practice in regard to religious matters remained unchanged. A vivid illustration of this point presented itself only a few months after the establishment of parliamentary life in Egypt.

In March 1924, the Grand National Assembly of Turkey finally decided to abolish the caliphate altogether, having already reduced it to a spiritual function entirely meaningless in the traditional Islamic view. This action of the Assembly, which, theoretically, should have had no effect at all on a sovereign independent Egypt, immediately stirred feverish activity by all sorts of committees, and raised a storm of discussion [4] on the validity of the act of the Assembly and its effect on the *bay'ah* — contractual obligation — of Egyptians to the deposed caliph! It might be useful to recall that Egypt's connections with Constantinople had been reduced under Muḥammad 'Ali and Ismā'īl to the symbolic act of payment of the tribute and the appointment of the Grand Qāḍī of Egypt by the Ottoman caliph. Ismā'īl had even managed to reduce the latter act to the payment of an honorarium to a Grand Qāḍī who remained in Constantinople, while he appointed a "deputy" for him in Egypt. Finally, in 1914, the declaration of the protectorate had formally severed all ties with Turkey and, nine years later, the Constitution declared Egypt to be a sovereign independent state.

The agitation finally sorted itself into two organized views. One was represented by the Ottomanophiles, led by Prince 'Umar Ṭūṣūn and supported by many *'ulama'* and publicists, who argued for the continued recognition of the caliphate of 'Abd al-Majīd and his rehabilitation in Egypt. The other view, represented by the official chief *'ulamā'* of al-Azhar and the religious institutions, argued that the caliphate of 'Abd al-Majīd had been invalid in Muslim doctrine, that Muslims were consequently absolved of their *bay'ah* to him, and that it was necessary to assemble a Muslim Congress to consider the whole question and choose perhaps a candidate "in conformity with the precepts of the Muslim religion and not too far from the Islamic regulations which Muslims have established for their governments." [5]

The latter view and initiative of the *'ulamā'* enjoyed the discreet encouragement and support of King Fu'ād, who entertained the ambition of becoming caliph himself.[6] This support unquestionably contributed to keeping the agitation about the caliphate alive, and giving it practical expression in the form of the actual assembling of a Muslim Congress; but it could not be taken as the explanation for it. For one thing, there was the agitation of the opposing group, as we have just mentioned, and it may very well be argued that the king entertained this ambition precisely because he thought he could capitalize on a popular issue to increase his power.

When the issue was first raised, Zaghlūl's government was in power; and even though Zaghlūl should at least have questioned the compatibility of a proper caliphate and of the discussion about an allegiance to a "foreign" sovereign with the concept of the nation-state enshrined in the Constitution, he contented himself with declaring the neutrality of the Egyptian state on the issue. Later, when his party was in the opposition, he commented privately that he was opposed to the caliphate, not on any secularist grounds, but mainly because it was a burden which even Turkey had proved unable to carry. At any rate, he preferred not to express his view in public because, he said, "this is a very touchy issue with the public; our opponents will try to give it a religious character in order to get at us. So we had better avoid that as long as possible." [7] Haykal, who quoted these words of Zaghlūl, reported that many members of his own party — the Liberal Constitutionalist — were opposed to the caliphate on exactly the same grounds.[8]

The conclusion of that episode was that a congress of the caliphate, composed of unofficial delegations from many countries, met in Cairo in 1926 and was unable to reach agreement even on the necessary requisites for the caliph.[9] But the whole affair showed how precarious were the principles of the Constitution, how distorted was the understanding of the real meaning of the caliphate among many Western-educated people, including Haykal and Zaghlūl, and how ready politicians were to capitalize on religious issues regardless of what the Constitution proclaimed.

During the first few years after Egypt had been ushered into parliamentary life, Turkey, under Ataturk, was undertaking drastic reforms in the spheres of religious life which culminated in the declaration of secularism as one of its fundamental principles. This activity did not fail to have its impact on Egypt and, in the first sessions of Parliament, proposals were made to adopt a secular code of law of personal status, the last and strongest fortress dominated by the Shar'ī law; to abolish family *waqfs*, and to cancel the position of Grand Muftī — which had been for many centuries the symbol of the submission of the state to the Islamic law. None of these proposals was applied in the course of our period of study; but Parliament did undertake reform legislation in the first two matters, which provides us with material to study concretely how the government actually conceived of its relation to the most important element in Islam: its surviving law.

The first major enactment of Parliament in the sphere of religious law was "Law No. 25 of 1929, Concerning Certain Questions Relating to Personal Status."[10] Its purpose was to correct some "abuses" in the Shar'ī marriage and divorce laws prevailing in Egypt. Because the subject was a touchy one and because it affected all Egyptians and was accompanied by a long Explanatory Memorandum, it provides excellent material for studying the question of the actual relation between the modern national governments and the Sharī'ah.

The first point to be clarified concerns the question of the relation between government and the Islamic law *in principle*: does the legislator consider himself legally bound by the principles of that law?

It is true that the very fact that the legislator issued a law in Shar'ī matters, quite apart from any change he might have introduced in the law itself, meant that the law was valid only by virtue of his will and already involved a reversal of the traditional doctrine: instead of the sovereign being subject to the Sharī'ah, the Sharī'ah itself became subject to the sovereign's will.[11] But the question is whether this principle, which had already been implied in the Constitution, received any explicit or practical support from the law itself, or from the Explanatory Memorandum, that the government was acting in religious affairs by virtue of its sovereign right.

The first impression that strikes the reader of the Memorandum seems to indicate just the contrary — that the legislator considered himself bound by Islamic law. This impression receives strong confirmation from such statements as: "Since in Islamic law the sovereign has the right to prohibit his *qāḍīs* from dealing with certain categories of issues . . . this Law extends that prohibition to . . . etc."; and, "Nothing in Islamic law opposes the adoption of the opinion of jurists other than those of the four schools." In fact, the entire Memorandum (eleven quarto pages) was an attempt to justify each clause of the new law by referring it to the authority of the Qur'ān or the rulings of Muslim doctors of jurisprudence, as the following examples point out:

> In the terms in which it has been regulated, repudiation must be pronounced numerous times (as the Qur'ān says): "Repudiation can be done twice. If you keep your wife, treat her in fairness; if you send her away, be generous towards her. . . . If a husband repudiates his wife three times he is not allowed to take her back until she will have married another husband. . . ." (Qur'ān:Sūrah of the Cow — 229–230).

Or, again:

> Multiple repudiation done at once by word or by sign is only a single repudiation. This is the opinion of Muḥammad ibn-Isḥāq and the opinion attributed to 'Alī, ibn Mas'ūd, 'Abd al-Raḥmān ibn 'Awf, and to Zubayr. It is also attributed to the doctors of Cordova, and so forth. . . .

Actually, however, the impression of supremacy of the Islamic law is a misleading one, for in the clauses where the Memorandum speaks of the general relation between government and the Sharī'ah, great care is taken to remain as evasive as possible:

> It is necessary to protect the Muslim law and to protect the people themselves against the temptation to violate this law which aims at procuring the happiness of men in this world and the next, and which, in its principles, can be applied to all nations at all times in all places if it is understood in its true sense and applied intelligently.
>
> The policy in regard to Muslim law is to facilitate for men the practice

of the law by interpreting it in a broad manner, and by consulting the *'ulamā'* whenever there is a question of finding a remedy to a social disease which has become difficult to cure, so that men may feel that the law offers a solution in every difficulty and relief in all adversity.

That is why the Ministry has thought of imposing restrictions on repudiation which would render it more in conformity with the principles and rules of the religion and with the doctrine of the *imāms* and the doctors, even those who do not belong to any of the four schools. It has elaborated this draft law in conformity with its principles.

It will be seen that each of the three paragraphs recognizes the validity of Muslim law but is deliberately ambiguous regarding its legally compulsory nature as far as the government is concerned. Thus, the first paragraph speaks of the necessity of protecting the Muslim law without clarifying what that "protection" involves, or specifying whether this necessity is legal or moral. Paragraph two speaks of the practice of the law as something autonomous and independent of the government's will at the same time that it implies that this practice is facilitated and tolerated as a matter of "policy," not obligation. Finally, paragraph three implies that the principles and rules of the religion are legally binding, only to qualify this in the next sentence by speaking of this approach as being founded on the [private] principles of the Ministry.

Certainly, one cannot find in this law an unequivocal statement by the government regarding its position *in principle* toward the religious law. But what about its practical position, its "policy" towards the religious law? What considerations guide it there?

It might have been assumed from the passages just quoted that whatever its attitude in principle toward the Islamic Law the government surely claimed for itself the right of *ijtihād* — free interpretation of the sources of the law. But a closer examination of these three passages alone dispels this view. The reader will notice, for example, that when the Memorandum speaks about the necessity of interpreting Muslim law it uses the indefinite person, and when it mentions specifically the initiative of the Ministry it does not use the term "interpretation" but speaks of the *imposition of restrictions* in order to make the law conform more closely to the principles of religion. It seems that here, too, the government chose to adopt a deliberately ambiguous position. On the one hand, it wanted to grant itself freedom of action by asserting the nonfinality of the Islamic law, and on the other hand it did not want to commit itself explicitly to the principles of *ijtihād* itself. Thus it took the unusual position of adopting the negative side of *ijtihād* — its critical spirit, its rejection of any final *ijmā'*, and of the binding character of the formulations of the four schools — and then, instead of proceeding to erect a new structure on the basis of the recognized principles of interpretation that form the positive side of *ijtihād*, the government resorted to a mixture of principles of its own. Where there was any authority at all for a certain point, the Memorandum eagerly referred to it for support; and where all authorities were opposed to what the government wanted to enact, the Memorandum explained the government's reasons for its action and added an injunction to the *qāḍīs* not to entertain cases opposed to the government's intentions.

One curious result of this procedure was that the Memorandum at several points bitterly denounced all the traditional authorities preparatory to an injunction to the *qāḍīs* not to hear cases based on their rulings, only to quote reverently one or more of these same authorities as support for another point a little later in the text. The following examples illustrate the government's tactics, or "policy," toward the Law and underline the actual considerations that guided its endeavor in reforming it.

The Memorandum criticized sharply the views of all Muslim jurists on the question of paternity. According to the rules hitherto in force, the child belonged to the husband no matter when it was born and regardless of any physical separation of the spouses. "Thus," the Memorandum commented wryly, ". . . the child born to a wife in the East belongs to the husband in the West even if the partners, married from afar, have never met in privacy . . . from the time of the marriage to the birth of the child. . . ." In regard to a child born after a woman had been divorced or widowed, the Muslim law attributes its paternity to the divorced or deceased husband if it was born within two years after the event. Commenting on the sources upon which the jurists based their view, the Memorandum said: "Most of them actually founded their opinion on this subject on nothing more than the sayings of some women that the gestation has lasted sometimes for so many years. . ." Still in the matter of paternity, Muslim law grants to the divorced woman the right of pension for up to three years after the divorce if she claims that she has had her menses once a year only, on the ground that she may be carrying from her divorced husband. The Memorandum rejected this view as "contrary to the normal physiological laws of women. . . ." In all these instances, the new law did not declare the traditional rulings invalid, but simply ordered the *qāḍīs* not to entertain cases where a year had elapsed after divorce or widowhood, or where more than a year had elapsed between private union of the married couple and the birth of the child. To be noted here is the role of modern science in leading to the modification of the traditional law.

The following examples from the Memorandum not only illustrate the method of criticizing one authority on substantive grounds in order to adopt the views of another, but also reflect all the considerations underlying the government's criticism of the traditional laws. The Ḥanafī doctrine, which applied in Egypt, envisages no relief for a wife whose husband absents himself for a long time without legitimate excuse, without repudiating her, and without asking her to join him. The Memorandum points out that "in general, it is contrary to a woman's nature to be able to live thus alone and preserve her honor and honesty intact even if her husband has left her the wherewithal to meet her needs during his absence." Accordingly, the new law rejected the Hanafī view in favor of that of Mālik, who allows the judge to grant the woman a divorce after a year of absence. Here, a concern for justice and a private ethics based on "human nature" are at the root of the modification.

In the case of divorce, the prevailing Shar'ī law had held conditional repudiation, repudiation on oath, and multiple repudiation pronounced at once, as valid and binding regardless of the husband's intentions. The Memorandum protested against this opinion of the great majority of jurists, holding it responsible for the breakup of marriages in a majority of cases:

> It is in such opinions that the woes of the family have their origin. From here stem the tricks to which the spouses have recourse. And it is through their inspiration that the casuists have ingeniously worked to multiply the means of blackmail. . . . The whole happiness of the spouses, the children, and the family is thus bound to acts alien to the intention of the chief of the family or the mistress of the home. . .

The law attempted to remedy this situation by adopting opinions of isolated jurists to invalidate repudiation on oath and some conditional repudiations, and to count multiple repudiations pronounced at once as a single repudiation. Care for the stability of the family and social considerations provide the motive in this instance.

Finally, in case of the disappearance of the husband, the prevailing Ḥanafī law presumed him alive for purposes of inheritance until all his contemporaries had died or until he reached the age of ninety. The Memorandum commented:

> . . . this rule . . . is no longer compatible with the progress in the means of communications achieved in our time. Mail, telephone, and telegraph and the spread of Egyptian consulates all over the world have facilitated

the search for the missing so that it is easy to ascertain in a short time whether they are alive or dead.[12]

Citing a minority opinion, the Law imposed a maximum limit of four years of waiting where the circumstances of the disappearance might presume death (in war, for example); in other cases it left the limit to be fixed at the discretion of the *qāḍī*. Technical advancement was summoned here to justify the relief of undue hardship.

It is time to summarize the lessons of this law. The new constitutional government, in the first major act that touched upon the most important preserve of religion, continued to maintain the practical, ambiguous position of the Constitution with respect to the fundamental relation between the modern government and religion. In one respect, the government worked within a modified religious juridical framework which, notwithstanding its questionable legality from a Muslim point of view, seems to imply subservience to the principles and some positive formulations of the religious law. On the other hand, it carefully avoided any definite indication as to whether it was doing so by choice, as a matter of policy, or because it considered itself bound by those principles and formulations. The considerations calling for modification of the law were scientific, technological, ethical, or social in character and were all bound to a newly found concern for social and moral problems on the part of a government acting on the basis of new ideas regarding its responsibility in matters which had hitherto been the preserve of religion. At the same time, this government made a show of justifying its action, at least technically, in terms of the principles of the religious law.

Thus, the government which claimed in theory absolute sovereignty in all spheres did not express this claim unequivocally in the religious sphere. The significance of the act of legislation itself could not be decisive in this respect since pre-Constitution governments, which had made no formal claim to absolute sovereignty, had also legislated in the same way and in the same spirit — the latest instance being the promulgation of the Marriage and Divorce Law of 1920. It seems that the new, fully sovereign constitutional governments simply followed the tradition and method of the preceding governments, which were ostensibly limited in their sovereignty, without bothering about the question of principle raised by their new status. This suggestion finds confirmation in the fact that it was the same permanent staff of the ministries in existence before the Constitution which continued to draft the laws after 1923. The result was a law that was not fully in conformity with either Islamic or Liberal Nationalist principles.

In terms of principles, method, and motivations, the basic pattern we have observed in the Law of 1929 applied to the other legislation in the sphere of religious law enacted during the period until 1952. This legislation included the Law of Inheritance of 1943, the Law of Testamentary Dispositions of 1946, and the Law of the *Waqfs* of 1949, besides the decrees of 1926 and 1931 modifying the code of procedure of the Shar'ī courts.[13] But if these laws were not more explicit on the matter of the principles in question, some of them involved a much more drastic application of the equivocal procedures used in the law of 1929 and introduced certain additional features which altered sharply the *objective* position of the religious law. Thus both the Law of Inheritance of 1943 and the Law of Testamentary Dispositions of 1946, pushing the method farther, introduced far-reaching "innovations" which served to undermine even more the notion of the stability of the religious law. Further, these laws represented complete codifications of their respective subjects, which considerably reduced the discretion of the *qāḍīs*. This, together with the fact that the laws were to apply to all Egyptians without distinction of faith, prepared the ground for transferring them entirely to the jurisdiction of the Civil Courts.[14] As for the Law of the Waqfs of 1949, the innovations it introduced were so drastic that the total abolition of family *waqfs* which followed a few years later caused no great surprise.[15] It is true that family *waqfs* did not have the same standing as the Marriage and Divorce Law since religious rulings could be found to the effect that the *waqfs* were not a matter of religion. It is also true that everyone, including the religious leaders and the beneficiaries of the *waqfs*, was deeply conscious of the serious abuses from which the *waqf* administration suffered, and that there had been several instances where the ruler — the most recent being Muḥammad 'Alī — had prohibited the formation of new family *waqfs*. Nevertheless, it should be emphasized that family *waqfs* had had a long and continuous existence from the very early days of Islam, that they came to be generally considered as religious objects, and that they were very popular, as is clearly indicated by their accumulation to an extent that required their abolition even after Muḥammad 'Alī's prohibition.

From our analysis of the Constitution, the episode of the caliphate, and the entire legislation in the sphere of religious law, it seems clear that the various governments tended in fact to view the surviving Islamic institutions and law as deeply rooted customs, to be treated with caution because of their association with religion in the minds of the people and because of their identification with the national heritage, but subject, nevertheless, to the reforming will of the legislator. In public, however, they were careful not to express this position in definite terms for tactical and political reasons, but resorted instead to the ambiguities we have described. The nearest approach to an explicit public expression of that position was made in 1949 in connection with the elaboration of a new civil code, which has become effective since that time. It was possible in this particular case because the code to be replaced had been entirely secular and because the tactical-political implications were of minor importance. In this instance 'Abd al-Razzāq al-Sanhūrī, who headed the committee of jurists chosen to elaborate the new code, argued for one based on principles which he had advocated since the thirties. He wanted the code to be founded on (1) selected portions of European codes, particularly the French and German; (2) judicial precedent in Egypt since 1850; and (3) Islamic law.[16] The Sharī'ah was to provide certain useful general concepts on a piecemeal basis in order to "perfect the fundamental bases of our legislation," to supply certain specific provisions in order to fill in some gaps in existing legislation,[17] and to serve as a residual source in default of any statutory rule or any relevant custom.[18] The provisions from the Sharī'ah were included, al-Sanhūrī explained, "because they are part of our heritage."[19]

In the absence of a definite stand on principles, the struggle between the nationalist governments and the forces representing the religious institutions took place on the level of concrete issues. In that struggle, the governments achieved important tangible successes; but since these were won by the manipulation of traditional concepts rather than by a frank proclamation of the actual guiding motives, the result was to weaken and confuse those concepts, without enhancing, in exchange, the Western-inspired principles and the socio-ethical considerations that motivated the government. One practical consequence of this equivocation was that the governments had to fight on every single law and every single article, and suffer in each case the prospect of an uncertain outcome and a state of constant tension. Thus, the Law of 1929 had originally been broached in 1926, but it contained certain clauses designed to restrict polygamy.[20] This aroused such opposition that the project had to be delayed for three years and was passed finally without some of the contested clauses. In the same way, the Ministry of Social Affairs had to fight in 1943 and again in 1945 for a draft-law designed to restrict divorce, without being able to push it through.[21] But more important than these setbacks was the fact that by using these equivocal methods, the government failed to give the relevant principles of the Constitution the support that might have endowed them with "rights of home" in the consciousness of the people and, instead, allowed those who wished, to persist in the delusion that the government was subject to the law of Islam and to judge it accordingly.

The only issue connected with the religious institutions which was fought on the grounds of principle was that of the control of Parliament over the appointment of religious leaders. We have seen that Muḥammad 'Alī had arrogated to himself as ruler the right to appoint the Shaykh of al-Azhar [22] and that Article 153 of the Constitution suggested leaving things as they were in the absence of new legislation.[23] When such legislation was finally envisaged, the king, in order to retain control of the religious institutions, invoked the clause which proposes following the established tradition, while the government argued from the total sovereign rights of Parliament to bring them under its own authority. The result was a kind of see-saw which tended to perpetuate the ambiguity and confusion attaching to the whole issue of religion and state. Thus a law of 1927 divided the right of appointing the religious leaders between the king and the ministry; but this was abolished by the law of 1930, issued by a government faithful to the king, which placed the right back in his hands. A new ministry abolished that law once more by the law of 1936, which, presumably, restored the law of 1927; but the king managed to appoint his own Shaykh even after that. The issue had not been definitely settled when the revolution of 1952 broke out.

Part Four

THE PROGRESS AND DECLINE OF LIBERAL NATIONALISM

CHAPTER 9

The Liberal Intellectuals and Their Task

In the preceding chapter we discussed briefly the prospects that control of state power opened to the victorious nationalists and examined in some detail the use that the national governments had made of this opportunity in the period between the revolution of 1919 and that of 1952. We concentrated our attention on those actions of the national governments that had a direct bearing on the relation between the new state and Islam, since traditional Islam, weakened as it was, was the ideology that Liberal Nationalism meant to supplant as the foundation for the political community. It goes without saying, however, that this activity was not the only kind of governmental action relevant to the task of consolidating the principles of Liberal Nationalism and converting them from formal clauses in the Constitution into an integral part of the people's world view. Public education and the actual operation of the Constitution to effect peaceful changes of government were obviously pertient to this end. So were other factors, less obviously connected, such as the approach of the successive governments and of the various Liberal Nationalist parties to the problem of completing Egypt's independence and fostering social justice and the well-being of the people. For, in the minds of the people, the performance of governments and parties in these areas was closely associated with the nature of the Liberal Nationalist regime itself. These additional activities of governments and parties will be examined in due course.[1] For the moment, we turn our attention to the work of the Liberal Nationalist intellectual leaders and analyze their contribution to the task of elaborating the principles implicit in the Constitution into a suitable general belief-system.

In describing Egyptian cultural development under the British occupation we have already referred in general terms to the emergence of the intellectual leaders to be studied now. Most of them were born during the first decade of the occupation and had grown up at the time when 'Abduh was seeking to reform Islam. They were therefore the first generation to benefit by his sanction of the pursuit of modern knowledge. They had all received an advanced Western-style education, and had reached the age of young manhood at a time when the ideas of nationalism, progress, evolution, and the aspiration to assimilate Western culture as well as Western techniques, had already taken root among some Egyptians. A relatively large number of them had spent a few years in Europe and had earned advanced academic degrees in European universities. Many of them had served a period of apprenticeship under Luṭfī al-Sayyid on *al-Jarīdah*. There were a few Christians among them, but we shall not be concerned with them since they did not share the ideological problem in the same terms as the Muslim majority, and, in the circumstances of Egypt after World War I, their ideas on the issue were bound to interest a restricted public at best.

By excluding Christian writers from our analysis on the ground of the limited impact of their ideas, we raise the question whether the work of the Muslim intellectual leaders, too, was not bound to remain confined to a relatively small proportion of the population since the majority of Egyptians could not be reached because of their illiteracy, if for no other reason. This question raises the issue of whether our whole inquiry is not futile or, to say the least, premature; and we must therefore digress for a moment to examine it.

It is true that most Egyptians were illiterate during the period under study; but it should be kept in mind that Egyptian society was at the same time in the process of rapid change, with education and general development continually nibbling at the intellectually inaccessible portions of society. If, therefore, the intellectual leaders could evolve a belief-system acceptable to the accessible portion, they would create a powerful core toward which those emancipated every year from illiteracy and from the complete hold of tradition would tend to gravitate. For, in relation to the rest of the population, the educated sector constituted an economically and socially dominant group to which the newly emancipated aspired to belong. Were the educated sector to make the ideological adjustment, the process of winning ever larger elements of society to its views would therefore have become almost irresistible. All this is not markedly different from the process by which any great change takes place in any society. Had not all the ideologies of the West since the capitalist and industrial revolutions, for instance, spread in ever-widening circles from the few who first formulated them to the larger groups who found them advantageous and suitable to the needs of the time, and, finally, to the great masses of the people, as the material realities to which these ideologies were related encompassed more and more groups?

This still leaves unanswered the question of whether the present study is not, perhaps, premature. Is it not too early to expect a settlement of the ideological conflict involved in the transition from one basic historical phase to another when in the West the same kind of conflict took centuries to resolve?

Indeed, a final resolution of the conflict was not to be expected by the end of the period under review. But this study is intended to turn our attention to the question of the relation between ideology and the stability of the political community, to clarify the nature of the ideological conflict affecting Egyptian society, to define the obstacles in the way of a solution, and to look for *beginnings* of approaches that might offer a means of meeting that conflict. Such beginnings could reasonably be expected more than a century after the disturbing factor of material change first began to manifest itself. The writers with whom we are concerned were themselves willing to see their work evaluated on the basis of this expectation since they repeatedly referred to themselves as pioneers and founders of a new Egyptian culture.

The cultural situation in Egypt at the end of World War I prescribed the newspaper column and the small booklet as the chief media of expression for the intellectual leaders. The limited size of the reading public and its lack of training in prolonged intellectual concentration militated against the long, thorough work and favored instead the brief, varied essay, article, or short story. Moreover, the writers themselves were so dazzled by the wealth of ideas, methods, and forms which their Western education had put within their reach, and were so eager to apply them to their own environment and culture, that they seized upon the short work as the best means of covering a broad area as quickly as possible. This explains how many of these writers managed to produce titles that are counted by the score. Concern for quick pecuniary profit and considerations of prestige had something to do with this rapid production, but these factors were less important than the cultural situation which made it possible to gain reward or recognition for such work.

The intellectual leaders not only wrote a great many short pieces, but also expressed themselves in a variety of literary forms — in articles, poems, short stories, novels, and impressionistic essays, as well as in scholarly dissertations. Most of them ranged wide in their choice of subjects, encompassing in their purview all branches of the humanities. They had their own views on society and local and international politics; on ancient and modern ethics; on religious and secular education; on literary criticism, history, philosophy, religion, and the art of all ages, places, and peoples. In addition to these cultural pursuits, all of them were actively engaged in practical politics at one time or another, and a few of them reached some of the highest positions in the state.

Clearly, then, these were not specialists in any single field of study addressing themselves to the initiated, nor were they scholars or artists removed from the din of the market place. They were creative writers, first, but they were also reformers and public educators-at-large who addressed themselves to the literate Egyptian. Their art and learning were placed in the service of the society in which they lived, and they were probably not averse to being judged on the basis of their success or failure in this endeavor. It is this commitment of the Egyptian intellectual leaders, together with the broad scope of their work, that makes them so nearly representative of Egyptian normative consciousness, and therefore such eminently suitable subjects for the study of the evolution of ideas and beliefs in Egypt. But these same qualities, unfortunately, were also partly responsible for a certain lack of depth in their thought and a rather disturbing disposition on the part of some to trim their intellectual sails too readily so as to catch the winds of public favor.

Before introducing these writers and undertaking an analysis of their work, it is necessary to make a second digression that is connected with two points of procedure. Hitherto we have analyzed the works of individual leaders separately because these leaders represented emerging basic trends of thought. Now, however, the primary issue is no longer the development of new tendencies but rather their evolution in the hands of those who inherited them. It would therefore seem more appropriate to state the main questions relevant to the Liberal Nationalist trend, and from that point to proceed to examine what the Liberal Nationalist writers collectively had to say about them. The questions chosen are grouped under the headings of politics, ethics, and history. The responses are examined in terms of their substance as well as the epistemological approaches underlying them. These last are crucial for underlining the distinctions and similarities between the approach of the writers and that of traditional and Reformist Islamic doctrine.

The other procedural consideration concerns the writers whom we shall study. It would be tedious and unnecessary to attempt to cover in our analysis all the writers whose views were connected with Liberal Nationalism. We are not interested, after all, in variety of expression, but rather, in substantive variety within a given trend. It seems reasonable, therefore, to concentrate on a limited group of writers who were most influential in their society, and who represented in the variety of their social background, their source of inspiration, course of career, and personal temperament, those other writers not included in our analysis. Following are the names and brief biographical accounts of the writers selected.

1. *Ṭāha Ḥusayn (1889–)*

Ṭāha Ḥusayn is a most remarkable figure by any standard of judgment. Born in a small village in upper Egypt and the seventh child of a minor employee in a sugar plantation, blind since the age of three, Ṭāha lived to become the undisputed dean of modern Egyptian and Arabic literature, to reach the positions of head of the Faculty of Letters of the University of Cairo, founder of the University of Alexandria, Minister of Education, and to be honored by Oxford and the Universities of Lyons, Rome, Madrid, and Athens.

Ṭāha began his education in the village *kuttāb* under various local religious teachers, who drilled into him the entire Qur'ān and other works believed necessary for entering al-Azhar. The plan was that he, too, would become a religious *shaykh.* At the age of thirteen Ṭāha was sent to that venerable but unreformed college where he spent the next six years of his life. He later recorded his experiences there, as well as his early life, in a masterly autobiography —*Al-Ayyām* (Days)—which has so far been translated into French, English, Russian, Chinese, and Hebrew. In 1908, when the Egyptian University opened its doors, Ṭāha was one of the first students to join it, and six years later he received the University's first doctorate. The subject of his thesis was Abū al-'Alā' al-Ma'arrī, a classical Arabic poet and writer who had also been blind.

While still at the University, Ṭāha had started writing for *al Jarīdah* and came under the influence of Luṭfī al Sayyid. Upon his graduation, the Egyptian University sent him to France to continue his studies. With Luṭfī's encouragement, he learned Greek and Latin and immersed himself in classical culture in the hope of encouraging its study in his own country later, and making it the foundation of Egypt's renaissance as it had been of the West's. He also attended courses at the Sorbonne and the Collège de France in history, philosophy, psychology, and sociology, and continued to pursue the work of orientalists as he had done in the university at home. In 1914, at the Sorbonne, he earned another doctorate, presenting a thesis on the social philosophy of ibn-Khaldūn. In the meantime he had married, with the permission of the Egyptian

University authorities, the young French lady who had served him as a reader.

On his return to Egypt, Ṭāha Ḥusayn was appointed professor of classical literature in the University. His efforts to promote classical culture, however, did not meet with an encouraging response and he was transferred to the faculty of Arabic letters after he had translated Aristotle's *Constitution of Athens*, several plays of Sophocles, and selections from other Greek works.

In addition to his teaching and his scholarly work, Ṭāha served as literary editor of *al-Siyāsah*, the daily organ of the Liberal Constitutionalist Party, which was modelled after Luṭfī al Sayyid's now defunct *al-Jarīdah*. Ṭāha wrote two weekly essays which constituted two series of studies, one on Arab cultural life in the first and second Islamic centuries and the other on contemporary French culture. These essays were later published in book form under the titles *Ḥadīth al-Arbi'ā'* (Wednesday Conversations) and *Qiṣaṣ Tamthīliyyah* (Theater Stories). This combination of teaching, journalism, translating, and writing scholarly and popular works on Arabic and French cultures, in addition to the novels he began later — all of it done in a didactic spirit — constituted the normal pattern of his activity, except when political events intervened, either to call him to high government office or to remove him from his university position.

In 1926, Ṭāha became the subject of a *cause célèbre* when he published a consciously defiant book — *Fī al-Shi'r al-Jāhilī* (On Pre-Islamic Poetry) — which infringed on certain basic Islamic dogmas.[2] Conservative elements and religious leaders of every shade accused him of apostasy, demanded his trial, and raised a tremendous uproar against the university that sheltered him, which they knew was to be the fortress of secularism and Liberalism. Fortunately for Ṭāha, Luṭfī al Sayyid, the rector of the university, stood firmly by him; moreover, the political parties were then engaged in a truce which prevented the exploitation of the incident for partisan purposes. Nevertheless, the agitation stirred up was so strong that the government found it necessary to go through the process of charging him before the court of attacking the religion of the state. Ṭāha felt compelled to leave the country for a year until the storm subsided, and, in the end, acquired a reputation as a heretic which took him many years and much effort to live down. Then, in 1931, Ṣidqī pasha, who had abolished the Constitution of 1923 and established one of his own, which he attempted to force on the country, managed to have the issue reopened and to use it as an excuse for dismissing Ṭāha Ḥusayn from the university. Luṭfī, who still stood by him, resigned in protest.

From 1931 to 1934 Ṭāha devoted much of his energy to fighting against Ṣidqī. He aligned himself actively with Ṣidqī's chief opponent, the Wafd Party, and lashed at him with fury from the columns of the Wafdist press. Ṭāha's services to the Wafd were rewarded, so that when he left the university again it was to become Secretary-General to the Ministry of Education in the Naḥḥās government of 1941–1945. Five years later he came back with the Wafd government of 1950–1952 as Minister of Education. In the meantime, he had founded a new literary review, *Al-Kātib al-Miṣrī* and had written several novels and many articles and essays.

Ṭāha's affiliation with the Wafd stood for a time between him and the new rulers who came to power after July 1952, but his prestige in the Arab world and his influence on a number of leaders of the revolution, including 'Abd al-Nāṣir, eventually brought him back into the councils of government. At present, he is serving in the General Directorate of Culture in the Ministry of Education.

The work of Ṭāha Ḥusayn is counted in scores of books. We shall refer to many of them in this study; most of the remainder are included in the bibliography. It will suffice to mention here that his work included translations, synopses, and critiques of dozens of French novels, plays, and studies; many original novels and some plays of his own; a few scholarly works and dozens of popular essays and articles on history, education, religion, criticism, and other subjects.[9]

2. *Muḥammad Ḥusayn Haykal (1889–1956)*

Haykal was born in the same year as Ṭāha Ḥusayn, and, like him, was a reformer who drew much of his inspiration from French culture. There were other formal as well as substantive similarities in the careers of the two men that will become apparent, but there were also important differences. Haykal was born into an old and well-to-do family of landowners from lower Egypt who had important connections with the "establishment," and he therefore moved smoothly up the paved path of his career. He received his primary and secondary education in governmental schools and went on to the law school in Cairo, from which he was graduated in 1909. While still in school he too had met Luṭfī al-Sayyid, who guided him and personally tutored him in his reading and writing. After graduation from law school, he went to Paris, where he spent three years and earned a doctorate in law in 1912. During this time he started working in French on a novel of Egyptian country life but then decided to write it in Arabic. He had the book published anonymously in Egypt under the title *Zaynab*. The novel drew the attention of critics as the first original novel ever written in the Arabic language. Haykal subsequently republished it, and this time proudly acknowledged his authorship.

For a while after his return to Egypt, Haykal practiced law in al-Manṣūrah, the chief city of his province, and in 1917 began to lecture in the Egyptian University while continuing his legal practice. In 1921 he published the first part of an intended trilogy on the life and work of Rousseau of which only two parts saw the light, the second appearing in 1923.

In 1922, when a few moderate nationalists from the ranks of the landowning aristocracy and the highly educated founded the Liberal Constitutionalist Party to counter Zaghlūl's monopoly over the direction of the nationalist cause, Haykal was among the founders and became chief editor of the party's daily paper, *al-Siyāsah*. Under his editorship, *al-Siyāsah* devoted several columns to basic literary and ideological discussion which were supplemented in 1926 by a weekly literary supplement. The two organs became the tribune of advanced Liberal thought and acquired an enormous influence among the educated public, not only in Egypt but in other Arab countries as well.

The similarities between the circumstances and purpose that prompted the formation of the Liberal Constitutionalist Party and those of the Ummah Party fifteen years earlier, and between *al-Siyāsah* under Haykal and *al-Jarīdah* under Luṭfī al-Sayyid, will not have escaped attention. As a matter of fact, these similarities were not accidental. As far as the broad intellectual character of *al-Siyāsah* is concerned, Haykal was deliberately following the policy of his master, Luṭfī, with whom he continued for some time to be in close touch. As for the strategy of the party, this was a nearly conscious duplication of the strategy that had enabled the Ummah Party to become the nucleus of the general nationalist movement after the war, and to reduce Muṣṭafā Kāmil's party to near insignificance, applied this time against Zaghlūl. It consisted of combining relative moderation in practical politics with strong emphasis on the primary role of long-range fundamental ideological reform, and was designed to enable its practitioners to pose as the seasoned and responsible leaders of Egypt and to reap the fruits of the concessions imposed on the British by Zaghlūl's more extreme party. In the case of the Liberal Constitutionalists, however, circumstances turned that policy into a slippery path to unprincipled opportunism; while Haykal proved himself to be of inferior moral stature to Luṭfī al-Sayyid.

In the abstract, the strategy of the Liberal Constitutionalists was more than defensible, much as the extreme nationalists disliked it. The desire to defeat one's political rivals is of the essence of politics and is legitimate as long as it finds its expression in recognized ways; while the policy of "take what you can get and then demand more" as a method of realizing the national aspirations might even be considered a sound one. The trouble with the whole conception was that it was no longer suitable to Egyptian realities in the post-war years. The policy of moderation and reason could be pursued with great success by the Ummah Party because the British, who were most likely to be impressed by it, also had it in their authority to grant power. But once Egypt had become formally independent, and the new legal master — the electorate — had decisively rejected the course of political moderation and reason, the Liberal Constitutionalists could only wait and hope for a change of opinion on the part of the electorate, or court the support of the king or the British who could grant power only illegally. When a succession of elections convinced the Liberal Constitutionalists that their hope for a change in public opinion was illusory, they decided to follow the other path and by so doing became largely responsible for undermining the experiment of democratic constitutional procedures in Egypt. In the councils of the party, when unconstitutional courses of action were discussed, Haykal objected halfheartedly but then went along with "the majority," while, to the outside world, he continued to speak loudly about the sanctity of the Constitution. Something of this moral weakness will also be seen in Haykal's intellectual work, where it had equally damaging consequences.[4]

Haykal's services to his party, together with the prestige he gained by his writings, brought him to the posts of Minister of State and Minister of Education. When the leader of the party, Muḥammad Maḥmūd pasha, died in 1941, Haykal succeeded him. He led the Liberal Constitutionalists into the coalition government that ruled Egypt in the crucial years, 1944–1949. His position during that time was President of the Senate. The revolution of 1952, with its hostility to all the parties of the old regime, brought an end to Haykal's political career. During the four years of his retirement he wrote his memoirs and a number of short stories, and published a novel. He died in 1956.

Because he was more deeply involved in politics, Haykal's literary production was not so prolific as that of Ṭāha Ḥusayn or other contemporary writers. Still, he managed to publish more than fifteen books, which included collections of some of his basic literary and philosophical articles in *al-Siyāsah*, his volumes on Rousseau, biographical studies, travel notes and reflections, two novels, two volumes of memoirs, and, in addition, a bulky study of the life of Muḥammad and a two-volume study of the life of the third caliph, 'Umar.[5]

3. *Tawfīq al-Ḥakīm (1899–)*

Tawfīq al-Ḥakīm belongs, with Ṭāha Ḥusayn and Haykal, to the French-educated and French-inspired school of writers. His social background was, perhaps, not so distinguished as Haykal's but was certainly far above that of Ṭāha Ḥusayn. His father was a judge and his mother a rich and forceful woman who took great pride in her Turkish aristocratic lineage. Tawfīq was born in Alexandria, not too far from the large estate on which his family lived.

After his primary education, Tawfīq was sent by his parents to Cairo for his secondary schooling and, subsequently, to attend law school. He was graduated in 1924 and was sent to Paris to continue his legal studies. His parents had evidently intended him to follow in his father's footsteps, but while he was still in law school Tawfīq had begun to discover that he was more interested in letters and in the theater than in law. He had become involved in theatrical activity and had written several unpublished plays for some popular ensembles. Once in Paris, al-Ḥakīm quickly gave up his legal studies for an artistic bohemian life and after four years returned to Egypt none the wiser in law, but with a considerable knowledge of novels and plays. Nevertheless, his first job was with the Ministry of Justice, where he served as prosecutor in a provincial town, and it was not until a few years later that he published his first literary work. He spent another period in the Ministry of Education in Cairo before he finally gave up official employment in 1936 to devote his whole time to writing.

In accordance with the prevailing general pattern, Tawfīq did not confine himself to any one particular branch of literature. He wrote free-lance columns on current political and social events for the press, philosophical and literary essays, as well as novels and plays. If Ṭāha Ḥusayn was at heart an educator and Haykal a politician, Tawfīq al-Ḥakīm was the one writer who was essentially an artist comparable to the familiar French prototype. He devoted particular attention to the play that was written to be read rather than acted on the stage. Through continued efforts he succeeded in perfecting it to a point which gained him considerable international recognition both for technique and for depth of inspiration.

Al-Ḥakīm wrote dozens of plays in addition to a few novels, several collections of stories and literary and philosophical essays. But not all his work is equally significant. In general, his output may be assembled in three groups: one consisting of light plays, essays, and stories; another consisting of more serious works of social and political criticism; and a third comprising tragedies and dramas of Greek inspiration and one or two very good social-philosophical novels.

Al-Ḥakīm's lack of affiliation with any of the political parties and his sharp criticism of the political and social regime stood him in good stead with the new rulers of Egypt. Shortly after the revolution of 1952, he was appointed Chief Director of the National Library and a member of the "Supreme National Council for Literature and the Arts." [6]

4. *'Abbās Maḥmūd al-'Aqqād (1899–)*

Al-'Aqqād, together with Ibrāhīm 'Abd al-Qādir al-Māznī, the Copt writer Salāmah Mūsā, and a few others, formed what might be called — from its initial inspiration — the English school of writers, in contrast to the French school of Ṭāha Ḥusayn, Haykal, al-Ḥakīm, and their contemporaries. Al-'Aqqād was born to a middle-income family in Aswan, where he received his primary education, and began, but never finished, his secondary education in government schools. At the age of fourteen he moved to Cairo where he held miscellaneous jobs with the government while beginning to educate himself by intelligent and well-selected reading in classical Arabic literature and in English and German literature and thought. Al-'Aqqād has never stopped educating himself and, paradoxically, this has become both his greatest asset and most conspicuous liability.

In the years after 1910, al-'Aqqād had progressed sufficiently in his education to become a teacher in a college preparatory school and to make a notable contribution to the evolution of modern Arabic literature. At the school he had met al-Māznī and had begun a long and fruitful intellectual association with him. The two men, together with 'Abd al-Raḥmān Shukrī, founded a new school of poetry which revolted openly against Shawqī and Ḥāfiẓ, the two deities who had reigned unchallenged over the Arabic poetry revival for many years. Al-'Aqqād and his friends assailed the work of the titans as formal, haphazard in its choice of themes, lacking, both in its totality and in its individual parts, unity of structure and meaning, insincere, seeking to impress the reader with verbal *tours de force* and unlikely or exaggerated imagery, rather than to communicate to him deeply sensed moods or feelings or securely grasped thoughts. In its place the three men advocated and promoted what they called "subjective" or "expressive poetry" such as that contained in the collections of poems which they published in 1911, 1913, 1914, 1916, and thereafter. Their criticism did not, of course, stop people from continuing to read and enjoy Shawqī and Ḥāfiẓ, but the influence of the new poetic concepts became so pervasive that even the two veteran poets modified their later work to bring it into accord with them.

After World War I, al-ʿAqqād and al-Māznī left teaching for journalism. Al-ʿAqqād met Saʿd Zaghlūl, who took a liking to him and made him one of the ideological spokesmen of the Wafd. Using the party's daily organ, *al-Balāgh*, and its weekly supplement, which the Wafd issued later to compete with the *al-Siyāsah* supplement, Al-ʿAqqād discussed literature, raised basic intellectual questions, and propounded his ideas on philosophy, society, religion, history, and aesthetics and a variety of other subjects, all of which he had culled from his vast reading. That he had not had a systematic education proved to be an advantage in this case. It gave his columns an engaging tone of enthusiasm and excitement at new discoveries and turned them into journeys for self-education in which al-ʿAqqād served his readers as guide. Selections of these writings were periodically collected and published in books, of which five appeared and, for the most part, enjoyed enduring success.

During the period of the Ṣidqī absolutism, al-ʿAqqād was in the forefront of the fighters for the restoration of liberties and the Constitution. He published a book extolling the virtues of democracy and arguing, against the opinions propounded by the government, that it was perfectly suitable for oriental nations. In the book, he attacked the king for abetting Ṣidqī's conspiracy against democracy, and this brought about his arrest and a nine-month sentence in jail. During his imprisonment, he wrote a book extolling freedom through the description of life in prison.

By the time the struggle against Ṣidqī was over and the Constitution of 1923 restored, al-ʿAqqād's youthful idealism began to subside and gradually gave way to a dark pessimism, a growing conservative antirationalism and a religiosity peculiar to himself. At this stage in his career, his lack of systematic education meant the lack of firm anchorage and a drift toward skepticism which he tried to counter with religion. At the same time he became increasingly misanthropic and megalomaniacal. In 1938 al-'Aqqād left the Wafd to join a group of dissenters who had broken away from the party to form the Sa'dist Front. He wrote for the Front's newspaper until it ceased to appear a few years later. He also became a Sa'dist senator for a time before he broke away and became a "party" unto himself. Since 1952 he has continued to write, choosing themes in keeping with the political orientation and interest of the regime.

Al-'Aqqād's books comprise no fewer than sixty titles. As might be expected, they cover an immense variety of subjects and differ greatly in quality. Among them there are four collections of poetry, five collections of articles, two books on religious philosophy, several historical studies, a few short texts on political theory, seven studies of "the genius" of some Muslim leaders and one on the "genius of Christ," half-a-dozen biographical studies, and various other subjects.

5. *Ibrāhīm 'Abd al-Qādir al-Māznī (1889–1949)*

Al-Māznī was born in Cairo to a family of modest means. His father, who was a humble Shar'ī judge, died when he was only a year old. Ibrāhīm grew up under the vigilant care of his mother. He attended primary and secondary school and then, unable to muster the means to go to law school, went to the teachers' college. He was graduated in 1909, having mastered the English language and read extensively in it, and was appointed to teach the art of translation in a secondary school. He, too, had been among the group of young authors who wrote for *al-Jarīdah* while still studying. Two years later he was transferred to the preparatory school where he met al-'Aqqād, and in 1914 and 1917 published the collections of poems which, as we have seen, inaugurated a new trend in poetry.

After the war, al-Māznī worked with al-'Aqqād on *al-Balāgh*. He wrote about the same subjects as al-'Aqqād and shared with him many ideas which they had evolved together. Beginning in 1931, al-Māznī worked independently, concentrating primarily on novels and stories, besides writing light journalistic satire on manners and society. In his fiction he developed to a high degree the character-study technique he learned from Russian writers, and tried to emulate the sarcastic wit of Mark Twain. He did some fine translations of Turgenev (from English) and various English short-story writers. His success with readers was considerable, but he never enjoyed the good fortune of some of his contemporaries and never attained any important public position.

Al-Māznī's work includes collections of articles gathered in four books, several collections of poems, a dozen collections of stories and novels, one play, and several translations, besides a vast number of uncollected press articles.[7]

6. *Aḥmad Amīn (1886–1954)*

Aḥmad Amīn represented a basically different type of writer from those mentioned before. He never had any immediate contact with Western culture, his education having been mainly Arabic-Islamic. His acquaintance with Western thought came to him indirectly, through his fellow writers, and his role consisted largely of reinterpreting the Arabic-Islamic intellectual heritage in the light of the modern ideas initiated or advanced by his contemporaries. For most of his life he succeeded admirably in the task that he had set himself, but the derivative character of his basic ideas, and his personal and educational background, made him more vulnerable than other writers to sudden loss of intellectual confidence and abrupt change of orientation.

Aḥmad Amīn was born in Cairo to a family of small farmers who had left the land to escape the burden of taxation and fled to the city. The proximity of his tradition-bound family through much of his life caused his deviation from tradition to weigh on his conscience and acted as a brake on his complete "modernization." He attended the *kuttāb* and public primary school and wanted to go on with his secular secondary education, but his father insisted on sending him instead to al-Azhar. After several years there, he went to the College for Shar'ī Judges, a modernized splinter of al-Azhar, from which he was graduated in 1907. He worked for a while as Shar'ī judge but then returned to the college to teach Islamic literature and ethical philosophy. Later, Amīn was invited to join the staff of the Egyptian University and teach the same subjects there. He accepted the post and, except for an interval in which he served as undersecretary in the Ministry of Education, spent the rest of his life as a teacher at the University until his retirement a few years before his death. During his period of service, he rose to the highest academic ranks and became for a while Dean of the Faculty of Letters. In 1918, at the age of thirty-two, he learned English well enough to use it for his scholarly work and research but not well enough, apparently, to enable him to immerse himself in Western culture.

Amīn's *magnum opus* consists of a seven-volume study and interpretation of the intellectual and social history of the first four centuries of Islam, which he wrote over a period of twenty years. Next in importance is a multi-volume collection of articles on literary, social, intellectual, and ethical questions which he had published in papers and magazines. Other important works include a collection of biographical studies of modern Muslim reformers, meditations in the form of letters to his son, and an autobiography. Amīn also wrote, alone or in collaboration with others, several textbooks on ethics, civics, and the history of Arabic literature for use in secondary schools.[8]

7. *'Ali 'Abd al-Rāziq (1888–)*

'Ali has not been a *littérateur* or an educator in the sense in which the writers mentioned earlier have been. He is included here mainly because of the importance of one of his early works and therefore needs no extended biography.

He was born in lower Egypt to one of the most distinguished among the big landowner families. His father was the first president of the Ummah Party. 'Alī entered al-Azhar at the age of ten after a preparatory religious education and remained for thirteen years. In his last two years at the college he also attended lectures by Nallino and Santillana at the Egyptian University. In 1912 he went to England where he spent a year learning the language and a year at Oxford studying economics and political science before returning to Egypt on the outbreak of World War I. He became judge in a Shar'ī court and lectured in the Islamic Institute of Alexandria while he undertook a study of the Muslim judiciary system. The first result of his study was his book on the caliphate, published in 1925, in which we are primarily interested. Subsequently, 'Alī became editor of the journal of *al-Rābiṭah al-Sharqiyyah* (The Oriental League) and a senator, and continued his investigation of the judiciary system, the results of which do not concern us here.

These, then, are the men whose work we will now examine. Before going into any detailed analysis, however, it might perhaps be useful to outline very briefly the general course of ideological evolution between 1919 and 1952.

Within the framework of the task of the intellectual leaders and the problems they had to deal with, their work may be divided into two phases which, as might be expected, were closely related to actual political, economic, and social conditions. In the first phase, which reached its height during the years of inspiring national unity and struggle right after World War I, amidst hopes for a brave new world and unprecedented economic prosperity, the work of the intellectual leaders was characterized by a vigorous rationalist spirit, a confident Western cultural orientation, buoyant ethical aspirations, and a bold assertion of Liberal Nationalist principles and themes. The writers themselves were unanimous in spirit and united in their effort. In the second phase, after a period of ambivalence, the work of the intellectual leaders reached a point that could be described as a complete retreat on all these fronts.

We shall see that the retreat from the first, progressive phase began on the level of basic intellectual outlook after an incident that had brought to a head the latent conflict between humanistic rationalism and the Muslim view of the Qur'ān and genuine Tradition as constituting in their entirety positive divine truth. In consequence of this clash, the intellectual leaders began, one after another, gradually to reorient their thinking so as to find a *practical* accommodation of the conflicting approaches, and they developed, in the process, a popular literature on Muslim subjects that served them as a medium through which to effect this accommodation. But the end result of the whole endeavor was disastrous. The writers had surrendered their previous guide and bearing — rationalism and a Western cultural orientation — without being able to produce viable Muslim-inspired alternatives.

As in the case of the progressive phase, the reaction went hand in hand with historical conditions and was reinforced by them. The process of reorientation took place in the context of a political, social and economic crisis which began in the thirties and persisted to the end of our period of study. As the crisis grew deeper, the reaction extended to more and more spheres and encompassed more and more writers so that at the end of World War II the whole ideological sphere was dominated by a romantic, vague, inconsistent, and aggressive Muslim orientation. The change of direction initiated by the intellectual leaders not only failed to meet the problem it was supposed to solve, but also provided assistance to a violent, religious, reactionary mass political movement which had developed on its own and was threatening to destroy everything for which Liberal Nationalism had stood and to involve society in an extremely dangerous experiment. The revolution of 1952 came in the nick of time to spare Egypt and other countries the dire consequences of the whole second phase.

The Progressive Phase

Political Thought

One of the important questions that faced the intellectual leaders after 1923 was the consolidation and extension of the two basic principles of the Liberal National state: (1) that the nation is the fundamental unit of the political order, and (2) that the sovereign people is the source of legislation. Both principles had been formally recognized in the Constitution. But, as we have seen in our discussion of the issue of the caliphate and of governmental legislation in the sphere of Islamic law, these principles were by no means secure and recognized in practice. If they were to have a chance of eventual assimilation by the people, therefore, they needed to be justified in principle and given a meaningful theoretical content.

One of the most important attempts made toward the justification of these principles of the Liberal National state was ʿAlī ʿAbd al-Rāziq's book, *al-Islām wa Uṣūl al-Ḥukm* (Islam and the Principles of Government). Published in 1925, the book appeared when the agitation about the abolition of the caliphate was at its height. This fact tended to concentrate attention on ʿAlī's views regarding this question even though his general thesis was far more fundamental than the question of the caliphate. Briefly stated, his thesis was that Islam is, on the one hand, an exclusively spiritual community and, on the other, a code of disciplinary and religious precepts binding upon the individual conscience without any relation to power and politics:

> Here below things are of too little importance in the eyes of Allah for Him to have considered it relevant to entrust their regulation to a prophet; while the prophets themselves appreciate these things all too well according to their true value to occupy themselves with them.[1]

Following these abstract rational reflections, ʿAbd al-Rāziq considered the career of Muḥammad and came to the conclusion that he had never envisaged the establishment of any specific political organization. His own political and military activities had nothing to do with religion and were carried out simply for the protection of the community and for its immediate material welfare. In fact, Muḥammad was not even very successful on the latter score; he did not improve the political organization of the Arabs and left them at his death in the same state of anarchy in which he had found them.[2] The caliphs who came after him were essentially temporal rulers and founders of empires. The particular form of government that they had chosen had nothing to do with religion:

> The truth is that the Muslim religion has nothing to do with the caliphate, which the Muslims generally recognize. The caliphate is not at all a religious office; neither are the offices of *qāḍī* and other posts of the state. All these are simply administrative offices with which religion is not concerned.[3]

As a matter of historical fact, not only was the caliphate a secular institution, but it was even harmful to the true interests of religion as well as to the welfare of the Muslims:

> Reason and history agree on the absolute incompatibility of the spiritual interests [of the religion] with the regime attributed to the caliphate. They testify to the indifference shown by the ancient caliphs to the true welfare of the religion. The caliphate was indeed the cause of the misfortunes of Islam [because] it became a source of discord and internal disorganization.[4]

Drastic as ʿAlī's thesis was, he had reached it only by pursuing some of ʿAbduh's key ideas to their logical conclusions. It was ʿAbduh who had hinted that the Prophet might be fallible in his activity beyond the transmission of Allah's message, and it was he who had rejected *ijmāʿ* as a binding principle of Islamic doctrine. To ʿAlī these views pointed to three conclusions. First, if the Prophet may be fallible in his political actions, then these actions are religiously irrelevant and should be evaluated in the light of history and reason. Secondly, if there is no *ijmāʿ*, then there is no foundation for the caliphate, and that institution should be judged in the light of reason and history. Thirdly, without *ijmāʿ*, there is no foundation for any universal interpretation of the Qur'ān and the Tradition and, therefore, these sources must have been intended to be understood individually and to bind only individual consciences. These conclusions were reinforced in ʿAlī's mind by general rational speculation as to the essentially ethical and spiritual function of religion which, again, is not a view alien to ʿAbduh's thought.

To the debate on the caliphate ʿAlī made this practical contribution, drawn from his study:

Nothing then prevents the Muslims from competing with other peoples in the scientific, social, and political spheres. It is up to them to decide whether they want to keep their archaic and cumbersome regime, or whether the time has come to lay the foundations for a new political organization according to the latest progress of the human spirit.[5]

'Abd al-Rāziq's book raised an uproar among the traditionalists and the orthodox, who were able to capitalize on a political conjuncture to punish the author by depriving him of his diploma of *'ālim* and causing him to be dismissed from his position as Shar'ī judge.[6] The intellectual leaders, however, defended the author publicly on the ground of freedom of opinion, and sponsored his views on appropriate occasions without necessarily using his arguments. Thus, in a different context, Haykal hailed the separation of church and state in modern Turkey as one of the "necessary foundations for any true democracy, a healthy social life, and for the upsurge of civilization." [7] Ṭāha Ḥusayn argued that "the Muslims realized a long time ago that religion is one thing, and state and culture another thing," and that they knew that the true foundations of the state are practical interests.[8] Aḥmad Amīn repeated in different words 'Abd al-Rāziq's argument in the course of his study of the social and cultural history of Islam.[9]

While 'Abd al-Rāziq's theory made an important contribution to the justification of the principles of the Liberal National state as embodied in the Constitution, it was nevertheless largely a negative one, seeking only to remove the obstacle of Islam's opposition to them. It was still necessary to provide a positive ideological rationale for a specifically Egyptian nationalism and for the specific institutions of popular sovereign rule adopted in Egypt.

In regard to the first need, the intellectual leaders attempted in two ways to justify and enhance a separate Egyptian nationalism. They endeavored, first, to reinterpret history so as to dissociate Egypt's past from that of the larger Muslim community, and then to endow a separate Egypt with a distinct cultural personality of its own.

In pursuing the first aim, most of the writers seized on the breakdown of the political unity of the Muslim empire under the 'Abbāsids through the ambition of various usurpers, in order to assert the establishment even at that early date of an Egyptian nation distinct from the *ummah*. Thus, Aḥmad Amīn argued in a book on civics, assigned in the Egyptian high schools, that the secession of ibn-Ṭūlūn (in the ninth century) from the Baghdad empire, or the establishment of the autonomous state of the Fāṭimids, and later of the Mamluks, represented assertions of the will to a specifically

Egyptian national independence against the Umayyad and 'Abbāsid conquerors.[10] Other writers, too, referred frequently to the Arabs as foreign intruders and subjugators of the Egyptian nation.[11] In a similar vein, Ṭāha Ḥusayn argued that

> . . . history shows that unity of religion and language does not necessarily go hand in hand with political unity. The Muslims realized this a long time ago. They established their states on the basis of practical interests, abandoning religion, language, and race as the exclusively determining factors before the end of the second century (A.H.) [eighth century (A.D.)] . . . Various national blocs and states emerged everywhere . . . on the basis of economic, geographic, and other interests. . .

He followed this with an assertion that Egypt under ibn-Ṭūlūn was among the first to establish itself as a state on these practical foundations.[12]

The pride that the writers took in the alleged fact of Egypt's early assertion of her geographical-political personality involved a real "transvaluation of values" in the common Muslim view of history, which always regarded the breakdown of the political unity of the *ummah* as one of the great disasters that befell Islam.[13] Still, the new view could at least lean on concrete historical events for support. Much more intricate and difficult was the attempt to establish a distinct Egyptian *cultural* personality. For, whatever her political and geographical status, it was obvious that Egypt belonged and had always belonged to the larger Islamic culture without any significant distinction in this respect. Most of the intellectual leaders followed the clue of Luṭfī al-Sayyid[14] and went beyond Islam to the ancient past, arguing that in the course of millennia, the Egyptian environment had molded a permanent "pharaonic core" or an "Egyptian mind" which gave Egypt a distinct and unassailable cultural personality. Some writers simply asserted this "fact," or took it for granted.[15] Others tried to give that "core" a specific content. Thus, Haykal argued that the essence of the pharaonic spirit was "the religious lights," the concern with things spiritual, and that this spirit found its culmination in Islam.[16] Ṭāha Ḥusayn maintained that the essence of the "Egyptian mind" was "Mediterranean," as materialist and as spiritual, as rational and as religious, as the "Western mind."[17] Both these views, however, failed to give their "core" or "mind" distinctively Egyptian characteristics since spirituality and "Mediterraneanism" were still transnational characteristics that Egypt shared with others. It was al-Ḥakīm who made the most impressive contribution in meeting this need.

Al-Ḥakīm expressed repeatedly his deep conviction that the

"Egyptian mind," deeply rooted in the soil and nourished by the Nile, had undergone very slight changes since ancient times.[18] The central idea of this conception and of all his pharaonistic work was that the Egyptian mind was obsessed with the notion of time and space in the way that the Greek mind had been obsessed with the notion of fate, and that its whole life-purpose was aimed at the conquest of those elements:

> Yes, Egypt cannot think of anything but the conquest of another life. She is metaphysical, always wrapped in religious philosophy, and ever obsessed with the fear of death and the hope of the triumph of the spirit over time and space. That triumph consists of a notion of resurrection, a resurrection not in a world that does not know time and space, but in this very world and this very planet. . . . Egypt did not need a Homer to write about that epic because the din of that battle cannot be described by a human pen. That din is the screams of the spirit which rise forever from the lines of *The Book of the Dead*.[19]

Al-Ḥakīm did not content himself with describing abstractly the *motifs* of the Egyptian mind, but devoted a great deal of effort to attempts to embody those notions in artistic works, as the Greek writers had done with the idea of fate. The most famous of these were two symbolistic dramas: *Ahl al-Kahf* (The People of the Cave) (1933), based on the legend of the four sleepers, and *Shahrazād* (1934), and a philosophical novel — *'Awdat al-Rawḥ* (The Rebirth), written in 1927 and published in 1933. In the first drama, al-Ḥakīm depicted the aspiration to conquer time, and in *Shahrazād*, the aspiration to conquer space; while in the novel, he expressed the continuity of the Egyptian mind, and tried to conquer time, as it were, by looking back into the ancient Egyptian "psychology" to explain the "mystery" of contemporary events. Because the novel is the more explicit, we shall discuss it briefly rather than the dramas.

Properly speaking, al-Ḥakīm's novel does not have a plot but depicts in a perceptive and often highly humorous way the life of Egyptians of various classes, backgrounds, and education at the time of the revolution of 1919. But al-Ḥakīm uses this setting in order to seek and suggest an answer to the puzzling phenomenon of the unanimous and spontaneous outburst of the nationalist spirit in that revolution. Through most of the novel, the author makes the point that there was nothing in the course of life in Egypt until the very eve of the uprising to forecast such a development — not even among well-educated middle-class officials and students. When his characters find themselves in the thick of events and finally land in jail under the shadow of death, they do not know exactly what had happened to them. But al-Ḥakīm had already put the explanation, long before the events, in the mouth of a French archeologist, in the course of a discussion with a British irrigation inspector. The two had been brought to the countryside, where, according to al-Ḥakīm, the Egyptian spirit is at its purest, and made to converse in sight of fellahin at work:

Fouquet (the archeologist): You doubt what I am saying? I will only tell you: Beware! Beware of this people, for it carries within itself a tremendous spiritual power . . . hidden in that well from which these pyramids have arisen . . . [These pyramids] about which Champollion said . . . 'I will only say that these men have built like giants a hundred feet tall . . .'
Black (the British inspector): All this came from a well? What sort of a well?
Fouquet: This! (and he pointed with his finger to the left side of his breast.)
Black: The heart?!
Fouquet: Yes. . . . We may be excused if we do not understand. For our language — we Europeans — is the language of sensual things. We cannot imagine the impulses which once made of this people one single person, able to carry on its shoulders for twenty years those huge rocks, with a smile on its lips and joy in its heart, content with pain for the sake of the worshipped one. Those thousands upon thousands of people who built the pyramids could not have been forcibly driven to work, as Herodotus has stupidly suggested. On the contrary: they flocked to work singing the hymns of the worshipped one in the same way as their descendants do at present in harvest time. Their bodies bled, but they felt the secret joy of sharing pain for the same ideal. They enjoyed the sight of blood dripping from their bodies not less than the sight of old wines sacrificed to the worshipped one. This collective joy and pain, this feeling of beautiful patience, of gay endurance of sufferings for the sake of a common cause, this feeling of faith for the worshipped one, and of sacrifice and unity in pain . . . this is their strength and their power. . . .[20]

At the Englishman's protest that there can be no relation between the ancient Egyptians and the present-day fellahin, the Frenchman, Fouquet, retorts emphatically:

And what a relation! I have already said, and I can repeat once more, that the core ever remains. These fellahin who sing with a single heart still feel the expression with which their ancestors mourned their dead:

> when time will become eternity
> we shall see you again,
> for you are bound for the beyond
> where all is one. . . .

Yes, Mr. Black, don't despise this poor people today. For the force is latent in it and needs only one thing in order to come to the fore. . . . The Worshipped One! This people needs only that man from its own ranks who would embody all its aspirations and feelings and serve for it as a symbol of the goal. When this happens, don't be surprised if this people, homogeneous, solid, suffering, and so ready to make sacrifices, brought about another miracle like that of the pyramids. . .[21]

The Worshipped One, al-Ḥakīm seemed to suggest, came in the person of Sa'd Zaghlūl, and that is how the "miracle" of the 1919 revolution took place.

Stimulated by the discovery of the treasures of Tut-Ankh-Amon, after the declaration of independence, and enjoying full official support, the pharaonic tendency enjoyed such a vogue among the educated classes that it seemed to have become accepted doctrine. In a biographical study of Sa'd Zaghlūl published in 1936, al-'Aqqād, for instance, felt he could assume without question the identity of ancient and modern Egyptians, and referred just as naturally to the Arabs as foreign invaders. But the development of the pharaonic movement was eventually checked by the intellectual and political crisis, which we shall examine later. After a brief transition, it was submerged under the markedly contradictory trend of an Islamic cultural orientation even though it was never explicitly and generally repudiated.[22]

In contrast to the attention devoted to the justification of a separate Egyptian nationality and the effort to endow that nationality with a mystique of its own, the intellectual leaders made very little effort to interpret and develop the other principles that the Constitution recognized even though most of them expressed their conviction on numerous occasions that no political reform would be of enduring worth unless it were assimilated by the people, and that it was their task to help make this assimilation possible.[23] General references to democracy, freedom of thought, and the rights of the nation can be found quite frequently dispersed in the writings of the intellectual leaders, but apart from a few collections of rather formal and scholastic synopses of theories of some casually chosen Western thinkers, very little political theorizing was done after Luṭfī al-Sayyid.

The explanation of this phenomenon lies in a number of tendencies which reflect important and enduring aspects of modern Egyptian thought. First among these was the attitude toward public education. The intellectual leaders, as well as their political colleagues, had an almost sacred esteem for public education, which reflected itself in the fact that, of all the social issues, it was the only one that was dignified with a special clause in the Constitution which made it universal and free. For a variety of reasons, they expected the spread of education to lead automatically to the acquisition of a democratic disposition and did not, therefore, feel a pressing need to devote much attention to interpreting the liberal-democratic principles of the Constitution. One of these reasons was a mistaken deduction made from the reversal of the true proposition that democracy cannot flourish in ignorance, leading them to expect the spread of knowledge to promote democracy. This expectation seemed to be confirmed from their own experience and from their observation that their closest readers and followers came from the ranks of the better educated. It also had the support of theorists of the French Enlightenment with whom they were acquainted — men like Condorcet, the father of modern French education, who asserted that the spread of the *lumières* would inevitably lead to the growth of the spirit of liberty. To the Egyptian intellectuals, therefore, the chief problem appeared to be the rapid quantitative expansion of the public school system and the inclusion of modern subjects in the curriculum. They failed to realize then that the accumulation of modern knowledge could be worse than futile if, as we shall see later on, it was inculcated in the form of general abstract formulas which the pupils and students memorized for the sole purpose of passing examinations.[24]

Another factor hampering the development of a political literature designed to interpret and promote the democratic principles of the Constitution was a tendency among large segments of the educated public to view political theorizing as a matter of legal interpretation of the Constitution reserved for the lawyers and the politicians. Scholarly books on constitutional law were many and relatively good,[25] in contrast to the dearth of works of political interpretation. Such a tendency is not a defect in itself; it characterizes, for example, much of American endeavor in political thought. But, as the American example precisely illustrates, it is an approach that is suitable to a society which has achieved agreement on principles, and need concern itself only with their evolution and application. This was hardly the case in Egypt. There, the legalistic approach became an attitude toward the Constitution not unlike that of the *'ulamā'* to the Sharī'ah, whereby the Constitution was viewed as a doctrine or a set of rules extrinsic to and above society, to be followed or circumvented, rather than as a combination of certain human ideals and principles of "political engineering" derived by mankind from experience.

Illustrative of this tendency is the treatment of the questions of sovereignty and the constitution in Aḥmad Amīn's civics test, mentioned above. The author starts by defining the concept of constitution in purely formal terms: "The constitution . . . is the fundamental principles determining the political regime, the power of government, the rights and obligations of individuals, the distribution of government's power and the way it should be used." [26] Then he goes on to describe the sources of the constitution in these formal and tautological terms:

> The constitution is issued by the power which possesses effective sovereignty in the state, so that if the state has a democratic inclination (*naz'ah dīmūqrāṭiyyah*), the nation possesses the sovereignty and it has the right to issue the constitution. . . . But if sovereignty belongs to the hereditary possessor of the throne, it is for him to grant his state a constitution. . . . It is also possible for the constitution to issue from a contract between the king and the representatives of the people, as happened in England. . . .[27]

A few pages later the author tells the reader that in Egypt it was the king who, in 1922, "gave orders to draw up a constitution which would include explicitly and frankly the establishment of a parliamentary regime in the country and realize the cooperation between the nation and the government in running the affairs of the country." [28]

A third reason for the neglect of systematic political theorizing was that when the intellectual leaders did concern themselves with political principles from other than a legalistic point of view, they tended to view them in an exclusively idealistic way and to subsume them entirely under ethics. It is true that all political theories are ultimately related to some ethical presupposition, but if a particular political system is to be justified, it is not enough to proclaim and extol the ethical principles on which it is founded. It is necessary, first, to justify those principles and then to show how the particular political system is designed to safeguard and realize them by means of political strategy. This the intellectual leaders failed to do. Political principles appeared to them as self-evident ethical imperatives, and political behavior as simply good or bad moral conduct. Here, too, it seems that the intellectual leaders were bringing into the field of modern politics the formal idealism and ethical approach of the traditional Islamic view of politics.[29] Aḥmad Amīn, for example, considered political rights and obligations as ethical values in themselves and enumerated them among values in general in a textbook on ethics which he had written for the Ministry of Education.[30] Elsewhere, he presented the evolution of the forms of government and of the ends of power as the progressive adherence by men to a succession of ethical positions, without any relation to material realities. He concluded his argument by saying, "The end of government has ceased [nowadays] to be ruling for the sake of ruling; its purpose has become the realization of justice and freedom even for the poor." [31] In a similar context, he defined a political party in Burkean terms as a group of peoples united for action by a common idea of the public good.[32]

Ṭāha Ḥusayn contended, in an article published as late as 1946 that the political history of the world in the preceding hundred years had consisted of a struggle between the two ethical norms of justice and freedom, and of men's inability to decide which of them should prevail: "Should the world proceed to realize justice or freedom? — That is the question. . . This is the problem that the nineteenth century posed to some minds in Europe. . . From the thinking class the problem trickled down to the middle and then to the lower classes and came, thus, to preoccupy all political thought in the last century. . ." [33] This struggle between the two norms was at the root of the two World Wars. Developments in Europe after World War II were only the result of countries wavering between the two norms, unable to follow either definitively. No formula for combining the two has so far been found, but, Ṭāha concluded optimistically, "Who knows? Perhaps some day that philosopher will appear who will invent [*sic*] for humanity that middle norm by which justice will be realized without violence, and freedom without oppression. . ." [34]

Other writers expressed differing views in a variety of contexts, but all shared the tendency that is so evident in the words of Aḥmad Amīn and Ṭāha Ḥusayn. With all of them politics was understood as a choice between norms; but none of them showed any awareness that a connection might exist between actual social forces and the alternative norms that present themselves at a given moment, or between the actual pursuit of some norm and such practical devices as balance of forces, organized opposition, checks and balances, and other institutional schemes. With such a view of politics, it is not surprising that the political education of the public became, in the eyes of the writers, a question of preaching certain ideals, a matter which did not require special attention apart from the endeavor to promote ethical values in general. Al-ʿAqqād and al-Māznī even went further and maintained that political education could be accomplished by the propagation of aesthetic values. Inspired by Schiller, they developed together an outline of a philosophy which conceived of freedom as the exercise of choice between alternative but inescapable necessities. But, since man is never nearer to being free than when he exercises choice between alternative manifestations of beauty, the development of an aesthetic sense is the highest education to freedom. In the words of al-ʿAqqād:

> One valuable painting evoking the admiration of the nation is more weighty proof that freedom is at the core of its nature than a thousand speeches, a thousand demonstrations, and a thousand paper constitutions which have no hold on its spirit and no effect on its dealings.[35]

The failure of the intellectual leaders themselves to perceive the indispensable role that the mechanics of democracy play in making possible the approximation of its ideals condemned the system of government embodied in the Constitution to remaining beyond the ken of the public's understanding. The exclusively idealistic understanding of democracy is one of the reasons for the strange phenomenon that was to be repeatedly observed in Egypt of various politicians and movements singing the praise of democracy while at the same time suppressing or even destroying altogether the institutions and procedures needed to make it function.

Intellectual Orientation, Ethics, History.

The justification of the Egyptian national state and the interpretation of the democratic system of government embodied in the Constitution formed only part of the task facing the intellectual leaders. Beyond these there was the problem of developing the philosophical, ethical, and historical views necessary to serve as a background for the specific political system adopted. We have seen, indeed, that the discussion of the political thought of the intellectual leaders inevitably spilled over into more general questions having to do with the readjustment and revision of traditional views. Thus ʿAbd al-Rāziq's theory led to a consideration of the role of reason as opposed to the traditional principles of validation, and the discussion of the various writers' views on nationalism and liberal democracy touched upon the subjects of ethics and the reinterpretation of history.

One of the fundamental questions facing the intellectual leaders with respect to this endeavor was the problem of working out acceptable principles of validation to take the place of revelation as traditionally understood. Without such principles no coherent world view could develop; no discussion could take place, and communication would be impossible. We know that the intellectual leaders did not have to start from the very beginning. They had before them the teachings of ʿAbduh which had narrowed very considerably the scope of what constituted revelation and had sanctioned reason as the criterion for its interpretation as well as for validating knowledge beyond its scope. But there was still the question of what the intellectual leaders would do with these teachings and how they would interpret them. And we have seen in our analysis of 'Abduh's thought that these teachings were susceptible to widely varying interpretations.

As we understand it, the spirit and intention of 'Abduh's teaching was to make reason the handmaid of revelation, even though, for practical purposes, he did give reason priority in case of seemingly irreconcilable conflict with revelation. Reason by itself, he contended, could discover the right norms and values for the moral life of society, but right reason, aware of the lessons of history and of its own fallibility, chooses to accomplish its work by subordinating itself to revelation. It takes a few steps on its own but always looks back to see that revelation gives its assent to them or, at least, does not oppose them. But even in 'Abduh's lifetime the tendency had developed to pursue reason and then to verify its results, not by referring to the letter of revelation, but by reference to its "spirit." This, of course, weakened considerably the effect that 'Abduh intended to achieve by the process of verification.

Examples of this tendency are abundant in the work of Qāṣim Amīn, a disciple and contemporary of 'Abduh, famous as the champion of the emancipation of women. In his *Taḥrīr al-Mar'ah* (The Emancipation of Woman),[36] for instance, he argued on various sociological and contemporary ethical grounds against allowing polygamy except in case of sterility or disability of the wife, and then asserted that certainly that was the spirit in which the Qur'ān had permitted it. "Otherwise, I see polygamy as nothing but a legal fiction designed to satisfy animal desires, an indication of corrupted morals or emotional imbalance, and of excessive indulgence in pleasure."[37] In the same way, he attacked the Shar'ī view of marriage as a contract by which man takes possession of part of the woman as "a horrible principle contrary to the spirit of the Qur'ān"[38] which, according to him, views marriage as founded on companionship, love, and partnership.[39]

Two decades later, the intellectual leaders dropped even the formalities of Qāṣim Amīn and began to speak of reason as sufficient in itself for validating any socially relevant conclusions. Some continued to consider religion as fulfilling a function that is essential for human happiness, but what they understood by religion was not any specific code of ethics — certainly not a specific law, nor even a specific creed. Religion to them, as to religiously inclined intellectuals everywhere, was a mystical faith in some divine essence which had little to do with practical life. That faith did not impinge on reason because it pertained to the realm of the metaphysical.

A clear expression of this view was given by al-ʿAqqād in an essay, published in 1924, in which he discussed the relation between reason and religion. He began by making a Kantian distinction between things as they appear to us and "things in themselves." Of the former we can know enough for the purposes of practical life and of "thought connected with that life," and with respect to them we can find certain definite criteria for distinguishing between true and false. With respect to matters pertaining to the realm of "things in themselves," however, we can have no such measure. But, al-ʿAqqād continued, this does not mean that we can have no contact with that realm, for not all contact is one of reason. Our relation with that realm is not, indeed, one of seeking to know it or of studying it logically, but rather of "seeking to be part of it and keep in touch with it"; and faith alone can fulfil this aspiration. That this relationship is possible in the first place is self-evident since "it is inconceivable that man should be the product of this universe and part and parcel of it in every atom of his being and yet remain without assurance about its truths, without belief in its secrets, and without connection with its essence." This confidence in the universe, al-ʿAqqād continued, is the foundation of belief and it is beyond the purview of rational criticism. As for the specific "religions, cults, and other ways of knowing the truths of the universe," these are subject to the criticism of reason and logic.[40]

We can gain some idea of the extent of al-ʿAqqād's rationalist commitment from the pains he took to justify the mere act of belief in some vague Supreme Being, even unrelated to any specific body of dogma. This commitment he shared with the other intellectual leaders, who developed their own rationalizations for belief in a similar "universal essence." But the writer who advanced the rationalist spirit farthest was Ṭāha Ḥusayn, who advocated in one of his famous books a rationalism which clashed head-on with some fundamental traditional conceptions.

The book in question was published in 1926 and bore the deceptively innocent title of *Fī al-Shiʿr al-Jāhilī* (On Pre-Islamic Poetry). But it had a deep religious significance stemming from the fact that pre-Islamic poetry had been used for many generations after the death of Muḥammad as a linguistic reference source for interpreting the terms of the Qur'ān and the Tradition, and as a historical source in its own right. As a result of his study, Ṭāha reached the conclusion that "this poetry proves nothing and tells nothing and should not be used, as it has been, as an instrument in the science of the Qur'ān and the *Ḥadīth*. For, undoubtedly it was tailored and invented all of a piece so that the *'ulamā'* might prove by it what they had set out to prove."[41] Thus with one stroke, Ṭāha cut the ground from under many hitherto unquestioned interpretations of the Qur'ān and the Ḥadīth, on which many laws and doctrines had been based, cast a shadow of doubt on the integrity of many revered authorities, and put in question the entire traditional processes of Qur'ānic exegesis.

More important than these conclusions was the method which Ṭāha expounded in that book: "I want to introduce in *adab* (literature) that philosophical method for investigating the truth of things which Descartes formulated at the beginning of the modern era. . ."[42] Its implications were starkly explained by the author when he said:

> Yes, when we engage in the study of the Arabic *adab* and its history, we must forget our nationality and everything which represents it, our religion and all that is related to it; we must not heed the question of what might contradict that nationality or that religion; we must be bound by nothing except the methods of true scientific investigation. . . .[43]

And lest there be any doubt about what the implications might be, Ṭāha undertook to spell them out. Speaking about "modernist" investigators like himself, he said:

> They do not allow themselves to follow the path of faith and trust — perhaps they just have not been granted faith and confidence; God has created for them minds which find delight in doubting, and pleasure in anxiety and perplexity. . . . the *necessary consequences* of this method are of utmost importance — they amount to nothing less than intellectual revolution. Just think that they doubt that which people have taken for certain and that they may rescind that which has been universally accepted as the indubitable truth. . . . They may end up changing history, or that which people have taken as history; and they may end up doubting in matters in which doubt had not been permitted. . . .[44]

In the body of the work, Ṭāha Ḥusayn missed no occasion to ridicule the Muslim thinkers, jurists, theologians, and rulers of the formative period of Islam for their naiveté in handling the sources, or their blatant trickery in manufacturing them. "I can only see you laugh with me at this verse which some Mu'tazilah had quoted in order to prove that Allah's throne . . . is His knowledge," he said in one passage. The verse in question is the saying of an "anonymous" poet: "Nor is the throne of God's knowledge created."[45] Elsewhere in the book he wrote, "The lies of the *ahl al-'ilm* (the 'ulamā') in attributing things to people of the pre-Islamic era are abundant and cannot be counted or exhausted."[46] More serious than all this was Ṭāha's barely disguised ridicule of the traditionally accepted idea that *jinns* exist and that they even composed poetry. Such ridicule implied an attack on the Qur'ān itself since it testified that *jinns* listened to the Prophet and believed in his message:

You may add . . . another sort of invented poetry which has been attributed not to human Arabs, but to pre-Islamic Arab *jinns*. For it seems that the Arab nation was composed not only of people descending from Adam, but that there was, besides this, another nation composed of *jinns* which was even better than that of the humans; indeed, its poets were sources of inspiration to the human poets. . . .[47]

But Ṭāha's worst offense, and his most challenging point, was his open denial of the veracity of certain facts asserted in the Qur'ān in the name of rational criticism. In the context of his argument concerning the language and style of some alleged pre-Islamic poetry, he made out the Qur'ānic stories about Abraham and Ishmael to be pure myths:

The Torah may speak to us about Ibrāhīm and Ismā'īl, and the Qur'ān may tell us about them too; *but the mention of these names in the Torah and the Qur'ān is not sufficient to establish their historical existence*, let alone the story which tells us about the emigration of Ismā'īl, son of Ibrāhīm, to Mecca and the birth of the arabicized Arabs there. We are compelled to see in this story a kind of fiction to establish the relation of Jews and Arabs on the one hand, and Islam and Judaism and the Qur'ān and the Torah on the other. . . .[48]

The appearance of Ṭāha Ḥusayn's book caused a tremendous uproar among the traditionalist and the orthodox *'ulamā'*. Rashīd Riḍā asserted that Ṭāha had "established his apostasy from Islam,"[49] and led a chorus of religious and conservative leaders demanding his dismissal from the Egyptian University. When they received no response, they turned their fire against the university itself as a haven for heretics and a breeding ground for atheism. In the end, Ṭāha was tried for attacking the religion of the state, but the court dismissed the charge. The book was withdrawn, the reference to Ibrāhīm and Ismā'īl was deleted, and the remainder, considerably expanded, was republished in 1927 under the title *Fī al-Adab al-Jāhilī* (On Pre-Islamic Literature). Five years later, however, Prime Minister Ismā'īl Ṣidqī was still able to use the incident to cause the dismissal of the author from the university.

Although Ṭāha Ḥusayn had been alone in stating his position in these challenging terms by juxtaposing reason and the Qur'ān and opting for reason, his views were only the logical conclusion of the ideas expressed by al-'Aqqād and others. At any rate, none of his colleagues took exception to his method even when, like al-Māznī, they disagreed with his conclusions.[50] All of them stood behind him in the agitation which ensued from publication of his book, if only on grounds of the right of freedom of thought.

But if some intellectuals were careful to avoid open clashes with specific fundamental religious tenets, such as the absolute veracity of the Qur'ān, all of them considered reason a sufficient guide for moral life and endeavored in their literature to foster such values as they had conceived on that basis. Thus, in an essay published shortly before 1933, Haykal defined the function of *adab* as discovering and propounding the good, the true, and the beautiful. These are eternal in their essence, he asserted, but assume different manifestations in various times and places, and it is the task of *adab* to discover and present the manifestations suitable to the environment in which it functions, without fear and without any restrictions.[51] In 1925, al-'Aqqād wrote that the function of *adab* is to transform the outlook of the nation on life. "Any reform in any aspect of the life of nations which does not deal with reforming their outlook on life is vain and worthless effort. . ." The function of *adab* is, therefore, "in the nature of creating the nations anew and is like unto the work of the gods. . . ." [52] Al-Māznī concurred with al-'Aqqād on the priority of moral and spiritual reform and described the modernist *udabā'* (littérateurs) as men who "understand true freedom, seek only the truth, and aim at nothing but arousing the best in human nature. . . . They are ready to battle anyone with solid arguments and decisive proofs. But, alas, the partisans of the old do not resort to logic and reason. . . ." [53] Again, Ṭāha Ḥusayn concluded a book on Greek thought published in 1929 and later assigned to the Egyptian secondary schools, in which he had set the intellectual history of mankind in terms of a continual conflict between religion and reason by stating with satisfaction that philosophy and politics have now replaced religion as the main guides to the human spirit:

The intellectual leadership remained with Christianity and Islam throughout the Middle Ages. But God has willed that philosophy and politics should resume that leadership once more and has destined Islam and Christianity to surrender it after having monopolized it during all those centuries. . . . The philosophers of Greece were in advance of their age. . . . But as soon as this philosophy spread among the moderns it brought forth its good fruits: it gave birth to a group of philosophers and political leaders who assumed the leadership of thought and brought about the French Revolution and the present conditions. . .[54]

All the views that we have presented show that the intellectual leaders were very strongly inclined toward idealism, not only in the epistemological and social-philosophical sense, but also in the popular sense of subscribing to lofty goals. This tendency was reflected in the ebullient, confident, assertive spirit of their work, as well as in the noble and heroic values they propounded. Thus al-'Aqqād indignantly attacked the traditional conception of ethics in which good and bad were defined by a will extrinsic to man, and morality was viewed as abstention from evil, expounding in its place an activist, euphoric ethical conception founded on human, willful choice.

. . . The vast majority of the Egyptian people . . . and many oriental peoples too . . . consider ethics as negative injunctions which keep man away from that which disgraces him; which forbid him to kill, to rob, and to attack others, or enjoin him not to be miserly or cowardly and not to indulge his passions. They also understand the ethical laws . . . as a power external to man, which dictates to him what to do and what to refrain from doing, without his having anything to do except obey and conform. We know of nothing more disastrous to ethics and more harmful to initiative than the entrenchment in the conscience of men of the view which considers man as the slave of the law who is pushed to do the good . . . and can do no better than to escape the bad and avoid the harmful. . . .[55]

Instead, al-'Aqqād suggested throughout his early works an eclectic ethics based on the ideas of evolution, on his own philosophy of freedom inspired by Schiller, and on certain Nietzschean concepts. The gist of his views may be presented briefly: Evolution is the law of the universe which mankind cannot escape and should not try to escape.[56] But society can, and should, control its operation by means of laws and ethics which do not contravene its purpose, and in this way transcend natural necessity by the exercise of social will. The individual can soar higher by *choosing* to obey the social laws, thereby transforming them from fetters to bracelets. For instance, in the course of evolution, woman has been formed into a creature inclined to impulsive and frivolous behavior. These characteristics are useful in the service of the perpetuation of the species and natural selection. Ethics and social laws should seek to discipline these inclinations, but should never try to suppress them — to do so would be to contravene the "law of God," and any ethics which does that "ought to be burned." Within these ethical and social laws, woman can still exercise choice, and thereby transform the element of necessity into one of freedom.[57] Thus, all ethics involve an overcoming of necessity by freedom or an assertion of the inner will against obstacles. Courage, patience, and other such qualities are praiseworthy only because they are indications that man possesses the freedom to command external events and act as one who is master of his affairs.[58]

Al-Māznī, who was a close colleague of al-ʿAqqād and collaborated with him in some of his writings, shared the latter's philosophy of freedom and necessity and also subscribed to an ethics based on "social Darwinism." However, he presented his ideas in a less involved way than al-ʿAqqād. Thus, in al-Māznī's view, men are dominated by instincts and passions which it is the function of reason and civilization to direct into social channels and embellish by art.[59] To surrender to the passions is weakness, and weakness is immoral because it is a handicap in the struggle for existence.[60] Nature made woman weaker than man — and consequently more subject to the influence of instincts — in order to fit her for her special function, the perpetuation of the species.[61]

Ṭāha Ḥusayn did not present in all his voluminous writings an explicit statement of his idea of ethics. But implicit in his work was a humanistic morality close to Hugo's which sympathized with human failure and saw moments of moral greatness even in sinful and corrupt lives. He, too, conceived of life as a constant battle between reason and passion, but, unlike al-Māznī, he understood and accepted passion as a part of human nature even when it led to moral aberrations. These views were, for the most part, communicated indirectly in his summaries of and comments on French novels and plays, and in his biographical sketches of French authors, which he began with his *Qiṣaṣ Tamthīliyyah* (Theater Stories) and continued intermittently throughout our period.[62]

Along with these studies of French literature, Ṭāha Ḥusayn, like the other intellectual leaders, undertook some analyses of classical Arabic poets. Unlike the others, however, Ṭāha used many of his studies to underline the dissent and deviation of his subjects from the real or alleged beliefs, norms, and customs of their times. He did so, not only to make his poets more human, but to facilitate a wider acceptance of the fluidity and permissiveness of the present by revising the traditional view of the classical Islamic times as the golden age of piety and greatness. His most popular work in this vein was *Ḥadīth al-Arbiʿāʾ* (Wednesday Conversations), a study of the work, life, and times of a number of poets from the first and second centuries of the *Hijrah*, which he published serially in *al-*

Siyāsah and collected in book form in 1927. One of the conclusions that he drew about the ethics of those times, for instance, was:

I do not want us just to concede that the second century, despite its many jurists, ascetics, and earnest doubters was also a time of skepticism, indulgence in pleasures, fascination, and deviation from the customary mores, the inherited habits, or even religion . . . but I want to give a representation of these dissenting, discontented men true to reality beyond any doubt. Then I want to show that these same men, although they may have been subject to the wrath of a few jurists and ascetics, were loved by all the people regardless of class, inclination, and sect, who enjoyed the humorous sayings they heard of them and the accounts of their amusing license of speech. Now, if these poets and their friends were so free in their opinions and indulged so much in pleasures and in their pursuit in public and in private, and yet were admired and liked by the people, then I would have no doubt that the times in which these poets and these people lived were not altogether times of faith and earnestness but were times of doubt and lightheartedness, of license and of pursuit of pleasures.[63]

Ṭāha further pointed out that the poets of that earlier time were also free thinkers and modern men who were not bound in any way to the heritage of the past:

Study that period well and read particularly the poetry and conversations which took place in the gatherings of poets and you will be amazed at . . . the degree of permissiveness, the free pursuit of thought, and the contempt for anything old, whether it be in religion, in mores, in politics, or in literature. Atheism made its appearance and spread to such a point that the 'Abbāsid caliphs were finally compelled to clamp down on the poets and the *udabā'* who were accused of atheism. . . .[64]

Al-Ḥakīm, like Ṭāha Ḥusayn, did not expound any specific principle or theory of ethics, but he too was preoccupied with the conflict between reason and passion and his work was suffused with Western humanistic values. Among these values, perhaps his chief concern was with the worth of human life and his feeling for human dignity, which he often emphasized by pointing out in scathing terms their neglect in Egypt.[65] Man's dignity, he wrote, can be asserted only by having reason prevail over the passions and by soaring beyond material, utilitarian considerations into the realm of spiritual aims, noble love, moral pleasures, intellectual nourishment, and so on. Otherwise man is indistinguishable from the animals.[66]

Haykal's thought was, more often than not, vague, confused, and confusing, and his ethical views were particularly inconsistent. The values he propounded were not actually different from al-Ḥakīm's or even from Ṭāha Ḥusayn's. But despite his practical commitment to reason, he was prone whenever he spoke of culture and civilization, to assert the need for the spiritual, the "religious element," essential for the well-being of society, which led him often to criticize the cults of nature, reason, humanity, and economic materialism, which he associated with the West, for having failed to make mankind happy.[67] His intention was, perhaps, only to criticize the *exclusive* adherence to these cults, but he never clarified his thought on the subject and, instead, wavered continually between what he apparently conceived to be opposite poles.

Aḥmad Amīn was the only one among the writers considered here who tackled systematically the subject of ethics. In his *Kitāb al-Akhlāq* (The Book of Ethics), published in 1929 and assigned as a text for secondary schools and for the teachers' college, he propounded an ethics based entirely on reason and intuition, in which religion was only one among many other factors — such as friends, habit, family, environment — serving as ethical controls.

One of the best ways of thanking God is to submit to the laws of ethics and act accordingly. For God has created this world and made its happiness dependent on things such as truthfulness, justice, and so on, and its misery on their opposites. He commanded [men] to follow that which leads to happiness and called it good and prohibited that which leads to misery and called it evil. . . .[68]

Amīn attacked specifically any ethics based solely on tradition and custom, and strongly implied that the new is always better than the old. "If people followed the principle of *'urf* (custom, tradition) the world would not have progressed over what it has been of yore. . ." Progress is achieved precisely by some people breaking away from mistaken *'urf*, and gradually rallying supporters to their views "until the right new takes the place of the wrong old." [69] In this particular work, Amīn reviewed the principles of hedonism, utilitarianism, stoicism, and Kantian intuitionism and chose the last: "We are inclined to a kind of intuitionism which sees that man was born with an inner force which tells him that some deeds are good and others are evil, not because of their consequent pleasure or pain but because these deeds are good or evil in themselves. . ." [70] Actually, however, the burden of all his writings indicates that he made an implicit distinction between public and personal ethics. In politics, as in all matters relating to the public welfare, he subscribed to a thoroughgoing utilitarianism that would even suppress truth or hold back its expression if necessary.[71] In personal ethics, he echoed the idealism of al-Ḥakīm and the emphasis on spirituality of Haykal, and adhered to the notion of the struggle between reason and passion to which all the intellectual leaders subscribed.[72]

Three important facts emerge from this summation of the ethical views of the intellectual leaders: One is that, underlying all the various ethical conceptions they propounded, there was general agreement, explicit or implicit, in rejecting any notion of ethics as founded on positive-divine revelation. Instead, all insisted on placing the source of morality in the individual faculties, whether reason, the will, or the heart. They also rejected explicitly or implicitly any idea of superhuman or other-worldly sanction and relied rather on the individual conscience, social responsibility, or the sanction of society to provide the necessary support for ethical norms. Finally, the authors drew their ideals entirely from Western sources, without making any attempt to disguise the fact. Even Haykal, who was already criticizing Western culture for its "materialism" and for the failure of its ideals to provide happiness, insisted that the education of the *adīb* must include the doctrines and systems of the West until the Arabs had assimilated the sciences and developed a philosophy suitable to the age.[73] Haykal's fellow-writers were lyrical in their praise of Western culture and zealous in their endeavor to spread and propagate it. These words of al-ʿAqqād were typical:

You, O reformer of *ādāb*; you who want men to set life in verses inspired by a heavenly composition, to make it an art among the creative arts . . . what are you to do amidst those beings, creatures of playful fate which charges you, O reformer, with the price of its playfulness? — Yours is the task to transport them from the buried world in which they live to the living world which is overflowing with ideals about which Aristotle meditated, which al-Ghazzālī worshipped, Shakespeare put in verse, Wagner sang, Leonardo sculpted, to which Nietzsche aspired . . . and thousands and millions . . . of their brethren in knowledge and consciousness have breathed. . . .[74]

We have already seen several instances of efforts by the intellectual leaders to reinforce their views by reading them back into history. These efforts culminated in an impressive work on Muslim social and intellectual history, written by Aḥmad Amīn, which provided valuable support to many of the main themes of the intellectual leaders, particularly to their positive attitude toward Western culture, their natural, earthy humanistic ethics, their assertion of the rights of reason, and their advocacy of a secular national state. This work, which occupied seven volumes and spanned an interval of seventeen years, was, perhaps, the most important production during the period under study.[75] Although much of it appeared at a time when reaction had already set it, logically it belongs to the progressive phase, and provides, in fact, an excellent summary of its spirit. This is because Amīn himself was the one among the intellectual leaders who had had least direct contact with Western cultures, and so tended to be a step or two behind the others and to rely on them for his inspiration. For this reason his work was essentially eclectic, incorporating not only the judgments and opinions of his fellow intellectuals, but also those of Western historians of Islam and Islamists. Nevertheless, he documented anew many of the theses he adopted and thus came out in the end with a product that was unmistakably his own.

One of the most important theses advanced by the Islamists, and echoed by Aḥmad Amīn, was the view that the elaboration of the Islamic law was not accomplished simply by a process of interpretation and deduction from the Qur'ān and the Tradition, but was achieved to a large extent by a process of "Islamicizing" norms and rules from Roman, Persian, and Jewish laws and the customary laws of Syria, Egypt, Iraq, and Persia at the time of the conquests. Amīn also documented anew and repeated the argument that the "Islamicization" was achieved through the acceptance, as genuine, of countless traditions which had been invented outright and attributed to the Prophet.[76] Far from seeing that process as subversive of Islam, Amīn commended it for its responsiveness to the conditions of the times [77] and used it to support the view that Islam followed the law of evolution [78] and should continue to do so.

Amīn coupled this revolutionary view with the equally revolutionary judgment that the breakdown of the political unity of the Muslim empire, which had been decried traditionally as an unmitigated disaster, was actually of great benefit both to Muslims and to Muslim culture. The partition of the empire may have weakened Islam internationally and may have hurt the caliphs, but it served the interests of the large masses of Muslims by leading to a better administration, by favoring a more equitable distribution of wealth, and by keeping each country's wealth at home rather than permitting it to be carried away to be squandered in Baghdad. Above all, he argued, it furthered the development of culture by multiplying its centers and fostering competition among them, by allowing greater freedom of expression, and by affording numerous places of refuge whenever thought was suppressed.[79] Amīn went even further and saw benefit in the multiplication of schools and sects, which had been regarded as disastrous by such men as Rashīd Riḍā and the conservatives. He deplored the violence of the sectarians but emphasized the beneficial effect of the diversity of opinions on thought and cultural life.[80]

Amīn adopted a similar position on the influence upon Islam of

Greek, Hindu, Jewish, and Christian ideas and cultures.[81] By stressing the blessings of that influence and the flexibility of Islam in its golden age, he wanted, of course, to justify and encourage the contemporary borrowings from Western civilization. On this score, however, Amīn was not altogether consistent. Sometimes he betrayed an implicit fear of the process, as when he praised and defended the Muʿtazilah for their crucial role in protecting Islam against the onslaught of Persian dualism and Jewish and Christian ideas. "God only knows the evil that would have befallen the Muslims if the Muʿtazilah had not been there to take their stand when the opponents of Islam attacked it with such strength. . ." [82] This element of ambiguity regarding the influence of foreign ideas was not peculiar to Aḥmad Amīn; it can be detected in the thought of most of the intellectual leaders and was to have crucial consequences later.

Amīn sympathized wholeheartedly with the general attitude of the Muʿtazilah, even though he took exception to some of their specific views. "In my opinion. . . ," he wrote frankly, "one of the greatest disasters that befell the Muslims and which they brought upon themselves was the extinction of the Muʿtazilah." [83] "Had the Muʿtazilah prevailed," he wrote elsewhere, "the Muslim position in history would have been entirely different from the actual one, in which surrender exhausted them, determinism paralyzed them, and fatalism sank them." [84]

Amīn adhered enthusiastically to the Muʿtazilah view of the unity of God which he characterized as "sublime and refined to the utmost." [85] He also endorsed their principle of the freedom of man as essential to the concept of the justice of God: "For God to create man and force him to act in a specific way . . . and then to punish . . . (him) has nothing just about it." [86] But he took exception to their attempt to impose a specific concept of justice on God, since such a concept can only be based on an invalid analogy with human justice, and he expressed reservations in regard to their exaggerated reliance on reason in working out matters of dogma.[87]

In the sphere of ethics, he agreed warmly with the Muʿtazilah view of the intrinsic nature of values and saw in it a fundamental principle of legislation akin to natural law:

> There is undoubtedly in this principle a liberation of the mind from petrification and from paralysis before canonic texts (*nuṣūṣ*). The legislator can thus use his own reason where there is no *naṣṣ* (text) to find out what is good and what is evil and to decide what to forbid and what to allow. Where there is no principle that can be followed by analogy, he can even know the nature of things. . . .[88]

Amīn pointed out approvingly a Mu'tazilah conception of crime that dissented from the traditional Islamic view which does not separate crime from tort, and emphasized instead that crime is a wrong done to society as well as to the victim.[89] But he took pains to refute their position which — leaning on the Qur'ānic verse enjoining the command of good and the prohibition of evil — empowered members of society to draw the sword to suppress what they consider evil. He approved of that measure only as a last resort against a tyrannical government, and only by consensus; otherwise, he contended, the function of suppressing evil should be left to the government, or else there would be total anarchy.[90]

On the question of the political order, Amīn took a view similar to that of 'Alī 'Abd al-Rāziq and maintained that the caliphate had been considered historically as a religious institution, but that this was only a result of what we may call demagogic manipulation. In truth, "religion did not bind the Muslims to any particular form or any particular person. All it did was to oblige them to consider the general interest. . ." According to Islam, the *ūlū al-amr* in the nation are to "consider what is suitable for each time and advance in understanding this suitability with the progress in understanding duties and rights. Differences of opinion among them would be political differences like those that prevail among political parties today. . . ."[91]

Altogether, then, Amīn attempted to use his history to foster the notion that the essence of Islam is found in its simple basic creed rather than in any specific dogmatic, legal, or ethical formulations. Such a creed should be based on a conception of a relationship with Allah that shuns over-rationalization, but is reasonable enough to counter the traditional Islamic view with its socially damaging emphasis on subjection, passiveness, and determinism. He also endeavored to shake the traditional Islamic conception of the *ummah* as the ideal unit by emphasizing the benefits of plurality; tried to weaken the traditional claim of the authority of Islam in all spheres of life by underlining the practical, nonreligious foundations of its political organization; sought to refute its assertion of the finality and divine basis of the Law by pointing out its eclectic and dated nature; and pointed to principles of adaptation by emphasizing the rational foundation of ethics, and the legitimacy of borrowing from foreign cultures.

CHAPTER 11

The Crisis of Orientation

The appearance of Ṭāha Ḥusayn's book on pre-Islamic poetry in 1926, the reactions it aroused, and the consequences to which it led marked a turning point in the unfolding of the ideological problem and the efforts of the intellectual leaders to meet it. The core of the problem was the need to replace an obsolescent belief-system founded on a conception of truth as something that is objectively defined in revelation, with a world view, more applicable to a new reality, that would be based on a conception of truth as something that is ascertained by the human faculties. Hitherto, the Liberal intellectual leaders had been able to achieve notable progress toward that goal without any serious fundamental difficulties by stretching two principles established by Muḥammad 'Abduh. One was the principle restricting the confines of what is to be considered as revelation; the second was the assurance that revelation could not be in contradiction with reason. The intellectual leaders relied on the first to narrow further the confines of revelation and on the second to indulge in their rational pursuits without bothering to verify their conclusions against revelation. But the point was bound to be reached when reason had to come up against the limitations inherent in 'Abduh's two principles, however liberally these might be interpreted. Application of the second principle, for instance, was limited by the fact that 'Abduh's assurance had really been based on à priori reasoning that revelation must be ultimately rational rather than on any concrete proof that this was actually so. Consequently, it was extremely likely that in the course of time some conflicts defying interpretive and formal reconciliation would emerge and require a substantial revision of the idea of what is to be viewed as revelation. The first of 'Abduh's two principles had its inherent limitation in a more literal sense; for, however liberally his view might be construed, he could not possibly be interpreted as having accepted anything less than the entire Qur'ān as divine revelation. Consequently, the time was bound to come when the obstacles that this conception of a core of positive revelation put in the way of the elaboration of a completely subjective belief-system would compel either its revision or a complete reinterpretation of the Qur'ān in harmony with the subjective view of truth. What Ṭāha Ḥusayn's book did was precisely to bring to a head both issues, to compel the adoption of new positions on the two principles, and so to determine the course of the ideological development in the next phase.

The new positions taken by the intellectual leaders varied substantially and, therefore, planted the seeds of the subsequent divergence of their efforts and disunity among their ranks. Ṭāha himself had, of course, recognized and even dramatized the possibility of conflict between the conclusions of reason and the content of the Qur'ān — at least in regard to some concrete historical matters — and had insisted that reason should prevail. Implicit in this approach was the suggestion that in the content of the Qur'ān itself distinctions should be made between those historical and, perhaps, legislative and other matters that might be verified and corrected by critical reason in the light of changing evidence and circumstances, and those universal ethical principles and metaphysical truths which might be accepted by emotional assent. Such a solution has been broadly adopted in the West in respect to the Scriptures and would have eliminated the interference of objective revelation with the development of systems of ideas, ideals, and norms based on subjective, humanly conceived truth. But, under the tremendous pressure that his book had provoked, Ṭāha was compelled to retract this position and he hastily adopted a new one which placed no limits on what might validly be accepted on faith.

During the height of the uproar stirred by the conservative *'ulamā'* and writers and the traditionalists of the camp of Rashīd Riḍā, Ṭāha Ḥusayn wrote a letter to the director of the Egyptian University, which was made public, in which he testified that he was a Muslim, believing in Allah, His angels, His books, His prophets, and the Day of Judgment.[1] But this confession did not mean that he had repudiated his own book altogether. The contradiction between book and letter he explained to the court appointed to look into his case in words which expressed concisely his new position: "Every one of us can discover within himself two distinct personalities, one a rational personality and the other a sentient personality. . . What is there, then, to prevent the first from being scholarly, inquisitive, and critical, and the other from being a believing, assured personality, aspiring toward the highest ideals?"[2] Ṭāha did not attempt, then, to establish any clear division between the two spheres of reason and revelation nor to work out any rules governing the relation between them. In fact, reason and revelation (and faith in general) were accepted as equally valid sources of truth, and the possibility that they might offer opposite teachings on the same subject was contemplated with equanimity.

Difficult as this new position was, it was not without precedent in history, though the precedent itself exemplifies how unviable it was. It was a position very close to that of the Latin Averroists of the thirteenth century. In his *Reason and Revelation in the Middle Ages*, Etienne Gilson described their reasoning in words that seem to paraphrase those of Ṭāha Ḥusayn:

> The conclusions of philosophy are at variance with the teachings of Revelation; let us therefore hold them as the *necessary* results of philosophical speculation, but, as Christians, let us believe that what Revelation says on such matters is *true*; thus no contradiction will ever arise between philosophy and theology, or between reason and Revelation . . . Why should not a man feel sure that Averroes cannot be refuted, and yet believe that the most necessary reasons fall short of the infinite wisdom of an all-powerful God? [3]

As Gilson pointed out, this position was not necessarily hypocritical, even though later Averroists finally succumbed to the seductions of necessary reason while continuing to echo hypocritically the teachings of revelation. Dante put Siger of Brabant, an early Averroist, in the Fourth Heaven of the Sun together with Albertus Magnus and Thomas Aquinas, which he would not have done had he entertained the least suspicion about Siger's integrity. But neither was this position of the Averroists logically safe, philosophically sound, or psychologically endurable. Above all, it was not one that was suitable to the requirements of the Egyptian situation which Ṭāha Ḥusayn faced. For it placed no limits whatsoever upon the conclusions that might be drawn from revelation and thereby opened the door to intellectual anarchy. It also imposed on men the very heavy burden of a dualism which was all the more difficult to withstand because of the lack of restraint on nonrational truth. And, if the theory was an accommodation that proved temporarily suitable for the defense and protection of a creed that was still generally viable, as Christian doctrine was in the early thirteenth century, it surely was not one that provided a principle by which a tottering belief-system could be preserved or regenerated. Still, Ṭāha's formula, weak as it was, might have been a tolerable temporary expedient if there had been an accepted authority, such as the head of the ecclesiastical hierarchy in Roman Christianity, who defined the content of faith and emotional truth. But no such authority was recognized in Egypt. The situation envisaged by Ṭāha was one in which every writer was to define for himself what that content was to be beyond the creed of the revelation of the Qur'ān.

Not long after the appearance of his controversial book, Ṭāha Ḥusayn gave substantial evidence that he took his new position seriously and thereby gave a concrete illustration of its perils. In 1934 he published the first book of a three-volume work on Muḥammad, the writing of which extended over a period of eight years. The work is entitled *'Alā Hāmish al-Sīrah* (In the Margin of the Prophet's Tradition) and was admittedly based on belief in the sayings of traditional authorities in all matters referring directly to the Prophet, and on a completely unrestricted weaving of legends around his birth and life.[4] In the introduction to the first volume, he cited his theory of dualism to justify this procedure and used the occasion to speak with contempt of unspecified potential critics who insisted on the position that he had previously held himself. "Those modernists who adulate and trust only reason," he wrote, and who insist that the intellectual leaders should "strive to turn the attention of the people away from the legends and tales and save them from their dangerous corruptive power over the minds" are sadly misinformed. "I wish those people to know," Ṭāha wrote, in refuting their objections,

> "that reason is not everything; and that men have other faculties which need to be fed and satisfied no less than the mind. These legends and tales do not satisfy reason and are not acceptable to logic . . . but the sensibilities, emotions, and imagination of the people and their naiveté . . . make them like and desire these legends and seek in them relief from the burdens of life." [5]

Ṭāha then went on to make a distinction between "one who addresses these legends to the mind, considering them as truths approved by science . . . and one who presents them to the heart, considering them as things which stimulate good inclinations. . ." [6]

The fallacies of the new position are evident from these lines. The reader will have noticed, for example, that Ṭāha Ḥusayn did not really answer the criticism about corrupting the mind with inventions that tend to assume the character of truths. To say that the people liked them because of their naiveté was to beg the question. And to make a distinction as to how these legends were addressed is scarcely relevant, since this distinction is known only to the writer and there is no assurance that his audience will understand it as he does. But even if it did, what was there to prevent other writers from presenting "to the heart" other legends or truths intended to stimulate undesirable inclinations? What grounds did Ṭāha have to defend his own legends or to criticize those of anyone else once he had exempted them from the rational principle of validation? It was perhaps these considerations, as well as a desire to defend the content of the Islamic revelation against attack by outsiders — which Ṭāha's theory had made impossible — that prompted Haykal to seek a different answer to the questions provoked by Ṭāha's book.

In his *Life of Muḥammad* (1935), Haykal tried to go back to Muḥammad 'Abduh's ideas concerning what is to be considered as revelation and the harmony of reason and revelation and tried to prove this harmony concretely. He attempted to prove that the life of the Prophet was perfectly ethical according to modern norms and that the Tradition and the Qur'ān were rational according to the modern scientific method. But he approached his task more in the manner of a defense counsel than of a philosopher, vitiating the rules of right thinking in order to reach preconceived conclusions, and by so doing actually subordinated reason to the teachings of an uncritically accepted belief. In the end, his work only confirmed the approach of traditionalists like Riḍā, who insisted à priori that Islam was superior to anything modern civilization could offer, and thereby weakened one of the foundations on which the intelletcual leaders' endeavor had rested.

In the introduction to his book, Haykal, like 'Abduh and al-'Aqqād, postulated a human craving for an "essential relationship" with the universe, without which happiness could not be attained — a relationship which, he affirmed, could be provided only by religion. Haykal went further than either of his fellow writers, however, and argued in a manner wholly inconsistent with his book that not only is this relationship itself beyond the purview of rational criticism, but that the means by which religion seeks to achieve that end are also beyond the power of science and reason to confirm or deny.[7] He must have sensed, however, that such a thesis would place black magic, for example, on the same level as the teachings of the Qur'ān because, in spite of his own argument, he went on and tried to prove that the fact of revelation, contact with angels, and the whole content of the Qur'ān, including Muḥammad's overnight trip to heaven, was scientifically explainable. The nature of his argument is familiar to the Western reader from similar attempts to interpret some of the informative material and myths of the Bible so as to make them accord with modern scientific views, and is of little interest to us beyond its indication of a commitment to both scripture and science. Much more important was Haykal's attempt to justify and defend as supremely rational and ethical all the acts of Muḥammad and all the controversial prescriptions of the Qur'ān, which have been viewed as divinely ordained norms. Here Haykal was defending Islam as it has always been lived by its adherents, that is to say, Islam as a binding moral authority and view of life. It is from these passages that we must take our examples.

Following the first engagement between Muḥammad and his Meccan opponents at Badr, the Prophet had approved the killing of two prisoners of war. To justify this action, Haykal invoked an argument which was a mixture of the notion that the end justifies the means and of *raison d'état*. Islam, he asserted, was nothing less than a revolution against paganism in the name of the unity of God and the brotherhood of men. If, in order to achieve that aim, it had to resort to unavoidable violence, then such violence was morally justified. Haykal did not actually use the terms "means" and "ends," but made a distinction between the "principles" of a revolution and its "policy":

> But the policy of a revolution is one thing and its principles are another. The policy may differ entirely from the desired principles. For if Islam wanted to proclaim the brotherhood of men on earth as its principle, it still had to follow its own way about (achieving) it even if this necessitated unavoidable violence.[8]

In speaking about Islam as a revolution, Haykal was seeking to establish an analogy with the French Revolution. He assumed that that revolution was ethically acceptable and thought that he needed only show wherein Islam was comparable to it in order to justify the violence that accompanied its rise. The assumption was, of course, gratuitous and the comparison questionable; but even if they were not, Haykal's argument still would not hold because he did not prove that the killing of the two prisoners promoted the cause of Islam or that it was unavoidable.[9]

In another instance, Haykal tried to defend Muḥammad for having "coveted" one of his client's wives. According to the tradition, Muḥammad had seen the woman in her home under tempting conditions and liked her. Upon learning this, his client divorced her and Muḥammad, who already had a number of wives, married her. Haykal justified this act by asserting that great men are not subject to the law.[10] If Moses and Jesus could break the laws of nature, he asked, why could not Muḥammad break a social law? Haykal cited some of the miracles attributed to Jesus and then, significantly, passed to the offensive and attacked Christian spokesmen for preaching belief in those infractions of the laws of nature, and even citing them as evidence of the greatness of Christ, while begrudging Muḥammad a departure from the lesser laws of society. Speaking of the miracle of the Immaculate Conception, he said:

> It is amazing that the Christian missionaries call for belief in this departure from the laws of the universe in the case of Jesus, while they blame Muḥammad for less than that; for something which amounts to no more than rising above submission [*sic*] to the laws of society, [a thing] which is permitted to all great men and which is granted to kings and chiefs of state by the constitutions, which make their person inviolable.[11]

Though the fallacies in Haykal's argument are apparent, it is worth while to point them out in order to show clearly the distortion of the thinking process that is entailed in apologetics. In the two instances just cited, Haykal's main device was to escape from substantial reasoning into formal analogies. He thus reduced Christ's miracles and Muḥammad's actions to infringement of the law and attempted to prove that a miracle is, if anything, more serious. But in so doing he clouded the substantial difference that is implicit in the fact that the essence of the miracle is precisely that it testifies to its divine authorship and that its function is to enhance the mission of the one who performs it; whereas Muḥammad's "breaking of the law" was purely personal in respect to authorship and function. Similarly, when Haykal invoked on behalf of Muḥammad the immunity that is accorded kings and chiefs of state, he confused immunity from criminal prosecution with moral irresponsibility, which no constitution can grant to anyone. Haykal's preoccupation with these devices was apparently so complete that it did not occur to him that if the great were not subject to any law, natural, positive, or moral, than his whole defense of Muḥammad was superfluous.

One more example. When speaking of the early part of Muḥammad's career, when he was still a pursued and persecuted pretender to prophecy, Haykal inveighed eloquently against the Prophet's tormentors. They were attempting to oppress a man who was only seeking "to assure the security and peace of the followers of his message and to gain for them the enjoyment of the freedom of conscience which others enjoyed. . ." he commented, and insisted that "only freedom can guarantee the triumph of truth." Any suppression of freedom is "a consolidation of the false and an advance of the armies of darkness which seek to destroy the ray of light in the human soul. . ." [12] But when he came to speak about the decree that Muḥammad issued, after he achieved predominant power in Arabia, to extirpate by the sword all the unbelievers within that territory, Haykal ceased apparently to be quite so sure that freedom guarantees the triumph of truth, for he endeavored to justify this use of force in violation of freedom. Freedom, he now said, is never an absolute right. The Western nations, for instance, fight and suppress Communism because it is evil; and if this limitation of freedom is justified when applied to people whose only offense is that they hold different economic opinions, how much more is it justified when it is applied against pagans, idolaters, adulterers, and so on, in the name of God's own truth? [13]

It is important to observe and keep in mind the qualities that characterize the kind of reasoning used in the apologetic enterprise of Haykal, for they will be encountered henceforth again and again and we shall have to draw important conclusions from them. The reader will have noticed, perhaps, the discrete quality of his thinking. Each issue was considered in isolation, and the same principles and facts were interpreted differently on different occasions to suit the purpose immediately at hand. Thus, Muḥammad's mission was nothing less than a revolution when it was necessary to justify some degree of violence, but it became a tame pursuit of the dictates of conscience when the measures taken against it by those who deemed themselves endangered by it were in question. Freedom of thought was absolute and indispensable on one occasion and relative on another, depending on who was to be the beneficiary. It will have been observed, too, how arguments were really settled beforehand by begging the question or distorting the descriptions. Thus, to Haykal, the Western nations suppress Communism simply because it is evil, and not because it actually refuses to commit itself to the rules of freedom by declaring its intention to overthrow the government by violent means. Communism is merely an economic doctrine. The victims of Muḥammad's decree are idolaters and adulterers; Muḥammad's message is God's own truth. Now it may be true, as Haykal said, that Muḥammad bore the word of God and that his opponents were in the clutches of the devil; but then, it may be asked, what do freedom of conscience and freedom of opinion have to do with the struggle between the forces of light and darkness?

Haykal's enterprise not only aimed at giving "scientific" explanations to some of the "supernatural" phenomena of revelation and at justifying the Prophet and his career for the benefit of those of his people who were waking up to new values and to rational ways of viewing the world, but was also intended to defend Muḥammad and Islam against foreign criticism. Understandably, this defense took the form of rebutting the charges of interested and prejudiced missionaries and then counterattacking, as we have seen in one of the illustrative passages quoted earlier. But Haykal went further than that and, taking a leaf from al-Afghānī's book, accused the Christian West in general of unrelenting hostility to Islam:

> Ever since (the first encounter between Muslims and Greeks) Muslims and Christians have faced each other in a position of political hostility in which history favored the Muslims for many centuries . . . until the time came for the wheels of history to turn. Then, the Christians expelled the Muslims from Andalusia, launched the Crusades against them, and began to attack and defame their Prophet in the ugliest manner. . . .[14]

Elsewhere in the book, Haykal insisted that "even though the Crusades have ended . . . the fanaticism of the Church against Muḥammad has remained most powerful to the present day . . . Many philosophers and writers in Europe and in America, although unconnected with the Church, have also taken up on their own account the fanaticism against Muḥammad." [15]

More important than these general attacks against the West, Haykal's defense of the Prophet and his exaltation of his message led him to denigrate and belittle, by way of contrast, the most important contributions that Western culture had to offer. Thus, in the introduction to his book, Haykal explained that science and rationalism, the hallmarks of Western culture, had failed to make mankind happy and had led Europe to an impasse from which it was desperately trying to escape by looking toward the spirituality of the East.[16] To Europe and to mankind Haykal offered Islam as the most suitable answer to their plight.

Later in the book, Haykal criticized severely Western ethics, which he identified with unsatisfying utilitarianism and the pursuit of material values, and contrasted them with the ethics of Islam which, he explained, consisted of spirit enlightening morality, which in turn enlightens action and utility.[17]

These attacks against Western culture were of crucial significance to the course of modern Egyptian thought and contributed to the initiation of an era of great intellectual confusion. The whole intellectual activity of the first phase, which offered promising prospects of an eventual communal ideology based on a Liberal Nationalist humanistic outlook, had been founded on two guiding principles. One was a strong tendency to refer to reason as the commonly accepted validating authority, and the other was a consensus among the intellectuals in favor of a comprehensive orientation toward Western culture. We have seen that Ṭāha Ḥusayn had already undermined the first principle by granting to unverified intuition equal validity with reason. With Haykal, now, the attempt to reconcile reason and revelation ended up as an apology for Islam which not only damaged the integrity of reason, but also weakened the second guiding principle by its denigration of Western culture, and thus denied subsequent intellectual activity any common center of gravity.

Haykal's retreat was made explicit and final in a subsequent work and in his whole intellectual endeavor until shortly after the revolution of 1952. In his *Fī Manzal al-Waḥy* (In the Birthplace of Revelation), published a year or two after his *Life of Muḥammad*, Haykal referred in the introduction to accusations leveled against him by some of his colleagues that ever since his book on the Prophet he had turned into a reactionary, after having stood in the forefront of the reformers. Responding to this criticism, he wrote that in so far as his colleagues meant that he had abandoned the comprehensive Western orientation and turned to Islam for inspiration, he pleaded guilty and was proud to do so. Haykal made a theoretical distinction between the "spiritual life" of the West, which he rejected, and its "rational life," which he still thought should be emulated. But in practice — that is to say, in the light of what he concretely rejected and accepted — this distinction seems to have been of little or no significance. It was probably intended to put his own reversal of opinion in a good light and to cast aspersions on those of his colleagues who continued to adhere to the Western orientation:

> It appeared to me at one time, as it still appears to my colleagues, that emulating the rational and the spiritual life of the West was our path for resurgence. I still agree with my colleagues that we still need to emulate as much as possible the rational life of the West; but I have come to disagree with them about the spiritual life and have come to see that what there is of it in the West is not good to emulate. For our spiritual history is different from the history of the West and our spiritual culture is different from its culture. The West has submitted from the outset to ecclesiastical thought as approved by the Christian papacy; while the East has been innocent of such thought. Nay, those (sectarian) creeds that attempted to establish in the Muslim world an ecclesiastical order were bitterly fought and therefore never gained a footing in it. . .[18]

One would think from these remarks that Westernizers — or he himself, before he had changed his views — had wanted to emulate Western ecclesiastical thought or import an ecclesiastical organization into Islam, and that this was the "spiritual life" he now rejected. This may have been the impression that Haykal wanted to convey, or perhaps his remarks had a meaning which he failed to communicate. At any rate, what he wanted to reject included everything that he had previously pleaded for, except Western science and industry, and what he wanted to promote was an Islamic orientation as he understood it:

"I had tried to bring over to those who share my language the culture and spiritual life of the West so that we might use them as models and guides. But after all the toil, I realized that I had planted my seeds . . . where the earth swallowed them but breathed no life into them. So I turned to our remote history, to pharaonic times, seeking inspiration to bring new life to this age. But I found that time and mental inertia had severed the bonds between us and that age . . . I then pondered and saw that our Islamic history is the only seed that grows and fructifies; for in it there is life which moves souls and stirs and activates them. . .

The Islamic idea differs from the idea that our world proclaims at present, which is one that sanctifies nationalities, views them as mutually competing units and causes destruction among them. We people of the East have been influenced by this nationalist idea and we have attempted to breathe a life-force into it in the belief that with it we could face that West which oppressed and humiliated us . . . The glitter of Western civilization has caused us to forget the deadly germs that this nationalist idea carries for any civilization that rests on it exclusively . . . But the proclamation of the divine unity which lit the souls of our ancestors has given us in inheritance from Allah's bounty a wholesome instinct which has led us to realize the danger in that which the West proclaims: that a nation whose present is not connected with its past is bound to lose its way . . . Hence, the chasm which had kept widening between the masses of the peoples of the East and those calling for ignoring our past and turning with all our might in the Western direction; and hence the revulsion of the masses at adopting the ideological life of the West while yet insisting on emulating its science and industry. But since ideological life is the foundation of existence both for individuals and for peoples, there was no escape from going back to our history in search of foundations for our ideological life so that we may emerge from our humiliating stagnation. . . .[19]

While Haykal and others who were beginning to follow him were turning their backs on Western culture and looking for ideological foundations in Islam by processes similar to those used by Haykal in his *Life of Muḥammad*, Ṭāha Ḥusayn, in 1938, published a book entitled *Mustaqbal al-Thaqāfah fī Miṣr* (The Future of Culture in Egypt) which was intended to stop what he considered to be a drift into intellectual chaos, and in which he pleaded once again the case for an unequivocal Western orientation. The contrast between its substance and purpose and the views of Haykal just quoted could hardly be more drastic. It reflected the deep division which had overtaken the endeavor of the intellectual leaders, and caused the prospects of achieving a consensus on a basic belief-system to recede indefinitely.

The book was composed of two parts, one theoretical and one practical. The latter, making up the bulk of the book, was essentially a blueprint for a reformed national educational program which recommended the unification and coordination of the school system, the reorganization of the curriculum, and the establishment of universal public education. The model that Ṭāha had in mind was the French system with its extreme centralization and total control by the state. One of the main targets of the reform was the system of religious schools which was controlled and led by al-Azhar and which continually replenished the cadres of the forces of conservatism. All these details, however are far less important for us than the fundamental orientation which Ṭāha urged both for the educational system and for all forms of intellectual activity in the country. This orientation was to be unconditionally Western, for reasons which he developed at length.

We have already had occasion to refer to one argument used by Ṭāha to support this position: He maintained that Egypt had a "cultural personality" consisting of a pharaonic core that had undergone the same Greek, Roman, and religious influences that had shaped the "Western mind." This, according to Ṭāha, placed Egypt definitely in the camp of Western culture and not in that of the irreconcilable rival which shared the world with it: the oriental culture of the Far East.[20] Other arguments Ṭāha drew from the course that Egyptian culture had followed since the nineteenth century. That course, he asserted, "although . . . still unclear in some respects, has an unmistakable modern orientation." Thus in technology, fashions, and manners Egypt had adopted "without discrimination and without distinction" everything European. "So far has the European ideal become our ideal that we now measure the material progress of all individuals and groups by the amount of borrowing from Europe." The absolutist government of Muḥammad 'Alī and the limited government of the khedives were based on European models. "They sought no guidance from the procedures of medieval Muslim kings and caliphs." The judicial, fiscal, and economic systems, and the administrative and ruling agencies adopted by them, were wholly European. "Until the modern era, Muslims had never heard of them," he wrote. The modern constitutional system was also adopted from Europe and became "an inseparable part of our being." The educational system "is also based on exclusively European methods." Even those few old Islamic institutions which survived because of their "more or less close association with religion" changed greatly under European influence. Such institutions as the Sharʿī courts or the *waqfs* would not be recognized by a *qāḍī* or an Azhar student from the previous century. All this, Ṭāha concluded, shows that "the dominant and undeniable fact of our times is that day by day we are drawing closer to Europe and becoming an integral part of it, literally and figuratively. This process would have been much more difficult than it has been if the Egyptian mind were basically different from the European." [21]

Given the basic concordance of the Egyptian mind with the European, and since Egypt has in fact been following European ideals and models which it is impossible to discard, Ṭāha Ḥusayn urged that these realities should be recognized and that the last, lingering resistance to a conscious and complete integration in Western culture should be overcome. Only thus can Egypt break out of the tension and the cultural crisis in which she finds herself, and get on the highway of progress which civilization has reached at the cost of centuries of labor:

> Let us admit the truth and banish hypocrisy: Only by eagerly welcoming the modern civilization can we have true peace of mind and a wholesome attitude towards the realities of life . . .
>
> This talk of a spiritual East is sheer nonsense. Egyptians who deride European civilization and praise the spirituality of the East are joking, and they know it. They would be the last to want to live like the Chinese or Hindus. Nevertheless, their arguments are dangerous and demoralizing, particularly to the youth. . . . My plea . . . is for nothing new. I simply want the apprehensive to be reassured and to accept, willingly rather than grudgingly, the inevitable. Stories about the East and West are told only by men with a superficial understanding of both. The younger generation must be protected from such false knowledge, and the best, if not the only, method is to provide it with sound education.[22]

Ṭāha conceded that there was a great deal of materialism in European civilization, but it would be absurd to deny that it also possessed great spiritual content. From men like Descartes and Pasteur, who devoted their entire lives to the exclusive pursuit of ideas, to the contemporary test pilots who risked horrible death in order to extend man's mastery over nature, there was a great imaginative and creative spirit at work.[23] Besides, he argued, the Near East had been the cradle of all the divine religions, those adopted by Europeans as well as those followed by the Near-Easterners. "Can these religions be spirit in the East and matter in the West?"

The sharpness and urgency of Ṭāha Ḥusayn's tone reflected his apprehensions about the strong reservations toward Western culture that were spreading in intellectual circles. Ṭāha referred to this phenomenon when he said:

Incidentally, I should like to refer to the irony that while al-Azhar . . . has been frantically rushing towards this civilization (the European), the Egyptian University . . . is inclining in the opposite direction, arguing that Egypt should progress at a measured pace, with forethought and deliberation. . . .[24]

Against that argument Ṭāha urged a course of outright, almost indiscriminate, assimilation in Western civilization:

In order to become equal partners in civilization with the Europeans, we must literally and forthrightly do everything that they do; we must share with them the present civilization with all its pleasant and unpleasant sides, and not content ourselves with words and mere gestures. Whoever advises another course is a deceiver or is himself deceived. . . .[25]

Some might have fears that Egypt would lose her national identity by Europeanizing. These fears, he said, were unfounded because "the controlling factors in Egypt's destiny are its geographical situation, religion, artistic heritage, unbroken history, and the Arabic language"; and these were all the more potent because they were now supported by a national and cultural consciousness:

The only time we might have been absorbed by Europe was when we were extremely weak, ignorant, and possessed of the notion that the hat was superior to the turban and the fez because it covered a more distinguished head! However, such fears are baseless now that we know our history and are aware of the essential similarities between ourselves and the Europeans.[26]

As for fears about damage being done to religion, Ṭāha argued that "our religion . . . will be best maintained by doing as our ancestors did and keeping it responsive to contemporary needs . . ." [27] Islam is "an evolutionary religion that is constantly striving to attain the ideal in both spiritual and material life. Its defenders and propagators must be equally flexible and idealistic." [28]

Europe today resembles the Umayyad and 'Abbāsid Near East in the richness of its civilization, which, like any human creation, possesses good and bad aspects. Our religion will not suffer from contact with European civilization any more than it suffered when it took over the Persian and Byzantine civilizations. In practice we are confronted with the choice of either repudiating our ancestors . . . or emulating their attitude towards Byzantium and Persia by adopting in full measure the motive-force of Europe. We have, in fact, been doing just this. . . . A reversal of this process would mean our end.[29]

Ṭāha's argument followed throughout the direction evident in the last two paragraphs. It combined a theoretical justification with arguments from actual practice and a warning against stopping in mid-course or attempting to go back: "The world has struggled for hundreds of years to attain the present stage of progress; it is within our power to reach it within a short time. Woe to us if we do not seize the opportunity." [30]

Ṭāha's book has been considered by some observers to represent the acme of Western cultural orientation in Egypt, when in fact it reflected only the deep crisis which that orientation — and, with it, the intellectual development of modern Egyptian thought — had reached.[31] Fifteen years before the publication of his book, Ṭāha's views had been essentially those of most of the intellectual leaders; whereas now the book itself and the whole tone of its argument betrayed the fact that its author had suddenly found himself rowing upstream.

To summarize and conclude this chapter, let us recall that the problem confronting Egyptian society was the need to develop a subjective, humanly oriented system of ideas, values, and norms that would serve as a foundation for a political community under new conditions of life, to replace the traditional system based on objective divine revelation. In such an endeavor the leaders had eventually to come to grips with the problem of the possibility of conflict between reason, as the main subjective principle of validation, and the content of divine revelation. 'Abduh had made a real contribution toward meeting the problem by narrowing down the scope of what was to be viewed as revelation, thereby reducing the area in which it might clash with reason. But the problem remained unresolved, at least as far as the Qur'ān was concerned, since the traditional view of its content as objective divine truth was unaffected by 'Abduh's modifications. And as long as this source of conflict remained, the ideological readjustment could never be complete and permanent.

During what we have termed the progressive phase of their endeavor, the intellectual leaders had tended to ignore this remaining problem since it had not as yet intruded upon their work. They did propound views that dissented by implication from the traditional view of the Qur'ān but they apparently were not aware that here a problem of grave importance was involved which required careful, even meticulous attention. This impression is reinforced by the fact that when Ṭāha Ḥusayn finally dealt with the issue directly, he did so in a way that showed more concern for the specific controversial conclusions his suggested method might entail than for the revolutionary character of the method itself, and with a bravado that was entirely inappropriate in the circumstance. This lack of awareness of the crucial importance of the problem of the Qur'ān to the issue of a fundamental intellectual reorientation was probably the reason why the response of the intellectual leaders to the crisis, when it finally broke out, was so woefully inadequate.

Having failed to see the problem in its broad ideological-cultural context, Ṭāha Ḥusayn responded to the crisis he had provoked by devising an individualistic solution which perhaps enabled him to set his own as well as his judges' mind at rest, but which destroyed the chief basis of the common ideological endeavor of the Liberal leaders. Having himself opened the gates of "emotional truth" unchecked by reason, and having himself plunged through them, he could not very well blame others for indulging in the same practice while going in different directions. That he published his *Future of Culture*, with its denunciation of the advocates of the "spiritual" vocation of Egypt, at the same time that he was issuing another volume of his *'Alā Hāmish al-Sīrah*, with its "truths addressed to the heart," only serves to point out how rare a virtue consistency had become.

As for Haykal, after having bravely chosen the harder task of attempting to interpret elements of the Qur'ān and the Tradition of the Prophet in the light of reason, he faltered in the execution and inevitably ended up by twisting reason and thinking to accommodate that which he had accepted on faith from the outset. And while he was defending the Prophet's Tradition and career in terms of the scientific principles, rational norms, and ethical values that he associated with Western culture, he was attacking and denigrating that culture in the name of Islamic "spirituality." This paradox, too, was a measure of the intellectual dislocation that overtook the Liberal leaders' work as a result of their failure to recognize the cultural implications of the problem of the Qur'ān, and for having failed to meet it adequately.

CHAPTER 12

The Historical Crisis of Liberal Nationalism

By the time Ṭāha Ḥusayn published his *Future of Culture*, the intellectual crisis which had begun on the level of the unsolved problem of the Qur'ān had already combined with strains in the actual social and political life of Egypt to produce the beginning of a general ideological-political crisis.

The faith in rationalism, Western values, and Liberalism which had characterized the progressive phase had been largely inspired by such factors as the tradition of orderly development under the British, the exhilarating idealism and expectations of national renovation stirred by the nationalist revolution, and faith in a Liberalism which was triumphant in the West. More concrete sources for this optimism were the example of the national transformation of Turkey and the unprecedented prosperity resulting from record-high cotton prices in the 1920's.

After that time, social developments in Egypt seemed to undermine the faith of the intellectual leaders in the adequacy of reason as a source, and of individual conscience and social responsibility as sanction, for ethical principles and behavior. Failures in the operation of Egypt's constitutional system and the clashes of ideology in the West raised doubts about the real value of the whole liberal democratic system. Moreover, an economic crisis, intensified by the strains and dislocations caused by the Second World War and its aftermath, shook the foundations of the entire political-social system and gave birth to powerful forces bent on its destruction.

All these developments tended to work in favor of the reorientation toward Islam advocated by Haykal and urged by the school of Rashīd Riḍā. Why this reorientation signified a crisis we shall see when we examine the nature of the Islam to which it turned. Before doing so, let us analyze briefly the developments that stimulated it.

The Strains of Social Restructuring and the Undermining of Social Controls

In the thirty years between the declaration of independence (1922) and the end of the period under study, Egyptian society went through an intensive process of social restructuring, accompanied by strains that endangered the whole social order and greatly aggravated the problem of evolving a basic ideological consensus. These strains were all the more severe because they proceeded not only from normal economic development, which was rather slow, but were to an even greater extent the by-product of extremely rapid population growth.

Between 1917 and 1947, the total population of Egypt increased by nearly 67 per cent; while the available crop area increased by only 20 per cent during approximately the same period.[1] The resulting pressure on the land caused a great acceleration of the movement from country to city. The number of inhabitants in Cairo increased from 791,000 in 1917 to 1,312,000 in 1937, and 2,091,000 in 1947; in Alexandria, from 445,000 to 686,000 to 919,000 in the same period.[2] By 1947, 19 per cent of the population lived in seven cities of 100,000 or more inhabitants each, and an additional 3.5 per cent lived in cities of between 50,000 and 100,000 inhabitants. In the decade 1937–1947, the rural population grew by 11 per cent, while the urban grew by 44 per cent.[3]

The doubling of the population of a city like Cairo in twenty years could not fail to have grave economic, social, and political consequences. The influx of cheap labor from the country kept down employment, wages, and living standards among the unskilled masses of the working people. It involved the uprooting, socially and psychologically, of large sections of the population from the controls of the still closely knit village society, and their inevitable drifting into the appallingly crowded city quarters,[4] where the collectivity that once existed had completely broken down and the social guidance that it provided had vanished.[5] In the absence of group life and moral and social restraints, the pursuit of the pleasures and attractions of the city and of the means to acquire them largely occupied the place of values, and the frustration met in their pursuit became the source of dangerous resentment. Idleness, precarious livelihood, rootlessness, crowding, desires in excess of reach, inadequate restraints — all contributed, in turn, to turning these people into responsive and easily accessible material for the political agitator and the social troublemaker, who were not lacking throughout this period.

A relatively small proportion of the new urban population was absorbed in newly established large-scale modern industry. Industrial enterprise had developed at a slow but steady rate since the tariff reforms of 1930. Capital invested in *industrial* joint stock companies grew from L.E. 16,300,000 (about $80 million) in 1938 to L.E. 56,000,000 (about $220 million) in 1950.[6] In 1947, there were 519 plants employing from 50 to 500 workers, making a grand total of 76,000 workers; and 64 plants employing over 500 workers each, adding up to 137,000 workers.[7] Of the total number of industrial workers, 24 per cent was concentrated in Cairo and Alexandria. This development, while not enough to provide an effective remedy to the problem of the excess population flowing into the cities, was sufficient to give birth to a new class of industrial proletariat having little or no connection with traditional society, and presenting difficult problems of its own. While fully exposed to the environment and discipline of modern life, its members yet lacked the education and experience to evolve or assimilate an intellectual and moral outlook capable of coping with them. Insecure in their livelihood, due to the vagaries of employment and the fluctuations of the real value of wages, and unable to protect themselves against large reserves of unemployed, they were easily susceptible to the appeals of the demagogue or the religious fundamentalist and ready to resort to violence. People in their condition represent an element difficult to assimilate in any political community; where the community itself was as shaky and uncertain as the Egyptian, they were even more disruptive.

The development of industry, together with the development of commerce and finance, gave rise to yet another new social group with its own special problems: an indigenous bourgeoisie in the real sense of the term. Until 1930, most of Egyptian industry had been owned by foreigners. After that time, most of the newly founded plants were owned by Egyptians, and by 1950 Egyptians owned most of the total industry.[8] Similarly, in commerce and finance, foreigners had led the way ever since the days of Muḥammad ʿAlī and Ismāʿīl in establishing modern shops and business houses which engaged in large-scale import-export and finance operations and catered to their own needs and to the demands of the Egyptian high-income groups. The growth of the cities, the spread of education, and the expansion of an indigenous clientele for modern goods encouraged Egyptians to follow suit. To be able to compete with the foreigners, Egyptian industrialists, merchants, and financiers had to abandon the traditional economic ethics with its notion of prohibited profits, such as those derived from interest or the sale of alcohol, its trust in a providence that preallocates *arzāq* (earnings), and the concomitant traditional customs — lack of initiative, unmindfulness of time, and confusion of capital with profits. They adopted instead their competitors' methods of accounting, rational organization, prospecting, advertising, and aggressive marketing, as well as their concept of interest as a central economic factor. But while the Egyptian bourgeoisie tended to separate business from religious ethics, they had no effective alternative rationale to sustain their activity, to give it moral worth, or to impose restraint in its pursuit. Such doctrines as the Protestant concept of vocation, or any of the numerous theories exalting the social role or the superior moral qualities of the entrepreneur and the business pioneer, which may have had some steadying influence on the bourgeoisie in the West, either could not or had not yet gained currency among them. Notions about the significance of their work from a nationalist point of view were still rudimentary and, in any event, could easily be given an exclusively negative interpretation to justify discrimination against the foreign competitor and recourse to unfair practices. The result was a tendency to view business as an occupation the sole purpose of which was the accumulation of wealth and in which anything was permissible. This tendency manifested itself in a particularly brutal fashion during World War II and in the years following it, when shortages and regulation of the economy by corruptible officials multiplied the opportunities for quick profit, and aroused the resentment and anger of the public. It was, in fact, the extension of ruthless business practice to the field of military supply during the Palestine war that ostensibly aroused the young officers and prompted them to bring down the whole system that permitted it.

Economic development, the expansion of the functions of government, the spread of education and the increased social mobility that resulted, led to an enormous expansion of the white collar, professional, and student groups. Together with the upper classes, they were all inclined to adopt without much discrimination many of the external aspects of Western civilization they observed in the cinema, in magazines and in the example set by the 250,000 foreigners who lived in their midst. Some of the habits they adopted — such as that of cleanliness — were beneficial; others, such as dress, fashions, home furnishings, certain styles of conversation, and social manners, were fairly innocuous. Much else, whether beneficial or harmful, touched upon some very important issues of social life such as sex, marriage, and family. Thus, relations between the sexes were substantially liberalized as women unveiled, mixed increasingly with men in the schools, in the street, and even on the beaches. Marriages were no longer prearranged exclusively by intermediaries, and young people insisted on knowing and choosing their partners. The traditional household composed of the agnatic family increasingly gave way to one formed by husband, wife, and children.[9] But all facets of Westernization had the crucial effect of creating a break between generations. Since change was the sign of the times, the younger generation viewed itself as up-to-date and its elders as backward. On the moral level, this cleavage between generations had the effect of weakening the authority of the parents, thereby undermining one of the most important social controls. On the political level, it tended to foster among the young an attitude of suspicion and impatience with the older political leaders and their methods, and a receptivity to simplified radical doctrines and violent measures. "I lived in times whose watchword was obedience. . ," wrote Aḥmad Amīn, addressing himself to the newer generations, "you live in times that have adopted rebellion as the watchword: rebellion against your parents, rebellion against your teachers, and rebellion against the authorities in charge of you in general. . ." [10]

Thus, among nearly all the major groups comprising the urban population, the general economic and social developments and the pressure of the population had the effect of weakening the main instruments of social control and of creating explosive social and political potentialities. Both of these effects were much aggravated by the circumstances of World War II and its aftermath.

The Second World War was bound to have a ravaging impact upon a society in which the controls of religion, social group, family, and parents were precarious. The millions of foreign troops that passed through the major cities of Egypt helped bring about a complete erosion of public morality. The mass of well-paid, easy-spending, pleasure-seeking soldiers, themselves torn from their social roots and controls, spread a mood of "eat and drink for tomorrow we die," which the populations of Egyptian cities were ill-prepared to resist. And while all those who could took full advantage of the opportunities for profit and pleasure, with little scruple, the general effect of this situation was extremely provoking to Egyptians. The sight of well-fed alien troops in the midst of widespread want and deprivation aroused the envy of the people, and their indulgence in the pursuit of sex and drink hurt the moral sensibilities of most Egyptians, inclined as they were to equate morality with sexual taboos. Moreover, the generally arrogant behavior of the troops stirred the nationalist and xenophobic feelings of the masses.

Other circumstances of the war had similarly damaging effects on public morality, and further intensified the growing tensions. Shortages, inflation, ineptly and corruptly administered rationing and economic controls, opened up vast opportunities for quick-profit through black-marketing, speculating, profiteering, jobbery, and all manner of devious dealing, which were exploited by all segments of the population. From the illiterate, veiled and cloaked slum-dwelling women who traded in food and clothing rations, through the petty shopkeepers, the newly risen small "businessmen," the big merchants and contractors, to minor and high government officials, the slogan seemed to be "grab what you can and don't be a fool." Society seemed to be engaged in a Darwinian struggle in which success went to those who were most cunning and ruthless. But since the whole struggle had started in the first place because supply was shorter than demand, its end result could only be to enrich a few at the cost of worsening the initially bad lot of the many. It was not as if a gold rush had undermined public morality. As far as the large masses of the people were concerned, the spirit of restraint was traded for an uncertain mess of lentils.

The process of social restructuring and the tensions it involved were reflected in cities whose appearance and character had been radically transformed. As any visitor could immediately see, the development of Egyptian cities was such that each grew to include two sections so different from one another as to constitute, in fact, two cities inhabited by two nations living uneasily side by side. The ancient town, with its old mosques, its bazaars, its walled quarters, its crumbling houses and shacks, its open gutters and filth, its narrow, teeming streets, its misery and disease, was abandoned to the poorer masses of humanity which were continually pressing on each other under the impact of the influx from the countryside and the increase in births which outpaced the ravages of disease. Here, the traditional corporate and communal organizations had broken down under the weight of crowding and the impact of economic laws. This breakdown and the lures of urban pleasures that could be had occasionally loosened the hold of religion on the conscience of these slum dwellers and set them adrift, even though their *general* attachment to Islam and its symbols and to the superstitions and practices that grew around them did not weaken.

Alongside the ancient town, and around it, there grew a modern city with its suburbs, spacious apartments, avenues, and parks, modern means of transportation and communication, department stores and skyscrapers, its modern hotels, cafes, bars, theaters, cinemas, its various clubs, its racetracks, its red-light districts, and all the contraptions of twentieth century urban civilization. It was in this milieu, in the anonymity of the big city, that, side by side with the foreigners, the young generations of Egyptians from the upper and middle classes grew up, in an environment in which the control of religion had weakened and that of family and parents had been undermined and in which they had only their own experience to guide them.

The juxtaposition of the two cities and the appalling contrast between them accelerated the development of specific class feelings among some of the inhabitants of the ancient town and stirred up in most of them a deep envy and resentment of the new city and its privileged dwellers. This resentment found expression in a massive lower-class movement which, by a process whose secrets Nietzsche had first unravelled, proclaimed a moral revolt against the pleasures and amenities supplied by the new city that were beyond the reach of the poor. It also expressed itself in eruptions of violence against the institutions that provided these pleasures and amenities and against the foreigners who were considered their main beneficiaries. The climax of these eruptions was reached in Cairo on Black Saturday (January 1952) when seven hundred hotels, bars, restaurants, cinemas, cabarets, department stores, fancy shops, auto show-rooms, banks, and modern commercial offices were systematically looted, destroyed, and burned within a few hours.

The Political and Social Failure of the Liberal Democratic Regime

At the time of the declaration of independence, the prestige of constitutional democratic government was so high that even leaders of religious opinion, conservative as well as traditionalist, were straining their minds to find in the Islamic heritage previsions of and justifications for such a form of government. This prestige was not so much due to a soundly founded conviction about the merits of the principles of democracy as it was the consequence of the association of the democratic form of government with the success and power of the European nations. The introduction of such a government was expected, in some mysterious way, to bring about equally felicitous results. Consequently, the fate of the regime inaugurated by the Constitution of 1923 was from the outset principally dependent upon the measure of practical success it could achieve in dealing with what important groups of Egyptians viewed as their most pressing problems. To all Egyptians, the national issue of achieving full independence was one such problem. Solving the problem of earning a livelihood, especially in times of crisis, was a question of utmost importance to the lower classes. Regulating satisfactorily the distribution and control of political power was a problem of primary interest to the upper classes and the politically conscious elements of the population. The religious issue was another question of general concern, but this we have already dealt with and will return to later.

Judged by its performance with respect to the three issues of complete independence, regulation of government changeover, and the social-economic problem, the record of the regime that began in 1923 and ended in 1952 proved to be an abysmal failure. By the time it reached the halfway mark in its career, it had been completely discredited on all three scores and attention had begun to turn to alternative forms of government. If the regime was still able to remain in precarious existence for another fifteen years, it was only because fortuitous circumstances helped it to do so and because the forces that could overthrow it had not yet fully matured. The process of its decline will be the subject of a brief analysis in the next few pages. For purposes of presentation, the political and the social criteria will be examined separately. But, of course, these and other issues were not separated in the minds of the people when forming their overall impression of the regime.

It will be recalled that constitutional life came to Egypt after the dissident aristocratic leaders — fearful of the social consequences of Zaghlūl's agitation and jealous of his rising power — had arranged a compromise with Britain that resulted in the declaration of limited independence. The aristocrats, who assumed the name of Liberal Constitutionalists after fathering the new constitution, expected the declaration of independence to take the wind out of Zaghlūl's sails and to restore power to their own hands. But the first general elections held in Egypt under the terms of the Constitution dealt them a shocking blow. Not only did Zaghlūl's party, now named the Wafd, win nearly all the parliamentary seats, but nondescript Wafdist candidates triumphed over the best-known figures from the ranks of the aristocrats. Former ministers and men who had wielded great power and prestige in the previous regime by virtue of birth, wealth, and education were defeated by semi-illiterate village heads, by humble *shaykhs*, school teachers, and budding lawyers. To the aristocrats the election returns seemed to suggest that the social revolution they had tried to avoid had come about as a result of their own actions. The conclusion seemed obvious, at any rate, that if governments were to be formed only by means of legal and fair elections, their chances of ever holding power for any length of time were virtually nil. The only escape from this predicament lay in devious alternatives.

One of these alternatives was the king, who had his own reasons to resent Zaghlūl and the Wafd's pretensions to supreme power. Under the Constitution, the king had the right to dissolve Parliament, dismiss the government, and appoint an interim ministry pending the holding of new elections. The interim period was too short to satisfy the ambitions of any politician, but it was crucial in that it permitted the incumbent government to run the elections while having at its disposal the means of pressure and influence available to the state. Another alternative was an appeal to the British, who, under the declaration of independence, had reserved to themselves the right to exercise absolute authority on certain issues pending the negotiation of a treaty concerning them. The British were already beginning to realize that only an agreement signed by the Wafd had a chance of becoming effective and, therefore, preferred to negotiate with that party. But since the Wafd remained uncompromising in its terms, the British were certainly not disposed to let it stay in power for long. For one thing, it was clear that they could not permit a party that was agitating against them to retain control of the police power. In addition, depriving the Wafd of power seemed an obvious means of compelling it to moderate its terms and to divert its fire from the British to its own internal opponents. To these alternatives the Liberal Constitutionalists began to turn as a result of the shock of the first elections. Their expectations did not take long to materialize.

In 1924, a little over a year after the formation of Zaghlūl's first government, the British compelled it to resign in the midst of a crisis caused by the assassination of the British commander of the Egyptian army. The king then entrusted the government to some of his men, headed by Ziwar pasha, to whom the Liberal Constitutionalists gave their support. This government exhausted every means of staying in power without parliamentary backing before calling for new elections. When the elections were held, the government and the Liberal Constitutionalists used every possible means to fix them, and managed to gain a formal majority of the deputies. But when Parliament assembled for the inaugural session, some of the deputies on whom the government had counted bolted to the Wafd, which thereby regained a majority. This time, the government, in which the Liberal Constitutionalists participated, reacted by having the king dismiss Parliament the same day and attempted to rule by decree, in flagrant violation of the Constitution. The Liberal Constitutionalists, who had been the fathers and self-appointed guardians of the Constitution, justified their action to themselves by saying: "We have suffered the greatest injustice and oppression under the Wafd's government. . . The tyranny of Parliament during the rule of Sa'd (Zaghlul) has rendered parliamentary life futile. . ." [11]

From that time on, Egyptian politics followed a regular pattern. Every half-free election was won by the Wafd, following which it was either compelled by a conflict with the British to resign or was dismissed by the king. Each new government suspended the Constitution, modified it, abrogated it, falsified elections, or ruled dictatorially until a quarrel with the king or a British decision to test the Wafd again caused new elections to be held, whereupon, the Wafd returned to power, and the cycle was repeated. Thus, in 1926, after another Wafdist victory, the British prevented the Wafd from ruling alone and compelled it to enter a coalition headed by a non-Wafdist. When that government fell, al-Naḥḥās pasha, who had succeeded the recently deceased Zaghlūl to the leadership of the party, formed a purely Wafdist government which was dismissed by the king after a few months in office. The king then allowed the new government, led by the Liberal Constitutionalists, to suspend the Constitution for two years and rule dictatorially. In 1930, after another initiative from Britain, the Wafd won the elections and returned to power only to be dismissed once more a few months later. This time the king entrusted the government to Ismā'īl Ṣidqī pasha, who made the most determined and most nearly successful attempt to crush the Wafd once and for all. He abrogated the Constitution of 1923 and replaced it with another which gave the king vastly expanded powers, drastically revised the electoral system, and brought the act of voting under strict control. He founded a new party, *Ḥizb al-Sha'b* (the People's Party), which naturally won the elections and gave his government a semblance of legitimacy. The principles underlying the new constitution were subsequently explained by Ṣidqī in his memoirs. They were founded upon an open repudiation of democratic doctrine in the name of ideas highly reminiscent of the doctrines of French politicians from the Restoration period, such as Royer-Collard and Guizot: "The truth is that voting is a function, not a right to which everybody is entitled. Consequently, the elector must have the necessary qualifications for making a good choice." [12] But even this new theory was given a twist which betrayed Ṣidqī's motives and intentions. Thus he maintained that a voter is disqualified from being able to make a good choice if he is "under the impact of an overwhelming personality, such as Zaghlūl's." [13]

Each time the Wafd was denied the fruits of its electoral victories, it reacted by boycotting the elections held by its opponents, sabotaging the results of any treaty negotiations, and agitating and fighting against the government, but it was forced to refrain from resorting to the ultimate means of revolution by fear of British intervention. In each case the Wafd succeeded in either bringing back into operation or restoring the Constitution of 1923. But by the time it brought about its restoration after Ṣidqī's challenge, the party had been out of office for seven years in succession, except for a very brief spell, its treasury had been exhausted, its ranks depleted, and its confidence in popular agitation badly shaken. This ordeal finally induced the Wafd to play the British game. To secure its future, it was now ready to reach a compromise agreement with Britain in order to have its hands free to deal with the king and its internal opponents without fear of outside intervention. This new disposition was encouraged by the aggravation of international tension which led the British to seek a settlement in earnest, and resulted in the Anglo-Egyptian Treaty of 1936. The treaty undoubtedly enlarged the sphere of Egyptian independence, but it still fell far short of the full nationalist demands. It did not, for instance, bring the Sudan under Egyptian sovereignty, and it recognized Britain's right to station troops in the Suez Canal zone for the next twenty years. More important, it made the evacuation of British troops from Egyptian towns contingent upon the Egyptian government's building of roads and installations for the benefit of British forces. And since this condition was not met in the years before the outbreak of World War II, the British remained in occupation everywhere, including Cairo, until 1946–1947 as a living denial of full Egyptian independence. It is no wonder, therefore, that soon after its conclusion, the 1936 Treaty came to be considered the symbol of the Wafd's betrayal of its custody over nationalist aspirations. As early as 1937, al-ʿAqqād, himself a Wafdist, bemoaned his party's betrayal of its trust, in a biographical study of Saʿd Zaghlūl, and attributed that betrayal to the lust for power, which, in his opinion, had caused the extremists of the earlier days to come around to the position of the moderates. The new leaders of the Wafd, he said, had lost contact with the people and had come to fear popular agitation. They had become skeptical about the ideals of self-determination, democracy, and the rights of the people. "These are very nice words . . . they say . . . but they should not be taken seriously by experienced, practical men." [14]

Since the Wafd was viewed as the chief upholder of the Constitution and the national cause, its compromise over the national issue reflected badly on the whole political system. The damage to the system might have been somewhat mitigated if, by neutralizing the British factor, the treaty had made possible the unhampered pursuit of political life in accordance with the Constitution. But this was not to be the case, and for several reasons. First, by the late 1930's democracy as such was badly discredited in Egypt as a result of the crisis suffered by the Western nations that practiced it. The great depression had given credence to the claims of Fascism, Nazism, and Communism that liberal democracy was a decaying system. The contrast between the misery, despair, and social discord that pervaded the Western democracies and the discipline, orderliness, and aggressive confidence that appeared to characterize the totalitarian regimes made a deep impression on Egyptians, who had seen in their own country a record of unmitigated failures of democracy. Consequently, the Wafd and other political groups, rather than seeking to reactivate the Constitution in earnest, began to turn their eyes to altogether different forms of political organization. In 1937–1938, the Wafd organized a paramilitary movement after the model of the S.A. and the Fascist phalanges which became known as the Blue Shirts and adopted all the paraphernalia of the German and Italian groups, including the Fascist salute, the swaggering, the hero-worship and the promotion of the *Fuehrerprinzip*. At about the same time, in an attempt to capitalize on the Wafd's surrender of the national cause, another organization, the Green Shirts, was formed with an ideology and a program copied from Fascism, which engaged in violent practices that recalled vividly the early days of the Nazi movement. In a different vein, but also reflecting the discredit of the democratic constitutional regime, the young king Fārūq, tutored by the Grand Shaykh al-Marāghī and advised by 'Alī Māhir pasha, entertained at the same time the notion of transforming the regime into an Islamic state with himself as caliph.[15]

All of these practical alternatives to the democratic regime came to naught simply by checkmating each other. But even then, constitutional political life did not proceed smoothly because the treaty did not, in fact, neutralize the British for long, nor did it weaken the position of the king as the Wafd had expected. On the contrary, the outbreak of war three years after the conclusion of the treaty made it more imperative than ever for the British to concern themselves with internal Egyptian affairs so as to ensure obtaining a government that would cooperate in making available to them the resources needed for the war and in keeping under control the activity of a clearly anti-British populace. As for the royal power, the death of king Fu'ād in the midst of the treaty negotiations brought to the throne his young son Fārūq who proved in the first years of his reign to be a much more formidable opponent of the Wafd than his father had been because he was infinitely more popular. One of the first acts of Fārūq upon assuming his full constitutional powers, after a brief period of regency, was to dismiss the Wafdist government in a manner that left no doubt in the mind of the public about his hostility to it, and to appoint a government led by the Liberal Constitutionalists to preside over elections. The returns brought a crushing defeat to the Wafd for the first time in its history. True, the elections were not entirely free, but neither were they significantly more fraudulent than previous elections that the Wafd had won. More important still, once a non-Wafdist Parliament was established, the king managed with consummate skill to keep the anti-Wafdist forces together for nearly four years, with the promise of more. For the declaration of martial law in the wake of the war offered an excellent excuse for prolonging indefinitely the exile of the Wafd from power.

In short, the conclusion of the Treaty of 1936 brought discredit upon the Wafd but did not modify substantially the old triangular power game to which the national aspirations, as well as the Constitution, had been sacrificed. The one element of change induced by the treaty was that the British and the Wafd were no longer inveterate antagonists. This *rapprochement* made it possible for the Wafd, in turn, to look up to the British to save it from the *cul de sac* into which the king had pushed it. In February 1942, the British fulfilled the Wafd's expectation. For reasons of their own, they paraded their tanks in front of Fārūq's palace and served him an ultimatum to appoint a Wafdist government or face both the loss of his throne and exile. The king succumbed and the Wafd came to power. The supreme irony of the spectacle could scarcely be exaggerated: The party that called itself custodian of the national aspirations, that for years had fought more ardently than any other on behalf of the democratic Constitution, was now accepting office through an act that was in flagrant violation of both Egyptian sovereignty and the Constitution! Nor could the discredit of the system that had come to such a pass be any greater.

The pattern of Egyptian social politics was not so obvious as the purely political, though the social issue was at least as important as the political failures just described in undermining confidence in the whole Liberal Constitutional regime. There were three reasons for the relative concealment of the pattern of Egyptian social politics, and these provide, at the same time, the keys to its essential features. First, there was little or no manifest conflict of economic interest among the groups that provided the leadership of the various political parties. Consequently, there was little or no competition among them to seek the support of the lower classes by means of alluring social programs. Bitterly as they fought against each other on political grounds, the various parties in fact presented a common front against the unprivileged groups in the social field. Secondly, among the lower classes themselves, social consciousness developed only slowly and ambiguously during the inter-war period, so that the underprivileged were unable to force a discussion of the social issue on the existing parties. In times of economic crisis, the lower classes were undoubtedly seized by a sense of unrest and discontent which expressed itself occasionally in outbursts against the privileged groups and the symbols of their power. But these outbursts were more in the nature of explosions of rage against accidental ill fortune, like primitive man kicking the stone upon which he had stumbled, than of action based on a consciousness of a collective interest, a concept of social justice and an awareness of denied rights. At any rate, the unrest tended to fizzle out once the crisis was over, or to relapse into fatalism after the outbreaks to which it may have led had been suppressed. Only after 1930, when an economic crisis began which continued uninterruptedly until 1952 and beyond, did the lower classes begin to assemble in a movement, outside the frame of the existing parties, which gave organized expression to their social grievances and sought to correct them by means of a comprehensive program. But then (and this is the third characteristic of Egyptian social politics and another reason why their pattern has not been clear) the grievances and the social program were considerably blurred by being integrated into a fundamental religious, moral and nationalist program and made dependent upon it, so that while the emotional energy stirred by economic discontent was marshalled behind a program which revolted against the existing order, the social issue did not even then receive the detailed treatment it deserved. All of these points will be elaborated and illustrated in the ensuing pages.

The most important characteristic of Egyptian social politics between the revolutions of 1919 and 1952 was the complete supremacy of the big landowning interest. In previous pages we have subdivided Egyptian society into several classes — an industrial-mercantile bourgeoisie, a white collar-professional class, the big landowners, the industrial proletariat, the urban *lumpenproletariat*, and the fellahin. But while this plural division was significant for the purpose of identifying attitudes toward the national question and cultural inclinations, and for discerning the trends in social restructuring, it is nearly meaningless as far as a statement of the basic conflicts of socio-economic interests and of the forces determining socio-economic policy is concerned. Here the only relevant division is that between the interests of the economically privileged groups on the one hand and the inchoate interests of the underprivileged masses of society on the other.

The reasons for this lay in some of the economic and social developments already mentioned. Among the privileged groups, the potential conflict of interests inherent in the rise of an industrial-mercantile bourgeoisie alongside the big landowners never materialized. Because the economic development of Egypt until World War II had been carried out primarily by foreigners who relied on their own governments to protect their interests, the indigenous bourgeoisie was too weak by itself to challenge the supremacy of the big landowners. Moreover, the Egyptian bourgeoisie itself had sprung up largely from the ranks of the landowner class and continued to have large land interests in addition to its mercantile and industrial enterprises. As for the white collar-professional class, this, though more numerous than the bourgeoisie and more influential because of its leading role in the nationalist struggle, had no interest that conflicted inherently with that of the landed gentry. Prominent members of this class aspired naturally to a share in power. But once this aspiration was satisfied, they used their position to lift themselves up to the ranks of the dominant class by marrying into it or by acquiring estates. This was how the Wafd, which had been dominated at the outset by lawyers and professionals, came to be effectively governed by landed interests very soon after. The first Wafdist delegation to Parliament had appeared to its opponents as shockingly plebeian; but in every subsequent delegation, an increasing number of members listed their main occupation as landowner.[16]

The supremacy of the landed interest reflected itself in a social policy which, for its one-sidedness and selfishness, had very few rivals in modern times. To list all the sins of omission and commission of the Egyptian ruling class during this period would be a depressing enterprise that would take us too far afield. The following two examples will suffice to illustrate the point.

It is generally agreed that one of the most important yardsticks for evaluating the social policy of a political system is the pattern of taxation that it follows in relation to the distribution of national wealth within it. Egypt's main source of wealth has always been its land. The inequity of its distribution has been documented at great length so that we need only recall here its bare outline. Out of a total area of 6,400,000 feddans of cultivable land in 1939, roughly seven-twelfths were owned by about 160,000 landowners, one-twelfth was under the control of the ministry of religious endowments, and the remaining four-twelfths were owned by about 2,500,000 small famers.[17] Most fellahin rented a large part of the land that they worked. About one million neither owned any land nor could afford to rent any, and constituted a growing class of wage agricultural workers. Now, to obtain the means necessary to make a dent in the appalling social problems of Egypt, a heavily progressive taxation of profits from land was necessary. The successive governments not only failed to do that, but did just the reverse. They loaded the whole taxation system in favor of the rich landlords and imposed the main burden of supporting the state on the consumers and the poorer classes. In 1899, a land-tax assessment put the average rental value of land at L.E. 3.595 per feddan and fixed the tax rate at 28.64 per cent of the rent. For the next forty years no new assessment was made, and the landlords continued to pay the same rate even though the rental value of land had in the meantime increased many times. A new assessment was finally made in 1939. This raised the average rental value to L.E. 5.750 per feddan, which was still much lower than the prevailing rates, but then it reduced the rate of taxation to 16 per cent. The same year, the income tax was introduced in Egypt for the first time, but agricultural profits were altogether exempted from it. In general, until 1939, taxes on income and wealth provided only 1.1 per cent of the revenue while indirect taxes which fell heavily on the lower classes provided 10.3 per cent.[18] During this period, we might recall, the Wafd held office four times.

Our second example is even more illuminating. All economists agree that the fundamental socio-economic problem of Egypt since the turn of the century has been the overly-rapid increase of the population in relation to the available land and resources. The number of men occupied in agriculture increased from 2.5 million in 1907 to 7.5 million in 1947. During approximately the same period, the crop area increased from roughly 7.7 million feddans in 1912 to 9.2 million feddans in 1948.[19] As a result of the gap between the over-all increase in population in relation to resources, the annual per capita income of the entire population declined from $109.50 in 1907 to $63.50 in 1950. This development called for many urgent comprehensive measures to prevent an already deep misery from getting worse. It called at least for steps to check the growth of population to keep pace with the available resources, Instead, all the successive governments were content to let the population multiply since this provided a cheaper and more abundant supply of labor and, by increasing the pressure on the land, caused the rents to go higher. This was not simply a matter of oversight or ignorance but of deliberate policy. Indeed, some governments even thought of taking measures to *stimulate* population growth. Thus, in 1932, in the middle of a depression that was ravaging the lower classes, a government commission appointed to examine the possibility of reducing the costs of cotton, urged in its report that measures should be taken to *stop* the decline in the rate of growth of the population which had begun to take place under the impact of sheer hunger and misery, on the ground that this was prejudicial to agriculture.[20]

To secure their total domination against a challenge from below, the ruling landed interest made it a criminal offense for agricultural workers of all sorts to organize in unions. Industrial workers, on the other hand, were allowed to form unions — a typical example of the generosity of the ruling class where its interests were not affected, and of the sort of challenge against which a strong, independent bourgeoisie might have retaliated by allowing agricultural unions. The industrial workers' unions might have provided an organizational sounding board from which the lower classes as a whole could have made their voices heard, as happened in other underdeveloped countries. But the existence of large reserves of unemployed sapped their strength and growth, and the intrusion in their leadership of political opportunists disrupted their unity and rendered them incapable of any but strictly local action. Thus, the power of the big landlords remained absolute to the end.

The fact that the lower classes were deprived of any legitimate means of expressing their economic and social grievances did not mean, however, that their grievances were without effect at all. Blocked along the normal conduits, they were diverted instead into the channels of nationalist and religious action where they were manifested in outbreaks of destructive violence. In 1919, for instance, the fellahin used the opportunity of the nationalist uprising to give vent to their resentment of both the official authorities that had despoiled them during the war and the big landlords who always exploited them. Fikrī Abāẓah, a prominent Egyptian journalist, described in an autobiographical novel[21] how the peasants in his home province of Asyūṭ arose in that year and sacked the offices of the government, then turned against the estates and persons of the big landowners. "The people of the great houses. . ." were compelled to barricade themselves in their own homes for fear of the revolution, "the revolution against the British and the revolution against wealth." The revolution against the British, he continued, was led by some enlightened people, while "the revolution against wealth was the work of some troublemakers and the poor. . ."[22] At some point in his narrative, Fikrī described how a group of fellahin assembled to burn down the house of Maḥmūd pasha Sulaymān, the father of Muḥammad Maḥmūd pasha, the future leader of the Liberal Constitutionalist Party, who was at that moment in exile with Sa'd Zaghlūl for his nationalist activities. When someone attempted to dissuade the mob by referring to the pasha's contribution to the nationalist cause, he received this illuminating reply: "Has Maḥmūd pasha Sulaymān ever given bread to the hungry? It is bread that we want."[23]

The tendency of social discontent to insinuate itself into the nationalist struggle was one of the reasons that had led the landed aristocrats to seek to liquidate that struggle by a compromise, which they were finally able to obtain in 1922. By then, however, the general economic situation of the country had begun to take a turn for the better due to a phenomenal rise in the price of cotton which enabled Egyptians to enjoy, for a few years, the highest standard of living they had ever attained. Thanks to this improvement, the Wafd was able to continue with its nationalist and political agitation unconcerned about its opponents' warnings that it was stimulating social anarchy. By 1930, however, the economic situation reversed itself abruptly as a result of the Great Depression. Cotton prices fell disastrously, bringing utter ruin to many small farmers who had borrowed money in what had seemed a safe gamble on high prices, and misery to the rest of the fellahin and the lower classes. The total value of the cotton crop dropped from L.E. 65 million in 1924 to L.E. 40 million in 1929 and L.E. 14.7 million in 1932. For the next five years it rose slowly to a maximum of L.E. 27.6 million in 1937, only to suffer a 20 per cent drop in the following year.[24] According to Issawi, the effect of the slump on money wages was to cut them down by 50 per cent. This fall was mitigated by a drop of 16 per cent in the cost-of-living index, which, however, contained many items outside the range of the poor classes. Corn, the staple food of the poor, on the contrary, rose by 11 per cent due to newly imposed tariffs.[25] Drastic as the fall in income was, those who experienced it were more fortunate than those who could get no jobs at all and did not have even the token relief of social security or national assistance. Among the jobless there were 11,000 holders of baccalaureat or higher degrees who comprised the most dangerous element in the whole unemployment situation. Under these circumstances, the Wafd too came to realize the danger of shaking public authority through nationalist agitation and availed itself of the first opportunity to follow in the path of its opponents and liquidate the nationalist struggle by the Treaty of 1936. This was the meaning of the words of al-ʿAqqād, quoted earlier, that the new leaders of the Wafd had grown fearful of popular agitation.[26]

As the depressed economic conditions continued and were aggravated by the dislocations of the Second World War and its aftermath, and as the nationalist agitation subsided in the wake of the treaty and, later, with the suspension of political activity by martial law after the outbreak of war, the grievances of the lower classes were channeled increasingly into a multitude of religious reform movements the most remarkable of which was the Muslim Brotherhood.[27] The philosophy of this movement, its place in the ideological evolution of Egypt, and its essential characteristics will be examined in some detail later. Here, it is necessary only to describe its aims and to outline its development and activity to the end of the period under study, in order to illustrate the popular reaction against the entire regime.

The Brotherhood was founded in Ismāʿīliyah in 1928 by an elementary school teacher, Haṣan al-Bannā. As a pupil in primary school, al-Bannā had taken part in the nationalist struggle. But the struggle to him was not simply a fight for independence; it was a fight to defend Islam itself against the threat of the godless British. He founded the Brotherhood as a movement to protect Islam by positive religious and ethical action designed to counter the spread of secularism and moral and religious laxity under the impact of modernization and imitation of the foreigners. At first, he directed his appeal exclusively to the lower classes who, he believed, were still uncorrupted at heart. As his movement grew, he moved its headquarters to Cairo in quest of a larger field of operation and began to appeal to other classes as well.

The Brotherhood first came to public notice in 1937 when it tried to organize assistance to the Arabs of Palestine who were then in open revolt. By then it had already expanded its program far beyond the initial religious and ethical issues. To ensure life according to the precepts of Islam, it now insisted that the whole political order must be transformed into an Islamic system whose constitution would be the Qur'ān. As the depression brought to the fore the problems of social misery, the Brotherhood incorporated in its platform a social program based, it said, on the conception of the solidarity of the *ummah* and the responsibility of the collectivity for the welfare of its members. And when the Wafd surrendered its leadership of the national cause by signing the Treaty of 1936, the Brotherhood picked up the fight for absolute independence and the evacuation and unity of Egypt and the Sudan, as steps in the liberation of the abode of Islam from the domination of the infidel. Thus, Islam remained, at least formally, the chief point of reference for the movement even when it in fact adopted principles which had been first promoted by movements of secular inspiration, or when it launched slogans which were dictated by the logic of the situation. This emphasis on the religious aspect proved of great service to the Brotherhood since it enabled it to continue to operate under martial law when other organizations that were avowedly political had to suspend their activity. It also intimidated hostile governments and made them hesitate before taking action against it for fear they might be accused of persecuting religion.

Events and circumstances connected with World War II and its aftermath gave the Brotherhood unique opportunities to grow and develop which it knew how to use. In the economic and social sphere, the war and its consequences confronted the successive Egyptian governments with problems that would have baffled far more honest, able, and unselfish rulers. Handled recklessly, heartlessly, and shortsightedly, these problems drove millions to despair, and hundreds of thousands to the ranks of the one organization that promised to eliminate the whole system.

The war eliminated temporarily the problem of unemployment only to make things much worse in the long run. The demand for manpower to staff the large number of military workshops established by the Allies and a large local industry which arose to substitute for the shrinkage of imports accelerated the usual movement of rural population to the cities. This led to a further crowding of the slums, especially since little new construction was undertaken. Immediately after the war, as the military workshops were dismantled and as many of the new industries shut down, most of the immigrants were reluctant to go back to their villages and the unemployment problem became worse than it had been before.[28] For now, in addition to the deprivation resulting from unemployment and the usual downward pressure that the unemployed exert on the wages of the employed, there was the increasingly hard pressure on the standard of living of wage earners and salaried employees caused by inflation. This pressure led to the eruption of waves of endemic strikes that encompassed workers, government employees, and even the police force. Many of these strikes were violently suppressed, leaving behind them a residue of tension and of bitterness against the government.

We have referred before to the effect on public morality of the shortages induced by the war and the dislocation and corruption of the system of distribution of goods. Their effect on the health, lives, and livelihood of millions of poor people was even more devastating. The extent of this devastation may be easily imagined if it is recalled that a malaria epidemic in upper Egypt in 1943–1944 took a toll of two hundred thousand lives. And the political-social consequences of this massive misery were made worse by the efforts of the factions of the ruling class to capitalize on it by mutual accusations about the responsibility for it. Thus in 1944, when Fārūq was finally able to dismiss the Wafdist government of al Naḥḥās pasha, he stressed in his formal message to the government that he was dismissing it for its failure to provide the people with food and clothing. At the same time, the smaller parties, called by the king to form a new government, launched against the Wafd an extremely violent campaign of vilification which disclosed a record of incredible corruption, profiteering, and ruthless exploitation of position among its leaders and hangers-on. A little while later, as the new government struggled hopelessly with the same issue for which the Wafd had presumably been dismissed, the latter had ample opportunity to take its revenge against it and its royal sponsor. Despite the restrictions imposed by martial law, it managed to stir up discontent with the social policy of the government and to promote a campaign of systematic destruction of the king's moral reputation. Whatever the degree of truth in all the charges and countercharges — and it varied considerably — their net effect was to destroy every shred of credit that remained to the system as a whole.

In 1938, even before the social crisis had reached its climax, Tawfīq al-Ḥakīm was moved to denounce democracy altogether for permitting such injustice and corruption to take place. "Democracy. . ." he wrote bitterly, "is a group of hungry, barefooted men paying a monthly salary of forty pounds to another group (meaning the parliamentary representatives) composed of wealthy men." [29] All the many parties of Egypt, he went on, represent only one class — the big landowners. This class alone makes its voice heard in Parliament; this class deprives all other classes even of the right to form unions to run their affairs and protect their rights; and this class represents only "a few hundred people who monopolize all the good, while leaving millions in the throes of nakedness and hunger." [30]

As the situation deteriorated, attacks of this kind spread among other writers and organs of opinion and increased in frequency and intensity. From the mid-forties on, the trend of social protest, together with the Muslim literature, accounted for virtually the whole field of literary activity. For example, between 1945 and 1950, Ṭāha Ḥusayn published seven books which dealt more or less directly with social injustice, political corruption, and resistance to oppression and exploitation, in addition to scores of articles in journals and in the daily press. In his *Mir'āt al-Ḍamīr al-Ḥadīth* (Mirror of the Modern Conscience) (1949), he observed that misery and injustice had not only ground down the people but had shaken their faith in the moral order of the universe. Until recently, he said, Egyptians had believed in a heaven and a hell which would be the lot of the virtuous and the wicked after death. Now they could see that there are heaven and hell on earth too, but the entry to either of them is not determined by one's merits.[31] Society, he wrote in his *Al-Mu'adhdhabūn fī al-Arḍ* (The Sufferers on Earth) (1949), is built on egotism and thus favors the self-seeking, the hypocrite, the turncoat, and the venal.[32] Political parties, he said in *Jannat al-Ḥayawān* (Animals' Paradise) (1949), are locked in an endless intrigue for particular interests which calls forth and rewards the qualities of sycophancy, cunning, and duplicity.[33] His *Jannat al Shawk* (Paradise of Thorns) (1945), a book of epigrams, his book on 'Uthmān (1947), dealing with resistance to a misguided ruler, and his *Al-Wa'd al-Ḥaqq* (The True Promise) (1950), on the resistance of the early Muslims to oppression, all labored on the theme of social injustice and warned the oppressors against the day of reckoning.[34]

Amidst all the misery and discontent, cynicism and despair, corruption and resentment, the Muslim Brotherhood appeared as the one movement offering grounds for hope for the future and opportunity for expressing immediate dissatisfaction with the regime. Not all who joined or supported it, needless to say, agreed with all its ideology and accepted its full program. There were those who were impressed by its moral and religious preachings at a time when society seemed to have reverted ethically to the rules of the jungle. These included the religiously devout and many disillusioned Liberals. Others, especially masses of lonely and uprooted slum dwellers and immigrants to the cities, found in its branch meetings and collective prayers a psychological haven that fulfilled the function previously accomplished by the Ṣūfī brotherhoods and the corporations. Educated nationalist youth from the middle classes saw the Brotherhood as the main heir to nationalist leadership at a time when the Wafd was abjectly collaborating with the forces of the Occupation that had made a mockery of the country's independence. Political opportunists of all sorts supported it or joined it in the hope of using it to further their own designs. Others were attracted by one aspect or another of the movement's activities and enterprises, which expanded ceaselessly as its membership grew. By the end of World War II, these activities included the founding and maintaining of sport clubs, boy scout groups, para-military squads, a secret apparatus for sabotage and terror, a daily newspaper and several magazines, clinics, welfare centers, schools, cooperative enterprises, and trade unions. The membership had reached at least half-a-million, an unprecedented size for a voluntary organization, and was organized in general branches and in overt and covert functional cells within the Army, workers' organizations, government service, and the schools. Though the bulk of the membership continued to be composed of working people, the directive layer came to comprise large numbers from the professional class — particularly teachers — and from the intelligentsia. A few years after the war, for example, students affiliated to the Brotherhood were able to gain control through open elections of the student councils of all the faculties of the Egyptian University.[35]

Having marshalled the elements of social, economic, political, and religious discontent into a powerful movement, the leaders of the Brotherhood chose to concentrate their first major effort on agitation for the national aspirations. This choice was a logical one, since the full realization of the movement's program depended on the overthrow of the current regime and the establishment of an Islamic state, and this was a risky, if not an impossible, feat to attempt as long as the British were present in force on Egyptian territory. It was even more sensible from a tactical point of view since it offered the movement the opportunity to mobilize a larger number of supporters behind a universally shared aim. It could also place the ruling parties in an embarrassing squeeze between the British and an aroused public, and it was bound to undermine public order and so open up revolutionary possibilities. As soon as the war in Europe was over, therefore, agitation for the British evacuation of Egypt and the unity of the Nile Valley was resumed with great vigor, spearheaded by a "national front" composed of the Brotherhood and other "popular" organizations. The government of the day, led by Nuqrāshī pasha, approached the British for negotiations to revise the Treaty of 1936, but the pressure of popular opinion was such that it could only take an intransigent position which led to the failure of the negotiations and the government's resignation. Another government, headed by Ṣidqī pasha, reopened the discussions and actually reached a compromise draft of a new treaty which was initialled by the two parties, but the agreement was repudiated by public opinion in Egypt, and Ṣidqī resigned. A third government within two years, again headed by Nuqrāshī pasha, took the Egyptian case to the Security Council of the United Nations, but failed to achieve any concrete results. When Nuqrāshī returned from Lake Success, he was expected either to resign or to initiate an active struggle against the British. The latter course seemed a hopeless as well as dangerous one given the existing state of extreme social tension due to the difficulties that we have described. Resignation was opposed by the king because it would have led to elections and the likelihood of the return of the Wafd. In these circumstances, the Palestine issue, which was coming to a head at that time, provided a welcome expedient to divert popular agitation, and the king and the government seized upon it.

Even before the United Nations adopted the partition resolution of November 29, 1947, the Egyptian government, together with the other members of the Arab League, had committed itself to resist its application even by force. When the resolution was passed and civil war broke out in Palestine, the Egyptian government believed that the Palestinian Arabs could win by themselves, with indirect assistance from the Arab countries. Together with other member-governments of the League, it took the lead in arousing its people, contributed moneys and arms, and encouraged the organization and dispatch of volunteers. By the spring of 1948, however, events in Palestine took an unexpected turn against the Arabs and it became obvious that the cause would be lost unless the regular armies of the Arab states intervened. The Egyptian government was reluctant to send its army to war; but the tremendous popular agitation which it had helped to incite, the necessity to confront the national issue if the Palestine problem were dropped, pressure from the king who feared the Wafd's return to power, and expectation of quick success in the war prompted it to overcome its hesitation. Once again the government took the lead in stirring up the enthusiasm of the public by premature announcements of success and reiterated commitments to fight until complete victory was won. But once again its calculations proved wrong. Not only was it impossible to win the war, but it became evident after the first forty days of fighting that every delay in ending hostilities exposed the Arab armies, the Palestinians, and what remained of Palestine to disaster. However, even as the disaster began to materialize, the government lacked the courage to admit failure and end the war. By that time, it was almost completely the prisoner of that *jinn* — mass opinion — which it had so recklessly unbottled.

During the whole agitation, the Muslim Brotherhood took advantage of the relaxation of the usual public security controls to collect arms and train its men. When it became evident that the war could not be won, and while the best units of the army were still occupied at the front, the Brotherhood began to plot the complete overthrow of the regime. Having begun with a campaign of terror against Jews and Jewish establishments which the government was too timid to repress, the Brotherhood extended its attacks against foreigners, and finally against Egyptians. It succeeded in undermining completely the morale and effectiveness of the police force after killing its chief and battling with it several times. By the autumn of 1948, it became the almost unchallenged master of the street and was about to deal its *coup de grace* when the government, in a spurt of determination, outlawed it and ordered its dissolution on the ground of conspiring against the existing order. Indicative of the power that the movement had attained and of the decline of public authority was the fact that the government did not dare arrest the leaders of the Brotherhood or bring them to trial. Not even when the movement retaliated by assassinating the Prime Minister did his successors dare to take such measures. Instead, they resorted to extra-legal means and had the leader and founder of the Brotherhood assassinated.

The liquidation of the Palestine war brought to the fore once more the Egyptian national issue which had been pushed aside in the preceding year-and-a-half. This, together with the disaster of the war, the crying social crisis, the continued underground activity of the Brotherhood, and the revelation of scandals in the handling of military supplies to the armed forces during the war, created an explosive atmosphere in the country and made the position of the government untenable. Partly for this reason and partly to embarrass the Wafd, the king called for new elections. In the absence of alternatives, he expected the Wafd to win, but he hoped at the same time to see it trapped between the British trenches in the Suez Zone and the highly agitated public. His expectations were justified. The Wafd returned to power, and, in the hope of expiating its spotty past and recapturing the leadership of the national struggle, it risked the danger of nationalist agitation in times of social crisis, which all parties had tried to avoid before, denounced unilaterally the Treaty of 1936, whipped nationalist feeling into hysteria and launched an ill-prepared guerilla war against the British forces. In the meantime, as part of a political bargain, it restored the legal status of the Muslim Brotherhood. But this time the forces that it unleashed were beyond its control. After an irresponsible order by the Minister of the Interior had led to a clash in the Canal Zone which cost the lives of scores of policemen, the wrath of the masses was turned inward and erupted in the burning of Cairo. The king had at last found the excuse he needed to dismiss the Wafd, but the ensuing crisis led directly to the July revolution and the complete overthrow of the whole regime.

The Failure of Public Education

Ever since Egyptian leaders first became aware of the challenge of modern conditions to the traditional ideology, education has been rightly viewed as the most important instrument for accomplishing the necessary readjustment. Religious reformists from al-Afghānī, through 'Abduh to Riḍā, and Liberal Westernizers from Luṭfī al-Sayyid, through the Constitution-makers to the most recent intellectual leader — all staked their hopes and aspirations on the reform and expansion of education. But whereas the religious reformists remained unable to control and reform education, the victory of nationalism gave the Liberal Westernizers a golden opportunity to realize their platform by means of a public education program.

We shall not be concerned here with the whole national education system established by the Liberal Nationalist governments, nor with its aims, methods, and failures. Our interest is only in its role in relation to the concrete strains that we have just described. Theoretically, education could fulfill a vital stabilizing function through its effect on a large segment of the population. It could ease considerably the strains caused by the process of restructuring Egyptian society by providing new ethical standards and controls in place of the decaying old ones. It could contribute to protecting the principles and the institutions of democracy from the tendency to ascribe abuses perpetrated in violation of them to a defectiveness inherent in them. What in fact did it accomplish?

Quantitatively, the progress of education since World War I was substantial. The total school population expanded from 324,000 in 1913 to 942,000 in 1933, and to 1,600,000 in 1951.[36] It is true that because of the increase in population, this expansion still left half the children of school age without any education at all. It is also true that for most of the school population, education, save for religion, consisted only of the three R's. But this portion of the population, as well as the completely unschooled, came from classes which were less seriously affected by the cultural-social changes, so that for them the problem of a new outlook and a new moral authority was not yet as crucial as for other segments. It was the section of the population that could give its children a better education that was most affected by the changes, and consequently, the problem was most pressing on the higher levels of education.

Proportionally speaking, the quantitative progress of higher education was more impressive than that of education in general. In 1913, only 2,500 students, all boys, studied in the government's secondary schools; in 1933, the number of students reached 15,000, 10 per cent of whom were girls; and by 1951 the total was 122,000, of whom 19,000 were girls. In 1913, the number of university students was negligible, but by 1951 there were 41,000 students studying in three Egyptian universities, and 1,400 studying abroad.[37]

Because of the character of Egyptian education during that period, however, the schooling at the secondary and university levels failed entirely to realize its potentialities. In fact, instead of easing ethical strains, it aggravated them by accelerating the breakdown of traditional influences without replacing them with any viable alternatives. And instead of contributing to the security of the democratic system, it only produced a large number of unemployed "intellectuals" who were foremost in their resentment of the system for its apparent lack of determination, and most active in the revolt against it. Thus Aḥmad Amīn testified solemnly that it has been his experience in his many years of teaching that

> . . . students in the secondary schools and the universities are Muslims only geographically. . . . Islam does not interest them much or little . . . they do not understand its nature and know nothing about its principles; nor do they even know many of its rites . . . they simply imitate the Europeans in their mode of living and behavior.[38]

As for the intellectual unemployment, by 1937 there were 11,000 jobless among holders of *baccalaureat*, or of higher degrees.[39]

The reasons why Egyptian education failed have been explained very well by an Egyptian scholar, Abū al-Futūḥ Raḍwān, in his excellent study in English entitled *Old and New Forces in Egyptian Education*,[40] so that we need not enter here into any detailed study of the question. Briefly, Raḍwān found that the fundamental defect of the system was precisely the feature which concerns us most, namely, that the teaching in the schools was entirely unrelated to the realities and problems of individual and social life. It consisted mainly of inculcating abstract or factual information, which was learned by rote in the traditional way, without any attempt to relate it to the problems of Egyptian society. The whole system was geared to passing factual examinations leading to the acquisition of diplomas that gave a right to official jobs. "The answers of students in examinations have become stereotyped, being very much alike in sense and words, as though they were answers of one and the same pupil. . . ," said a report of the Ministry of Education quoted by the author.[41]

At the root of these deficiencies, Raḍwān found many social, psychological, organizational, and technical reasons which do not concern us here. But he also stressed the baleful effect on education of a certain outlook prevalent among the responsible political and intellectual leaders which is important for us. We have already referred to the tendency of these leaders to assume that there was an organic and automatic relation between mere knowledge and the acquisition of a democratic attitude.[42] Raḍwān amply substantiated this point and indicated that this tendency applied to all social problems: "any social need or problem has been conceived as a token of ignorance in some single field of knowledge. The next step has been to thrust a new school subject into the curriculum. . ." This was how civics, political economy, philosophy, psychology, and logic found their way to the secondary school program.[43] Raḍwān drew this conclusion about the system as a whole:

> In a word, schools are more of ivory towers where the students are seldom bothered by the realities of life surrounding them. They teach ready-made and imported subject matter. When the students graduate, they know all about books but little about the society or the concrete features of the physical environment into which they are defenselessly thrown.[44]

The only lessons related to social and political life which the students learned well was an intransigent, negative nationalism and an understanding of patriotism as a readiness to commit and suffer violence in the name of the nationalist slogans.

The control of parental authority had been shaken, that of the religious authority weakened, and that of society undermined by the transformation of the social structure. Hence the failure of education to instill any guiding principles of personal behavior left the growing generations from the middle classes in a moral and spiritual vacuum which they filled by opportunism, reckless pursuit of pleasure, and destructive political adventures or agitation.[45] In the face of this situation some intellectual leaders lost their faith in reason and joined the traditionalists in blaming everything on the influence of the irreligious, materialistic West. Others looked for ways to temper the Westernized education with religious additions. All of them went back to Muslim tradition in the hope of finding a substitute or supplementary guidance there.

CHAPTER 13

The Reactionary Phase

The actual strains and crises under which the liberal democratic regime lived after the early thirties had the effect, on the ideological level, of favoring the position adopted by Haykal and discrediting that urged by Ṭāha Ḥusayn after the orientation crisis. Ṭāha Ḥusayn's advocacy of an unequivocal and total Western cultural orientation proved to be embarrassing even to its author, in the face of the manifest failure of the constitutional system to take root in Egypt and to secure a modicum of political stability and social justice, the breakdown of the hegemony that liberal democratic philosophy seemed to hold in Europe into a confusion of warring ideological systems, the increasingly evident failure of the Western-modelled system of education to produce the results expected from it, a reawakened hostility against Britain for violating Egypt's national rights, and a deep resentment against the West for its support of the foundation of Israel. On the other hand, Haykal's argument that the Egyptian cultural soil was inhospitable to any but Muslim-inspired ideals and values seemed to receive resounding confirmation from the events and met enthusiastic approval from the public.

Haykal's *Life of Muḥammad* encountered such great success that he and other authors followed it with one work after another of a similar nature until the whole Egyptian literary endeavor came to be dominated by works on Muslim subjects.[1] Thus Haykal followed his book on Muḥammad with a book on the experience of a pilgrimage to Mecca (1937), one on the first caliph, Abū Bakr (1942), a two-volume work on the second caliph, 'Umar (1945), and a book on the third caliph, 'Uthman (1946).[2] The weekly *al-Siyāsah*, which he had once used as a medium for expounding liberal thought, changed both its look and its outlook, adopting a cover of Muslim design and giving large coverage to Muslim subjects. Ṭāha Ḥusayn followed his *'Ala Hāmish al-Sīrah* (1937) with two more volumes bearing the same title (1938, 1943), a book on 'Uthmān (1947) and a book on the martyrs of Islam (*al-Wa'd al-Ḥaqq*, 1949) which was subsequently made into a motion picture with the approval of the religious authorities. Al-Ḥakīm joined the trend with his play *Muḥammad* (1936), and subsequently wrote many articles and essays on Islam,[3] and al-ʻAqqād followed in 1941 with his *ʻAbqariyyat Muḥammad* (The Genius of Muhammad), to which he added nearly a dozen works on illustrious figures from the first century of Islam.[4] Nearly all the books by these writers met with great success and went into several printings. In addition, many less known writers contributed scores of items to the stream of Muslim literature, and the Muslim Brotherhood produced hundreds of books, pamphlets, and articles expounding its own point of view and exhorting its followers.[5]

All of this literature purported, in fact, to interpret Islam anew; [6] but except for some purely technical, legal, and historical studies, most of it suffered from the same basic contradictions to be found in Haykal's *Life of Muḥammad*, and only served to increase the ideological confusion. Like Haykal, its authors attempted a rational defense of those aspects of the Islamic heritage to which they were committed à priori on faith, while at the same time they attacked Western rationalism. When a writer could do so, he defended elements of the Muslim tradition in terms of Western values; and when the contradiction between the two seemed to him insurmountable, he attacked and denigrated Western culture and ethics. Since these writers chose to stress different elements of the traditional heritage as essential, and to understand them differently, and since the likelihood of reconciling them with reason or with Western ideals depended on the ingenuity of the individual writer, there was little that was common to the total product and therefore little that could serve as part of a common belief-system. The only clear and universal aspects of that literature were a general emotional glorification of a vague Islam, and an aggressive attitude toward its antithesis, the West. These points, together with some analytical comments on their effect on the pursuit of a basic belief-system, will be elaborated in some detail as we examine once again examples of the intellectual leaders' work in the spheres of ethics, political thought, and history.

Ethics

It will be recalled that, in the initial phase, the intellectual leaders had gone beyond Muḥammad ʻAbduh's views in regard to the relation between ethics and religion. ʻAbduh had given ethics a rational foundation, but at the same time insisted on linking it sociologically to revelation. In the ebullient progressive phase, the intellectual leaders severed this link and counted on the individual's conscience and sense of social responsibility to provide the sanctions for a rationally founded body of ethics. The intellectual development of the leaders and their exposure to new intellectual winds from Europe that challenged and contradicted their initial liberal humanistic values, as well as the realities of social behavior in the environment in which they lived, made them more hesitant to continue trusting purely subjective sanctions. Realizing the wisdom of ʻAbduh, they turned back to Islam in order to mobilize its affective power in the service of ethics (and politics). But the Islam to which they returned was not ʻAbduh's Islam of revelation, dogma, and a carefully interpreted law, but an Islam based entirely on emotion and focused on the personality of Muḥammad, which they adorned with all the virtues and interpreted arbitrarily. In this way they attempted to avoid having to face squarely the problem raised by the traditional creed concerning revelation and its potential conflict with the implications of modern reality.[7]

The perplexity of the intellectual leaders at the time they began to turn toward the Muslim tradition was expressed by al-ʻAqqād before he joined in the trend toward Muslim literature. In his biographical study of Saʻd Zaghlūl, al-ʻAqqād contrasted nostalgically the generation of his hero with that of his own times. Although education and progress were less widespread in Zaghlūl's time, he wrote, that generation was distinguished by the solidity of its principles, its confidence, and its assurance. In contrast,

> Today, there is no principle and no belief which people do not repeatedly submit to the whetstone of criticism and analysis. What is good and what is evil? What is virtue and what is baseness? What is justice and what is oppression? To all these questions there have been given many answers, opposing arguments, and clashing views so that doubt has torn the whole matter and consensus has become impossible. . . .
> Sixty years ago, the accepted tradition in these matters was along a straight, unquestioned path. The permissible was evident and the prohibited was obvious . . . In either case, the decisive authority was the religious prescription which was operative for the religious as well as the non-religious people.[8]

In his usual vague and misty style, Haykal stated in the introduction to his book on Muḥammad that his study was intended, among other things, to foster those ethical and social values which reason alone had failed to promote:

> ". . . what is life, what is being, what is man . . . what are the common tenets which inspire moral force in the groups . . . all these are questions which have been submitted to pure logic . . . but you will find their solution (as given) in the life and teachings of Muḥammad more apt to bring man the happiness he seeks. . . ."[9]

The grafting of ethics onto the personality of Muḥammad involved a fundamental retreat from the position which the intellectual leaders had taken in the progressive phase, a retreat which handicapped the construction of any viable ethical outlook. It also denied them any distinct rational principle and condemned the authors to pursue discrete, unrelated values. Because the corpus of traditions and legends relating to the Prophet was vast and often inconsistent, it permitted a very considerable degree of latitude in the choice of references. At the same time, since the Prophet's life involved certain incontrovertible facts — his armed struggles, his taking of many wives, and so on — the authors were compelled to tailor their values to suit those facts, or to engage in their defense at a considerable sacrifice of integrity, clear thinking, and the highest ethical principles.

We have already had occasion to point out an example of apologetics that was destructive of ethics in the case of Haykal's argument about ends and means.[10] We have also seen in his case a few instances of the vitiation of the intellectual processes in his attempt to defend Muḥammad's actions at all costs. Here we will supplement these examples with several from al-ʿAqqād's book on Muḥammad.

Until the appearance of this book, al-ʿAqqād had been distinguished by the vigor of his thought, the breadth of his knowledge, and his judiciousness. Even in this book his lucidity, poise, and balance contrasted very favorably with Haykal's romantic excursions, his vagueness, and his self-contradictions — until he came to deal with two controversial positions of Muḥammad: his resort to violence to spread his message and his relations with women.

Al-ʿAqqād published his book in the middle of the Second World War so that it was especially important to absolve Muḥammad of any aggressiveness and violence. He began by making the generalization that Muḥammad never used force to impose his faith. To support this assertion, he referred to the first converts to Islam, who had, indeed, come of their own will and stood by Muḥammad despite all the persecutions they suffered. Here, al-ʿAqqād was implying, misleadingly, that this was the rule in regard to all those who adopted Islam.[11] But then, as he came to the undeniable fact of the wars that Muḥammad launched against the Meccans, al-ʿAqqād quietly introduced a qualification without correcting his previous implication. The operations against the Meccans, he now explained, were not undertaken by Muḥammad in order to impose his creed by force, but only to eliminate obstacles in the way of spreading his message. This did not involve any suppression of freedom of conscience or of expression, because the Meccans did not oppose to Muḥammad's message any creed of their own, but only a corrupt and dissolute way of life.[12] The subsequent wars waged to establish Islam in the Arabian peninsula were not religious wars either, he contended. They had nothing to do with spreading the faith as such, but were related solely to the establishment of civil order. For it must be remembered, he wrote, that "Islam is a religion and a political order; and in the latter capacity it has, like all political orders, the right to enforce obedience and to prevent revolt." [13] Christianity did not need to establish a constitutional and a political order because they were there already, "not because worldly affairs and constitutions are not the concern of religion." [14]

These illustrations are not the worst by any means. But they suffice to illustrate what Gibb, in writing of the apologists, has called "the disregard of all objective standards of investigation and historical truth" which, he said, "debauched the intellectual insight and integrity of their fellow-Muslims." [15]

Al-ʿAqqād, like Haykal, sanctioned and defended the killing of the prisoners-of-war, contending that these were not usual prisoners, but notorious enemies of Islam. The protection accorded to prisoners-of-war in modern international law is based on the anonymity of the soldiers; but in this case, the captives had been known to have committed specific acts of aggression against the Muslims. The fact that Muḥammad rejoiced at the sight of the slaughtered enemies after the battle was no proof, al-ʿAqqād asserted, that he sought plain vengeance; it simply showed his great relief after the severe trial he had undergone; and "the rejoicing of the victor in his victory is human nature and is unblameable. . ." [16] Further, al-ʿAqqād expressed astonishment at the fuss the Westerners make about these prisoners when they glorified and adulated Napoleon who had slaughtered thousands of prisoners in Jaffa and elsewhere.

For the massacre of the Jews by Muḥammad, and the enslavement of their womenfolk, al-ʿAqqād had another answer: They had violated their commitment to the Prophet and collaborated with his enemies; therefore, they could no longer be trusted alive. In any event, they had accepted an arbitrator who judged them according to their own Torah.[17]

It will be noticed that al-ʿAqqād faced each event separately and adapted his moral judgment to suit it. There is no common principle underlying the whole; the judgment is dictated by the situation to be justified.

On the subject of women, al-ʿAqqād defended Muḥammad personally for taking many women on the grounds that he did so for political reasons or for charitable and humane considerations.[18] He wanted only to give those poor women refuge and protection at great cost and sacrifice to himself. As for Muḥammad's legislation permitting polygamy, this, again, was due entirely to humane considerations and a regard for the sick and sterile women: "There is no doubt that taking a wife in addition to one that is sterile or sick is better than abandoning her to the bitter struggle of life without a husband or a protector." On second thought, al-'Aqqād decided to insert a line regarding polygamy where the first wife was healthy and not sterile, by saying that "the same was the case with the despised woman." This he added, is at any rate better than prostitution, which the Westerners allow, and better than their practice of having one or more mistresses, besides their wives.[19]

The absence of any over-all guiding principle or rational foundation led authors to attribute qualities and values to the Prophet according to their own whim. Al-'Aqqād, writing during World War II, devoted a great deal of effort to emphasizing the military genius of Muḥammad, which he compared to that of heroes who had captured his own imagination: Napoleon and Hitler.[20] But the best illustration of the point can be drawn by comparing the qualities attributed to Muḥammad by two authors — al-'Aqqād and al-Ḥakīm, for example. To be sure, both accorded him the cardinal virtues of friendship, devotion, truthfulness, generosity, forgiveness, and the like. For the rest, however, al-'Aqqād's Muḥammad is, but for his martial genius, the good father or the benevolent patriarch who protects the weak, is just and wise, moderately cheerful and well-disposed, warm and modest with his wives. For al-Ḥakīm, on the other hand, Muḥammad is a classical Greek hero, generous and magnanimous, but in an unpredictable way. He is harsh and ruthless in battle, expert in leadership, and wise in counsel. He is terrible in his wrath, awe-inspiring in his strength, but magnificent in his forgiveness and touching in his weakness. He is the model of patience in adversity and selflessness in the service of his people. But he is also a lustily joyful man and a super-potent lover. Thus, many of the actions of Muḥammad which al-'Aqqād sought to excuse and justify at great cost to his intellectual honesty and to historical truth, were taken by al-Ḥakīm at their face value and presented as virtues in Muḥammad's personality, inspiring examples of heroic greatness.

As long as the dogma of the Qur'ān as integral divine revelation was maintained, any rational principle had to be subordinated to the specific content of the Book. This meant that reason could not operate freely and consistently to evolve certain general guiding ethical principles. Under these conditions, the attempt to graft ethics onto the Prophet's personality could only produce a conglomeration of values, arbitrarily ascribed to Muḥammad, lacking any coherence and system, and therefore offering no sure guide for action. Thus, recourse to religion by the intellectual leaders offered only the illusion of security and solidity, a faith in a noble but vague Islam, and provided that romantic backward look on which reaction thrives.

Political Thought

The clash between rationalism and the traditional creed concerning the *Qur'ān*, projected to the level of a conflict between the West and Islam, had been at the root of the Muslim orientation. Once the clash had been brought to that level, the antagonism toward the West fed on the failure of Western liberal institutions in Egypt and on their tribulations in Europe, on the internal social-ethical crisis which was attributed to the invasion of European "materialistic" values, and on the political clashes with Western powers in Egypt and in Palestine. At first the ideological reaction against Western culture tended to confine itself to the defense of such Islamic elements as the traditional creed, which were considered to have been challenged by Western rationalism. As the political and social crises which fed the reaction grew more and more intense, it expanded to include the assertion of ethics in a Muslim garb, and finally, towards the end of our period, the reaction sought to encompass political values too and bring them under the aegis of Islam.

By then the Muslim orientation had become predominant, and the opposition to Western culture on the ideological level had become nearly total, even though in practice imitation of the surface aspects of that culture remained as widespread as ever. But as in the attempt to graft a new ethics on to Islam, the attempt to implant modern political ideals in the Muslim tradition resulted in severe distortions of both that denied either of them any value as effective guiding principles, and only fostered an emotional commitment to and pride in a Muslim political system, without giving it any substantive content.

The best example of the intellectual consequences of the reversal to traditionalism in the sphere of political thought is provided by al-'Aqqād's book, *al-Dīmūqrāṭiyyah fī al-Islām* (Democracy in Islam) published in 1952, just prior to the July revolution. The book may also serve as a summary of the technique and method of apologetics in general.

Al-ʻAqqād indicated in the introduction that he was aware of the political-ideological vacuum left by the failure of the Liberal constitutional system and the disenchantment with Western culture, and sought to fill that vacuum by embedding the principles of democracy in the Muslim tradition. The Muslim nations, now awakening and progressing, he wrote,

> . . . are in greatest need at this particular stage for (an understanding) of freedom which is harmonized with and integrated into their faith. Because freedom without faith is a mechanical or animal thing, closer to anarchy and chaos than to good effort and work that lead to a purpose. It is therefore beneficial that the Muslim nations always keep in mind that, with them, freedom is part of the true faith and not simply something useful and borrowed. . . .[21]

The book may be logically divided into three parts. In the first, al-ʻAqqād purported to make a comparative study of the various Western democracies and "Islamic democracy." In fact, this study was distorted from the outset by its apologetic and polemical approach: He started by examining very briefly the democracy of the Greek city states; and after reviewing sketchily the formal constitutional arrangements, lumping together various states and epochs, he reached the conclusion that democracy in Greece was not considered a human right or universal principle, but was simply "an expedient measure and an inescapable arrangement for the maintenance of order in the state. . . ." This view, he continued, was frankly stated in "the writings of the Greek philosophers." Thus Plato viewed the citizens as minors who need guardians and may be deceived like children, and Aristotle spoke of equality as something that assures good government rather than as a universal human right. The same was true of the Roman state and of the Roman thinkers, except, perhaps, Cicero, who developed some notion of natural equality. But even in Cicero's case, his concept of equality was "merely an equality in the sphere of reason and natural qualities"; and, "all that Cicero meant by it was that the laws must be based on nature and should be applied on the basis of justice and equality. . ." This view found currency among Roman legislators and jurists, "because of their concern with establishing the principles of law. They all agree (for instance) that the law of nature is common to men and animals. . ." At any rate, al-ʻAqqād added, the Romans did not grant equality of rights to their subjects except under the pressure of circumstances.[22]

From Greece and Rome, al-ʻAqqād jumped all the way to the nineteenth and twentieth centuries and then disposed of all modern democracies by stating that they extended the franchise only gradually and not until the elements to be enfranchised had attained a degree of power which the rulers could not ignore. From this survey al-ʿAqqād concluded:

> It is evident, then, that [Western] democracy, ancient and modern, was not based on a human right universally recognized. It was closer to practical necessity than to ideological or ethical principles. . . . A democracy imposed by necessity owes as much thanks to nature as it does to legislation. For nobody can claim credit for the freedom of the bird and that of the Bedouin. . . . They have simply taken that which nobody had given them and nobody could take away from them. This is not what we mean when we look for credit for the establishment of rights and the principles of constitutions.[23]

It would be a waste of time to point out the specific deficiencies in al-ʿAqqād's analysis. But certain general comments relating to his intellectual approach and his understanding of democracy need to be made.

Al-ʿAqqād tended to view democracy, which he understood to mean as essentially the right to vote, as a primary natural right rather than as a system expressing and applying certain fundamental ideals. This conception, of course, whether deliberately chosen or not, suited his purpose since, as we shall see later, he intended to interpret the general *bayʿah* of Islam as the equivalent of the right to vote, and hence as evidence that Islam is democratic. Here, then, is an example of the apologist finding refuge in formalism and thereby misunderstanding and misrepresenting the essence of democracy.

Because al-ʿAqqād did not understand that democracy is both the expression and practical application of certain ideals, he tended to show a marked contempt for questions of expediency and practicality. He strongly suggested that the fact a certain doctrine is in harmony with social and political facts is a point against the nobility of that doctrine. He even thought that if certain rights or laws are based on universal reason and nature, this would be a point against them. Here again what al-ʿAqqād had at the back of his mind was the exaltation of the Islamic ethical-political doctrine which asserts its norms but makes no provision for realizing them. Instead of learning the value of practical procedures from the utter failure of the Islamic political doctrine, which was largely due to their neglect, al-ʿAqqād went just the other way and criticized Western doctrine for taking these practical matters into account. Here, then, is apologetics combined with an idealistic approach leading to another vitiation of thought and missing the most crucial lesson of Islamic political history. Al-ʿAqqād's concentration on apologetics prevented him from asking himself why, if democracy was a compelling, almost natural, necessity in the West, that same democracy never appeared necessary and never took roots in Islam; or why it took place in some Western countries and not in others.

Having disposed of Western democracy, al-ʿAqqād went on to discuss "Islamic democracy" and concluded his discussion with a statement confirming all our previous remarks:

> We can now . . . assert that the *Sharīʿah* of Islam was the first to establish the humanistic democracy; *viz.*, the democracy that man enjoys because it is his own right, which allows him to choose his government, not the mere tactic of government seeking to avoid danger or prevent rebellion, nor a mere measure which is taken by the government in order to facilitate obedience and benefit from the services of its employees and workers.[24]

The substance of "Islamic democracy" consists of four principles which, according to al-ʿAqqād, are essential to every democracy. These are: 1) individual responsibility; 2) "generality of rights" and equal rights; 3) the duty of *shūrā* (consultation) incumbent upon the rulers; 4) the solidarity of citizens belonging to the various classes and communities.[25]

It is somewhat strange that, after defining democracy as consisting of the right to choose the government, Al-ʿAqqād did not include this right specifically among the principles of "Islamic democracy." He did not abandon it, however, but returned to it later. Its omission here and in subsequent statements and arguments must be ascribed to a weakness which we shall meet again in the course of his book, and that is the discrete character of al-ʿAqqād's approach.

It will be readily seen that the four principles of "Islamic democracy" are not necessarily related to each other or to any common principle. The duty of consultation incumbent upon the ruler does not, for instance, derive from the rights of the people, whatever these may be; and the solidarity of classes, by which al-ʿAqqād meant the Qur'ānic injunction to command that which is good and forbid that which is evil, is not related to any of the other principles. Each principle stands by itself and relies on verses and traditions, which al-ʿAqqād quoted abundantly. Nothing in the system prevents the addition of other principles to it, based on verse and tradition, since the system has no logic of its own and merely rests on discrete, positive injunctions. In fact, according to al-ʿAqqād, its greatness lies precisely in the fact that it has no logic of its own but consists of outright positive norms.

With the same discrete approach, al-'Aqqād discussed two concepts, essential to any liberal doctrine, which he tried to read back into Islam. He sought to assert the notion of the inviolability of the human personality, which certainly is not alien to the ethical spirit of the Qur'ān but had been lost in the long tradition of arbitrary rule which characterized the political history of Islam:

> Good government is not merely a commendable thing urged by the faith among other virtues . . . it is a principle which runs in the nature of things and applies to all things. References to good government are oft-repeated and government is described in terms of justice and avoiding arbitrariness only in order to entrench in the depth of the conscience that there is an inviolability in human beings which raises them above the play of passions and the tyranny of the powerful.[26]

Disregarding the question of the adequacy or inadequacy of the foundation which al-'Aqqād attempted to give to that ideal, he did not try to relate it to the political system, but again left it standing by itself as another independent norm.

The second concept he attempted to revive was the notion of man's freedom of will. Al-'Aqqād asserted God's omnipotence, but emphasized His unchanging custom and His justice, which allow man to act freely. "To the Muslim, then, the government of the universe is one that follows laws . . . not anarchy and arbitrariness . . . and does not convict anybody without previous warning."[27] Although the Muslim believes that the *sunnah* of Allah is above everything, he also believes that "he is one of the elements of the divine custom and is neither a parasite nor a plaything in the universe."[28] This concept might have served to establish a foundation for all the other principles, and lead to a democracy inspired by Islamic ideals, but al-'Aqqād contented himself with preaching that view also discretely and autonomously.

In the second part of the book, al-'Aqqād took up the fundamental concept of sovereignty and, by developing it along lines of modern Western political thought, he presented a theoretical system which bore no relation in logic, in method, or in tone either to his previous discussion or to what followed. The explanation of this puzzle is that al-'Aqqād was presenting here the views of a Pakistani political leader, Dr. Ishtiyāq Ḥusayn Qurayshī, to which he was giving his assent with some minor modifications. Since he approved of those views, he inserted them in the middle of his book apparently unaware of their inconsistency with his own.

Al-'Aqqād claimed that the theory he was presenting was "identical with the views of the orthodox *'ulamā'*," whereas in fact it had nothing in common with any orthodox view. He began by defining sovereignty as "the reference which gives the law or a leader the right to be obeyed," and then went on to describe some Western theories of social contract — Hobbes' and Locke's in particular — and a particular Muslim theory which held that sovereignty resided in the religious leaders. He then concluded that "nothing in Islam enjoins the rejection of any of these doctrines of legitimation of authority . . . except the doctrine which claims for the ruler divine authority, or an authority which cannot be withdrawn." [29] Thus, al-'Aqqād simply reversed things, since the traditional Islamic doctrine recognized *only* the concept that the caliph's authority derived from God.

While many doctrines of social contract are acceptable to Islam, al-'Aqqād continued, the doctrine which seems nearest to it is that which views sovereignty as being founded on a dual contract: one between men and God, committing men not to obey anything which contravenes His prescriptions; the other between the people and the ruler by virtue of which the people delegates to the ruler the right to legislate in its name without infringing on its contract with God. Four kinds of sovereignty are involved in this theory: 1) divine sovereignty, which means simply the recognition of God's mastery in the universe; 2) "real sovereignty," which is represented by the Qur'ān and the Tradition; 3) "political sovereignty," which resides in the people; and 4) "legislative sovereignty," which is exercised by the legislators chosen by the people. Put in different terms, the people is "the source of sovereignty," and the Qur'ān and the Tradition are "the sources of legislation." There is no conflict between the two because

> . . . it is the *ummah* which understands the Book and the Tradition, acts according to them and considers its own conditions to see where there should be application, where there should be suspension, and where there should be amendment, and because it is the *ummah* which approves or rejects the rules that the *imām* issues.[30]

Al-'Aqqād justified both his conception of the social contract and the wide legislative prerogative of the people by referring to the concept of *ijmā'*, or consensus.[31] There is the general *ijmā'*, he argued, which is reflected in the election of governments and in the approval of their legislation, and there is the special *ijmā'* which consists of the agreement among the legislators. But by this argument, he modified the concept of *ijmā'* in two crucial ways so that it bore little relation to the traditional concept except in name. First, he made *ijmā'* a political as well as a judicial concept, and extended its validity to "the thing which comes nearest to it" (that is, majority); [32] secondly, he made of *ijmāʿ* a programmatic concept, resting on deliberate will, instead of the traditional *ex-post-facto* sanction of change already established, resting on the divine assurance that the community would never agree on what is wrong.

Al-ʿAqqād tried to defend the idea that popular sovereignty is at the root of the Islamic political conception against objections based on the recognition by Islamic doctrine of "the right of the sword," which seems to view the legitimacy of power as residing in itself. Such right, he argued, does not preclude popular sovereignty — it means only that the wielders of the sword might compel the people to use its sovereignty according to their will for as long as they can effectively enforce it. When they are no longer able to do so, the people resumes, as a matter of course, the free exercise of its sovereignty. Al-ʿAqqād defended this process by arguing that "Islam recognizes the right of the sword; but this right is contingent upon more important things — such as preventing revolutions, avoiding anarchy, protecting property, and compelling the depraved and the sinners to obey the Sharīʿah." [33]

The end result of all this discussion of sovereignty was a complete justification of the existing political regime: "general *ijmāʿ*" was equivalent to electoral majority; "special *ijmāʿ*," to parliamentary majority; "divine sovereignty" was divorced from "political sovereignty"; and the rulings of the Qur'ān and the Tradition ("real sovereignty") were made morally binding upon the Parliament ("the legislative sovereignty") but susceptible in practice to reinterpretation, suspension, or amendment. Despite al-ʿAqqād's protestations to the contrary, this system was, of course, radically different from, and in some fundamental senses opposed to, the traditional Islamic belief; but this did not negate its value as a foundation for a political doctrine that could rationalize effectively the transition from the traditional to the existing system. But it is, perhaps, the clearest illustration we have of the damaging effect of the apologetic and polemical method that al-ʿAqqād left his discussion of sovereignty where it stood, and went back to discussing discretely, inconsistently, and in isolation certain political concepts which should have been related to the theory of sovereignty, in order to prove that Islam is democratic or that Islamic democracy is indeed superior to the Western. As might have been expected, the result was only a confusion of issues and a waste of the gains he had made.

In the third and last section of the book, al-ʿAqqād discussed a series of topics chosen without any apparent order or any connection to his discussion of sovereignty. The choice of topics seems to have been influenced by two considerations: Some he chose because they were central concepts in the traditional Islamic doctrine; others, with the intent of justifying and defending the principles of "Islamic democracy" which he had discussed in the first part of the book.

Accordingly, the next concept discussed by al-ʿAqqād was that of the *imām*, which he examined in the formal traditional way. He began, as usual, by considering the qualifications of the *imām*, and asserted that "everybody capable of leading men and maintaining the *aḥkām* (law) is eligible for the *imāmah* in Islam." He then proceeded to the matter of appointing the caliph and maintained that no special body had the exclusive right to do so. In looking at the *bayʿah*, — contract of appointment — he strongly suggested that the appointment of the *imām* was accomplished not by the special *bayʿah* of those with "the power to bind and loosen," but by the general *bayʿah* — traditionally the merely formal profession of allegiance by the leaders of the community and the public at large after the appointment of the caliph. Still following the traditional order, he next examined the question of obedience to the *imām* and agreed that it was compulsory unless the *imām* contravened the Sharīʿah. Injustice should be borne only to avoid revolutions.[34] He then turned to the problem of contesting pretenders to the *imāmah* and took the opportunity to suggest that "belief in popular sovereignty" might be a solution in such situations, because

> . . . . if it becomes impossible to give the *bayʿah* to a single, generally accepted caliph, the Sharāʾiʿ will not fall and rights will not be forfeited since the ruled would then be the source of government and the *nations* the source of authority in every state. Otherwise, all right will revert to the sword and power — a right which unbelievers as well as believers hold.[35]

Here, as in his discussion of sovereignty, al-ʿAqqād interpreted arbitrarily the traditional Islamic concepts. The last paragraph quoted, for example, postulates the existence of many "nations" within Islam, a supposition that begs the question and is alien to traditional doctrine. But while his reinterpretation of the concept of sovereignty served at least to make that concept relevant to modern conditions, his reinterpretation of the principles governing the *imāmah* achieved no such purpose. It would appear that al-ʿAqqād attempted it only because the principles of the *imāmah* were the sole topic of traditional political doctrine. By doing so, he contributed to the survival or revival of empty forms to which others could give a completely different content. This was all the more likely to happen since the content he gave them was not founded on clear, systematic principles. In discussing sovereignty, for example, he had argued vehemently that political sovereignty was inherent in the people, but here he seems to concede that it resides in the *imām*, though he suggested that as a practical expedient in times of emergency, this should be "believed" to reside in the people.

The next topic discussed by al-'Aqqād was "political democracy." The appropriateness of taking up such a subject after his discussion of sovereignty might be questioned if his apologetic purpose were not so apparent. He defined "the essence of political democracy" as consisting of "the liberty of the ruled to choose their own government"; all the rest — constitutions, electoral laws, parliaments, and so on — he dismissed as incidental.[36] By this definition he seemed to retreat from the position he had taken in his discussion of sovereignty, where he insisted on participation in legislation, directly or through representation, as a necessary manifestation of popular sovereignty; but this was precisely what he needed to do in order to introduce and glorify the concept of *shūrā*, which he had mentioned as one of "the four principles" of Islamic democracy.

The idea of the *shūrā* has a great appeal to all modernists because it is mentioned in the Qur'ān and because it is susceptible to democratic interpretation. Al-'Aqqād naturally considered the *shūrā* as an injunction incumbent upon the ruler rather than as useful advice. He regarded it as the supreme manifestation of "true democracy, not the sham democracy of weights and numbers." (He seems to have forgotten his insistence that only the liberty of the ruled to choose the government is essential to democracy. But that definition was apparently adopted only when his purpose was to deny that the right of participation in legislation was an essential feature of democracy.) The *shūrā* was not intended to express the opinion of the majority, nor was it meant to bring forth the truth — truth is not to be found in multitudes nor in the din of controversy, but with the learned few. Its real function is to express the organic relation between ruler and ruled:

> The political democracy of nations is a matter of life, not of weight and numbers. Once this is clear, the wisdom of Islam in ordering the *shūrā* and in distinguishing it from numbers and truth becomes evident . . . *shūrā* is the coalescing of the forces of those who advise and those who are advised instead of bickering and biting each other.[37]

Al-'Aqqād next dealt with the concepts of "democratic legislation," "judicial democracy," and "economic democracy." His discussion of these subjects, like that of "political democracy," which we have just reviewed, was aimed at proving that his four specifically "Islamic" principles — individual responsibility, generality and equality of rights, the duty of *shūrā*, and solidarity of the subjects — were in perfect harmony with a proper understanding of these general concepts. But his proofs amounted, in fact, to nothing other than defining each of these concepts in such a way as to include beforehand in the definitions that which he set out to prove. "Democratic legislation," for example, is defined as legislation which is "general as to its source and its application" — meaning that it should have a generally accepted source, such as the Qur'ān, and that it should apply to everybody, as the Qur'ān does — [38] which is essentially just what he meant by the principle of general and equal rights. In other words, what appears to be a discussion of general concepts aimed at testing certain specific principles turns out to be a circular game of arbitrary definitions.

Because of this implicit connection between concepts and principles, his discussion of the concepts suffered from the same defects that we have noted in the principles. Each of the concepts appeared as a discrete theory unrelated to the others, and, taken together, presented no consistent whole that had any logical relation to his concept of sovereignty. Thus, while popular sovereignty appeared as a fundamental idea in his discussion of sovereignty, it seemed incidental and optional in his discussion of the *imām*, and once again essential in his discussion of political democracy. Similarly, participation in legislation was an essential attribute of popular sovereignty, unessential to political democracy, and once more essential for democratic legislation.[39] In short, the entire work was actually more a collection of inconsistent *ad hoc* definitions than a coherent exposition of a political doctrine.

In the concluding chapters of his book, al-'Aqqād undertook to defend certain Islamic institutions presumed to be anti-democratic, such as slavery and *jihād*. With respect to the former, al-'Aqqād offered the familiar justifications: He compared the mild lot of the slaves in Islam with their situation prior to Islam, which he painted pitch-black; he emphasized the religious recommendations to treat the slaves well and to set them free; he contrasted the Muslim concept of slavery as partial legal disability with Aristotle's view that some men were by nature born to slavery. He then concluded by attacking the West, which, he wrote, boasts of having emancipated the slaves when it had done so only because economic necessity no longer required their subjugation, whereas Islam had recommended setting them free despite economic necessity.[40]

In regard to *jihād*, al-'Aqqād argued that its purpose was not to compel conversion to Islam, nor to fight all infidels. It was directed only against those forces that stood in the way of propagating the message of the Prophet and against the enemies of Islam who had made no covenant with it. That Muḥammad had fought against his Meccan opponents and had compelled them to adopt Islam could not be construed as a contradiction since the Meccans did not oppose any ideas to Muḥammad's message but only certain traditions which they exploited in order to perpetuate their power. Besides, he went on, history has proved that "power is indispensable for the realization of the programs of reformers and revolutionaries. . ." and, in any case, the Muslims had been the victims of the sword before they turned it against their enemies. Finally, power as used by the Muslims in the service of man guiding man cannot be compared to power as used by the West solely for economic expansion, ambition, domination.[41]

These last arguments are good examples of the apologetic spirit pervading most of the book, overshadowing and confusing its potentially constructive parts. In his attempt to put one side in the most favorable light and the other in the most unfavorable, al-'Aqqād does not hesitate to distort history and to select and ignore facts at will, to "reconcile" contradictions by verbal manipulation and resort to spurious comparisons, to mix norm with fact and principle with emotional argument, and constantly to shift his ground. In short, reason degenerates into casuistry and the ruses of the defense counsel.

Altogether, al-'Aqqād's work represented neither a justification of the existing system nor a concrete alternative based on a reinterpretation of the traditional doctrine. His argument about sovereignty might have served to clothe the existing constitutional regime in Muslim garb and so facilitate its assimilation by Muslims; but his subsequent effort to defend the principles of "Islamic democracy" caused him to disparage some of the essential procedures of constitutionalism and involved a retreat from the initial position of the intellectual leaders, who sought with great effort and at some sacrifice to establish the separation of Islam from the political order and to lay the foundations for an Egyptian nationalist mystique. Thus he stated on several occasions that the Qur'ān must be the source of legislation. He strongly implied that certain Muslim procedures and institutions in their historical form, or as he imagined them, were part of the faith and binding upon Muslims, thereby rejecting, by implication, the concept of the nation as founded on geography, ethnic origin, and political organization, in favor of the traditional view holding religion to be the primary determinant of the political unit. Neither did the "Islamic principles" that he suggested offer any coherent alternative to the existing system. They were unrelated to each other, inconsistently interpreted, purely formal and idealistic. They betrayed a lack of understanding of the dynamics and real foundations of democracy and constitutionalism as a result of the subordination of the need to understand them to the urge to defend and glorify Islam.

Here, then, as in the case of ethics, the attempt to ground the Liberal ideas in Islam resulted only in reinforcing faith in an Islam presumably capable of assuring the best government and the best order, but lacking any concrete guiding principles. More than in the case of ethics, the glorification of the ideal Muslim political system, whatever that was thought to be, pointed to the existing government and the existing political order as the main obstacles in the way of the realization of the ideal and hinted at revolutionary action. This was precisely the sentiment that impelled the Muslim Brethren in their drive to bring down the existing political order by violent means.

History

The most extreme ideological consequences of the retreat of the intellectual leaders were reflected in a work published by Aḥmad Amīn in 1952, concluding his series of volumes on the social and cultural history of Islam. The work is entitled *Yawm al-Islām* — (The Day of Islam). In the initial rationalist-humanist phase, we have seen that Amīn summarized the constructive views of the intellectual leaders and read them back into Muslim history. Now, in the reactionary phase, his concluding reflections on ancient and recent Muslim history may be viewed as exemplifying in an extreme fashion the ideological failure resulting from the intellectual leaders' retreat from rationalism and their loss of orientation.

The most prominent feature in Amīn's book is the drastic change of attitude towards the West. Whereas in his previous work Amīn had hailed the interplay of cultures in early Islam in order to justify the recent Western orientation of Egyptian thought, here he launched a bitter attack against the "Christian peoples" of the West of all categories, times, and places.

> Christians hate Muslims and treat them as enemies even more than they do the Jews. Their enmity continues to this very day and is evidenced in their support of the Jews against the Arabs in tearing off Palestine from their hands.[42]
>
> The spirit of the Crusades is residing in them today even as it was in the heart of Peter the Hermit. Fanaticism is still abiding in their tissues, permeating their entrails, and circulating in their veins. . . .[43]
>
> All the Christian peoples are unanimous in their enmity to Islam. The

spirit of enmity is embodied in a constant secret effort to crush Islam utterly.[44]

Amīn did not spare even the Islamists, with some of whom he had worked personally in the Fu'ād University: "One might have expected the orientalists to correct the Europeans with their research and science; but it has become evident that they are made of the same stuff as the Crusaders." [45]

His bitterness against the West was so great as to cause him to lose all his previous sense of human fellowship. He did not hesitate to write with brutal frankness that during World War II, "the Muslim world quenched its resentment because the fighting took place between the Christian nations and because it knew that victors and vanquished alike were losers in that war." [46] He then went on to say that only God knows what would happen if a third world war broke out, and added: "But perhaps the Muslim world might expect some good from the violent strife between the . . . capitalist countries and communist Russia. For the conflict between the two opens the door for it and allows it to cut its way between the two creeds. It can benefit from both rivals if it acts wisely and thoughtfully." [47]

With his attacks on the West, he also turned against fellow-intellectuals and former colleagues in the university, retracting or reversing most of the ideas that he had shared with them.

"Those Europeanizers who preach separation on the basis of language, ethnic origin, and country are more vicious than those who preach separation on the grounds of creeds. . ." [48] he wrote, retreating from his previous nationalism. He denounced the modern Western-style education and publicly accused the university in which he had taught of responsibility for creating whole generations of students who "are Muslims only geographically." [49] He made it a point to emphasize, contrary to what he had previously maintained, that he did not agree with 'Alī 'Abd al-Rāziq that Islam is concerned only with spiritual affairs and that it has nothing to do with political power. He insisted now that Islam is both a religious and a temporal order, although the elaboration of a constitutional law for such questions as the succession of the caliphate was left to the leaders of each generation to decide.[50] Forgetting his previous views on the exploitation of religion by politicians, he vehemently opposed the separation of politics from religion and argued that "it is essential that religion enter into politics in order to mitigate and improve it. . ." [51] Europe, he said, abandoning his historian's role and relapsing into that of the preacher, "fell victim to repeated wars only because it separated religion from politics, for in so doing, it separated politics from ethics." [52]

Amīn expressed vigorous disagreement with Ṭāha Ḥusayn's statement that the East, to which Egypt belongs, does not differ from the West. He stressed the "materialism" of the West, which he understood in the sense of rationalism, and opposed it to the "spirituality" of the East with its concern for the purpose of life, of existence, and of the after life. The West, he contended, studies the heart in terms of its physiology, the East is concerned with its meditation.[53]

Amīn completely reversed his previous position about the desirability of a plurality of Muslim political centers. Now, he asserted repeatedly that the only hope for Muslims was in their banding together in a Muslim League which would take over unconditionally Western achievements in science and technology in order to fight for its own existence and protect Islam from the impending danger.[54] This, and the recommendation to open the gates of absolute *ijtihād* in order to reestablish Islam as the foundation for a religious-social order,[55] were the only concrete steps he had to suggest for the regeneration of Islam.

Thus, as a remedy for Muslim countries, Amīn was unable to do better than echo the general propositions first suggested by al-Afghānī. All the experience gained in three quarters of a century of national life, and all of the progress made in ideological development — much of it in pursuit of al-Afghānī's ideas — was either ignored or rejected. Although Amīn's is admittedly an extreme case of regression, for which personal reasons were partially responsible,[56] he still reflects the ideological failure of his times, without which such regression would perhaps have been unlikely.

Part Five

THE THREAT OF TRADITIONALIST REACTION

CHAPTER 14

The Ideology and Mentality of Mahdism

In the chapter on the historical crisis, we have described briefly the rise of the Muslim Brotherhood to a position of first importance in Egyptian society and we have referred to its role in political developments since the war. In the present chapter, we shall attempt to elucidate the positive aspects of its program and its ideology and point out the essential characteristics and the place of the movement in the ideological development of Egypt.[1]

In discussing the work of the intellectual leaders during the reactionary second phase,[2] we have qualified this movement as dangerous and have consequently considered the intellectuals' indirect contribution to its growth as one of the most damaging by-products of their Muslim orientation. The Muslim Brotherhood was dangerous not because of its terroristic and revolutionary activities as such. Violence may sometimes prove the only means to redress an unbearable evil, even though history has repeatedly shown that the unleashing of violence carries with it great social risks. The danger of the Brotherhood lay in the mentality governing its use of violence and in the ideology and program in whose name it was ready to commit it. In general, it can be said that members of the Brotherhood knew bitterly and well what they were opposed to, but they knew very little of what to put in its place. They believed that a state and a society based on the Qur'ān and the Tradition would cure all the ills of their people, but they had no real knowledge of what must be done to build such a state. Worse still, they were not aware of their ignorance because they had no clear idea of the intricate problems of a modern state and a modern society, and were consequently disposed to consider anyone who objected to their program, even on technical grounds, as an enemy of Islam who deserved to be struck down by force.

The ideology of the Brotherhood was essentially a version of the views of Rashīd Riḍā and the Manārists reduced to a simple creed, grounded more on faith than systematic thought, cast into the frame of a militant movement inspired and activated by negative nationalism, and reinforced by concern with the bitterly felt social misery.

The leader of the Brotherhood, al-Bannā, had in fact known Riḍā and attended his circle frequently during his years as student in Dār al-ʿUlūm, in Cairo. But where Riḍā had been preoccupied with the *doctrinal foundations* for returning to the Islamic sources, al-Bannā simply went back to the bare Qur'ān and Tradition; where Riḍā had tried to work out the *principles* of Islamic ethics, al-Bannā asserted the prohibitions and injunctions of the Qur'ān in their stark simplicity; and where Riḍā had concerned himself with the *doctrine* of the Islamic State, the *bases* for the unification of the Law and the restoration of the unity of the *ummah*, al-Bannā and the Brotherhood began to agitate for a Muslim State and a Muslim social order which they perceived only intuitively and tried to understand pragmatically in the course of time by reference to the Qur'ān and the Tradition. Al-Bannā and the Brotherhood had in common with Riḍā an unwavering faith that Islam is perfect and provides all the answers to the problems of mankind. They also shared a deep conviction that Islam was in mortal danger from the hostile machinations of the Christian West and its blind puppets, the Westernizers. This latter belief was greatly intensified in the case of the Brotherhood because it merged with the active nationalist struggle, and became a cardinal point in its whole thinking.

Throughout the period of al-Bannā's leadership, the Muslim Brotherhood was concerned mainly with preparation, organization, and action in several spheres. After the suppression of the movement in December 1948, and the assassination of al-Bannā a few months later, the movement went through a period of persecution and underground activity from which it emerged again into legality in 1950 on the condition that it abstain from political activity. During the next two years, reorganized and led by a well-educated former magistrate, Ḥasan al-Huḍaybī, the movement made a supreme effort to appeal to the educated public by establishing its ideological position on the crucial problems of the time.

Dozens of books and pamphlets were published by its leading members, bearing such titles as *Islam and the Political Conditions, Islam and Financial Matters, Islam and the Socialist Programs, Islam and Political Despotism, Labor Regulations in Islam, Islam and the Rules of War* and so on.[3] Despite their deceptively learned titles, however, these books actually had no common theoretical foundation and spelled out no concrete program. On the whole, the works to which this writer has had access [4] said little more than that Islam was in harmony with the best ideals and practices in these matters, which were actually understood in a very superficial way, and restated the favorite themes of the Brotherhood. As an illustration we will examine the political-social views of the Brotherhood as expressed in one of the most important books in the series, written by an eminent *idéologue* of the movement.

The book in question is entitled *Min Hunā Na'lam,* (translated into English as *Our Beginning in Wisdom*). It was written by *shaykh* Muḥammad al-Ghazzālī and was published in 1950. Al-Ghazzālī had also written three books on political–social subjects — *Islam and the Economic Conditions, Islam and Political Despotism, Islam and the Socialist Programs* — and dozens of articles in the Brotherhood's periodicals; so that he was well qualified to represent the Brotherhood's political thinking. *Min Hunā Na'lam* is particularly appropriate for our purpose because it was written in refutation of a book by *shakyh* Khālid Muḥammad Khālid, *Min Hunā Nabda'* (From Here We Start), which directly challenged the fundamental political and social ideology of the Brotherhood. (Khālid had restated and elaborated 'Alī 'Abd al-Rāziq's thesis that Islam had nothing to do with the political and social order and that the few prohibitions mentioned in the Qur'ān could very well be accommodated in a secular state; he had energetically attacked the religious state, which, he said, must lead to the collusion of clerics and tyrants against liberty, justice, and progress; he had insisted on the indispensability of secular, national government and socialism for reconstructing a healthy and prosperous society; and he had advocated the further emancipation and education of women, giving them equal rights, and establishing birth control). In examining al-Ghazzālī's rebuttal, we shall not bind ourselves to the polemics or the logical order of the book; we shall simply take it as a statement of the position of the Brotherhood on some social and political questions and as an illustration of the mode of thinking of its leaders.

Typical of the ethos of the Brotherhood is the fact that one of the dominant themes in the book is a fervent belief that Islam, being the expression of divine wisdom, is the most perfect guide to all mankind in all their endeavors: Islam is a religion "that saves civilization and is the guardian of its noble pillars." [5] It is

> . . . a body of general principles valid for all, irrespective of race, color or nation. It is a gift from God . . . to all mankind. It is based on the conviction that God alone is king and Lord in a realm where no difference separates Arab from foreigner, where His word is law and His will is reality, where all believers are equal, and where there are neither tyrants nor dictators, neither philosophers of power nor advocates of terror. . . .[6]

These and similar assertions of a general nature are familiar from the writings of Rashīd Riḍā and others. But it must be kept in mind that the Muslim Brotherhood was a militant (and armed) movement, and that such utterances had, therefore, a quite different significance in its case. They did not simply express pious boasting or devotional cant, but reflected a messianic vision which the Brethren proceeded to bring into being sword in hand.

From the level of generalities, al-Ghazzālī moved to the narrower area of state and society and asserted that Islam is a complete political-social system — as complete as the Communist doctrine and ideology — and therefore needs power to fulfill its purpose.

> Islam . . . is a comprehensive program presented to man for the purpose of a general reconstruction of societies and states in accordance with practical as well as spiritual principles. It would be idle to claim that in a program of reconstruction there is no place or need for worldly government. . . .[7]

He compared Islam with the French Revolution [8] and asserted that the latter "did not realize its program through preaching alone, but overthrew the government, seized power, and effected its principles. . . ." [9] The same was true of the Bolshevik Revolution. Now, "Islam," he wrote, "came to us with principles far more important than those of both revolutions. If success is to be achieved, the method of reconstruction that Islam commands cannot be different from that of world reformers at other times and places." [10] In the present situation, state power does not belong to Islam, but "any attempt to justify this . . . is an attempt to induce religion to accept the crime that has been perpetrated against one half of its being. . ." [11]

The author gave numerous definitions of the nature of the Islamic State. "The State of Islam is the embodiment of an idea by and for which it lives, as Communist Russia is the embodiment of an idea by which its internal and foreign policies are regulated and according to which . . . it lives." [12] The state in Islam is not merely a utilitarian institution. "The purpose of state rule is not only the administration of justice and the maintenance of public services; it also includes certain religious duties that are not separable from the state. . ." [13]

But what precisely are the functions and the organization of the Islamic state? (This was Khālid's specific challenge to the Brotherhood.)

In regard to the specific functions of the Islamic State, the Muslim Brethren had placed themselves in a rather difficult theoretical position. Since they had brushed aside the whole compendium of Islamic law and had gone back to the Qur'ān and the Tradition, there were, in fact, few concrete functions left for the Islamic State, as such, unless new ones were formulated. Indeed, notwithstanding the general assertions that Islam is as complete a system as that of the Communist society, the author was able to specify only a few concrete functions peculiar to the Islamic State; otherwise, he tended to evade the challenge by insisting that "the duties of the state are clearly and precisely outlined in the Qur'ān and the Tradition. . ." [14] Such duties as he was able to list included a mixture of some general and a few specific elements. They are mentioned below in the author's own words:

The government established by Islam was based upon definite principles; it bore the Islamic idea and sought to realize it on earth. If such a government seeks power, it is in order to *hold prayer, give alms,* and to *command what is good and prohibit what is evil.*[15]

In Islam, there are personal duties of worship which individuals can perform directly and through their own personal effort alone. Such are prayer, fasting, and other related duties. But there are, in addition to these, social duties which individuals cannot discharge alone and which require the instrumentality of the state. Of these there are *Jihād, punishment, charity, and others.*[16]

In the economic field, for instance, Islam *prohibits usury and monopoly*; in the political, it *prohibits despotism and tyranny*; in the moral, it *prohibits disbelief and corruption.* Islam further demands that its men, both rulers and ruled, *observe prayer and the other commandments of God.* If the state carries out this teaching in its entirety, Islam will live securely therein and it will not matter whether that state is called nationalist or religious.[17]

The justifications for the necessity of an Islamic State which the author stressed most, however, were the two related functions of "the defense of Islam" and *jihād.* These constituted in fact a reinterpretation of nationalism in Islamic terms which were familiar only to the lower classes. The Brotherhood thus transposed into the context of the nationalist struggle the traditional notion underlying *jihād* of the division of the world into two hostile camps — the abode of Islam and the abode of war; and manifested an intensive conviction of the eternally active hostility of the Christian-imperialist-West to Islam, which suggests irresistibly the Soviet obsession with the idea of a capitalist encirclement during the thirties. It seems, indeed, that the notion of the hostile Christian West fulfilled for the Brotherhood the same function of marshalling the energy of the people and silencing the opposition that its counterpart fulfilled for Soviet Russia. Following are a few illustrations:

At last it has become clear to us that there exists a widespread conspiracy plotted by religious and cultural imperialism against Islam. The purpose of this plot has been to destroy the position which Islam occupies in the heart of the faithful. . . .[18]

The aim of Europe is the destruction of Islam as a religion once it has succeeded in destroying it as a state. . .[19]

The hostility and aggression of the West against Islam was not merely political or imperialistic; it was religiously motivated and was controlled by the Church:

The West surely seeks to humiliate us, to occupy our land, and to begin destroying Islam by annulling its laws and abolishing its traditions. In doing this, the West acts under the Church. . . . In the West . . . we have seen how Christianity indirectly controls the government.[20]

The power of the Church is operative in orienting and directing the internal and foreign policies of the Western bloc led by England and America. . . . A hundred years ago, the situation was one of enmity between the state and Christianity. Today, however, the relation is obviously a cordial alliance.[21]

The function which this conviction of Western hostility fulfilled for the Brotherhood is clearly reflected in the following passages. If Christianity controls the Western states and means to destroy Islam, what is more logical than that Islam, too, should have its united state to counter the attack?

Seldom, if ever, has Islam needed the state more than today — not merely because the state is an integral part of it, but also because Islam is threatened with extermination in a world where only the strong can survive.[22]

The denial to Islam of its absolute right to rule and its consideration as a religion separate from the state is the effect of the traditional enmity that Europe has always felt for Islam and its people.[23]

If (Marxist) unbelief has its political state that gives its false logic life and power, then all the more so should faith not be left without a political stronghold to give it protection, to defend it against its enemies, and to champion the cause of believers everywhere.[24]

Furthermore, if the West was bent on destroying Islam, all those who opposed the Brotherhood's program to counter the threat were, wittingly or unwittingly, the enemies of Islam. As the chief lieutenant of the Supreme Guide said of Khālid's book in his introduction to *Min Hunā Na'lam*:

From Here We Start is a book the purpose of which was neither the drawing up of a healthy program nor the depiction of an ideal. Rather, it has provided the enemies of Islam with weapons and ammunition to retard the advance of any reform program.[25]

Referring to the Westernizers in general, al-Ghazzālī dubbed them again and again as puppets of the enemies of Islam.

Undoubtedly imperialism has succeeded in creating a generation of Muslims who cooperate with the enemies of Islam to destroy their own religion. . . .[26]
. . . . The faction which works for the separation of Egypt from Islam [that is, the secular nationalists] is really a shameless, pernicious, and perverse group of puppets and slaves of Europeans.[27]

The notion that a different interpretation of Islam amounted to helping the ever-pressing enemy suggests, again, the Stalinist-communist idea of the "objective guilt" of deviationists against the Soviet system as a whole. This is even clearer in the following words of the author, referring to 'Ali 'Abd al-Rāziq's book: [28] "The soldiers of Islam recognized in it an instrument by which its author had, intentionally or not, served the cause of Christian imperialism. It was for this reason that al-Azhar withdrew the title of *'ālim* from *shaykh* 'Abd al-Rāziq." [29]

It is not surprising that the Muslim Brotherhood should place great emphasis on the injunction of *jihād*. We have seen in the chapter on "Islamic Background" that *jihād* was the only civic function envisaged in the Islamic political and social doctrine. It was only natural, therefore, that this function should again become predominant with the awakening of the political consciousness of the masses and the reassertion of the Islamic ideal in general. The Muslim Brotherhood liberated that injunction from all the interpretations of reformists like Riḍā who sought to internalize it,[30] and Westernizers who sought to soften and apologize for it,[31] and reasserted it in its simple, literal meaning as an obligation to fight to defend and spread God's faith. The aggressive character of that injunction was of no concern to the Brotherhood but was simply lost in its fervent avowal of the absolute truth and excellence of the cause for which Holy War was to be waged, and was implicitly explained away by the conception of a general plot to destroy Islam. Offense and defense were thus fused in one concept.

Truly, the wars of conquest were in perfect accordance with Islam's constitution and nature. Islam does not meet aggression with silent protest; nor does it allow peoples to suffer under their despots and merely shed its tears over their fate . . . The Great Prophet began building a state that would adopt the right cause everywhere and defend it against tyrants of the earth. As soon as he was able to order the people in line for prayer at the mosque, he led them in ranks to the battlefield.[32]

The injunction of *jihād* was so important in the Brotherhood's ideology that al-Ghazzālī not only used it as one of the main justifications for the indispensability of the Islamic State, but made it the foundation of the "economic policy of Islam." Indeed, *jihād* provided the practical link between the religious-political and the social functions of the Islamic State, or what the author called "Islamic Socialism."

The author saw the theoretical foundation of Islamic socialism in two principles of the Islamic dogma and ethics: "Islamic socialism is based on the cardinal points of monotheism and the brotherhood of all men." This meant, he continued, that "there can be no pecuniary or class discrimination among the people. . . ."; [33] and that "the state is responsible for the realization of the brotherhood of men and the abolition of every circumstance that runs counter to it. . ." [34] The first idea he understood as implying, for instance, that "no person may be preferred to another and no opportunity may be given to one unless it is given to another; nobody may work unless everyone else has the opportunity to do likewise. . ." [35] As for the responsibility of the state to realize the brotherhood of men, this he understood to mean that the state should undertake action to uproot luxury and extravagance, establish a self-sufficient economy, and maintain full employment.[36]

Full employment is to be assured by two means: the first is that the state should undertake public works — "this is a measure of common sense (and) there is nothing in it contrary to Islam"; the other is peculiarly Islamic, and consists of a "*jihād* economy." "Islam prescribes economic mobilization along with military mobilization for the service of truth, virtue, and faith. . . Such total mobilization would put an end to unemployment and social injustice. All workers would be true Holy Warriors." [37]

On the question of socialism, the author conceded that apart from these general principles and suggestions the matter must be left to the state to work out in detail. According to Islam, it is fully empowered to take all the necessary measures:

> Islamic socialism is first concerned with realizing the more basic principles that Islamic doctrine teaches. Only after these are assured will it devote care to discover and establish the detailed economic regulations compatible with it. To this end, it fully sanctions the use of legislative and executive power . . . Perhaps these requirements will force the state to extend its control in a manner similar to the Russians and the Americans. But this is perfectly legitimate as long as its general purpose and motives are purely Islamic.[38]

Although the author, in speaking of what we might call the "positive side" of Islamic Socialism, contented himself with asserting the few principles and suggestions already mentioned, on the negative side he was very forceful in his condemnation of the existing socio-economic order. Here, as in other aspects of the program, the author and the Brotherhood knew much better what they were against than what they were for. The author concurred with Khālid's scathing criticism of the Egyptian social system and added a few of his own:

> Oriental capitalism . . . is alone responsible for most of our present sufferings and for our extremist inclinations. Everybody knows that capitalism is founded on robbery and, what is worse, that it spends all it steals on the satisfaction of base desires and the spreading of moral, social, and political chaos. . . .[39]
>
> The land Islam occupies on the earth is a wretched wilderness where flocks of miserable people labor endlessly under most inhuman conditions for the benefit of a few decadent aristocrats. Is this the fate of those whose religion is monotheism and justice? 'Accursed be that which they have given to themselves. God has condemned them to eternal fire.'[40]

With respect to the functions peculiar to the Islamic State, then, the Brotherhood had in actual fact a few specific ideas, such as the application of the few legal prescriptions, prohibitions, and punishments prescribed by the Qur'ān, as well as collection and distribution of the alms and the promotion of observance of some rituals; a more general notion of establishing social justice and of enforcing an atmosphere of decency and austerity in public manners;[41] and a still more general notion of defending Islam against disbelief and external enemies and of propagating the faith. Otherwise, the Islamic State embraced presumably all the other functions of a modern state:

> Islam regards it as the duty of the state to protect the faith and spread it at home and abroad, to apply its rules, to look after the believers, to bring up new generations in true devotion to the faith, and to employ the benefits of modern civilization in the service of Islam itself.[42]

The author's views regarding the constitutional and political organization of the Islamic State were less specific than his views of the functions of the state. They consisted largely of broad ideas and generalities, with only occasional references to the details of organization. Such references as there were revealed for the most part a lack of appreciation of the importance and complexity of the mechanical side of politics and government that spelled grave danger for Egyptian society if the Brotherhood succeeded in its aim of achieving power — as it almost did.[43]

At the beginning of the book, al-Ghazzālī expressed a gratifying awareness of the importance of establishing constitutional controls to restrain abuses of power. He attributed the decline of Islam and the sufferings of the Muslim peoples to the lack of a definite constitution:

It was, perhaps, the absence of such a constitution that enabled one of the Muslim rulers to abolish by a stroke of the pen the legislation of the Qur'ān and the Sunnah and replace it with the . . . infidel *Code Napoléon.* And it was likewise the absence of this constitution that made it possible for a number of absolute rulers to govern not only the Muslims, but Islam itself, according to their own inclinations and whims.[44]

He also expressed the opinion that such a constitution should be worked out afresh. Thus, after commenting on some of the laws and procedures in Saudi Arabia and rejecting the claim that that country's government was Islamic because it enforced the Qur'ānic prohibitions, he concluded by saying: "We have seen that criminal and financial ordinances are only a branch of the general constitution which must be first decided upon and in which the rights and obligations of ruler and ruled should be defined. . . ."[45] Later, however, he revealed that the constitution and the restraints which he had in mind were essentially of a moral nature. He then suggested the following principles as the foundations of "an original constitution"—that is to say, an Islamic constitution that would not be copied from some foreign culture:

Wherever Islamic rule is established it must be based on the following truths or principles:

The world has but one Master unto Whom all reverence, all love and all obedience is due; He is the one great God. All peoples are one single nation. No origin, race, color, or country shall differentiate them. Their superiority to one another lies only in the sphere of morals and of achievement.

The sole lawgiver is God. No man shall legislate for or judge another. Human beings are all one in their submission to divine authority. . . . The divine revelation is the basis of justice in the affairs of individual and society. Where there is no justice, there is neither revelation nor divine law. . .[46]

An indication as to how the restraints implicit in this passage were to operate was provided by the author's response to the criticism that religious government allows no opposition in the modern sense, which is generally recognized as one of the best guarantees against despotism and tyranny. Our author's answer was that, on the contrary, the teachings of Islam demand "the creation of a benevolent and daring opposition which allows no wrong to pass without criticism. . . . Islam does not want a despondent, ignorant, and passive society which is incapable of disciplining its rulers. . . ." [47] In other words, he assumed that right and wrong according to the Qur'ān are absolutely clear and that the people, knowing this, and knowing its own and the ruler's rights and obligations, will check him in case of transgression.

This conception of truth and right as absolute, monistic, and clear, was made explicit in al-Ghazzālī's refutation of the contention of critics of the Muslim Brotherhood that the Qur'ān was liable to many interpretations. He made a distinction between verses which refer to God and His attributes and those having to do with doctrines, principles, anecdotes, and narratives. The former are beyond reach of reason and relate to faith; the latter, which alone are "the source of legislation and the groundwork of government," are clear and final in what they say "and are not susceptible of any interpretation." All the historical conflicts and sectarian wars, he asserted, that were allegedly due to differences of interpretation were in fact due to the malicious intentions of one or both parties. "We only impute to the Qur'ān the ambiguity that really exists in our minds. . ." [48]

The consequences for the social order of encouraging militant opposition on the basis of such views are easy to imagine. The author gave a glimpse of them when he said in a tone of self-criticism: "When the righteous dispute with the unrighteous and each party advances the same verse in its support, we sit with folded hands instead of smiting the shameless misinterpreter and restoring right where it belongs." [49] What this amounts to, in fact, is to let power and the sword decide what is right. It is a return to the beginning of Islamic history when the Khārijites, expounding the same views, started the tale of violence and anarchy which largely constituted Muslim history and which ended with ruthless despotism on one side and passive submission on the other.[50]

Apart from the general principles of the Islamic constitution mentioned before, the author made no detailed reference to the exact form of government and the institutions which should apply it. The Islamic state was to be ruled by an *imām*, limited in his powers only by the principles and implications of the Qur'ān and the Tradition, and by the people's obligation to correct him. The book abounds with references to the ethical limitations which Islam imposes on the ruler, and with advice in the form of assertions that in Islam the ruler is an employee, a benevolent, merciful father, an *imām* not different from the *imām* in his mosque, and so on,[51] all of which point to an exclusively moral approach to politics that ignored completely the lessons of historical or human experience. At one point, the author considered the objection to an *imāmah* on the grounds that since history had shown virtuous caliphs to be extremely rare it would be safer to adopt a democratic form of government which would establish solid guarantees against tyranny; but instead of answering this objection or thinking in terms of endowing Islamic government with similar guarantees, al-Ghazzālī went on to compare the behavior of Western democratic governments with that of Muslim governments, and reached the conclusion that "the first Muslim conquerors were angels. . ." and that ". . . despite all its ills and mistakes, [the historical] Islamic rule was still a blessing for the whole of mankind. . ." [52]

One of the main ideals of the Islamic Constitution mentioned above was the opposition to nationalism in the name of the community of Islam. Although the Muslim Brotherhood became the champion of the nationalist struggle in Egypt, and provided the most zealous soldiers to the cause, it equated what we called positive nationalism with godlessness and considered it responsible for all the corruption of modern Muslim society; ". . . Every growth of nationalism, racialism, and infidel patriotism is a loss of Islamic faith as well as of Islamic rule. The revival of such evil fanaticism is a plot against God's religion and a return to the first *jāhiliyyah* with its injustice and criminality." [53] Here, as everywhere in the book, the author saw the hand of the enemies of Islam plotting its destruction: "Nationalism is only a ruse of war and a strategy espoused and encouraged by heathenism for the purpose of overwhelming and obliterating Islam." [54] If the nationalist state is not concerned with the political, economic, social, and moral teachings of Islam and gives Islamic civil and criminal law no place, then, he declared, "the state is utterly irreligious and it is impossible to expect Islam to accept it." No Muslim, he went on, is under the obligation to respect such a government. "On the contrary, Islam demands of Muslims who live under such regime to fight it to the end and institute in its place a government that actually observes the teachings of Islam and strives to realize its ideals." [55]

To conclude our examination of the views, mode of thinking, and ethos of one of the ideological leaders of the Brotherhood we should, perhaps, emphasize once more the two themes noted at the beginning of this analysis as most characteristic of the spirit of the movement. One is the messianic tendency, or the quality of intense faith, born of a burning desire for relief from unbearable conditions, cavalierly dismissing contradictory facts. This substitution of faith and wishful thinking for causality is well expressed in the following remarks of the author on the wickedness of modern nationalism:

> In Turkey, a miserable reactionary movement was started for the purpose of reviving the Turkic nationality. It succeeded in dissolving the Caliphate and in separating religion from the state. But what good did that do?
>
> Under the Islamic Caliphate, the Turks inspired terror in their Russian neighbors, and, for centuries, they waged war on Russian soil. Today, Turkey is a petty state which begs for its arms from America and lives in the orbit of the dissolute democracies. The Turks live under constant fear of the outside world and possess less than ten percent of their empire. To what good has their unbelief led them? [56]

Implicit in the author's questions is the belief that if only Islam were faithfully followed, then all good would follow. This belief filled the gap between the actual, rather simple and general program of the Brotherhood, and their expectation of realizing the Kingdom of God on Earth.

The second theme we wish to emphasize is the readiness to support the messianic aspiration with violence. We have seen some expressions of this readiness, but none is as indicative of the mood of the Brotherhood as this passage from al-Ghazzālī's book:

> The spirit of resistance throbs in the heart of all of us, individuals and groups; and we are resolved to live as Muslims under the Book and the Tradition or die. But if we are to die in the course of this struggle, we shall not perish alone. The enemies of Islam shall perish before us.[57]

From what has been said of its political activity, we may conclude that the Muslim Brotherhood was essentially a movement of violent reaction against the ideological failure of the intellectual leaders of whatever tendency and against the political–social failure of the Liberal Nationalist regime. The Brotherhood itself did not provide a positive response to the ideological and political problems facing Egyptian society nor did it even begin to understand them. Its assertion that the Qur'ān was a sufficient guide to the establishment of an Islamic utopia was based on faith, not on rational demonstration. Its success in rallying the lower classes and its resort to violence were, perhaps more than anything else, a measure of the social failure of the Liberal Nationalist regime. Its great success among the educated youth and among some of the professionals, after World War II, was a measure of the failure of the Liberal Nationalist ideology and of the betrayal of the nationalist cause by the Liberal political leaders. Viewed from a broad perspective, the phenomenon of the Muslim Brotherhood — its rise, its ideology, its violence, and its success — seems to us a negative confirmation of the original premise upon which this study was based: that the stability, smooth functioning, and well-being of a political community require a generally accepted ideology which explains and justifies the existing order of things. Because such an ideology failed to emerge in Egypt, the Brotherhood sought to fill the vacuum with faith; and because the existing order remained alien to the people, failure of function was taken as failure of principles, and led the Muslim Brotherhood to seek its destruction.

CHAPTER 15

Retrospect and Prospect

In comparing the response to the challenge of modernism by the Western Christian countries with that of Egypt we conceded at the beginning of this study that in examining the efforts of Egypt's intellectual and political leaders to evolve an ideology adapted to modern conditions of life, in place of the obsolescent traditional belief-system of Islam, we could not justifiably expect complete success in the relatively short time that these leaders have had to grapple with the problem. Therefore, we shall not stress here the conclusion which plainly emerges from our analysis — that the Egyptian leaders failed to work out any such viable ideology — but will attempt instead to summarize the difficulties that have led to that failure.

In making our comparison between Egypt and the West, we have emphasized that the problem was aggravated for Egypt by three factors: (1) that she had to undergo change at a more accelerated rate than the Christian West; (2) that the forces of change were of foreign importation at a time when foreign powers were encroaching on her; and (3) that Islam had been from the beginning far more involved in the politico-social order than Christianity. Speaking in the most general terms, we may conclude that these three points of difference proved to be precisely the factors most responsible for Egypt's failure to evolve a viable modern ideology. For they were reflected in a faster rate of material — as opposed to intellectual — development; in the rise of a nationalist movement dominated by what we have called the "negative element;" in a greater resistance to modern ideas because of their Western-Christian label; and in a readiness to associate the protection of the religious sentiment with the necessity to preserve or restore specifically Muslim forms of political organization. But if we are to draw conclusions that might help in understanding present and future developments in Egypt, we must attempt to review in greater detail the manner in which these three factors manifested themselves in the specific course of Egyptian political and intellectual development.

In the strictly political sphere the most striking characteristic of the period under study was the failure of liberal democracy to take root after it had been constitutionally established. A number of intellectual and historical reasons have been advanced for that failure in the course of our analysis, but to understand its implications for the present and the future, its deeper causes must be examined more closely.

Intellectually, the liberal thinkers did not grasp the essential meaning and dynamics of democracy and constitutionalism. They looked upon the Constitution as a legal document beyond their purview, or understood its provisions in exclusively moral-idealistic terms rather than as an attempt to realize certain desirable ideals by means of practical political devices. This attitude may have been partially rooted in the approach of traditional Muslim political doctrine, but it was also due to other contingent factors. Among these were the relatively recent beginnings of secular intellectual activity in general, the character of the writers as *belles-lettristes* rather than specialized social or political thinkers, and, most important, the fact that democracy had not only been imported ready-made into Egypt but had been instituted altogether too soon. These facts are also at the root of the *historical* failure of the regime established by the Constitution.

From a moral and short-range point of view, there is no doubt that through their actions and behavior the chief political protagonists — the British, the king, the Wafd, and the small parties — all shared in the responsibility for the failure of the Liberal Constitutional regime. From a broad historical perspective, however, that failure must be seen to have had its roots in the Egyptian social structure as it affected and was in turn affected by Egyptian nationalism.

In the West, for example, the ideas of democracy had had a long history before economic transformations brought forth large and powerful middle classes to champion them in the course of their struggle against the traditional political authorities and systems which obstructed their interests. Only after this process had culminated in the French Revolution did modern nationalism emerge as a by-product of democratic ideas. In Egypt, on the other hand, the democratic ideal was itself the by-product of the nationalist movement. For, by the end of World War I, the ideas of democracy had had only a very brief and limited existence in Egypt, and economic development had not yet given birth to a bourgeoisie whose interests clashed with those of the traditionally dominant group and which had therefore a stake in the promotion of the democratic ideal. Rather, in so far as the Constitution of 1923 represented a victory of liberal democracy, this was only because a small middle class of professionals, officials, and intellectuals who had espoused democratic views mainly on idealistic grounds had managed to ride to power on the wave of "negative nationalism." This is why the constitutional regime could have only a precarious existence.

The absence of any conflict of interests between the group which had lately come to power on the wave of nationalism and the traditionally dominant landowners caused the two groups to merge in due course, left the internal programs and policies of the various parties biased in favor of the landed interests and with little difference in other respects, and turned politics into a relentless struggle for power between a few personalities and their supporters. The only issue existing, or believed to exist, between the parties was related to the nationalist tactics and gave the party struggle the almost exclusive character of inflammatory agitation by the "outs" countered with violent repression by the "ins." Thus nationalism was instrumental in the premature institution of democracy in Egypt, gave to the party system its *raison d'être,* while it contributed to its failure to fulfill the functions of parties in a democratic system.

In the broader ideological sphere, after the first intellectual groupings, the problem of the relation between reason and revelation, and the related question of the dogma of the integral revelation of the Qur'ān emerged, objectively, as the fundamental issues. The positions taken in regard to them had a decisive effect on the method of thinking, the orientation, and the efforts of the leaders of all persuasions to evolve an ideology adaptable to the realities of modern life.

With 'Abduh, Islamic Reformism faced the problem of the relation between reason and revelation consciously and deliberately; however, because 'Abduh took as premises the traditional dogmas, the solution that he suggested was more formal than real. He attempted to reconcile science and reason with revelation primarily be deductive reasoning from the à priori conceptions that the Qur'ān in its entirety is divine revelation and that the religion revealed through Muḥammad is perfect.

In the case of science, his argument was basically that since the Qur'ān is the word of God, and since it permits the pursuit of science, the latter cannot be contrary to it. Therefore, 'Abduh's act of "reconciling" science with revelation amounted chiefly to quoting chapter and verse to show that the Qur'ān urges scientific study, rather than demonstrating concretely the harmony in method, teachings, and ethos between the two through an understanding of science and a reinterpretation of revelation.

In the case of reason, 'Abduh did go some way toward showing concretely how its teachings could be in harmony with revelation; but his confidence that the two would always be in agreement rested ultimately on the tacit syllogism: true religion ought to be in harmony with reason; Islam is the most perfect, true religion; therefore, the teachings of Islam *are* in harmony with reason.

Thus ʿAbduh's contribution toward meeting the challenge of modernism, though still undeniably great, remained essentially negative. He accomplished the necessary step of reopening the traditional doctrine for fresh inquiry and inspired confidence in the vitality and liberality of Islam, but he failed to reconcile *concretely* and objectively the content of revelation with the driving forces of modern life.

ʿAbduh's successor in the Islamic Reformist camp — Rashīd Riḍā — let the question of the relation between science and revelation stay substantially where ʿAbduh had left it, and retreated from ʿAbduh's aim and endeavor to prove that the teachings of right reason were in harmony with those of revelation. He applied ʿAbduh's deductive reasoning in a new direction to argue that the politico-social system envisaged by the Islamic revelation (as he conceived and understood it), was by definition more perfect than anything that fallible reason and human invention could suggest. His successors in the Reformist tradition — the Muslim Brethren — took a few more steps backward, refusing even to recognize that there existed a problem of conflict between reason and revelation which needed solution, and denying arbitrarily that there was any need for methodical rational procedure in the interpretation of revelation. They simply asserted — without substantially demonstrating — the superiority of the teachings of Islam in all the spheres of life by dint of their divinely revealed origin.

The Islamic Reformist alternative, then, has been severely handicapped in its aim of adjusting Islam to modern life by the dogma of the Qur'ān as the integral and perfect revelation of God's word. It was by deductive reasoning from that dogma that ʿAbduh had given the assurance that science and reason were in harmony with revelation. But since, in actual fact, the results reached by Western-educated Muslims pursuing reason were not always in harmony with the teachings of revelation, ʿAbduh's successors in the Islamic tradition could only blame the perverse influence of the West on the reasoning of those Muslims or attribute the results plainly to their wickedness. At the same time, the Muslim Reformists spoke more and more deprecatingly of the power of reason in general, and endeavored to fan the spark of faith in the dogma of the perfection of the teachings of Islam and in the capacity of those teachings to serve as foundation for the City of God on earth.

With the liberal intellectual leaders, the difficulties which gradually distorted their position were as much due to their failure to grasp the epistemological significance of the problem of the dogma of the Qur'ān and their consequent casual treatment of it, as they were due to the problem itself. Until the appearance of Ṭāha Ḥusayn's book, *On Pre-Islamic Poetry*, they had given scant attention to the question of reason and revelation, their relation to each other, and their place in their work. They had proceeded rationally, it seems, as a natural consequence of their Western education without manifesting any serious awareness of problems of epistemology. They had made some general statements about the distinction between the universal metaphysical essence of religion in general, which was beyond the purview of reason, and its specific content, which was open to criticism, but they never applied that theory to Islam and the Qur'ān specifically.

Even when Ṭāha Ḥusayn dealt with the problem of reason in its relation to Islam, his treatment of it betrayed a lack of awareness of its full importance. He propounded his Cartesian rationalist method with a bravado which appeared to reflect a more immediate concern with its provocative effect on the conservatives than any serious interest in the place that method might have in the context of a problematic ideological situation. He also gave the impression that he thought of his method as having more a narrow scholastic application than a broader philosophical one. Finally, his treatment of the Qur'ānic story of Ishmael as legend, which involved the crucial step of making critical distinctions with respect to what in the Qur'ān is to be seen as divinely sanctioned and what is to be viewed as subject to revision, was undertaken casually and without elaboration, so that he was able to drop it from subsequent editions without affecting at all the argument of the book.

The uproar aroused by Ṭāha's book brought the problem of the dogma of the Qur'ān to the attention of intellectual leaders and called for its thorough examination. But their weak grasp of its grave ideological and epistemological implications was reflected in the temporizing solutions they suggested. Ṭāha Ḥusayn's theory of man's double personality restated rather than solved the problem, and reaffirmed in the process the dogma of the integral revelation of the Qur'ān. Haykal's forced attempt to prove that everything found in the Qur'ān was rational and to defend all of Muḥammad's acts as supremely ethical amounted in fact to strengthening the dogma of the perfection of the revelation without really solving anything. It was a return to 'Abduh's conception of the harmony between reason and revelation but without 'Abduh's genuine commitment to Islam as the main guide of life. The difficulties encountered by Haykal in the process of trying to substantiate that conception involved him in attacks against the reasoning and outlook of the West, just as the conflicts between the findings of reason and the teachings of revelation had involved the Islamic Reformists in attacks against the Westernizing intellectuals.

With the dogma of the integral revelation of the Qur'ān and of the perfection of Islam generally reaffirmed, the Muslim literature which emerged, and which encountered enthusiastic popular response, had to resort to the damaging intellectual devices that we have underlined in the course of this study in order to comply with that dogma. The result was that the Liberal intellectual leaders joined the Islamic Reformists, and even the orthodox, in subordinating reason to the faith, but with this difference: that whereas, to the orthodox, faith was really a way of perceiving the truth, and its content was a practical guide to life, to the "repentant" Liberal Nationalists faith only remained as a limitation on the intellect, and the interpretation of its content a means of vain intellectual aggrandizement.

Thus, the dogma of integral and perfect revelation has led Islamic Reformism away from the initially mild and cautious rationalism, which was at least aware of the problematic nature of the cultural situation, and toward an emotionalism in which that awareness was dissipated in simple assertive faith. And it has led Liberalism away from its first rational and Westernizing orientation, which had made some progress in evolving a modern Liberal humanist and nationalist ideology, and toward a romantic Muslim orientation which lacked any real direction or serious constructive purpose, and dissipated many of the gains previously achieved. In the case of Liberalism, the retreat was effected by the intellectual leaders without ever having seriously come to grips with the problem.

Although the intellectual aberrations of both Islamic Reformism and Liberal Nationalism were factors of first importance in leading to the abortive ideological evolution, it would be misleading to understand that evolution and to envisage the problems and needs of present and future ideological development only in intellectual terms. An intellectual elite might devise a right or a wrong formulation, but the fate and consequences of either depend greatly on the circumstances and forces at work in the environment that receives them. The Mu'tazilah, for instance, had a more refined conception of the unity of God, a more stimulating view of morality and justice, than their opponents, and their view of the Qur'ān as created was more consistent with the absolute monotheism of Islam than that of the Ḥanbalites or the Ash'arites; yet it was the views of the Ash'arites that triumphed on all scores, largely because the Mu'tazilah's ideas had been evolved in response to intellectual challenges from without, by non-Muslims, which did not affect the people at all.

Broadly speaking and in terms of its relation to the two main ideological trends studied in this book, the Egyptian historical environment was dominated by two opposing forces, each favoring potentially one of the two trends. The balance between those two forces in the actual process of their unfolding had a crucial influence on how each of the parallel ideological trends fared.

Immediately after the First World War, the section of the population which constituted by occupation and education the recruiting material of Liberalism was a small minority in comparison to the large masses of people whose lives had not been seriously affected by modern conditions and who were still, by education or inertia, under the sway of traditional Islam. However, because that minority was economically dominant and was more active intellectually and politically, it succeeded in rising to power on the wave of nationalism and in imprinting its liberalism on the country's regime. Henceforth, the balance between the two forces hung on the effects of education, economic and social developments, and the nationalist struggle. Education, which was supposed to favor the Liberal trend, failed to bring about the expected results for reasons that we have examined. The growth of the middle classes, which was expected to work in the same direction, was handicapped by the foreign domination of the country's industrial and big mercantile development and by the bias of the landowner-dominated government in favor of agriculture.

Working in the opposite direction, the country-to-city migration and the nationalist struggle activated large parts of the tradition-bound population, permitting them to make the impact of their religious attitude felt; and the basic economic deterioration as well as temporary dislocations from which they suffered most encouraged them to give organized expression to their resentment in the context of that religious attitude. The same dislocations, the failure of education, and the betrayal of the nationalist cause also drove to the ranks of the organized lower classes important elements from the intelligentsia and the middle classes. These historical developments had a great deal to do with deterring the intellectual leaders from questioning the dogma of the Qur'ān, compelling them instead to adjust their thinking and their method to accommodate it, and impelling them to pursue the Muslim orientation.[1]

If the analysis developed in this study and summarized in the preceding pages is correct, then the following factors should be watched as most relevant to present and future progress toward the evolution of a political community in Egypt.

In the intellectual sphere, the primary factor to be observed is any development touching the question of the relation between truth that is reached through the human faculties and revealed truth, especially as such development affects the dogma of the Qur'ān as perfect integral revelation. Another crucial factor to be observed is the development of an understanding of the essence of the ideological problem that sees its ultimate relevance to the establishment of a viable modern political community. Such understanding must discern the objective, historically determined, inevitable character of the problem of transition and the central role that the dogma of the Qur'ān plays in it, and must not confuse it with a subjective conflict between East and West, or some similar antithesis. All this implies the development of a critical historical approach to the Islamic heritage, and the mitigation of the overwhelming idealism and formalism that have hitherto characterized all ideological activity in Egypt, by the injection of strong doses of inductive reasoning and philosophical materialism.

In the practical political-social sphere, in addition to the attitude of the government itself toward the ideological problem and its practical understanding of it, all the factors bearing upon the balance between the tradition-bound and modern-oriented sectors of the population are of great relevance to the ultimate resolution of the ideological problem. Will the growth of the economy, the changes in the social structure, the expansion of public education, and the spread of the media of mass communication increase significantly and rapidly the proportion of those who have been sufficiently liberated from the hold of tradition to envisage an essentially different outlook on life? Will promised and actual economic and social benefits for the masses be substantial enough to palliate their sense of alienation from the political-social order while the ideological problem is being met? Will constitutional provisions, the pattern of internal politics, and the national policy of the government restrict or enlarge the possibilities for the tradition-bound masses to make a decisive impact on the general orientation of society? The answers to all these questions are obviously of prime importance in determining the chances of a successful and relatively peaceful ideological readjustment, assuming that a valid intellectual formulation of a solution were found.

It is still too early to attempt any final assessment of the developments in Egypt since 1952 in the light of the previous criteria. Given the heritage of intellectual confusion left from the previous era, it would obviously be futile to scrutinize the intellectual activity of the last eight years in search of evidence for such major readjustments of thinking as we concluded were necessary. As for questions relating to developments in the political-social sphere, though the course of events here is more rapid, and new tendencies are more easily discernible, it is still difficult to distinguish definitely what is likely to prove enduring from what is likely to prove only transitory, and it is, therefore, hazardous to project trends and rates of development. For the young authors of the revolution who have presided over Egypt's destinies for the last eight years came to power with no guiding political philosophy beyond a few generalities, and little in the way of a positive program beyond good intentions. They proceeded to work out philosophy and program in a pragmatic, experimental fashion, fighting at the same time against forces of reaction and counter-revolution and struggling among themselves for predominance in their own councils. The result was many false starts, mistaken courses, abrupt reversals, and a high degree of uncertainty. It is only in the last few years, with the emergence of 'Abd al-Nāṣir as the unchallenged leader, the elimination of all the obvious centers of opposition, and the accumulation of experience that a period of conscious, planned development on all fronts has been inaugurated. The accomplishments of this period are still too uncertain to warrant the drawing of any definite conclusions. It is with all these reservations in mind that we proceed to conclude our study with some remarks about the general tentative trends since 1952.

In the intellectual sphere, there has been no substantive progress in dealing with the fundamental questions relating to the ideological problem. On the other hand, the dangerous drift toward the emotional Muslim orientation has been decisively stopped, apparently by government fiat, ever since the suppression of the Muslim Brotherhood. Since 1955, little new work has appeared exalting the perfection of allegedly Islamic political, social, and ethical principles and contrasting them to Western-imported ideas and values, or implying that the application of Islam to Egyptian life would solve all problems. The Muslim literature that has appeared has treated strictly technical and devotional subjects or glorified the scientific, artistic, and, above all, the military feats of Muslims and Arabs.

Another favorable development, also tangential to the main ideological problem, has been the growth of the spirit and method of scientific inquiry in certain fields of the social sciences, notably sociology and education. In the last years of the previous regime, a few highly qualified sociologists who had been trained in Britain and the United States had already begun to wrest certain subjects of inquiry from the hands of the ubiquitous *belles-lettriste* intellectuals and to attract some student followers. The new regime, with its technocratically minded officers at the helm, and its experimental social projects, has encouraged this tendency to such an extent that there has been some dilution of quality due to the rush to fill the growing need.

A more dubious development affecting intellectual activity has been its increasing control by the government. At first, this control was mainly negative and was applied through censorship to suppress opposition to the regime. But as the government began to feel its way toward a philosophy and a program, it began to exert positive control by means of inducement, and then by outright compulsion. In addition to the Ministry of National Guidance, a "General Directorate of Culture" was set up within the Ministry of Education which established in all fields of intellectual and artistic endeavor a vast number of prizes and awards to encourage works that promoted certain specified goals and values. In addition, numerous official and semiofficial institutions bought and published manuscripts on all sorts of subjects on which they wanted to instruct the people. The effect of these measures was such that even before the government took the final step of fully subsidizing artists and writers and of "nationalizing" all the newspapers and popular magazines — in addition to the radio, which has always been nationally controlled — the dominant trend in all creative activity became a kind of "social realism" in which, however, the main *motif* was patriotism or Arab nationalism. Now, in so far as these actions indicate an awareness on the part of the government of the need to unite the political community in a common belief-system they constitute, perhaps, a step in the right direction. But to the extent that they concentrate on current politics and promote the ideas of Arab nationalism, while ignoring altogether the fundamental issues involved in the problem of ideological readjustment, they tend to degenerate into superficial pamphleteering and propaganda.

In the political-social sphere, the actions of the government have tended, with one important exception to be noted presently, to create conditions that are likely to facilitate the resolution of the ideological conflict by radically altering the previous balance between the modern and the tradition-bound camps. With a few bold strokes the revolution destroyed the exclusive power of the big landowners, thus opening the door for more rapid economic development by freeing land-bound capital and redressing the excessive bias of government policy toward agriculture. It opened vast new opportunities for the growth of the indigenous middle classes, which are less bound to traditional Islam, by encouraging the development of industry, "Egyptianizing" many big enterprises previously owned and staffed by foreigners or members of minority groups, and by multiplying the opportunities for army careers. It accelerated the growth of the proletariat and enlarged the class of cooperatively organized peasant proprietors by means of land redistribution and so brought large sections of the tradition-bound population into the circle of modern life.[2] In the sphere of education, the revolution consolidated the unification, achieved in the final days of the previous regime, of the dual school system which had been largely responsible for creating an unbridgeable gap between the graduates of the two systems, and proceeded to expand education at a very accelerated rate. Provided the content of education and the methods of teaching are also improved along the lines suggested for a long time by many Egyptian critics, this development might offer the best prospect for an eventual ideological readjustment. Finally, the revolution eliminated the obstructive power of the religious leaders by submitting all religious institutions to the strict control of the state and cancelling the bargaining position which the *'ulamā'* had enjoyed under the previous regime owing to the multiplicity of the centers of power.

The revolution of 1952 liberated the two dominant forces of nationalism and Islam from the particular historical forms in which they had manifested themselves, and its leaders endeavored to overcome the conception that they were largely antithetical forces. It broke the association of nationalism with the Western-modeled Liberal constitutional regime by abolishing the old political order, and it fought the identification of the Islamic ideal and Muslim loyalty with the Muslim Brotherhood by destroying and then defaming that movement. Instead, the men who made the revolution have tried to combine some of the basic elements of both Liberal Nationalism and Islamic Reformism into a new indigenous nationalism to serve as the foundation of a modern Egyptian community.

The leaders of the revolution rejected the over-all conception of Islamic Reformism advocated by the Brotherhood, which maintained that the realization of the just and successful society could be achieved only by founding it on the principles and doctrine of Islam, in favor of the Liberal Nationalist conception of an order based on the absolute sovereign will of the people and of "an atmosphere where there are no dictates save those of conscience and reason." [3] They followed the practice of the previous regime in regarding the surviving Islamic law and institutions as deeply rooted custom, subject ultimately to the will of the sovereign, but they asserted this view unequivocally and acted upon it in a much more drastic fashion than their predecessors.[4] But, having rejected any notion of the supreme and imperative character of any specific Islamic legal, social, or political regulations, they endeavored to mobilize the Muslim sense of solidarity and even religious xenophobia in the service of nationalism as they understood it.[5] They revised their conception of the nation in accordance with the popular view to encompass all the Arab peoples, if not all the Muslim community. The final product seems to be a new nationalism, which, though it feeds on Muslim emotion, is, nevertheless, intolerant of Muslim tradition whenever that tradition seems to conflict with the course of the desired modernization.

All these developments tend, as we have said, to create a political-social situation in which it might be possible some day to reexamine some of the delicate questions involved in the relation between revelation and humanly conceived truth, without arousing storms of religious agitation and reaction. But one factor which has come to occupy a central position in the orientation of the revolutionary government might prove an obstacle to such an eventuality, if it would not indeed preclude it altogether. This factor is the pan-Arab character of the new nationalism. It is not that Arab nationalism is logically and in principle opposed to any particular formulation on that basic question. However, given the past history of the problem and the political-social dynamics affecting intellectual activity that we have analyzed in this study, the pursuit of a pan-Arab nationalism is likely to lead once again to a confusion of the basic ideological problem with extrinsic issues, and might unleash forces that would make the realization of the necessary intellectual adjustment impossible.

In Egypt the idea of a union of the Arab countries had its roots in a religious motive. The first serious consideration of such an idea took place in 1924–1925, in the course of the agitation over restoring the caliphate, which had just been abolished by Ataturk. Prior to that time, the possibility of an Arab caliphate was broached in Egypt only to be rejected as disruptive of the larger Muslim union under the Ottoman caliphate.[6] Despite the failure of the agitation of

1924–1925, the proposal was revived time and time again with the encouragement of the king, who expected it to bring him not only an enlarged realm but enlarged powers as well. Each time, however, the idea of an Arab caliphate was resisted by the Wafd and the other nationalist parties on the grounds of principle as well as of party self-interest. In the meantime, the promotion of the cause of an Arab union preliminary to a Muslim union was taken up by independent popular organizations, such as the Association of Muslim Youth and the Muslim Brotherhood. During the Second World War, propitious political circumstances in the Levant, the encouragement of the British, the spread of the idea of an Arab union along with the growth of the Brotherhood, and the fear that the king might take the initiative himself, induced the Wafdist government to abandon its negative attitude and to seek some form of Arab cooperation that would satisfy the growing pan-Arab pressure without sacrificing Egypt's sovereignty and its own constitutional order. The result was the pact of the Arab League. The intricate succession of steps which led from the formation of the Arab League to the full commitment of Egypt to the promotion of the cause of Arab nationalism and the formation of the United Arab Republic does not concern us here. It need only be said that behind this commitment there was the same combination of driving forces that prevailed at the foundation of the Arab League — a broad, popular, religious-inspired sense of Muslim solidarity which is given outward expression in secular and political terms by the leaders of the country.

Given these components of the driving force of Arab nationalism, the question is whether the leaders would be able to control the religious impulse that moves the masses or whether in the course of the struggle for the emancipation of all the Arab peoples they would be compelled to speak increasingly the language of their own followers. So far, the record of the leaders' behavior in this respect is not too reassuring. They have all too lightly invoked the *jihād* to arouse the people, and their simple division of the world into imperialists and anti-imperialists is a disconcerting echo of the facile dichotomies of East and West and "the abode of Islam and the abode of war." And even if the leaders retain the direction of their immediate followers, will they risk alienating other, more conservative, Muslim Arab countries by permitting a radical resolution of the question of the relation between Islamic dogma and humanly conceived truth? Or will they subordinate the essential, but not immediately perceptible, problem of ideological adjustment to immediate political expediency? Nearly four decades ago, Ataturk realized that if Turkey were to find her place in the modern world, she must free her hands by divesting herself of her responsibilities to the Muslim world beyond her own frontiers. Can Egypt find her own place in the new world by imposing upon herself responsibilities that she has not had before?

BIBLIOGRAPHY

NOTES

INDEX

Bibliography

Small bibliographies relevant to specific topics are included in the notes. These topics are listed immediately below with chapter and note references. Other primary sources and some selected works are given in the pages following.

The traditional Islamic world-view (Chapter 1, note 1).
The traditional view of the Law (Chapter 1, note 5).
The traditional view of history (Chapter 1, note 6).
The traditional view of the state (Chapter 1, note 7).
Egyptian society in the eighteenth century (Chapter 2, note 1).
Muḥammad ʻAlī (Chapter 2, notes 1–12).
Ismāʻīl (Chapter 2, note 14).
Al-Afghānī (Chapter 3, note 4).
The "Constitutionalists" (Chapter 3, note 10).
The rise of modern literature in Egypt (Chapter 4, note 7).
Muḥammad ʻAbduh (Chapter 5, note 1).
Rashīd Riḍā (Chapter 5, note 27).
The nationalist movement and the revolution of 1919 (Chapter 7, note 1).
Modern legislation in the sphere of religion (Chapter 8, note 13).
The Muslim Brotherhood (Chapter 14, note 1).

OTHER PRIMARY SOURCES

Abāẓah, Fikrī, *al-Ḍāḥiq-al Bākī* (To Laugh or to Weep?), Cairo, 1933.
ʻAbd al-Rāziq, ʻAlī, *al-Islām wa Uṣūl al-Ḥukm* (Islam and the Principles of Government), Cairo, 1925; French translation in *Revue des études islamiques*, 1934, pp. 353–391, and 1935, pp. 163–222.
Amīn, Aḥmad, *Fajr al-Islām* (The Dawn of Islam), 2 vols., Cairo, 1928–1931.
——— *Ḍuḥā al-Islām* (Islam's Morning), 3 vols., Cairo, 1933–1936.
——— *Ẓuhr al-Islām* (Islam's Noon), 2 vols., Cairo, 1945–1947.
——— *Yawn al-Islām* (Islam's Day), Cairo, 1952.
——— *Fayḍ al-Khāṭir* (Inspirations), 5 vols., Cairo, 1938–1951.
——— *Ḥayātī* (My Life), Cairo, 1950.
——— *Ilā Waladī* (To my Son), Cairo, 1951.
——— *Kitāb al-Akhlāq* (The Book of Ethics), Cairo, 1929.
——— *al-Naqd al-Adabī* (Literary Criticism), Cairo, 1952.
——— *Zuʻamāʼ al-Iṣlāḥ fī al-ʻAṣr al-Ḥadīth* (Leaders of Reform in the Modern Age), Cairo, 1948.
——— and al-Bishrī, ʻAbd al-ʻAzīz, *al-Tarbiyyah al-Waṭaniyyah* (Civic Education), Cairo, 1934.
Amīn, Qāṣim, *Taḥrīr al-Marʼah* (The Emancipation of Women), Cairo, 1899.
——— *al-Marʼah al-Jadīdah* (The New Woman), Cairo, 1901.
al-ʻAqqād, ʻAbbās Maḥmūd, *ʻAbqariyyat Khālid* (The Genius of Khālid ibn al-Walīd), Cairo, 1944.

——— *'Abqariyyat Muḥammad* (The Genius of Muḥammad), Cairo, 1942.
——— *'Abqariyyat al-Ṣaddīq* (The Genius of Abū Bakr), Cairo, 1943.
——— *'Abqariyyat 'Umar* (The Genius of 'Umar), Cairo, 1942.
——— *Abū al-Shuhadā'* (The Father of the Martyrs — al Ḥusayn, the son of 'Alī), Cairo, 1944.
——— *'Alī al-Safūd* (On 'Ali, the Fourth Caliph), Cairo, 1944.
——— *'Amru ibn-al-'Āṣ*, Cairo, 1944.
——— *al-Ṣaddīqah bint al-Ṣaddīq* (On 'Ayshah, Muḥammad's Wife), Cairo, 1943.
——— *'Abqariyyat al-Masīḥ* (The Genius of Christ), Cairo, 1943.
——— *Allāh*, Cairo, 1949.
——— *al-Falsafah al-Qur'āniyyah* (The Qur'ānic Philosophy), Cairo, 1948.
——— *al-Dīmūqrāṭiyyah fī al-Islām* (Democracy in Islam), Cairo, 1952.
——— *al-Murāja'āt* (Reviews), Cairo, 1925.
——— *Muṭāla'āt fī al-Kutub wa-al-Ḥayāt* (Readings in Books and in Life), Cairo, 1924.
——— *Sā'āt Bayn al-Kutub* (Hours with Books), Cairo, 1929.
——— *Sa'd Zaghlūl, Sīrah wa-Taḥiyyah* (Sa'd Zaghlul, Biography and Tribute), Cairo, 1936.
——— *Raj'at Abī al-'Alā'* (The Return of Abū al-'Alā' al-Ma'arrī), Cairo, 1939.
——— *Athar al-'Arab fī al-Ḥaḍārah al-Awrubbiyyah* (The Arabs' Influence on European Civilization), Cairo, 1946.
——— *Falāsifat al-Ḥukm fī al-'Aṣr al-Mu'āṣir* (Contemporary Political Philosophers), Cairo, 1950.
Badawī, 'Abd al-Raḥmān, *Humūm al-Shabāb* (Troubles of Youth), Cairo, 1946.
Badawī, al-Sayyid Muḥammad, *Naẓariyyat al-Taṭawwur al Ijtimā'ī* (The Theory of Social Evolution), Cairo, 1952.
Fahmī, Manṣūr, *Khaṭirāt Nafs* (Reflections), Cairo, 1930.
al-Ḥakīm, Tawfīq, *Ahl al-Kahf* (The Cave-Dwellers), Cairo, 1933.
——— *'Awdat al-Rawḥ* (The Resurrection), Cairo, 1933.
——— *Shahrazād*, Cairo, 1934.
——— *Muḥammad*, Cairo, 1936.
——— *Taḥt Shams al-Fikr* (Under the Sun of Thought), Cairo, 1938.
——— *Yawmiyyāt Nā'ib fī al-Aryāf* (Diaries of a Country Prosecutor), Cairo, 1937; English translation by A. Eban under title, *Maze of Justice*, London, 1947.
——— *Sulṭān al-Ẓalām* (The Rule of Darkness), Cairo, 1941.
——— *Brāksa, aw Mushkilat al-Ḥukm* (Praska, or the Problem of Power), Cairo, 1939.
——— *Masrahiyyāt al-Mujtama'* (Theater of Society), Cairo, 1950.
——— *Shajarat al-Ḥukm* (The Tree of Power), Cairo, 1953.
Haykal, Muḥammad Ḥusayn, *J. J. Rousseau*, 2 vols., Cairo, 1919–1921.
——— *Waladī* (My Son), Cairo, 1931.
——— *Thawrat al-Adab* (The Revolt of Literature), Cairo, 1933.
——— *Tarājim Miṣriyyah wa-Gharbiyyah* (Biographies of Prominent Egyptians and Westerners), Cairo, 1929.
——— *Ḥayāt Muḥammad* (The Life of Muḥammad), Cairo, 1935.
——— *Fī Manzal al-Waḥy* (In the Birthplace of Revelation), Cairo, 1936.
——— *al-Ṣaddīq Abū Bakr* (The Life of Abū Bakr), Cairo, 1942.
——— *Mudhakkirāt fī al-Siyāsah al-Miṣriyyah* (Memoirs on Egyptian Politics), 2 vols., Cairo, 1952–1953.

Ḥusayn, Ṭāha, *Qisas Tamthīliyyah* (Theater Pieces), Cairo, 1924.
——— *Hadīth al-Arbi'ā'* (Wednesday Conversations), 3 vols., Cairo, 1937–1945.
——— *Qādat al-Fikr* (Leaders of Thought), Cairo, 1925.
——— *Fī al-Shi'r al-Jāhilī* (On Pre-Islamic Poetry), Cairo, 1926.
——— *Fī al-Adab al-Jāhilī* (On Pre-Islamic Literature), Cairo, 1927.
——— *'Alā Hāmish al-Sīrah* (On the Margin of the Prophet's Tradition), 3 vols., Cairo, 1933–1943.
——— *Min Ba'īd* (From Afar), Cairo, 1935.
——— *Laḥaẓāt* (Moments), 2 vols., Cairo, 1943.
——— *Mustaqbal al-Thaqāfah fī Miṣr*, Cairo, 1938; English translation by S. Glazer under the title, *The Future of Culture in Egypt*, sponsored and published by the American Council of Learned Societies (Washington, D.C., 1954).
——— *Riḥlat al-Rabī'* (Spring Journey), Cairo, 1948.
——— *Ṣawt Bārīs* (The Voice of Paris), 2 vols., Cairo, 1943.
——— *Jannat al-Shawk* (Paradise of Thorns), Cairo, 1945.
——— *al-Mu'adhdhabūn fī al-Arḍ* (The Sufferers on Earth), Cairo, 1949.
——— *Mir'āt al-Ḍamīr al-Ḥadīth* (Mirror of the Modern Conscience), Cairo, 1949.
——— *Jannat al-Ḥayawān* (Animals' Paradise), Cairo, 1949.
——— *Alwān* (Miscellany), Cairo, 1952.
——— *'Uthmān* (On the Third Caliph, 'Uthmān), Cairo, 1947.
——— *'Alī wa-Banūh* ('Alī — the Fourth Caliph — and his Sons), Cairo, 1953.
——— *al-Ayyām*, 2 vols., Cairo, 1929–1939; English translation of Vol. I by Hilary Wayment under the title, *The Stream of Days*, London, 1948.
——— *Etude analytique et critique de la philosophie sociale d'ibn Khaldūn*, Paris, 1917.
Jum'ah, Ibrāhīm, *al-Qawmiyyah al-Miṣriyyah-al-Islāmiyyah* (Egyptian-Muslim Nationalism), Cairo, 1944.
Khalīl, 'Uthmān 'Uthmān, *al-Niẓām al-Dustūrī al-Miṣrī* (The Egyptian Constitutional Order), Cairo, 1942.
——— *al-Mabādi' al-Dustūriyyah al-'Āmmah* (General Constitutional Elements), Cairo, 1943.
Khālid, Khālid Muḥammad, *Min Hunā Nabda'*, Cairo, 1950; English translation by I. R. el-Faruqi under the title, *From Here we Start*, Washington, D.C., 1953.
al-Māznī, Ibrāhīm 'Abd al-Qādir, *Ḥaṣād al-Hashīm* (Harvesting Stalks), Cairo, 1925.
——— *Qabḍ al-Rīḥ* (Grasping, or Collecting, the Wind), Cairo, 1928.
——— *Ḥukm al-Ṭā'ah* (The Rule of Obedience), Cairo, 1949.
Mūsā, Salāmah, *Naẓariyyat al-Taṭawwur wa-al-Insān* (The Theory of Evolution and Man), Cairo, 1952.
——— *Tarbiyyat Salāmah Mūsā* (The Education of Salāmah Mūsā), Cairo, 1950.
Nāṣif, 'Isām al-Dīn Ḥifnī, *Naẓariyyat al-Taṭawwur* (The Theory of Evolution), Cairo, 1952.
Ṣabrī, Aḥmad, *Qanā' al-Fir'awniyyah* (The Mask of Pharaonism), Cairo, 1943.
Ṣabrī, al-Sayyid, *al-Lawā'iḥ al-Tashrī'iyyah* (The Legislative Statutes), Cairo, 1944.
——— *Mabādi' al-Qānūn al-Dustūrī* (Elements of Constitutional Law), Cairo, 1940.

al-Sayyid, Aḥmad Luṭfī, *al-Muntakhabāt* (Selections), Cairo, 1945.
——— *Ta'ammulāt fī al-Falsafah, wa-al-Adab, wa-al-Siyāsah, wa-al-Ijtimā'* (Reflections on Philosophy, Literature, Politics, and Society), Cairo, 1946.
Shumayyil, Shiblī, *Falsafat al-Nushū' wa-al-Irtiqā'* (The Philosophy of Evolution), Vol. I, in *Majmū'at al-Duktūr Shiblī Shumayyil*, 3 vols., Cairo, 1910.
al-Zayyāt, Aḥmad Ḥasan, *Waḥy al-Risālah* (Collected articles originally printed in the review, *al-Risālah*), 3 vols., Cairo, 1938–1950.

SELECTED WORKS

Adams, C. C., *Islam and Modernism in Egypt*, London, 1933.
'Allūbah, Muḥammad 'Alī, *Mabādi' fī al-Siyāsah al-Miṣriyyah* (Elements of Egyptian Politics), Cairo, 1941.
Ammar, Hamed, *Growing Up in an Egyptian Village*, London, 1954.
Arkoun, M., "Les tendences de la litterature arabe moderne," *IBLA*, 2nd quarter, 1952.
Ayrout, H. H., *The Fellaheen*, Alexandria, 1953.
——— *Moeurs et coutumes des fellahs*, Paris, 1938.
Berthier, F., "La rencontre de l'Islam et du monde moderne," *Lettres nouvelles*, IV, Nos. 39 and 40, 1956.
Blackman, W. S., *The Fellahin of Upper Egypt*, London, 1927.
Cachia, Pierre, *Taha Husayn*, London, 1956.
Cahiers du Sud, *L'Islam et l'occident*, Numero special, 1947.
Chegne, A. C., "Some Aspects of Islamic Nationalism," *Islamic Literature*, August, 1956.
Colombe, Marcel, *L'Evolution de l'Egypte*, 1924–1950, Paris, 1951.
——— "Ou va l'Egypte?" *L'Afrique et l'Asie*, 4th quarter, 1948.
——— "Ou en est le Wafd?" *L'Afrique et l'Asie*, 2nd quarter, 1950.
——— "L'Egypte et les origines du nationalisme arabe," *L'Afrique et l'Asie*, No. 14, 1951.
——— "L'Islam dans la vie sociale et politique de l'Egypte contemporaine," *Cahiers de l'orient contemporain*, No. 21, 1950.
Coon, Carleton S., *Caravan, the Story of the Middle East*, New York, 1951.
——— "The Impact of the West on the Middle Eastern Social Institutions," *Proceedings of the Academy of Political Science*, Vol. XXIV, 1952.
Ḍayf, Shawqī, *al-Adab al-'Arabī al-Mu'āṣir* (Contemporary Arabic Literature), Vol. I, Cairo, 1957.
Dodge, Bayard, "Western Education and the Middle East," *Proceedings of the Academy of Political Science*, Vol. XXIV, 1952.
Dubois-Richard, H., "L'état d'esprit des étudiants egyptiens et leur role dans la vie politique," *Entretiens sur l'évolution des pays de civilization arabe*, Paris, 1937.
Gardet, Louis, *La cité musulmane, vie sociale et politique*, Paris, 1954.
——— "Raison et foi en Islam," *Revue Thomiste*, 1937–1938.
——— "La mesure de notre liberté, chapitre de théologie musulmane," *IBLA*, 1946.
Gibb, H. A. R., *Modern Trends in Islam* (Chicago, 1947).
——— *Muhammedanism*, London, New York, and Toronto, 1949.
——— "La réaction contre la culture occidentale dans le Proche Orient," *Cahiers de l'orient contemporain*, 1951.

Hartmann, R., "Islam und Nationalismus," *Abhandlungen der Deutschen Akademie der Wissenschaften zu Berlin*, 1945–1946.

Heyworth-Dunne, J., *Introduction to the History of Education in Modern Egypt*, London, 1939.

——— *Religious and Political Trends in Modern Egypt*, Washington, D.C., 1950.

Ḥusayn, Aḥmad, *al-Ittijāhāt al-Waṭaniyyah fī al-Adab al-Miṣrī al-Ḥadīth* (Nationalist Trends in Modern Egyptian Literature), 2 vols., Cairo, 1954–1956.

Ḥusayn, Ṭāha, "Les tendences religieuses de la litterature egyptienne d'aujourd'hui," special issue of *Cahiers du Sud*, 1947.

Issawi, Charles, *Egypt, an Economic and Social Analysis*, London, 1936.

——— *Egypt at Mid-Century*, London, New York, and Toronto, 1954.

——— "Economic and Social Foundations of Democracy in the Middle East," *International Affairs*, Vol. XXXII, 1956.

Jomier, J., "La place du Coran dans la vie quotidienne en Egypte," *IBLA*, 1952.

Khadduri, Majid, "Governments of the Arab East," *Journal of International Affairs*, Vol. VI, 1952.

——— "The Role of the Military in Middle Eastern Politics," *American Political Science Review*, Vol. XLVII, 1953.

al-Khawlī, Amīn, *Fī al-Adab al-Miṣrī* (On Egyptian Literature), Cairo, 1943.

Klingmuller, E., *Geschichte der Wafdpartei*, Berlin, 1937.

Kramers, J. H., "L'Islam et la démocratie," *Orientalia Neerlandica*, Leyden, 1948.

Lacouture, J. et S., *L'Egypte en mouvement*, Paris, 1957.

Lammens, H., "La crise intericure de l'Islam," *Etudes*, 1926.

Lane-Poole, S., *Cairo*, London, 1898.

Laoust, H., "L'évolution politique et culturelle de l'Egypte contemporaine," *Entretiens sur l'évolution des pays de civilization arabe*, Paris, 1937.

Manḍūr, Muḥammad, *Fī al-Mīzān al-Jadīd* (Literature in the New Balance), Cairo, 1944.

Massignon, L., "L'étude de la presse musulmane et la valeur de ce témoignage social," *Annales d'histoire économique et sociale*, 1930.

Médawwar, P. K., "En Egypte: L'Islam religion d'état. Quelques consequences," *al-Macarrat*, April, 1940.

al-Miṣrī, Ibrāhīm, *al-Adab al-Jadīd* (The New Literature), Cairo, 1930.

Moussa, Salama, "Intellectual Currents in Egypt," *Middle Eastern Affairs*, Vol. II, 1951.

Naguib, Mohammed, *Egypt's Destiny*, New York, 1955.

Radwan, Abu al-Futouh Ahmad, *Old and New Forces in Egyptian Education*, New York, 1951.

Rizzitano, U., "Spirito faraonico e spirito arabo nel pensiero di Tawfik el-Hakim," *Annali*, Vol. III, 1949.

el-Sadat, Anwar, *Revolt on the Nile*, London, 1957.

Safran, N., "The Abolition of the Shar'ī Courts in Egypt," *The Muslim World*, Vol. XLVIII, January and April, 1958.

Shafīq, Aḥmad, *Mudhakkirātī fī Niṣf Qarn* (My Memoirs in Half a Century), 2 vols., Cairo, 1934–1936.

Schoonover, K., "A Survey of the Best Modern Arabic Books," *The Muslim World*, Vol. XLII, 1952.

——— "Contemporary Egyptian Authors," *The Muslim World*, Vol. XLV, January and October, 1955.
Ṣidqī, Ismā'īl, *Mudhakkirātī* (Memoirs), Cairo, 1950.
Smith, W. C., *Islam in Modern History*, Princeton, 1957.
——— "The Intellectuals in the Modern Development of the Islamic World," in *Social Forces in the Middle East*, Ithaca, 1955.
Warriner, Doreen, *Land and Poverty and the Middle East*, London, 1948.
Young, T. C., ed., *Near Eastern Culture and Society*, Princeton, 1951.
Zaydān, Jurjī, *Tarājim Mashāhīr al-Sharq* (Biographies of Eastern Celebrities), 2 vols., Cairo, 1920.

Notes

Introduction

1. Hobbes's effort to establish a theory of the state based solely on power rested on the principle that no agreement is binding unless it is backed by force. The founding contract is valid only in so far as it is supported by the sword. The rights of the sovereign extend only as far as his sword can reach. But then, when Hobbes came to the question of providing the means by which the sovereign can maintain his force, he argued that the subjects "ought" to will them since they have willed the ends for which sovereign power is established. It is obvious that behind that "ought" there is nothing but a rational imperative which implies also a dependence of the sovereign on the continually renewed, freely given consent of the subjects.

2. See the essay entitled "Politics as a Vocation" in H. H. Gerth and C. Wright Mills ed. *From Max Weber*, Galaxy edition (New York, 1958), pp. 77–83.

3. To the best of the author's knowledge, the approach adopted in this study has not been previously taken by any writer on Middle Eastern or Islamic subjects. H. A. R. Gibb, in his *Modern Trends in Islam* (1947), W. C. Smith, in his *Islam in Modern History* (1957), and Daniel Lerner, in his *The Passing of Traditional Society* (1958), have dealt with some topics closely related to subjects studied in this work, but their basic approach has been essentially different from the one followed here.

Gibb has written a masterly critique of the efforts of Muslim thinkers in several countries to reformulate the doctrine of Islam in the light of modern intellectual tendencies. Underlying his analysis is his conviction that only a resuscitated and revitalized Islam can rescue Muslim societies from their present spiritual crisis. W. C. Smith has taken a similar position though, unlike Gibb, he has sought to emphasize the psychological-historical heritage of Islam, rather than its doctrine or law, as the decisive factor in the life of Muslim societies.

Both studies have contributed enormously to our understanding of the subjects under discussion, but the author cannot but disagree with their exclusive stress on Islam as the only strategic category both for the Muslim societies themselves and for the outsider seeking to understand their problems and orientation. Like all classical Islamists, they tend excessively to look upon Muslim societies as subject to a *sui generis* approach.

Daniel Lerner, in his work, serves to correct this perspective to some extent. In applying general sociological categories to the societies he analyzes, however, he goes too far to the other extreme, that of reducing the Islamic outlook to the "traditional outlook" in general. In Lerner's approach, the religion of these societies could just as well have been Christian, Hindu, or Jewish. And, while Lerner had many insights, his over-all diagnosis and prognostication suffer from the lack of thorough appreciation of the specifically Islamic historical dimension.

In a sense, the present study seeks to synthesize the three views of Gibb, Smith, and Lerner by submitting a particular Muslim society to an analysis based on general political-sociological categories, which, however, takes account of the specific ways in which the Islamic background has affected the operation of these categories. Sebastian de Grazia's work *The Political Community* (Chicago, 1948) has been of great help in suggesting a framework within which the synthesis could be attempted.

CHAPTER 1. The Islamic Ideological Background

1. Our presentation of the five concepts mentioned owes much to the following works, although the responsibility of the particular authors is restricted to the views specifically attributed to them: Aḥmad Amīn, *Duḥā al-Islām* (The Morning of Islam) (Cairo, 1935), Vol. II; T. J. de Boer, *Geschichte der Philosophie in Islam*, English trans. F. R. Jones (London, 1903); F. Buhl, *Das Lebens Mohammeds*, English trans. H. H. Shaeder (Berlin, 1930); L. Gardet, "La Mesure de notre liberté; chapitre de théologie musulmane," in *IBLA* (Tunis, 1956); H. A. R. Gibb, *Muhammedanism* (London, New York, and Toronto, 1949); I. Goldziher, *Le Dogme et la loi en Islam* (Paris, 1920); G. von Grunebaum, *Islam — Essays in the Nature and Growth of a Cultural Tradition* (Chicago, 1955); *Medieval Islam — a Study in Cultural Orientation* (Chicago, 1953); D. B. Macdonald, *The Development of the Muslim Theology and Constitutional Theory* (London, 1903); *The Religious Attitude to Life in Islam* (Chicago, 1912); G. Quadri, *La filosofia degli Arabi nel suo fiore* (Florence, 1939); L. V. Vaglieri, *Islam* (Naples, 1946); A. J. Wensinck, *The Muslim Creed* (Cambridge, England, 1932).

2. For an excellent study of al-Ghazzālī's reconciliation of Ṣūfism with Sunnī theology, see L. Gardet, "Raison et foi en Islam," in *Revue Thomiste*, 1937–1938.

3. G. von Grunebaum, *Islam*, p. 13.

4. See below, pp. 169f, 214.

5. The section on law draws much from J. Schacht, *Origins of Muhammedan Jurisprudence*, 2nd ed. (Oxford, 1953); the essays by the same author: "Pre-Islamic Background and Early Development of Jurisprudence," and "The Schools of Law and Later Development of Jurisprudence," in *Law in the Middle East*, ed. M. Khadduri and H. J. Liebesny (Washington, D.C., 1955); E. Tyan, *Histoire de l'organisation judiciaire en pays d'Islam*. 2 vols. (Paris, 1934–1943); Goldziher, *Le Dogme et la loi en Islam*; Gibb, *Muhammedanism*.

6. Our interpretation of the Islamic view of history has much in common with that of von Grunebaum in *Islam*, pp. 1–29.

7. Our interpretation of the theory of the Islamic State and government makes use of material and views in the following works: T. W. Arnold, *The Caliphate* (Oxford, 1924); L. Gardet, *La Cité musulmane* (Paris, 1954); H. A. R. Gibb, "Constitutional Organization," in Khadduri and Liebesny, *Law in the Middle East*; "Al-Māwardi's Theory of the Khilāfah," in *Islamic Culture*, XI (1937); "Some Considerations on the Sunnī Theory of the Caliphate," *Archives d'histoire du droit oriental*, III (1948); M. Godefroy-Demombynes, *Muslim Institutions* (London, 1950); R. Levy, *An Introduction to the Sociology of Islam*, 2 vols. (London, 1931–1933); E. Tyan, *Institutions de droit public musulman*, Vol. 1, "Le Califat" (Paris, 1954); Jalāl ud-Dīn Dawwānī, *Akhlāq-i Jalālī*, trans. W. F. Thompson, under the title, *Practical Philosophy of the Muhammadan People* (London, 1930); Abū Ḥāmid al-Ghazzālī, *Ihyā 'Ulūm al-Dīn* (Cairo, 1933); *al-Iqtiṣād fī al-I'tiqād* (Cairo, 1320 H.); Badr al-Dīn ibn-Jamā'ah, *Taḥrīr al-Aḥkām fī Tadbīr Ahl al-Islām*, ed. H. Kofler, in *Islamica*, VI (1934)–VII (1935); 'Abd al-Raḥmān ibn-Khaldūn, *al-Muqaddimah* (Cairo, 1867), Vol. I; Abū al-Ḥasan al-Māwardī, *al-Aḥkām al-Sulṭāniyyah* (Enger edition, Bonn, 1853).

8. Quoted by von Grunebaum in *Islam*, p. 10.

9. Al-Māwardī, pp. 5–7; quoted by Arnold in *The Caliphate*, p. 72.

10. Arnold, *The Caliphate*, p. 72.

11. *Ibid.*

12. See E. Tyan, "Judicial Organization," in Khadduri and Liebesny, *Law in the Middle East*, p. 236f.

13. See below, pp. 32, 36, 109f.

14. From 'Abd al-Qāhir al-Baghdādī, *Uṣūl al-Dīn* (Istambul, 1928), cited by Gibb in Khadduri and Liebesny, *Law in the Middle East*, p. 8.

15. al-Māwardī, cited by Arnold in *The Caliphate*, p. 71.

16. al-Baghdādī, cited by Gibb in *Law in the Middle East*, p. 11.

17. *Ibid.*, p. 15.

18. Arnold, *The Caliphate*, p. 77f.

19. See Gibb, in *Law in the Middle East*, p. 21f; Arnold, *The Caliphate*, p. 107f.

20. See Arnold, *The Caliphate*, p. 55f.

21. al-Ghazzālī, *Ihyā'*, II, 124.

22. al-Ghazzālī, *Iqtiṣād*, p. 107.

23. See al-Dawānī, cited by Gibb in *Law in the Middle East*, p. 26.

24. See E. Tyan, "Judicial Organization," p. 236f.

25. See below, pp. 81, 220, 223, 240.

26. See Tyan, *Institutions*, II, 436f; Schacht, "The Schools of Law and Later Development of Jurisprudence," in *Law in the Middle East*, pp. 59–60.

27. In a very interesting discussion of Islam and democracy, J. H. Kramers also expressed the belief that, despite the fundamentally democratic Islamic ideals of the equality of the believers and the submission of both rulers and ruled to the divine law, democracy was rendered ineffective in Islam by the absence of any social bodies having autonomous power that were sanctioned by the doctrine to counterbalance the caliph's authority. He attributed this fact, however, to the traditional idea of divine omnipotence: "The omnipotence of God, delegated to his vicar on earth, cannot bear the existence of any power derived from another source. . . ." No independent source of authority can exist any more than intrinsic ethical qualities. This theory is tempting, but, in our view, Kramers pushed his logic too far. For, as we have seen, later Islamic doctrine recognized God's will in the facts of history, and it would not have been an insuperable problem to endow autonomous power groups with that kind of divine sanction, had such groups emerged and successfully asserted themselves. Kramers is right when he says that the legal doctors of Islam had a "blind spot in their visual organ" when it came to the possibility of autonomous powers, but this was only because they were immersed in a moralistic view of the world which could see good government only as the result of good rulers, and not because autonomous powers were altogether inconceivable. (See J. H. Kramers, "L'Islam et la démocratie," in *Orientalia Neerlandica*, 25th Anniversary Volume (Leiden, 1948), pp. 223–239.

CHAPTER 2: Political, Economic, and Social Transformations

1. For a detailed and well-documented study of the religious, political, and social structures and relations in Egypt at the end of the eighteenth century, see H. A. R. Gibb and H. Bowen, *Islamic Society and the West* (London, 1950), Vol. I, Part I, pp. 200–235; 258–280; and Part II (London, 1957), pp. 59–69, 157–164. See also E. W. Lane, *Manners and Customs of the Modern Egyptians* (Everyman's edition, London, 1908).

2. In regard to Muḥammad 'Alī's attitude to power and reforms, see H. Dodwell, *The Founder of Modern Egypt* (Cambridge, Massachusetts, 1931), p. 220: "He began by seeking only to raise money. He ended by seeking, however mistakenly, to develop and civilize the country."

3. See G. Guémard, *Les Réformes en Egypte* (Cairo, 1936) and H. Dodwell, *The Founder of Modern Egypt.*

4. See Moustafa Fahmy, *La Révolution de l'industrie en Egypte et ses consequences sociales au 19eme siècle (1800–1850)* (Leiden, 1954).

5. *Ibid.*, pp. 96–97.

6. See chapter entitled "Bureaucracy," in *From Max Weber*, ed. Gerth and Mills (Galaxy Edition, New York, 1958).

7. For a well-documented, though sometimes careless, study of the development of modern Egyptian education from the beginning of Muḥammad 'Alī's reign through the end of Ismā'īl's, see J. Heyworth-Dunne, *Introduction to the History of Education in Modern Egypt* (London, 1939).

8. See 'Abd al-Raḥmān al-Rāfi'ī, *Tārīkh al-Ḥarakah al-Qawmiyyah fī Miṣr* (History of the Nationalist Movement in Egypt) (Cairo, 1929), Vol. 3. Al-Rāfi'ī draws extensively on the narrative of al-Jabartī, *'Ajā'ib al-Āthār*, which was written in part during Muḥammad 'Alī's reign. Al-Jabartī's work has been translated into French by Chafīq Manṣūr bey and others, under the title, *Merveilles biographiques et historiques, ou chronique du cheikh Abd el-Rahman el-Djabarti.* 9 vols. (Cairo, 1886–1896).

9. Aḥmad Shafīq pasha, who was chief of the khedivial cabinet under 'Abbās II, mentions in his memoirs that he and Buṭrus pasha Ghālī had attended the same *kuttāb*. Buṭrus was a Copt. This shows how the *kuttābs* had come to be viewed largely as regular elementary schools. See *Mudhakkirātī fi Niṣf Qarn* (My Memoirs in Half a Century) (Cairo, 1934), I, 6.

10. See J. Heyworth-Dunne, "Printing and Translation under Muḥammad 'Alī," *Journal of the Royal Asian Society*, July 1940.

11. Al-Rāfi'ī, III, 93.

12. See J. Deny, *Sommaire des archives Turques* (Cairo, 1930), pp. 33–34.

13. Rashīd Riḍā, *Tārīkh al-Ustādh al-imām al-Shaykh Muḥammad 'Abduh* (History of Muḥammad 'Abduh) (Cairo, 1908), II, 282–289.

14. For a well-documented work and a favorable judgment on Ismā'īl's reign and achievements see 'Abd al-Raḥmān al-Rāfi'ī, *'Aṣr Ismā'īl* (The Age of Ismā'īl), 2 vols. (Cairo, 1937). See also, A. Sammarco, *Les Règnes de Abbas, de Said, et d'Ismail*, in *Précis de l'histoire d'Egypte par divers historiens et archéologues* (Cairo, 1932–1935) Vol. IV; G. Hanotaux, *Histoire de la nation égyptienne* (Paris, 1938), Vol. VI; G. Douin, *Histoire du règne du khedive Ismail.* 3 vols. (Rome, 1933–1939); M. H. Haykal, *Tarājim Miṣriyyah wa-Gharbiyyah* (Egyptian and Western Biographies), (Cairo, 1929), pp. 54–108.

15. Charles Issawi, *Egypt at Mid-Century* (London, New York, and Toronto, 1954), pp. 21–22. Data in the rest of this paragraph and in the next two paragraphs are taken from the same source, pp. 21–25.

16. J. Heyworth-Dunne, *Education in Modern Egypt*, pp. 360, 405.

17. *Ibid.*, p. 381.

18. *Ibid.*, p. 436.

19. For the privileged position of the foreigners, the organization and nature of the mixed jurisdiction, see J. Brinton, *The Mixed Courts in Egypt* (New Haven, 1930).

20. Aḥmad Shafīq reports in his memoirs a story told to him by his father about the beginnings of the assembly. When it met for business for the first time, the secretary invited the members to divide themselves into three groups, or parties: one, which would include the supporters of the government, should sit to the right; another, which would include those who opposed the government, should sit to the left; and

a third, which would include the moderates, should sit in the center. When the secretary finished, all the members rushed to the right, saying: "How can we be against the government?" See *Mudhakkirātī*, I, 28–29.

CHAPTER 3: Challenge and Response, The First Formulations

1. See the chapter entitled "The Types of World-Views and their Unfoldment Within Metaphysical Systems, *in Dilthey's Philosophy of Existence*, ed. W. Kluback and M. Weinbaum (New York, 1957).

2. The extent to which the new laws and new legal procedures were alien to the people is reflected in Aḥmad Shafīq's remark in his memoirs that during Ismā'īl's days, the people of the good families would not marry their daughters to lawyers because of the latter's low status, a view based on "the prevalent belief that the lawyer is a man who turns right into wrong and wrong into right." (*Mudhakkirātī*, I, 74). A generation later, this attitude had not changed significantly. 'Abd al-Raḥmān al-Rāfi'ī reports in his memoirs that when, in 1904, he wanted to enroll in the law school, his father opposed him vehemently. As 'Abd al-Raḥmān's relatives tried to dissuade the father, he replied indignantly: "Would you want him to graduate from the law school and become a judge in the national courts, issuing sentences not in accordance with the *Sharī'ah?*" Subsequently, the attitude toward lawyers and the legal profession improved somewhat, but the laws with which they dealt and the legal procedures followed in the modernized or non-Shar'ī courts remained remote and alien to the people. See, for example, Tawfīq al-Ḥakīm's *Yawmiyyāt Nā'ib fī al-Aryāf* (Diaries of a Country Prosecutor), translated into English by A. Eban under the title *Maze of Justice* (London, 1947).

3. See W. C. Smith, *Islam in Modern History* (Princeton, 1957), Chap. I.

4. The essay on Jamāl al-Dīn al-Afghānī is based largely on the following material: Jamāl al-Dīn al-Afghānī, *al-Radd 'alā al-Dahriyyīn*, translated into French by A. M. Goichon as *La réfutation des matérialistes* (Paris, 1942); also, an article answering a lecture by E. Rénan on science and religion in which Rénan had maintained that Islam was intrinsically inimical to scientific inquiry. Rénan's lecture and al-Afghānī's answer are given in the translation of Goichon; two essays on absolutist governments published in *al-Manār*, Vol. III; articles from *al-'Urwah al-Wuthqā*, the review published by al-Afghānī and 'Abduh in Paris in 1884, ed. Dār al-'Arab (Cairo, 1954); a detailed biography and appreciation of al-Afghānī in G. E. Browne, *The Persian Revolution* (Cambridge, 1910), Chap. I; a biography by Muḥammad 'Abduh, al-Afghānī's foremost disciple, published in Rashīd Riḍā's biography of 'Abduh, *Tārikh . . . Muḥammad 'Abduh* (Cairo, 1907), Vol. I; A. Amīn, *Zu'amā' al-Iṣlāḥ fī al-'Aṣr al-Ḥadīth* (Modern Reform Leaders) (Cairo, 1948), chapter on al-Afghānī; C. C. Adams, *Islam and Modernism in Egypt* (Cairo, 1948), pp. 4–17; L. Massignon, in *Revue du Monde Musulman* (1910), XII, 561f; I. Goldziher, "Djamāl al-Dīn al-Afghānī," in *Encyclopedia of Islam* (1913); E. Rossi "Il Centinario della nacitá di Jamal u'Din," in *Oriente Moderno* (1940), Vol. XX; O. Amin, *Muhammad 'Abduh* (in French) (Cairo, 1944), Chap. I; B. Michel and M. 'Abd al-Rāziq, *Risālat al-Tawḥid, exposé de la théologie musulmane* (Paris, 1925), Introduction; M. al-Makhzūmī pasha, *Khaṭirāt Jamāl al-Dīn* (Beirut, 1931); Qadrī Hāfiẓ Ṭawqān, *Jamāl al-Dīn al-Afghānī* (Jerusalem, 1947); Aḥmad Shafīq pasha, *Mudhakkirātī* (Cairo, 1934), Vol. I.

5. See al-Afghānī, *Al-Radd.*

6. Shafīq, *Mudhakkirātī*, I, 109.

7. *Ibid.*, pp. 38–39.

8. *Ibid.*, p. 109.

9. *Ibid.*, pp. 100–110.

10. The material on Sharīf, the Constitutionalists, and the 'Urābī movement is based primarily on the following sources: Article in Jurjī Zaydān, *Tarājim Mashāhīr al-Sharq* (Biographies of Famous Men of the East) (Cairo, 1922); 'Abd al-Raḥmān al-Rāfi'ī, *'Asr Isma'īl*, Vol. II, and *al-Thawrah al-'Urābiyyah* (The 'Urābī Revolution) (Cairo, 1937); M. Sabri, *La Genèse de l'esprit national egyptien, 1863–1882* (Paris, 1924); Lord Cromer, *Modern Egypt* (London, 1908), Vol. I; W. S. Blunt, *Secret History of the English Occupation* (London, 1907); M. Rifaat, *The Awakening of Modern Egypt* (London, 1947); M. H. Haykal, *Tarājim*, Introduction, and pp. 54–108; B. Young, *Egypt* (London, 1927); H. Kohn, *History of Nationalism in the East* (New York, 1928); M. T. Symons, *Britain and Egypt, the Rise of Egyptian Nationalism* (London, 1925); Aḥmad Shafīq pasha, *Mudhakkirātī*, Vol. I.

11. Quoted by Shawqī Ḍayf, *Al-Adab al-'Arabī al-Mu'āṣir* (contemporary Arabic Literature), (Cairo, 1957), I, 197.

12. Alfred Milner, *England in Egypt* (London, 1894), p. 16.

13. Shafīq, *Mudhakkirātī*, I, 147.

CHAPTER 4: The Making of Modern Egypt

1. Ch. Issawi, *Egypt at Mid-Century*, p. 55.

2. *Ibid.*, p. 34. The crop area is larger than the cultivable area because perennial irrigation makes possible more than one crop a year.

3. *Ibid.*, p. 35.

4. *Ibid.*, pp. 34–39.

5. *Ibid.*, p. 52.

6. *Ibid.*, pp. 50–51.

7. For studies of the Egyptian literature written during this period see: Shawqī Ḍayf, *Al-Adab al-'Arabī al-Mu'āṣir* (Contemporary Arabic Literature) (Cairo, 1957), Vol. I; Aḥmad Ḥusayn, *Al-Ittijāhāt al-Waṭaniyyah fī al-Adab al-Miṣrī al-Ḥadīth* (The Nationalist Trends in Modern Egyptian Literature), 2 vols. (Cairo, 1954–1956); Pierre Cachia, *Ṭāha Ḥusayn* (London, 1956), pp. 1–38; A. S. Eban, "The Modern Literary Movement in Egypt," *International Affairs*, April, 1944; H. A. R. Gibb, "Studies in Contemporary Arabic Literature," B.S.O.S. IV (1928), 745–760; V (1929), 311–322, 445–466; VII (1933), 1–22; T. Khemiri and G. Kempffmeyer, "Leaders in Contemporary Arabic Ltierature," *die Welt des Islams*, Vol. IX (1930); M. J. Lecerf, "Renaissance de la langue et de la litterature arabes," in *Entretiens sur l'évolution des pays de civilization arabe* (Paris, 1936) and "Shiblī Shumayyil, métaphysicien et moraliste contemporain," in *Bulletin des études orientales* (Damascus, 1931), Vol. I; H. Pérès, *La Litterature arabe et l'Islam par les textes: Les XIXe et XXe siècles* (Alger, 1938) and *Litterature arabe moderne. Grands courants. Bibliographie* (Alger, 1940); *La Revue du Caire, "Cinquante ans de litterature egyptienne,"* special issue, February, 1953; short notes on Egyptian authors and books may be found in C. Brockelman, *Geschichte der arabische Litteratur*, II (Berlin, 1902), 469–522; Supplement, II (Leyden, 1938), 718–896, and III (Leyden, 1942), 1–499.

8. M. Zwemer, "Present-day Journalism in the World of Islam," *The Muslim World Today*, J. R. Mott, ed. (London, 1914), p. 129f.

9. Qāṣīm Amīn, *Taḥrīr al-Mar'ah* (The Emancipation of Women) (Cairo, 1899), p. 118.

CHAPTER 5: Reformist Islam

1. The study of the life and thought of Muḥammad 'Abduh is based on the following sources: Primary: Muḥammad 'Abduh, *Risālat al-Tawḥīd* (Treatise on the Unity of God), 5th ed. (Cairo, 1346 H.); *al-Islām wa al-Naṣrāniyyah Ma' al-'Ilm wa al-Madaniyyah* (Islam and Christianity vis à vis Science and Civilization), 3rd ed. (Cairo, 1923); and *Tafsīr al-Manār* (Commentary on the Qur'ān). The Tafsīr was to have embraced the whole Qur'ān but was carried during 'Abduh's lifetime only as far as Chap. 4, verse 125. Rashīd Riḍā continued it as far as Chap. 9, verse 93. The Tafsīr first appeared in *al-Manār* and then in a work of 10 volumes (Vol. X, 1931); Muḥammad 'Abduh, miscellaneous writings, collected in Vol. II of Rashīd Riḍā's *Tārīkh al-Ustādh al-Imām al-Shaykh Muḥammad 'Abduh* (History of M. 'Abduh) (Cairo, 1908). Volume I of Tārikh contains a biography of 'Abduh by Rashīd Riḍā (Cairo, 1907).

The secondary sources include: C. C. Adams, *Islam and Modernism in Egypt* (London, 1933): an analysis of the life and work of M. 'Abduh and of his influence; O. Amin, *Muhammad 'Abduh—Essai sur ses idées philosophiques et religieuses* (Cairo, 1944); H. A. R. Gibb, *Modern Trends in Islam* (Chicago, 1947) devotes a central part to 'Abduh's work; I. Goldziher, *Die Richtungen der Islamischen Koranauslegung* (Leiden, 1920), pp. 320–370; M. Horton, "Muhammad 'Abduh; sein Leben und seine theologischphilosophische Gedankenwelt," *Beitrage zur Kentniss des Orients*, XIII (1915), 85–114 (biography), and XIV (1916), 74–128 (doctrine); J. Jomier, *Le Commentaire coranique du Manār* (Paris, 1954); B. Michel and M. 'Abd al-Rāziq, French translation of 'Abduh's *Risālat al-Tawḥīd* (Paris, 1925), contains a biographical study and an excellent summary of 'Abduh's ideas; Aḥmad Ḥusayn, *Al-Ittijāhāt*; Aḥmad Shafīq, *Mudhakkirātī.*

2. Muḥammad 'Abduh's remarkable courage is revealed in the following incident reported by Aḥmad Shafīq: A *kiswah* (robe) of honor became vacant with the death of one of the grand *'ulamā'* of al-Azhar. By law, the *kiswahs* are awarded by the board of directors of al-Azhar. Yet, when this one became vacant, the khedive gave an oral order that it be granted to *shaykh* X. The board, however, did not heed the khedive's order, presumably upon 'Abduh's instigation, and granted the *kiswah* to some other *shaykh.* A while later, when the board members gathered in the khedive's palace for their usual bi-weekly visit, the khedive said angrily to its president, the Shaykh al-Azhar; "Didn't I order you to give the *kiswah* to *shaykh* X?" The Shaykh al-Azhar mumbled some excuse; whereupon Muḥammad 'Abduh intervened by saying: "What the board of directors decided *is* Your Highness' order as it is stated in the law crowned by Your Highness' signature. The board cannot rely on oral orders. Now, if Your Highness wishes that *kiswahs* be granted according to your personal wishes, let Your Highness issue a new law saying: 'The *kiswahs* are to be granted by order from us.' " When the khedive heard this, his face turned red and he promptly stood up, indicating the end of the visit. (*Mudhakkirātī*, Vol. II, pt. 2, pp. 34–35)

3. For a report about the machinations of 'Abduh's enemies, see Aḥmad Shafīq's *Mudhakkirātī*, II, 34f. As an example of their unscrupulousness, we may mention the incident, reported by Shafīq, of those *shaykhs* who secured a tricked photograph of Muḥammad 'Abduh in company of a European lady and took it to Lord Cromer, 'Abduh's protector, in an effort to persuade him to withdraw his support from 'Abduh on the grounds that the latter had compromised himself in the eyes of his fellow-Muslims. Cromer, of course, saw through the trick and laughed the matter off. Some-

time later, certain newspapers in the pay of 'Abduh's enemies printed drawings of 'Abduh in the company of a woman in bathing dress and accused him of outright apostasy. Those responsible were duly prosecuted and punished. The khedive persisted in his hostility to 'Abduh until the latter's death. He reprimanded Shafīq severely for having paid 'Abduh final honors by marching in his funeral.

4. Reprinted in *Tārīkh*, II, p. 36f.
5. *Risālah*, pp. 176–177.
6. *Ibid.*, p. 224.
7. *Ibid.*, pp. 90–91.
8. *Ibid.*, p. 142.
9. *al-Islām*, p. 51.
10. *Risālah*, p. 143.
11. *Ibid*, pp. 73–80.
12. *Ibid.*, p. 80.
13. *Ibid.*, p. 140.
14. *Ibid.*, pp. 9–10.
15. See above, p. 10.
16. *al-Islām*, pp. 49–50.
17. *Risālah*, p. 67.
18. *Ibid.*, p. 67.
19. *Ibid.*, p. 61.
20. *Tārīkh*, I, 11–13.
21. Quoted by B. Michel, p. XLII.
22. *Tafsīr*, III, 8–12.
23. *Tārīkh*, II, 167f.
24. *Tafsīr*, II, 296–300.
25. We are using the expression in a strict philosophical sense. Practically, there is, of course, room for progress according to 'Abduh's views; but that would be only in relation to the existential present, which happens to fall short of the static ideal of the age of the prophets. Western philosophical conceptions of progress, such as Condorcet's or Kant's, envisaged progress as advance toward an infinite perfection. Hegel did have a terminal point for progress when the Idea finally realizes itself; but then, unlike 'Abduh, regression from that point is inconceivable to him.
26. W. S. Blunt, *Secret History of the British Corporation* (London, 1907), pp. 624–628.
27. The study of Riḍā's thought is based on the following sources: Muḥammad Rashīd Riḍā, *al-Khilāfah aw al-Imāmah al-'Uẓmā* (The Caliphate) (Cairo, 1923), French translation with notes and comments by H. Laoust, *Le Califat dans la doctrine de Rashīd Riḍā* (Beirut, 1938). The notes in this section refer to the French translation; Muḥammad Rashīd Riḍā, *Kitāb al-Wiḥdah al-Islāmiyyah* (The Book of Muslim Unity) (Cairo, n.d.); and miscellaneous writings in various issues of *al-Manār*.

Secondary sources: C. C. Adams, *Islam and Modernism in Egypt*, pp. 177–247; J. Jomier, *Le Commentaire coranique*; H. Laoust, "Le Reformisme orthodoxe des Salafiyyah et les caractères généraux de son orientation actuelle," *Revue des études islamiques* (1932), pp. 175–224, and *Essai sur les doctrines sociales et politiques de Taki-d-Din Aḥmad ibn Taimiya* (Cairo, 1939), Bk. 3, which is dedicated to ibn Taimiya's influence on the Wahhābi movement and the Manārists.

28. For more details about these periodicals, see H. Laoust, "Le réformisme orthodoxe. . ."
29. For more details on these societies, see *Whither Islam*, Gibb and Kempffmeyer,

ed. (London, 1932); J. Heyworth-Dunne, *Religious and Political Trends in Egypt* (Washington, D.C., 1950); *Oriente Moderno*, 1936, p. 504f.

30. See below, pp. 94–95.
31. *Kitāb al-Wiḥdah*, p. 140f.
32. See, for example, *al-Manār*, I, 586–587.
33. *al-Khilāfah*, p. 52.
34. *al-Manār*, IV, 209–210.
35. *Ibid.*, XXVIII, 650.
36. *Ibid.*, IV, 215.
37. *Ibid.*, I, 766–767; II, 322–324.
38. See below, Chapter 14.
39. *al-Khilāfah*, p. 61.
40. *Ibid.*, p. 61.
41. *Ibid.*, p. 76.
42. *Ibid.*, pp. 77–81.
43. *Ibid.*, pp. 209–210.
44. *Ibid.*, p. 220.
45. *Ibid.*, pp. 35–41.
46. *Ibid.*, p. 103.
47. *Ibid.*, p. 116.
48. *Ibid.*, p. 116.
49. *Ibid.*, p. 224; also *Kitāb al-Wiḥdah*, pp. 139–142.
50. *al-Khilāfah*, p. 55.
51. *Ibid.*, p. 116.
52. *Ibid.*, p. 100.
53. See Aḥmad Taymūr pasha, *Naẓrah Tārīkhiyyah fī Ḥudūth al-Madhāhib al-Fikriyyah wa-Intishārihā* (A Historical Glimpse at the Rise of the Schools of Thought and Their Spread) (Cairo, n.d.).
54. See *al-Manār*, II, 321f.
55. *Ibid.*, XXXII, 18f.
56. *al-Khilāfah*, p. 106.
57. *al-Manār*, XXVII, 27, 119.
58. *al-Khilāfah*, p. 144.
59. *Ibid.*, p. 144.
60. *Ibid.*, p. 114.

CHAPTER 6: Liberal Nationalism

1. We do not use the term "liberalism" in the sense in which it was understood in the nineteenth century, with its limitation of the role of the state and its emphasis on individualism and the sanctity of property. Liberalism in this sense could hardly have a place in Egypt given her still embryonic capitalism and her long tradition of state action, even though some political leaders and thinkers, notably Luṭfī al-Sayyid, came at times near to it. We use the term to refer to a general commitment to the ideal of remolding society on the basis of an essentially secular conception of the state and rational-humanitarian values.

2. From a speech in Alexandria, May 21, 1902, reprinted in ʻAbd al-Raḥmān al-Rāfiʻī, *Muṣṭafā Kāmil, Bāʻith al-Ḥarakah al-Waṭaniyyah* (M. Kāmil, The Resuscitator of the Nationalist Movement) (Cairo, 1939), p. 466.

3. Incidentally, it is perhaps significant that Muṣṭafā Kāmil used the term "*waṭaniyyah*" in his speeches and writings and adopted it for the name of his party.

For, strictly speaking, *waṭaniyyah* means patriotism rather than nationalism. The Arabic term for the latter is *qawmiyyah*, and is the one used by Luṭfī al-Sayyid. It is therefore a mistake to translate the name of Muṣṭafā Kāmil's party as the Nationalist Party. But to start changing the accepted translation now would only cause confusion.

4. From a speech in London, July 24, 1906, in al-Rāfiʻī, *M. Kāmil*, pp. 466–467.
5. *Ibid.*, pp. 466–467.
6. From speech in Cairo, January 1898, in al-Rafiʻī, pp. 112–113.
7. al-Rāfiʻī, pp. 392–393.
8. From a speech in Alexandria, June 1900, al-Rāfiʻī, p. 146.
9. *Ibid.*, p. 93.
10. *Ibid.*, p. 497.
11. *Ibid.*, p. 439.
12. *Ibid.*, p. 465.
13. Biographical details on Luṭfī al-Sayyid, as well as on other writers mentioned later, are taken from Shawqī Ḍayf, *Al-Adab al-ʻArabi*, Vol. I.
14. Aḥmad Luṭfī al-Sayyid, *Ta'ammulāt fī al-Falsafah, wa al-Adab, wa al-Siyāsah, wa al-Ijtimāʻ* (Reflections on Philosophy, Literature, Politics and Society), a collection of essays published in *al-Jarīdah* in 1912–1914 (reprinted, Cairo, 1946), p. 56.
15. *Ibid.*, p. 56.
16. *Ibid.*, p. 73.
17. *Ibid.*, p. 49.
18. *al-Muntakhabāt* (Selections), a collection of essays originally published in *al-Jarīdah* in 1913–1914 (reprinted, Cairo, 1945), p. 82f.
19. *Ibid.*, p. 87.
20. *Ibid.*, p. 71.
21. *Ibid.*, pp. 71–74.
22. *Ibid.*, p. 31.
23. *Ta'ammulāt*, p. 75.
24. *Muntakhabāt*, p. 60.
25. *Ibid.*, p. 66.
26. *Ibid.*, p. 66.
27. *Ibid.*, p. 107.
28. *Ibid.*, pp. 75–76.

CHAPTER 7: The Anatomy of the Liberal Nationalist Triumph

1. There is virtually unanimous agreement among observers of all nationalities that the uprising of 1919 was universal. The literature on the reawakening of Egyptian nationalism is so vast and so repetitious that we cannot and need not list here all the works consulted. Following is a partial list of titles by way of suggestion: A. M. al-ʻAqqād, *Saʻd Zaghlūl, Sīrah wa Taḥiyyah* (S. Zaghlūl, a Biography and a Tribute) (Cairo, 1936); ʻAbd al-Raḥmān al-Rāfiʻī, *Thawrat 1919* (The Revolution of 1919), 2 vols. (Cairo, 1937) and *Fī Aʻqāb al-Thawrah-al-Miṣriyyah* (In the Wake of the Egyptian Revolution) (Cairo, 1947); M. Colombe, *L'évolution de l'Egypte, 1924–1950* (Paris, 1951); Earl of Cromer, *Modern Egypt*. 2 vols. (London, 1928); P. G. Elgood, *The Transit of Egypt* (London, 1929) and *Egypt and the Army* (New York, 1924); B. G. Gaulis, *Le Nationalism egyptien* (Paris, 1928); Groupe d'études de l'Islam (Centre d'études de politique étrangère), *L'Egypte independente* (Paris, 1938); E. Klingmuller, *Geschichte der Wafdpartei* (Berlin, 1937); Lord Lloyd, *Egypt since Cromer*, 2 vols. (London, 1933); E. W. P. Newman, *Great Britain in Egypt* (London, 1928); M. Rifaat, *The Awakening of Modern Egypt* (London, 1947); M.

Sabri, *La Révolution egyptienne*, 2eme partie (Paris, 1921); M. T. Symons, *Britain and Egypt* (London 1925); Tawwaf (pseud.), *Egypt, 1919* (Oxford, 1919) (a day-to-day account of the revolution by an eyewitness); S. Wihīda, *Fī Uṣūl al-Mas'alah al-Miṣriyyah* (On the Principles of the Egyptian Problem) (Cairo, 1951); B. Young, *Egypt* (London, 1927).

2. See, for example, 'Abd al-Raḥmān al-Rāfi'ī's *Mudhakkirātī* (Memoirs) (Cairo, 1952), p. 33, where he expressed his own surprise and the surprise of Muḥammad Farīd at the "scale, speed and force" of the Revolution of 1919. Al-Rāfi'ī and Farīd were leaders of the intransigent Nationalist Party founded by Muṣṭafā Kāmil.

3. See Hamed Ammar, *Growing up in an Egyptian Village* (London, 1954) pp. 72–73.

4. See, for example, E. W. P. Young, Newman, P. G. Elgood, Lord Lloyd, M. T. Symons, cited in note 1 above.

5. See al-Rāfi'ī, *Tārikh*, Vol. I.

6. Muḥammad Shafīq mentioned in his memoirs that in 1906, the prices of land had risen tremendously. For example, he had bought a few *feddans* at the price of L.E. 100 each and sold them at L.E. 1,300 each! There were times when prices changed between morning and evening. It is worth recalling that 1907 was the year when the heightening of the Aswan dam was undertaken, and that the dam itself had been built five years before. (See *Mudhakkirātī*, Vol. II, Pt. II, p. 125).

7. See below, p. 197.

8. See below, pp. 113f, 141f, 154f.

CHAPTER 8: The Role of Nationalist Governments in the Evolution of Ideology

1. The text of the Constitution, issued in the *Journal officiel* No. 42, August 20, 1923, is found in many books and journals; see D. H. Miller, *Constitutions, Electoral Laws, Treaties of States in the Near and Middle East* (Durham, North Carolina, 1947); M. Colombe, *L'Evolution de l'Egypte*, Appendix 1, pp. 282–304.

2. For an interesting illustration of some of the practical consequences of the vagueness of these articles see P. K. Mudawwar "L'Islam religion d'état: quelques consequences," in the Copt Egyptian review *al-Macarrat* (April, 1940). The author reviews the case of a Copt who had converted to Islam and then reconverted to his original religion. Somebody brought the case before the *Shar'ī* courts, asking that the children of the "apostate" be put under custody in accordance with Islamic procedure in such cases. The court of first instance and the court of appeal ruled in favor of the petitioner. This raised a great deal of indignation on the ground that it constituted an infraction of the freedom of conscience guaranteed by the Constitution. Finally, the government, without deciding on the issue in principle, prevented the application of the sentence by an administrative act and prohibited the religious courts hearing in the future *ḥisbah* (guardianship) cases except with the permission of the Ministry of Justice. It should be noted that, throughout the period under study, the various governments never tried to enact fundamental legislation concerning apostasy, which therefore remained, in theory, subject to Islamic law, even though the issue was raised in Parliament several times.

3. Emphasis added, here and below.

4. See, for example, the articles by Rashīd Riḍā in *al-Ahrām*, March 3, 1924 and by 'Abd al-'Azīz Shāwīsh in *al-Akhbār*, March 4, 1924; manifesto of the "Society of the Solidarity of the *'Ulamā'*" in *al-Ahrām*, March 13, 1924; article by the former Grand Muftī in *al-Sayāsah*, March 27, 1924; declaration of "the Assembly of the Senior *'Ulamā'* of Egypt," in *al-Siyāsah*, March 27, 1924.

5. *al-Siyāsah*, March 27, 1924.

6. See M. H. Haykal, *Mudhakkirāt fī al-Siyāsah al-Miṣriyyah* (Memoirs on Egyptian Politics) (Cairo, 1951), I, 259; also al-'Aqqād, *Sa'd Zaghlūl . . . , ibid.*, p. 470.

7. Haykal, *Mudhakkirāt*, I, 259.

8. *Ibid.*, pp. 288–289.

9. See A. Sékaly, "Les Deux congrès musulmans de 1926," *Revue du monde musulman*, LXIV, 1–123.

10. The text of the Law and the Explanatory Memorandum are given in the *Revue des études islamiques*, No. 1, (1929), p. 137f.

11. This point was originally made by J. Schacht, "L'Evolution moderne du droit musulman en Egypte," in *Mélanges Maspero* (publications de l'institut français d'archéologie orientale) (Cairo, 1935).

12. For all the preceding quotations, see the text of the Law and the Memorandum in *Revue des études islamiques* (1929).

13. For an analysis of these laws from the point of view of their relation to Islamic law and method, see J. N. D. Anderson, "Recent Developments in *Shar'ī* Law," in *The Muslim World*, Vol. XL (October 1950); Vol. XLI (January, April, July, October, 1951); Vol. XLII (January, April, July 1952). For a detailed analysis of the *waqfs* in Egypt, their history, their effect on economy and society, and the successive policies towards them, see A. Sékaly, "Le problème des Waqfs en Egypte," *Revue des études islamiques*, Vols. I–IV (1929). For an analysis of the Law of 1931 reorganizing the procedure of the religious courts, see L. Mercier, "Reorganisation égyptienne de la justice du Chraa," *Revue des études islamiques* (1931), p. 125f. For an analysis of the Waqf Law of 1949, see G. Busson-de-Janssens, "Les Waqfs dans l'Islam contemporain," *Revue des études islamiques* (1951), pp. 1–72. Also, by the same author, "Les vicissitudes des fondations pieuses dans le monde musulman." *Afrique-Asie* (1954), pp. 7–22. For Law No. 180 of September 1952 abolishing the family *waqfs* altogether, see J. Chlala, "La Suppression du *waqf ahlī* en Egypte," *Revue internationale de droit comparé* (1953) p. 682f.

Among other material on modern legislation in the sphere of Islamic law the following studies are noteworthy: A. D'Emilia, "Intorno alla moderna attivitá legislativa di alcuni paesi musulmani nel campo del diritto privato," in *Oriente Moderno*, July 1953; J. N. D. Anderson, "The Religious Element in Waqf Endowments," *Royal Central Asian Journal*, Vol. XXXIX (October 1951), "The *Sharī'ah* and Civil Law," *Islamic Quarterly*, Vol. I (April 1954), and "Law Reform in the Middle East," *International Affairs*, Vol. XXXII (January 1956); H. J. Liebesny, "Religious Law and Westernization in the Muslim Near East," *American Journal of Comparative Law*, Vol. II (Autumn 1953); R. Clemens, "Changes in Social and Legal Systems in the Near East as a Result of Technological Development," *International Social Science Bulletin*, Vol. V, No. 4 (1953); J. Linant-de-Bellefonds, "Immutabilité du droit musulman et réformes législatives en Egypte," *Revue internationale de droit comparé*, No. 1 (1955).

14. See Nadav Safran, "The Abolition of the Shar'ī Courts in Egypt," *The Muslim World*, Vol. XLVIII (January 1958).

15. See J. Chlala, "La Suppression du *waqf ahli* en Egypte," cited in note 13.

16. See Abd el-Razzak el-Sanhoury, "Le droit musulman comme élement de reforme du code civil egyptien," in *Introduction à l'étude du droit comparé; recueil en l'honneur d'Edouard Lambert*, (Paris, 1938), II, 622–624.

17. *Ibid.*, p. 628.

18. See H. J. Liebesny, "Religious Law and Westernization in the Muslim Near East," *American Journal of Comparative Law*, Vol. II (Autumn 1953), p. 499.
19. el-Sanhoury, p. 628.
20. These would have allowed wives to introduce stipulations in the marriage contract which would permit them to obtain dissolution of their marriage if the husband should take another wife. Also, they provided that a man might not marry a second wife without the consent of the *qāḍī*, and enjoined the *qāḍī* not to permit this until he made sure that the applicant was able to support two wives and was capable of treating them both fairly.
21. The draft-law envisaged prohibiting administratively any divorce without the consent of the *qāḍī* and enjoining the *qāḍī* not to give his consent before investigating the causes of the friction and attempting reconciliation. It should be noted that the draft-law did not invalidate a divorce undertaken in defiance of the law, but imposed penalties for administrative violation.
22. See above, p. 32.
23. See above, pp. 110–111.

CHAPTER 9: The Liberal Intellectuals and Their Task

1. See Chapter 11 below.
2. An analysis of the views expressed in this book is given below, pp. 153–155. The intellectual consequences of the book are discussed in Chapter 11.
3. For further details on Ṭaha Ḥusayn's life, see his autobiographical recollections, *Al-Ayyām*, 2 vols. (Cairo, 1929–1939); first volume translated into English by Hilary Wayment under the title, *The Stream of Days* (London, 1948). See also Sami al-Kayyālī, *Ma' Ṭāha Ḥusayn* (Cairo, 1951), and Pierre Cachia, *Ṭāha Ḥusayn* (London, 1956).
4. See below, pp. 169–175.
5. For additional details on Haykal's life, see his own memoirs, *Mudhakkirāt* . . . 2 vols. (Cairo, 1952).
6. For additional details on the life of Tawfīq al-Ḥakīm, see Shawqī Ḍayf, *Al-Adab al-'Arabī*, Vol. I.
7. For additional details on the life of al-Māzinī, see Shawqī Ḍayf, *Al Adab al-'Arabī*, Vol. I.
8. For details of Aḥmad Amīn's life, see his autobiography, *Ḥayātī* (My Life) (Cairo, 1950).

CHAPTER 10: The Progressive Phase

1. 'Alī 'Abd al-Rāziq, *al-Islām wa-Uṣūl al-Ḥukm* (Cairo, 1925), pp. 78–79.
2. *Ibid.*, p. 81f.
3. *Ibid.*, p. 103.
4. *Ibid.*, p. 36.
5. *Ibid.*, p. 103.
6. "This is a new heresy; a diabolical error which no Muslim, orthodox or dissenter, had dared to profess . . . " wrote Rashīd Riḍā in *al-Manār* (XXVI, 98). The political conjuncture was that King Fu'ād was personally interested in the caliphate at the time and was, therefore, naturally opposed to a work which denied its religious necessity and denigrated its role. At the same time, Sa'd Zaghlūl, the leader of the Wafd, which was then in opposition, sided with the *'ulamā'* in an attempt to

embarrass some members of the government who supported 'Abd al-Rāziq and, perhaps, drive the Ministry to resign. (See al-'Aqqād, *Sa'd Zaghlūl*, p. 518.

7. M. H. Haykal, *Waladī* (My Son) (Cairo, 1931), pp. 207–211.

8. T. Ḥusayn, *Mustaqbal al-Thaqāfah fī Miṣr*. English translation by S. Glazer, *The Future of Culture in Egypt* (American Council of Learned Societies, Washington, D.C., 1954), p. 5. All references to this work are from the English translation. Permission to quote has been gracefully granted by the Council.

9. A. Amīn, *Ḍuḥā al-Islām* (Cairo, 1936), III, 4–5.

10. A. Amīn and A. A. al-Bishrī, *al-Tarbiyyah al-Waṭaniyyah* (Civic Education) 6th ed. (Cairo, 1934), pp. 201–204.

11. See, for example, T. al-Ḥakīm, *'Awdat al-Rawḥ* (Cairo, 1933), pp. 23–25; al-'Aqqād, *Sa'd Zaghlūl*, pp. 19, 25, and 27.

12. T. Ḥusayn, *Future*, p. 5.

13. See pp. 15–16, 19–22, above for an account of the efforts of traditional doctrine to preserve the fiction of Muslim political unity; and pp. 78f, for Rashīd Riḍā's views and efforts to restore Muslim unity.

14. See above, p. 95.

15. See, al-'Aqqād, *Sa'd Zaghlūl*, pp. 18–36.

16. M. H. Haykal, *Thawrat al-Adab* (The Revolt of Literature) (Cairo, 1933), pp. 146–152.

17. T. Ḥusayn, *Future*, *passim*.

18. See, for example, *Taḥt Shams al-Fikr* (Under the Sun of Thought) (Cairo, 1938), p. 8f.

19. *Ibid.*, pp. 106–108.

20. *'Awdat al-Rawḥ*, pp. 51–56.

21. *Ibid.*, pp. 51–56.

22. The neglect of the Pharaonic trend did not preclude momentary flickers of interest in it afterward. Recently, for example, the present government installed a huge statue of one of the Pharaohs in one of the main squares in Cairo amidst great pageantry. Among the most recent discussions of Pharaonism and Islam we may mention Aḥmad Ṣabrī's *Qinā' al-Fir'awniyyah* (The Mask of Pharaonism) (Cairo, 1943), which tries to show that the Pharaonic culture was diametrically opposed to Islam and Ibrāhīm Jum'ah's book, *Al-Qawmiyyah al-Miṣriyyah-al-Islāmiyyah* (Egyptian—Islamic Nationalism) (Cairo, 1944), which endeavors to show a continuity of Egyptian national feeling in ancient Egyptian and in Islamic times.

23. See, for example, al-'Aqqād, *al-Murāja'at* (Reviews) (Cairo, 1925), p. 79; al-Māznī, *Haṣād al-Hashīm* (Harvest of the Stalks) (Cairo, 1925), p. 37; Haykal, *Waladī*, pp. 219–221; Ṭ Ḥusayn, *Future*, p. 61f.

24. See the excellent study of Abū al-Futūḥ Aḥmad Raḍwān, *Old and New Forces in Egyptian Education* (New York, 1951), especially pp. 82–133.

25. See for example Al-Sayyid Ṣabrī, *Mabādi' al-Qānūn al-Dustūrī* (Elements of Constitutional Law) (Cairo, 1940); and *Al-Lawā'ih al-Tashrī'iyyah* (Legislative Statutes) (Cairo, 1944); 'Uthmān 'Uthmān Khalīl, *Al-Niẓām al-Dustūrī al-Miṣrī* (The Egyptian Constitutional Order) (Cairo, 1942) and *Al-Mabādi' al-Dustūriyyah al-'Āmmah* (General Constitutional Elements) (Cairo, 1943).

26. Amīn, *al-Tarbiyyah*, p. 16.

27. *Ibid.*, pp. 16–17.

28. *Ibid.*, pp. 20–21.

29. See our discussion in the first chapter, pp. 17–18. We have also seen that the traditional view of politics as a function of ethics was predominant in the thought of Muḥammad 'Abduh (pp. 73–74) and Rashīd Riḍā (pp. 80–81); and we shall see

later that the same approach was predominant in one of the rare works on political theory by one of the intellectual leaders (p. 217f). All this gives ample material for reflection on the continuity of the underlying influence of the traditional disposition, despite many other changes in the mode of thinking of the Western-educated Muslims.

30. A. Amīn, *Kitāb al-Akhlāq* (The Book of Ethics) (Cairo, 1929), pp. 65–91.

31. *Ibid.*, p. 269.

32. *Ibid.*, p. 141.

33. See "al-'Adl wa al-Ḥuriyyah" ("Justice and Freedom") in *al-Kātib al-Miṣri,* Vol. II, (1946); reprinted in *Alwān* (Miscellany) (Cairo, 1952), pp. 223–250.

34. *Ibid.*

35. al-'Aqqād, *Muṭāla'āt fī al-Kutub wa-al-Ḥayāt* (Readings in Books and Life) (Cairo, 1924), p. 54. Al-'Aqqād's philosophy of freedom underlies all his essays in this book, and also his *al-Murāja'āt.*

36. Qāsim Amīn, *Taḥrīr al-Mar'ah* (The Emancipation of Women) (Cairo, 1899). See also his other work on the same subject, *al-Mar'ah al-Jadīdah* (The New Woman) (Cairo, 1901).

37. *Tahrīr,* p. 157.

38. *Ibid.*, p. 140.

39. *Ibid.*, p. 140.

40. al'Aqqād, *Murāja'āt,* pp. 237–243.

41. T. Ḥusayn, *Fī al-Shi'r al-Jāhilī* (on Pre-Islamic Poetry) (Cairo, 1926), p. 10.

42. *Ibid.*, p. 12.

43. *Ibid.*, p. 12.

44. *Ibid.*, pp. 5–6; emphasis added.

45. *Ibid.*, p. 78

46. *Ibid.*, p. 78.

47. *Ibid.*, p. 70.

48. *Ibid.*, p. 26; emphasis added.

49. *al-Manār*, XXVIII, 378

50. See al-Māznī, *Qabḍ al-Rīḥ* (Grasping the Wind), 2nd ed. (Cairo, 1948), p. 165f.

51. Haykal, *Thawrat al-Adab*, p. 21f.

52. al-'Aqqād, *Murāja'āt,* p. 273.

53. al-Māznī, *Haṣād,* pp. 44–45.

54. T. Ḥusayn, *Qādat al-Fikr* (Leaders of Thought) (Cairo, 1929), pp. 250–253.

55. al-'Aqqād, *Murāja'āt,* pp. 111–112.

56. It may be worth mentioning specifically that the ideas of evolution, both in the Darwinian version and in their social application, were among the Western ideas that achieved the widest acceptance in Egypt. After Shiblī Shumayyil and Ya'qub Ṣarrūf introduced the ideas of evolution at the turn of the century, they became part of the intellectual baggage of most Egyptian writers from all sectors of opinion. 'Abduh had been such an admirer of Herbert Spencer that he went to considerable trouble to make a personal visit to the aging and retired philosopher. Since then, Qāsim Amīn, Luṭfī al-Sayyid, al-'Aqqād, al-Māznī, al-Ḥakīm, Haykal, Ṭāha Ḥusayn, and Aḥmad Amīn expressed on numerous occasions their adherence to the ideas of evolution. A number of other writers have taken over from Shumayyil and Ṣarrūf the task of propagating the ideas of evolution with something approaching missionary zeal. Notable among these are the Coptic writer, Salāmah Mūsā (see his *Naẓariyyat al-Taṭawwur* [The Theory of Evolution], Cairo, n.d.); see also Ḥasan Ḥusayn, *Faṣl al-Maqāl fī Falsafat al-Nushū' wa al-Irtiqā'* (A Last Word on the Philosophy of Evolution) (Cairo, 1924), Ismā'īl Maẓhar who translated *The Origin of the Species* (*Aṣl al-Anwā'*, Cairo, 1928),

al-Sayyid Muḥammad Badawī, *Naẓariyyat al-Taṭawwur al-Ijtimā'ī* (The Theory of Social Evolution) (Cairo, 1952), and 'Iṣām al-Dīn Ḥifnī Nāṣif, *Naẓariyyat al-Taṭawwur* (The Theory of Evolution) (Cairo, 1952).

57. *Muṭāla'āt*, especially pp. 109–117.

58. *Murāja'āt*, p. 66.

59. *Haṣād*, pp. 50–51.

60. *Ibid.*, pp. 92–98.

61. *Ibid.*, pp. 85–92.

62. See his *Qiṣaṣ Tamthīliyyah* (Theater Stories) (Cairo, 1924), *Laḥaẓāt* (Moments) 2 vols. (Cairo, 1942), *Ṣawt Bāris* (The Voice of Paris), 2 vols. (Cairo, 1943).

63. T. Ḥusayn, *Hadīth al-Arbi'ā'* (Wednesday Conversations) (Cairo, 1927), p. 184.

64. *Ibid.*, p. 27.

65. See, for example, his *Yawmiyyāt Nā'ib fi al-Aryāf* (Diaries of a Country Prosecutor). Translated into English by A. Eban as *Maze of Justice.*

66. See his *'Awdat al-Rawḥ (passim)*; *Shahrazād*, (Cairo, 1934), *Taḥt Shams al-Fikr*, p. 65f; *Sulṭān al Ẓalām* (The Rule of Darkness) (Cairo, 1941), p. 23f.

67. See *Thawrat*, pp. 12f. 21f.

68. A. Amin, *Kitāb al-Akhlāq*, p. 100.

69. *Ibid.*, p. 25.

70. *Ibid.*, p. 58.

71. See, for example, *Fayḍ al-Khāṭir* (Inspirations), I, 296; *al-Tarbiyyah*, p. 30.

72. See A. Amīn, *Fayḍ al-Khāṭir*, I, 135–136.

73. *Thawrat*, p. 33.

74. *Murāja'āt*, p. 276.

75. A. Amīn, *Fajr al-Islām* (The Dawn of Islam), 2 vols. (Cairo, 1928–1937), *Ḍuḥā al-Islām* (The Morning of Islam), 3 vols. (Cairo, 1933–1936), and *Ẓuhr al-Islām* (Islam's Noon), 2 vols. (Cairo, 1945–1947).

76. See, for example, A. Amīn, *Ḍuḥā*, II, 163–165, 238–239.

77. *Ibid.*, pp. 174–175.

78. *Ibid.*, pp. 361–362.

79. *Ẓuhr*, I, 93–94.

80. *Ḍuḥā*, II, 297; *Ẓuhr*, I, 93f.

81. *Ẓuhr*, I, 96f.

82. *Ḍuḥā*, I, 207.

83. *Ḍuḥā*, II, 207.

84. *Ibid.*, p. 70.

85. *Ḍuḥā*, I, 68.

86. *Ibid.*, p. 69.

87. *Ibid.*, pp. 69–70.

88. *Ibid.*, p. 71.

89. *Ḍuḥā*, III, 85.

90. *Ḍuḥā*, I, 73–74.

91. *Ḍuḥā*, III, 4–5.

CHAPTER 11: The Crisis of Orientation

1. See Sāmi al-Kayyālī, *Ma' Ṭāha Ḥusayn* (Cairo, 1951), p. 59.

2. From article in *al-Siyāsah*, July 17, 1926.

3. Etienne Gilson, *Reason and Revelation in the Middle Ages* (London, 1950), pp. 57–58.

4. Pierre Cachia, in his study of Ṭaha Ḥusayn, noticed the shift in Ṭāha's posi-

tion from an out-and-out rationalism opposed to religion to a rationalism which was willing to live side by side with the emotionally inspired truths of religion (see *Ṭāha Ḥusayn*, p. 80f). But Cachia was not accurate and clearly missed the significance of *'Alā Hāmish al-Sīrah* when he saw it as "the most impious of Ṭāha Ḥusayn's books" because it tacitly assumed the material it dealt with to be mythological and exploited it for entertainment (p. 198). In fact, Ṭāha scrupulously refrained from touching any material relating to the Prophet's life and simply restated traditional accounts of it. Thus he made it a point to pay his respects to the traditional beliefs. What he embroidered and embellished was material in which the Prophet was not involved; and there was little impiety in this.

5. Ṭāha Ḥusayn, *'Alā Hāmish al-Sīrah* (On the Margin of the Prophet's Life), Vol. I (Cairo, 1934), Introduction.

6. *Hāmish*, Vol. I, Introduction.

7. Haykal, *Ḥayāt Muḥammad*, pp. 20–24.

8. *Ibid.*, p. 240.

9. The author wishes to make it clear that his criticism of the reasons that Haykal, or other writers, used to defend this or that aspect of Islam is undertaken strictly for the purpose of analyzing their thought on the subject. It is not meant to imply any stand on his part in regard to the specific aspects at issue.

10. Haykal, *Ḥayāt Muḥammad*, p. 285.

11. *Ibid.*, p. 285.

12. *Ibid.*, p. 186.

13. *Ibid.*, p. 446f.

14. *Ibid.*, p. 9.

15. *Ibid.*, p. 3.

16. *Ibid.*, p. 20f.

17. *Ibid.*, pp. 490–494.

18. Muḥammad Ḥusayn Haykal, *Fī Manzal al-Waḥy* (In the Birthplace of Revelation) (Cairo, 1936), Introduction

19. *Ibid.*

20. T. Ḥusayn, *The Future of Culture*, p. 3.

21. *Ibid.*, pp. 11–13.

22. *Ibid.*, p. 19.

23. *Ibid.*, p. 21.

24. *Ibid.*, p. 19.

25. *Ibid.*, p. 15.

26. *Ibid.*, p. 27.

27. *Ibid.*, p. 20.

28. *Ibid.*, p. 136.

29. *Ibid.*, p. 19.

30. *Ibid.*, p. 18.

31. Thus, Pierre Cachia wrote of the period in which the book appeared: "This was also a period when Egypt scored some spectacular successes on the international scene . . . The Egyptian Renaissance was attracting some attention in the West . . . It seemed that the time for reaping had come and Ṭāha Ḥusayn's earlier works, dedicated to educating the Egyptian reading public in fundamentals, now gave way to others of more intrinsic immediate appeal reflecting self-confidence and even satisfaction . . ." (*Ṭāha Ḥusayn*, p. 63).

In fact, at about the same time, Aḥmad Amīn was writing: "I am afraid the leaders of opinion among us have grown tired of resisting and have surrendered . . . They have given up looking forward and have begun to lead the public where it wants to go rather than along a road of their own choosing. If this is what happened indeed, what a defeat." (See *Fayḍ al-Khāṭir*, I, 358–359).

Amīn's opinion seems to jibe more than Cachia's with the urgent warnings of Ṭāha Ḥusayn and with the spread of the popular but retrogressive Muslim orientation which was already evident at that time.

CHAPTER 12: The Historical Crisis of Liberal Nationalism

1. The exact figures as given by Issawi are: Population, from 11,287,000 in 1907 to 19,022,00 in 1947; crop area, from 7,717,000 *feddans* in 1912 to 9,165,000 *feddans* in 1948 (*Egypt at Mid-Century*, p. 55 and p. 102 respectively).

2. Issawi, *Mid-Century*, p. 60.

3. *Ibid.*, p. 60.

4. Jean and Simone Lacouture give the following figures about the crowding of the "popular" quarters of Cairo: Over the city as a whole, the density of the population is 19,000 to the square mile. In the working-class districts it amounts to 36,800. In some particular old quarters it is much more than that. Thus, in the 'Abdīn quarter the density is 94,000 to the square mile, while in the Bāb al-Sha'riyyah quarter it reaches 179,600 persons to the square mile. (See Lacouture, *Egypt in Transition*, New York, 1958), p. 409.

5. In an interesting novel by 'Abd al-Raḥmān al-Sharqāwī about village life and problems, the author gave ample evidence that villagers who had lived for some time in the city and then had to return to their village could no longer reintegrate themselves in its life. Their speech, manners, way of dressing, and aspirations had all changed. Above all, their values had been corroded. They came to despise agricultural work and ridiculed the issues that were of utmost concern to the fellahin of the village. They transformed the loose woman of the village into a regular prostitute. They talked nostalgically about the city and dreamed of returning to it soon. They sought to impress the villagers with their "conspicuous consumption." The villagers, in their turn, looked on them with contempt, and occasionally with envy. See *Al-Arḍ* (The Land) (Cairo, 1951).

6. Issawi, *Mid-Century*, p. 142.

7. *Ibid.*, p. 157.

8. *Ibid.*, pp. 207–208.

9. For a fuller description of the social changes, see C. S. Coon, "The Impact of the West on Middle Eastern Social Institutions," *Proceedings of the American Academy of Political Science*, Vol. XXIV (January 1952); H. A. R. Gibb, "La Réaction contre la culture occidentale dans le Proche Orient," *Cahiers de l'orient contemporain*, Vol. V (1951); F. Berthier, "La Rencontre de l'Isalm avec le monde moderne," *Lettres Nouvelles*, Vol. IV, Nos. 39–40, (1956).

10. Aḥmad Amīn, *Ilā Waladī* (To My Son) (Cairo, 1951), p. 130.

11. Haykal, *Mudhakkirāt*, I, 214.

12. Ismā'īl Ṣidqī pasha, *Mudhakkirātī* (My Memoris) (Cairo, 1950), p. 47.

13. *Ibid.*, p. 30.

14. al-'Aqqād, *Sa'd Zaghlūl*, pp. 254–258.

15. See Haykal, *Mudhakkirāt*, II, 155f.

16. Issawi, *Egypt: An Economic and Social Analysis* (London, 1947), p. 173.

17. Issawi, *Mid-Century*, pp. 124–129.

18. *Ibid.*, pp. 233–236.

19. *Ibid.*, p. 102.

20. Issawi, *Economic and Social Analysis*, p. 196. Other examples of the bias of

the regime in favor of landowners are found in Issawi, pp. 173–174. The selfishness of the big landowners made a deep impression on the consciousness of the men who made the revolution of 1952. Wrote Muḥammad Naguib: "Instead of investing their savings, legal or illegal, in productive enterprises in Egypt, the big landowners either exported their savings or invested them in inflated urban and rural real estate. The result was a land boom in the midst of unprecedented suffering on the part of the great majority of Egypt's 22 million people . . ." (*Egypt's Destiny*, New York, 1955), p. 14.

Anwar al-Sādāt, another revolutionary leader wrote: "The ruling class of Egypt were the great landowners . . . They behaved in a manner which was already out of fashion in Europe in the nineteenth century. Landowning was a speculative business. The land was let and sublet at exorbitant rates . . . Vast feudal fortunes were achieved by exploitation of the fellahin . . . In 1939, two million Egyptian tenant farmers were so poor that they did not own the simple tools which they needed to till their fields." (*Revolt on the Nile*, London, 1957).

21. Fikrī Abāẓah, *Al-Ḍāhiq-al-Bākī* (To Laugh or to Weep?) (Cairo, 1933).

22. *Ibid.*, p. 62.

23. *Ibid.*, pp. 60f.

24. Issawi, *Economic and Social Analysis*, pp. 63, 117.

25. *Ibid.*, p. 77.

26. See above, p. 191.

27. For a full history of the Brotherhood and a description of its ideas, see Isḥāq al-Ḥusaynī, *Al-Ikhwān al-Muslimūn* (The Muslim Brethren) (Beirut, 1952). For further bibliography, see Chapter 4 below, Note 1.

28. The withdrawal of the Allied troops after the war led to an estimated unemployment of 250,000 persons (Issawi, *Mid-Century*, p. 262).

29. Tawfīq al-Ḥakīm, *Taḥt Shams*, p. 118.

30. *Ibid.*, p. 136.

31. Ṭāha Ḥusayn, *Mir'āt al-Ḍamīr*, pp. 108–109.

32. Ṭāha Ḥusayn, *Al-Mu'adhdhabūn*, p. 27.

33. Ṭāha Ḥusayn, *Jannat al-Ḥayawān*, p. 34.

34. For other instances of attacks against the corruption of the social and political order, see Tawfīq al-Ḥakīm, *Masraḥiyyāt al-Mujtama'* (Plays about Society) (Cairo, 1950); Aḥmad Ḥasan al-Zayyāt, *Waḥy al-Risālah* (The Inspiration of *al-Risālah*), Vol. II (Cairo, 1944). Between 1945 and 1952, almost all the press carried articles and editorials on the social problems. Some of these articles, particularly those published by the review *Roza al-Yūsūf* and by the organs of the former Miṣr al-Fatāt party, made shocking revelations about misery and corruption and had an extremely virulent tone.

35. Al-Ḥusaynī, *Al-Ikhwān*, p. 66.

36. Issawi, *Mid-Century*, p. 167.

37. *Ibid.*, p. 67.

38. Aḥmad Amīn, *Yawm al-Islām* (The Day of Islam) (Cairo, 1952), p. 153.

39. Issawi, *Mid-Century*, p. 261.

40. Abū al-Futuḥ Raḍwān, *Old and New Forces in Egyptian Education*, Columbia University Series on Education (New York, 1951).

41. *Ibid.*, p. 128.

42. See above, p. 148.

43. Raḍwān, *Old and New Forces*, p. 124.

44. *Ibid.*, p. 126.

45. For a good description of the state of mind of the better-educated youth of

the time, see the novel by 'Abd al-Raḥmān Badawī, *Humūm al-Shabāb* (The Troubles of Youth) (Cairo, 1946). Badawī's young hero is besieged by conflicting ideals and intellectual confusion. He feels within himself a restless, boundless energy but is unable to find a satisfying outlet for it and blames his society for its waste. In his frustration, he wishes he were "a bomb that would blow up the whole universe." He becomes involved in a secret society which seeks to establish contact with the Germans during World War II, at the same time that he gets involved with a fallen girl who turns out to be an informer in the pay of the British. He ends up dying in jail. In actual fact, after the war, terrorist and subversive secret societies mushroomed in Egypt. Anwar al-Sādāt, one of the leaders of the 1952 revolution, mentions four or five of them in his book, *Revolt on the Nile*. Naguib mentions two others in his *Egypt's Destiny*. Many murders and attempts at murder of high personalities and acts of sabotage are attributable to these societies. In many respects, the whole situation was reminiscent of nineteenth-century Russia, with its conflicts between the Slavophiles and the Westernizers, its sharp contrast between the opulence and irresponsibility of the few and the misery of the masses, the spread of a painful consciousness of social injustice, the frustration of the intellectual youth, and the rise of nihilism and terrorism.

CHAPTER 13: The Reactionary Phase

1. See Umberto Rizzitano, "Studi di storia Islamica in Egitto," *Oriente Moderno*, November, 1953. The author listed and commented briefly on about one hundred titles on Muslim history, biography, and related titles by about half as many authors. Some of the works were undoubtedly *bona fide* critical history, but most of them represented varying degrees of compromise between a critical historical method and a restatement of traditional material more or less arbitrarily interpreted. About one third of the titles were clearly works of popularization.

2. See bibliography under Haykal.

3. See, for example, his *Taḥt Shams al Fikr*, where he justified the Muslim apologetic literature by saying: "The question is not simply one of religion, but is a matter of nationality and patriotism . . . The defense of Islam is not always a defense of a creed and a religion, but is the defense of that bloc which the Westerners call 'the East' . . ." (p. 19) "The defense of our personality and faith is a defense of our life; therefore, writings which aim at this purpose should be encouraged" (p. 21)

4. See bibliography under al-'Aqqād.

5. From the time the Muslim Brotherhood acquired importance on a national scale — sometime during World War II — until 1952, the Central Bureau of the movement published one hundred fourteen booklets dealing with subjects related to Isalm, the titles of which are to be found in Muḥammad Shawkat Zakī, *Al-Ikhwān al-Muslimūn fī al-Mujtama' al-Miṣrī* (The Muslim Brotherhood in Egyptian Society) (Cairo, 1953).

6. The nature of this reinterpretation and its bearing on Islam from a religious point of view have been studied by H. A. R. Gibb in his *Modern Trends in Islam* (Chicago, 1947), and by W. C. Smith in his *Islam in Modern History* (Princeton, 1957). Our analysis here is bound to overlap theirs, even though our approach is basically different. We are not interested in the ideas broached in this reinterpretation in terms of their effect on Isalm as a religion, but only in terms of their validity as possible elements of a belief-system for a political community.

7. In an article published in a French journal in 1947, Ṭāha Ḥusayn argued that the Muslim literature, far from representing a retreat from the rational liberalism of

the initial phase, represented in fact the consecration of its triumph. The struggle between "modern liberalism" and "orthodox traditionalism," which had reached its climax in the 'Abd al-Rāziq–Ṭāha Ḥusayn episodes, had ended in a complete victory for liberalism, according to Ṭāha. Thereafter, "once assured of their right to express their thought freely, the modernists took a pause, and then began to think over the ancient history of Islam. They did that as free men . . . and from this there was born . . . a whole literature of religious inspiration." ("Les Tendances religieuses de la litterature egyptienne d'aujourd'hui," *Cahiers du Sud*, numero special *L'Islam et l'Occident*, 1947). Actually, it is almost certain that this opinion was designed expressly for foreign consumption if it did not represent mere wishful thinking on the part of Ṭāha Ḥusayn. For he himself had often expressed the opinion that the Egyptian writers lacked freedom of expression in religious subjects: "The subjects that are taboo outnumber those that are not . . . ," he wrote in his *Future of Culture* (p. 147). A year before the French article, Ṭāha had said that "the modernist movement had failed because the mind has not yet attained control over instinct and will" (*Al-Kātib al-Miṣrī*, II, May 1946, 569–570). See, in this connection, Aḥmad Amīn's judgment about the modernist writers previously quoted (see Note 31, Chap. 11).

8. al-'Aqqād, *Sa'd Zaghlūl*, pp. 45–46.
9. Haykal, *Ḥayāt*, p. 24.
10. See above, p. 170.
11. al-'Aqqād, *'Abqariyyat Muḥammad* (Cairo, 1942), p. 42.
12. *Ibid.*, p. 54.
13. *Ibid.*, p. 60.
14. *Ibid.*, p. 57.
15. *Modern Trends in Islam*, p. 77. Desmond Stewart reported in his *Young Egypt* (London, 1958) a pertinent remark made to him by a professor in an Egyptian university: "Too many of my students need a period of mental disinfection . . ." (p. 177).
16. *'Abqariyyat*, pp. 92–93.
17. *Ibid.*, p. 97.
18. *Ibid.*, pp. 160–191.
19. *Ibid.*, p. 192–193.
20. *Ibid.*, pp. 61–76.
21. al-'Aqqād, *al-Dīmūqrāṭiyyah fī al-Islām* (Democracy in Islam) (Cairo, 1952), p. 8.
22. *Ibid.*, pp. 17–19.
23. *Ibid.*, pp. 20–21.
24. *Ibid.*, p. 43.
25. *Ibid.*, p. 43.
26. *Ibid.*, p. 56.
27. *Ibid.* p. 57.
28. *Ibid.*, p. 51.
29. *Ibid.*, p. 60.
30. *Ibid.*, p. 65.
31. al-'Aqqād used *ijmā'* in a sense that is reminiscent of Rousseau's General Will. It may not be amiss to compare and contrast the two concepts. Both of them do represent a *vox populi* and are infallible. But whereas the General Will has its sanction in itself, the traditional *ijmā'* derives its sanction from a divine assurance that it will not be wrong. Also, unlike the General Will, the *ijmā'* is not a programmatic instrument but an *ex-post-facto* realization that consensus had occurred.
32. *Ibid.*, p. 66.

33. *Ibid.*, p. 68.
34. *Ibid.*, pp. 68–70.
35. *Ibid.*, p. 73.
36. *Ibid.*, p. 74.
37. *Ibid.*, p. 84.
38. *Ibid.*, p. 84f.
39. See pp. 84–93.
40. *Ibid.*, p. 136f.
41. *Ibid.*, p. 425f.
42. Aḥmad Amīn, *Yawm al-Islām*, p. 107.
43. *Ibid.*, p. 109.
44. *Ibid.*, p. 110.
45. *Ibid.*, p. 111.
46. *Ibid.*, p. 148.
47. *Ibid.*, p. 148.
48. *Ibid.*, p. 151.
49. *Ibid.*, pp. 153, 172.
50. *Ibid.*, p. 154.
51. *Ibid.*, p. 189.
52. *Ibid.*, p. 189.
53. *Ibid.*, pp. 173–175.
54. *Ibid.*, pp. 110, 143.
55. *Ibid.*, p. 189.
56. See, for instance, his autobiography, *Hayātī* (Cairo, 1950), where he appears as shy, melancholy, and brooding, inclined to mysticism and to oppressive feelings of guilt. He seemed to be particularly conscious, somewhat painfully, of the excessive liberty and permissiveness of his children. In his last years, he was handicapped by the loss of his sight.

CHAPTER 14: The Ideology and Mentality of Mahdism

1. Our study of the Muslim Brotherhood is based on the following sources: I. M. al-Ḥusaynī, *al-Ikhwān al-Muslimūn* (The Muslim Brethren) (Beirut, 1952); M. Sh. Zakī, *al-Ikhwān al-Muslimūn fī al-Mujtama' al-Miṣrī* (The Muslim Brethren in Egyptian Society) (Cairo, 1954); J. Heyworth-Dunne, *Religious and Political Trends in Modern Egypt* (Washington, D.C., 1950); L. Gardet, *La Cité Musulmane*; H. A. R. Gibb, *Modern Trends in Islam*, Chap. VI; W. C. Smith, *Islam in Modern History*, Chap. III; Ḥasan al-Bannā, *al-Ikhwān al-Muslimūn Taḥt Rāyat al-Qur'ān* (The Muslim Brethren under the Banner of Qur'ān) (Cairo, 1951), *Muqaddimah fi al-Tafsīr* (Introduction to Qur'ānic Interpretation) (Cairo, 1951), and *Thalāthat Rasā'il* (Three Epistles) (Cairo, 1951); Muḥammad al-Ghazzālī, *al-Islām wa al-Manāhij al-Ishtirākiyyah* (Islam and the Socialist Programs) (Cairo, 1950) and *Min Hunā Na'lam* translated into English under the title *Our Beginning in Wisdom* by Isma'il el Faruqi for the American Council of Learned Societies (Washington, D.C., 1953); 'Abd al-Qādir Udā, *al-Islām wa Awḍa'unā al Siyāsiyyah* (Islam and our Political Conditions) (Cairo, 1951); *al-Ahrām*, reports on the trial of the leaders of the Muslim Brotherhood, October, November, 1954.
2. See above, p. 226.
3. See above, Note 5, Chapter 13.
4. See bibliography, in Note 1 above.

5. *Our Beginning in Wisdom, p. ix.* All references are to the English edition. Permission to quote granted by the Council.

6. *Ibid.*, p. 35.

7. *Ibid.*, p. 3.

8. Incidentally, we can see in our author's comparison a concrete instance of the indirect contribution that the intellectual leaders made to the effort of the Muslim Brotherhood. Haykal had first made the comparison of Islam with the French Revolution in the course of his defense of Muḥammad. He had not intended, however, to carry his comparison to the not illogical conclusion advanced by al-Ghazzālī. Another instance is expressed in a remark made by the lieutenant of the Supreme Guide of the Brotherhood, Ṣāliḥ 'Ashmāwī, in the Introduction to the book under discussion. He took seriously Haykal's attack against Western civilization and, consequently, asserted the obligation to live integrally according to Islam. "The advocates of the Islamic idea [that is, the Brotherhood] came to this realization [the perfect guidance of Islam] when they saw Western civilization crumbling, and realized that it has failed to give men security and happiness. They rose to demand that those in power observe Islam. . ." (p. viii).

9. *Ibid.*, p. 3.

10. *Ibid.*, pp. 3–4.

11. *Ibid.*, p. 6.

12. *Ibid.*, p. 13.

13. *Ibid.*, p. 26.

14. *Ibid.*, p. 10.

15. *Ibid.*, p. 4. Emphasis added here and below.

16. *Ibid.*, p. 25.

17. *Ibid.*, p. 89. The last statement was made as a summary of the difference between national rule and religious rule. It omits some of the cardinal points which the book asserted repeatedly throughout, such as defense of Islam, *jihād*, religion, and the rejection of the principle of "nationality." The statement that a state that would apply the principles mentioned is acceptable should not be understood as indicating a willingness to give up the principles that were omitted. In this, as in some other rare instances, the author was talking specifically of the existing system, and in such situations he tended to be more cautious and less demanding than when talking about the Islamic state in general.

18. *Ibid.*, p xv.

19. *Ibid.*, p. 4.

20. *Ibid.*, p. 15.

21. *Ibid.*, p. 22.

22. *Ibid.*, p. 15.

23. *Ibid.*, p. 4.

24. *Ibid.*, p. 14.

25. *Ibid.*, p. viii.

26. *Ibid.*, p. 5.

27. *Ibid.*, p. 54.

28. See above, p. 141f.

29. *Ibid.*, p. xvi.

30. See above, p. 82.

31. See above, p. 224f.

32. *Ibid.*, pp. 42–43.

33. *Ibid.*, p. 135.

34. *Ibid.*, p. 136.

35. *Ibid.*, p. 135.
36. *Ibid.*, pp. 130, 136–137.
37. *Ibid.*, p. 130.
38. *Ibid.*, pp. 136–137.
39. *Ibid.*, p. 134.
40. *Ibid.*, p. 143.
41. This refers particularly to relations between the sexes and the regulation of the public appearance of women: ". . . We wish to make clear . . . that women, when they go away from home, should be fully dressed but not over-dressed or over-adorned. Showing their face is not a sin as long as they are not painted or perfumed . . . In truth we are anxious to keep temptation away from the people, away by any judicious means. . ." (p. 17). Also, "Would a religious government be exceeding the limits of its nature if it sought to fight indecency and nudism on the beaches, for instance, and took the necessary steps thereto?" (p. 28)
42. *Ibid.*, p. 27.
43. It may not be insignificant in this respect to point out that the Brotherhood, which ran its organization and enterprises as a state within the state, developed serious rifts within its ranks as soon as the founder died. These rifts did not heal to the end and played in the hands of the enemies of the movement. Also, during the trial of some of its leaders after the attempt on the life of 'Abd al-Nāṣir, it transpired that certain sections of the organization, particularly the secret apparatus, often acted on their own in opposition to the policies of the central organs. These failures point out concretely the consequences to be expected from a constitutional organization which depends entirely on personality and is heedless of the "engineering" side of power.
44. *Ibid.*, p. 2.
45. *Ibid.*, p. 8.
46. *Ibid.*, p. 38.
47. *Ibid.*, p. 18.
48. *Ibid.*, p. 20.
49. *Ibid.*, p. 20.
50. Once more, the parallel with Stalinist communism is striking. Since "truth" is embodied in Marxist "science," any dissenting opinion is suspicious if not malicious. The right interpretation of the true doctrine is, of course, that of the party which has force on its side.
51. See, for example, pp. 43, 44, 31, and 140.
52. *Ibid.*, pp. 51–64 and especially p. 54.
53. *Ibid.*, p. 35.
54. *Ibid.*, p. 80.
55. *Ibid.*, p. 32. The author was careful to camouflage this open invitation to revolt by stating immediately after: "It should be noted that the present constitution of Egypt provides for the rule of a wise Islamic government. It is to disbelief rather than to faith that we should impute the crime of attempting to overthrow the form of government." (p. 32) There is no doubt that this is a camouflage since the Egyptian state hardly fulfills the requirements of the Islamic state mentioned before. Note also the ambiguity of the second sentence, which can easily apply to the Egyptian government itself attempting to "overthrow" the wise Islamic provisions of the Constitution. At any rate, threats and invitations to revolt are not lacking in the book even though they were not addressed specifically to the Egyptian regime. See immediately below.

56. *Ibid.*, p. 37.
57. *Ibid.*, p. xv.

CHAPTER 15: Retrospect and Prospect

1. Viewed in this light, Islam appears undoubtedly as a force of first importance in Egyptian life; but it is an Islam whose manifestations are very closely related to the concrete historical environmental forces. We do not, therefore, see any justification for the opinions of some Islamists and philosophers of religion prognosticating definite solutions to the adjustment problem of Muslim societies in terms of conceptions derived from an intellectual analysis of the history of Islamic doctrine. (Such, for instance, is L. Gardet's position in his otherwise excellent study *La Cité Musulmane.* On the basis of an analysis of Islamic political and social doctrine, Gardet reached the conclusion that the solution of the problem of Islam must be in terms of the realization of a new Muslim City on Earth based on the model of the Ideal Muslim City. He suggests a reinterpretation of Islamic doctrine in terms of a neo-Thomistic conception of natural law as the most appropriate approach for such a solution.) Our opinion coincides rather with that of H. A. R. Gibb who does not prejudge the solution but insists on the need for Muslims to master the historical critical method before they can work out any viable solution (see his *Modern Trends in Islam*, Chap. VI).

2. The character and orientation of the present regime are illustrated by the composition of the National Assembly "elected" under the terms of the Constitution of 1956. (The author has had no access to data for later representative bodies.) Out of 341 members, the Assembly comprised only 15 landowners, 19 members of the mercantile and industrial bourgeoisie, 45 "agriculturers," 19 ministers and under secretaries, 48 army and police officers, 45 officers of provincial administration, 134 civil servants, members of the professions and private employees, and four workers. It included two women and only one man of religion (see *Oriente Moderno*, July, 1957).

3. See preamble to the Constitution of 1956, *Middle Eastern Affairs* (February, 1956), VII, 2.

4. See N. Safran, "The Abolition of the Shar'ī Courts in Egypt," *The Muslim World*, Vol. XLVIII, January and April, 1958. See also the Preamble to the Constitution of 1956, in which the clause of the 1923 Constitution guaranteeing freedom of conscience has been changed to one guaranteeing "freedom of worship." The former text is more liable to interpretation in a sense that would require the preservation of the Islamic institutions. Recently, in the Constitution of the United Arab Republic, the clause about Islam being the "religion of the state" was altogether dropped. The views of the revolutionary leaders were expressed by Anwar al-Sādāt in the following terms: "The problem is to get Egypt out of the Middle Ages, to turn it into a modern, ordered, viable state, while at the same time respecting the customs of the people. On this last point, respecting the customs of the people does not mean chaining them to a dead past; it means respecting the essential and invisible continuities in a nation's life. We would conserve anything that did not impede the real progress of the community." (*Revolt on the Nile*, p. 53)

5. The press of the period is replete with reports about Friday Sermons delivered by members of the junta or by religious preachers invoking *jihād*, particularly during the recurrent flare-ups in Palestine.

6. In his *al-Mas'alah al-Sharqiyyah* (The Eastern Problem) (written before 1900), for example, Mustafā Kāmil referred to a proposal broached by W. S. Blunt to establish an Arab caliphate, headed by khedive 'Abbas II, under British protection only

to reject it vehemently as a project designed to eliminate the Ottoman obstacle in the way of perpetuating the occupation of Egypt (see pp. 19–22).

In 1912, Kāmil's successor, Muḥammad Farīd, denounced khedive 'Abbās in the French newspaper *Le Siècle* for plotting against the Ottoman empire with the view of establishing himself as head of an Arab caliphate under British protection (see Shafīq, Vol. II, Part 2, p. 269).

Index

90566

HARVARD POLITICAL STUDIES

Administration of the Civil Service in Massachusetts. By George C. S. Benson. 1935

The President's Control of the Tariff. By John Day Larkin. 1936

Federal Commissioners. By E. Pendleton Herring. 1936

The Physiocratic Doctrine of Judicial Control. By Mario Einaudi. 1938

The Failure of Constitutional Emergency Powers under the German Republic. By Frederick Mundell Watkins. 1939

The Regulation of Railroad Abandonments. By Charles R. Cherington. 1948

Muddy Waters: The Army Engineers and the Nation's Rivers. By Arthur Maass. 1951

American Conservatism in the Age of Enterprise. By Robert Green McCloskey. 1951

National Minorities: An International Problem. By Inis L. Claude, Jr. 1955

The Politics of Distribution. By Joseph Cornwall Palamountain, Jr. 1955

The Politics of German Codetermination. By Herbert J. Spiro. 1958

The President's Cabinet: An Analysis from Wilson to Eisenhower. By Richard F. Fenno, Jr. 1959

Egypt in Search of Political Community. By Nadav Safran. 1961

HARVARD MIDDLE EASTERN STUDIES

1. *Desert Enterprise: The Middle East Oil Industry in its Local Environment.* By David H. Finnie. 1958
2. *Middle Eastern Capitalism: Nine Essays.* By A. J. Meyer. 1959
3. *The Idea of the Jewish State.* By Ben Halpern. 1961
4. *The Agricultural Policy of Muḥammad 'Alī in Egypt.* By Helen Anne B. Rivlin. 1961
5. *Egypt in Search of Political Community.* By Nadav Safran. 1961

LIBRARY
OF
MOUNT ST. MARY'S
COLLEGE
EMMITSBURG, MARYLAND

JAN 15 1971